ATTRIBUTION:

Perceiving the Causes of Behavior

ATTRIBUTION :

PERCEIVING THE CAUSES

OF BEHAVIOR

Edward E. Jones
David E. Kanouse
Harold H. Kelley
Richard E. Nisbett
Stuart Valins
Bernard Weiner

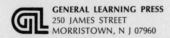 GENERAL LEARNING PRESS
250 JAMES STREET
MORRISTOWN, N J 07960

ACKNOWLEDGMENTS

In August 1969 the six editors of this book met at the University of California at Los Angeles to discuss attribution theory. Out of these proceedings there developed a decision to prepare the chapters that appear in this book. They reflect the issues discussed at our first meeting and also the further problems raised when we met again in New Haven the following January. Subsequently, mutual criticism has been exchanged in the extensive correspondence during the period of final preparation of the chapters. Thus, each contribution owes much to the comments and suggestions of each of the other chapter authors.

In addition, each chapter reflects the helpful suggestions of other persons not mentioned among the authors. Grateful acknowledgment is made to John Thibaut for his comments on "Attribution in Social Interaction." Both that chapter and "Causal Schemata and the Attribution Process" reflect many stimulating discussions with Jae-Ho Cha. Norman Anderson made a number of constructive suggestions that improved "Order Effects in Impression Formation." The authors of "Perceiving the Causes of One's Own Behavior" are indebted to Irving Janis and Mark Lepper for valuable criticism of an early draft. "The Actor and the Observer" reflects suggestions made by Gordon Baer, Judy Grumet, James Jones, and Camille Wortman. For their comments on drafts of "Attribution Processes in the Development and Treatment of Emotional Disorders" the authors are grateful to Gerald Davison, Larry Gross, Reid Hastie, Irving Janis, Mark Lepper, John Neale, Donald Quinlan, Lee Ross, and Michael Storms.

Finally, the initial support of the National Science Foundation must be gratefully acknowledged. Grant GS-2613 made possible the UCLA Workshop from which this effort evolved. Other research grants made possible the preparation of particular papers: NSF Grant GS-1121X—the chapters on "Attribution in Social Interaction" and "Causal Schemata in the Attribution Process"; NSF Grant GS-114X—the chapters on "Order Effects in Impression Formation" and "The Actor and the Observer"; NSF Grant 2587 (to Nisbett) and NIMH Grant 14557 (to Valins)—"Perceiving the Causes of One's Own Behavior" and "Attribution Processes in the Development and Treatment of Emotional Disorders"; Grant MH 12603-05 from NIH and Grant CG 9938 from the Early Childhood Research and Development Center, Los Angeles Division—"Perceiving the Causes of Success and Failure."

CONTENTS

v

Introduction

THIS BOOK is about the basic processes involved in perceiving the self, other persons, and the settings in which people function. Each chapter combines evidence with speculation in an attempt to shed light on particular social psychological problems. How do individuals integrate conflicting evidence in forming impressions of others? How do we account for our own successes and failures? for the outcomes of others? How do verbal habits help to mediate generalizations from specific behavioral instances? How does the setting influence the subjective meaning of emotional experience? How do group members impute to one another motives of friendly cooperation rather than, or aggressive competition? How do we allocate responsibility for an action between the actor and his environment? What are some of the consequences of believing that a person is or is not responsible for a particular event?

Each of these questions may arise when an observer causally interprets a given set of information to arrive at an *attribution*. The information concerns behavior, behavioral consequences, and the circumstances under which behavior occurs. The attribution has the effect or result of placing this information in a cause-effect context. It provides an answer to the question: what caused the observed behavior and its consequences?

The following chapters investigate the processes intervening between information and attribution. A central thematic concern throughout the book is an analysis of the assumptions and expectations the attributor brings to his task of causal understanding. These assumptions and expectations shape the attribution process by filling gaps in informaion, relating behavioral data to comparative standards, and effecting shifts in attention or emphasis. Because attributions go beyond the information given, the attributor's causal interpretations may be accurate or in error, functional or dysfunctional. Analysis of the attribution process takes on special practical importance because people frequently draw erroneous inferences about the causes of social events and act in accordance with these inferences.

General Orientation of Attribution Theory

Attribution theory deals with the rules the average individual uses in attempting to infer the causes of observed behavior. Thus it concerns what Heider has called "naive psychology"—the cause-effect analyses of behavior made by the "man in the street." Scientific psychology, of course, is also broadly concerned with the causes of behavior, but the domain of attribution theory within psychology is more delimited; attribution theory examines the layman's analysis of behavioral causation for the purpose of understanding how his analysis affects his own behavior.

Attribution theory is related to a broader field called "psychological epistemology," a science analyzing the processes by which man "knows" his world. As it has been developed to date in social psychology, however, attribution theory deals only with that portion of this broad area that has to do with gaining knowledge about people—including knowledge about others and knowledge about the self. Thus, it is not "naive physics" or "naive cosmology" but a naive version of psychology itself.

At present attribution theory is an amorphous collection of observations about naive causal inference. Although Jones and Davis (1965) and Kelley (1967) have attempted to construct a systematic framework drawing together some of these observations and insights, and Kelley's discussion of causal schemata (Chapter 9) represents a further attempt at systematic theorizing, the reader of this book should not expect to come away with a firm grasp of interrelated deductive principles. The intent is, instead, to illustrate a mode of approach, a way of thinking about human behavior that can illuminate the origins and consequences of the actor's own cognitions. The attribution approach treats the actor as a constructive thinker searching for causes of the events confronting him and acting upon his imperfect knowledge of causal structure in ways that he considers appropriate.

Attribution theory grows out of a number of converging lines of inquiry in social psychology. The research along these lines can be roughly classified according to emphasis on certain broad concerns.

[1] The factors motivating the individual to obtain causally relevant information,

[2] the factors determining what cause will be assigned for a given event, and

[3] the consequences of making one causal attribution rather than another.

Research of the first type includes Festinger's analysis of the role of social comparison processes [1954] in the assessment of one's own ability and in the evaluation of the validity of one's opinions (that is, whether or not their "cause" lies primarily in properties of the external world). A closely related example is Schachter's (1959) study of affiliation under fear arousal. Schachter and his colleagues found that subjects under stress want to associate with others facing the same threatening situation. This desire to affiliate stems at least partially from the need to evaluate one's own feelings—to determine, through subtle comparisons with others, a response appropriate to the causal properties of the threatening situation. This work was later extended by Gerard and Rabbie (1961) who showed that an individual's affiliative tendencies were strong to the extent that he lacked information regarding his own emotional reactions.

Examples of the second line of inquiry on factors affecting the assignment of cause, include Heider's theoretical writings (1958) on the attribution of intention, ability, and task difficulty. Another example is Thibaut and Riecken's classic study (1955) of relative status and the assignment of responsibility for a compliant act. Also in this category is the analysis by Jones and Davis (1965), based on earlier works such as that reported in Jones, Davis, and Gergen (1961), concerning the factors influencing the intentions and attitudes attributed to a person. A related example is Bem's studies (1965, 1967) of the attitude inferred from a person's behavior in the light of the circumstances under which the behavior occurred.

Schachter and Singer (1962) initiated a distinctive line of research investigating the labeling of experienced emotions. They were able to show that drug-induced autonomic arousal can be experienced as either anger or joy depending on the surrounding circumstances. In Chapter 4, Nisbett and Valins examine such findings in attributional terms. They argue that the direction and intensity of emotion will vary with the subject's assignment of causation. Thus, for example, if a person believes that his autonomic symptoms are drug-induced, he will not experience intense emotion toward stimuli that would otherwise produce an affective reaction.

A number of studies deal simultaneously with the determinants and the consequences of causal attribution. Strickland (1958) investigated the effects of surveillance and its interference with the development of trust in a supervisory work setting. In this context, lack of trust is equivalent to the belief that the desirable behavior of the worker under observation is caused by the supervisor's surveillance rather than being spontaneous or voluntary. If the supervisor attributes causation to his own surveillance, he will continue to monitor the worker's performance as a consequence of his lack of trust. Thus surveillance is both a determinant and a consequence of the causal attribution. Another example of research dealing with both determinants and consequences is provided by Valins (1966) who showed that an experimentally induced covariation between heart rate changes and photographs of attractive girls was effective in producing differential feelings of attraction to the girls. Thus causal attribution was determined by the variation in heart rate with attraction toward the girls varying as a consequence.

The third type of research has focused more exclusively on the consequences of causal attribution. For example, many studies in the dissonance area have been concerned with identifying the post-decisional consequences of subjective volition (i.e., of perceived control over one's own behavior). Attitude change occurs after a person has acted in a way that is at variance with his current beliefs if he realizes that he had other behavioral options (cf. Brehm and Cohen 1962, Aronson 1969). A second example of attributional consequences is Storms and Nisbett's demonstration (1970) of an apparent reduction in insomnia resulting when the insomniac reattributes the cause of his sleeplessness. A final example is Shomer's finding (1966) that skill-attributed differences in contributions of group members to a group product result in differential division of the group's rewards in favor of the more skillful group member.

At a very general level, the lines of work defined by the preceding examples are based on three broad assumptions:

I. The individual attempts to assign a cause for important instances of his behavior and that of others; when necessary, he seeks information that enables him to do so.

II. His assignment of causes is determined in a systematic manner.

III. The particular cause that he attributes for a given event has important consequences for his subsequent feelings and behavior. The "meaning" of the event and his subsequent reaction to it are determined to an important degree by its assigned cause.

With respect to the *first* of these assumptions, concerning the motivation underlying the attribution process, attribution theory stands in sharpest contrast to theories of cognitive consistency (Abelson, et al. 1968). Attribution theory begins with man's motivation to understand the cause and effect relations that underlie and give stable meaning to the shifting surface of events. It assumes a need to have a veridical understanding of these relations (a *reality* orientation to the world) and a need to predict and apply them (a *control* orientation).

In attribution theory, consistency is not necessarily the desired end-product of cognitive work. Consistency is rather a *criterion* for understanding, a criterion for when the causal explanation is thought to be sufficient. In the various cognitive consistency theories, on the other hand, consistency serves other purposes, such as to "justify" or render reasonable one's own past decisions (cognitive dissonance theory), or to achieve certain "good" figural properties (balance theory). Furthermore, the nature of the "consistency" is different. Kelley (1967) has proposed that the ultimate criterion for "knowing" involves *consistently* being able to make *distinctive* responses to informational patterns. This implies active comparison between responses made on different occasions and by different modalities. There is no assumption that priority is given to past decisions or commitments as the particular responses with which current responses must be consistent. Nor are the particular patterns of consistency specified by "balance" or "congruity" principles assumed to be especially comfortable or stable.

While there are clear differences between attribution theory and theories of cognitive consistency, their intellectual roots have much in common. Many basic ideas of the former derive from the two major cognitive consistency theorists, Leon Festinger and Fritz Heider. We have already noted the ties between attribution theory and Festinger's theory of social comparison processes. Festinger's 1954 paper drew together his earlier notions of the social validation of opinions and extended them to include the role of social comparisons in evaluating one's own ability. It was only later that his theory of cognitive dissonance was proposed (1957) and the relations between social comparison and dissonance theory have never been clearly spelled out.

It is to Heider more than to any other single individual that attribution theory can be "attributed."

His early paper on phenomenal causality (1944) emphasized the human motive to stabilize the perceived environment by appropriate cause-effect assignments. Heider's 1946 paper was a clear forecast of balance theory, with no attempt to link the discussion of "attitudes and cognitive organization" to causal attribution. In his influential *Psychology of Interpersonal Relations* (1958), the naive analysis of action, intention, ability, and environmental properties is more central and important than the concept of "balance." Heider's conception of the relations between attribution and balance is not clearly delineated in his writings, but it might be suggested that the balance "principles" form one possible vehicle, among many, for making causal inferences. In any event, Heider's later writings show him as more of a cognitive functionalist than a configurational Gestaltist and therefore closer in spirit to Brunswik than to Koffka.

Attribution theory, with its emphasis on the reality and control orientation of the individual, does not supplant the cognitive consistency theories. To propose that the individual seeks information enabling causal attribution does not imply that this information search is unaffected by other motives suggested by cognitive consistency theories—self-justification or the maintenance of preferred cognitive configurations.

Nor does attribution theory involve any assumption that the individual is always acting as an "attributor." Certainly, the importance of causal understanding to the individual depends on the amount of information available and the action requirements and role constraints of the situation. Jones and Thibaut (1958) have pointed out that a person may make interpersonal judgments under different inferential sets. Some of these sets involve naive causal analysis more directly than others. Heider himself has noted the existence of different levels of attribution as a function of developmental maturity. It is not a far leap to assume that adults function at different levels of attributional complexity at different times and under different conditions. Moreover, the work by Seeman (1963) on internal locus of control as it relates to information seeking implies that there are important differences among individuals in their orientation toward understanding and controlling their worlds. This same assumption is apparent in Rotter's (1966) work.

These notions about situational and individual variations in making attributions should sensitize us to the possibility that our research findings in attribution studies are not representative of most people or most situations. An "attribution-making set" is highly appropriate in most psychology experiments, and college student subjects are probably atypically high on internal locus of control. Therefore, the research to date may lead to the impression that attribution processes are more important and common than they actually are. This in no way reduces the significance of studying these processes, particularly if it can be shown that they are especially likely to come into play at crucial decision points in the individual's life. But these limitations of our research evidence do suggest the importance of studying this particular type of motive and process within the broader context of other motivational and information-processing systems.

A final caution concerns the fact that attribution theory has obvious limits in explaining the complexities of human behavior. Perhaps the most that can be reasonably claimed is that attributional analyses may be propaedeutic to the application of other theories, for the simple reason that attributions arouse a diversity of other motives and mediate numerous other processes—such as aggression, guilt, or motivational changes. While attribution theory itself has nothing to say about these processes, an attributional inquiry may indicate which process is likely to be involved.

BIBLIOGRAPHY

Robert P. Abelson, Elliot Aronson, William J. McGuire, Theodore M. Newcomb, Milton J. Rosenberg, and Percy Tannenbaum, eds., *Theories of Cognitive Consistency: A Sourcebook.* Rand McNally, 1968.

Elliot Aronson, "The Theory of Cognitive Dissonance: A Current Perspective." In Leonard Berkowitz, ed., *Advances in Experimental Social Psychology*, Vol. 4. Academic Press, 1969.

Daryl J. Bem, "An Experimental Analysis of Self-Persuasion." *Journal of Experimental Social Psychology*, 1965, 1:199–218.

Daryl J. Bem, "Self Perception: An Alternative Interpretation of Cognitive Dissonance Phenomena." *Psychological Review*, 1967, 74:183–200.

Jack W. Brehm and Arthur R. Cohen, *Explorations in Cognitive Dissonance.* Wiley, 1962.

Leon Festinger, "A Theory of Social Comparison Processes." *Human Relations*, 1954, 7:117–140.

Leon Festinger, *A Theory of Cognitive Dissonance.* Stanford University Press, 1957.

Harold B. Gerard and Jaap Rabbie, "Fear and Social Comparison." *Journal of Abnormal and Social Psychology*, 1961, 62:586–592.

Fritz Heider, "Social Perception and Phenomenal Causality." *Psychological Review*, 1944, 51:358–374.

Fritz Heider, "Attitudes and Cognitive Organization." *Journal of Psychology*, 1946, 21:107–112.

Fritz Heider, *The Psychology of Interpersonal Relations*. Wiley, 1958.

Edward E. Jones and Keith E. Davis, "From Acts to Dispositions: The Attribution Process in Person Perception." In Leonard Berkowitz, ed., *Advances in Experimental Social Psychology*, Vol. 2. Academic Press, 1965.

Edward E. Jones, Keith E. Davis, and Kenneth J. Gergen, "Role Playing Variations and Their Informational Value for Person Perception." *Journal of Abnormal and Social Psychology*, 1961, 63:302–310.

Edward E. Jones and John W. Thibaut, "Interaction Goals as Bases of Inference in Interpersonal Perception." In Renato Tagiuri and Luigi Petrullo, eds., *Person Perception and Interpersonal Behavior*. Stanford University Press, 1958.

Harold H. Kelley, "Attribution Theory in Social Psychology." In David Levine, ed., *Nebraska Symposium on Motivation, 1967*. University of Nebraska Press, 1967.

Julian B. Rotter, "Generalized Expectancies for Internal versus External Control of Reinforcement." *Psychological Monograph*, 1966, 80 (1) (whole no. 609).

Stanley Schachter, *The Psychology of Affiliation*. Stanford University Press, 1959.

Stanley Schachter and Jerome E. Singer, "Cognitive, Social, and Psychological Determinants of Emotional States." *Psychological Review*, 1962, 69:379–399.

Melvin Seeman, "Alienation and Social Learning in a Reformatory." *American Journal of Sociology*, 1963, 69:270–284.

Robert W. Shomer, "Effects of Chance and Skill Outcomes on Expectancy, Recall, and Distributive Allocations." Ph.D. thesis, University of California, Los Angeles, 1966.

Michael D. Storms and Richard E. Nisbett, "Insomnia and the Attribution Process." *Journal of Personality and Social Psychology*, 1970, 16:319–328.

Lloyd H. Strickland, "Surveillance and Trust." *Journal of Personality*, 1958, 26:200–215.

John W. Thibaut and Henry W. Riecken, "Some Determinants and Consequences of the Perception of Social Causality." *Journal of Personality*, 1955, 24:113–133.

Stuart E. Valins, "Cognitive Effects of False Heart-Rate Feedback." *Journal of Personality and Social Psychology*, 1966, 4:400–408.

1 · Attribution in Social Interaction

HAROLD H. KELLEY

University of California, Los Angeles

IN the course of my interaction with other people, I often wonder why they act as they do. I may wonder how to interpret a compliment a student makes of a lecture I recently gave, why my friend is so critical of a certain common acquaintance, or why my colleague has not done his share of the work on our joint project. These are questions about the attribution of the other person's behavior—what causes it, what is responsible for it, to what is it to be attributed? In all such instances, I not only ask these questions but I myself—through my actions, characteristics, social status, and so on—provide some of the possible answers. It is a special feature of social interaction that each participant is both a causal agent and an attributor. His own behavior may be a cause of the behavior he is trying to understand and explain.

In some manner, each individual answers these attributional questions for himself, and in each case the answer he reaches undoubtedly affects his subsequent behavior in the interaction and his attitudes toward the other person. This assertion is based not only on introspection and common experience but on numerous experiments in social perception and interpersonal relations. The purpose of this paper is to review this research and to summarize its conclusions and implications. This review is guided primarily toward determining *how* the person arrives at his answer to the question "Why?" The aim is to summarize what we have learned about the "attribution process" as it occurs in social interaction and the facts that affect its course. Our special interest will be in attributions made by the participants in ongoing social interaction. However, much of the relevant literature deals with simpler situations, as in the case of a third party observing the interaction between two other persons.

The reader must be alerted to several problems encountered in assembling this review because most of the relevant studies are primarily concerned with other dependent variables and only incidentally with attributions. Thus, the typical investigation links stimulus cues or conditions to some dependent variable such as liking or helping behavior. The observed relationship is assumed to be mediated by an attributional link (for example, "He is responsible for the aid I have received so I will help him in return"), but the link is not always directly assessed. In interpreting many of the studies, therefore, it is necessary to infer the mediating attributions. Few have employed explicit measures of the assumed attributions (for example, perceived causality, responsibility) or even indirect measures (such as perceived freedom, honesty, blameworthiness).

A second problem in assessing the relevant literature has to do with the unclarity of the theoretical statements. Concerned not only with attribution but with its consequences, the theoretical statements often reflect a complex interweaving of ideas about perceived causality and ideas about, say, the bases of interpersonal attraction. By trying to deal with several problems at once, as they pertain to attribution, the theories are often not entirely clear. It is perhaps debatable, but I believe the analysis of the attributional process can and should be separated from the other phenomena. To emphasize this point, attribution theory is *not* a theory of interpersonal attraction, even though a large majority of the relevant studies employ liking or evaluation as a main dependent variable.

A final problem is that the typical study has not dealt systematically with the antecedents of attribution. Consequently, we are left to piece together the propositions about the determinants of the attribution process. This review attempts to remedy this neglect, emphasis being given to propositions about information patterns that form the basis for various attributions. Another facet of this last problem is that much of the literature is highly redundant in terms of its relevance for attribution theory. For example, numerous studies show that behavior is attributed less to the actor when there is also present a plausible external cause for that behavior than when no such cause is present. While these various studies make interestingly different points for other purposes (for example, for the analysis of attraction), for our present goal there is little purpose to be served by reviewing them in detail. For this reason, some of the "classic" areas of research relating to attribution receive cursory review and more attention is paid certain less well-known studies that allow us to draw a wider range of generalizations about attribution. This inevitably results in reliance upon the isolated, unreplicated study or the pair of studies that, though done for different reasons, are now found to point to the same conclusion. Thus, the tenor of this paper is highly speculative. Its purpose is to change the direction of research in this field— to move it out of the several grooves in which it has been moving and to encourage research that is specifically designed to test attributional hypotheses and that concerns itself with a broader range of attribution phenomena.

The general substantive outline of this discussion is as follows. We consider first several types of attribution phenomena in which the attributor makes use of the information at his disposal in a highly reasonable manner. An earlier paper on attribution theory outlined a model for the attribution process, describing it in terms of an analysis of covariation very much like that a scientist employs in identifying cause and effect relations [Kelley 1967]. In the first case to be considered here, the lay attributor (at least as represented by our university student subjects) generally acts like a good scientist, examining the covariation between a given effect and various possible causes. Under the press of time and the competition of his other interests, however, he often makes incomplete analyses, settling for small samples of data and incomplete data patterns. In these instances, even though his available information does not permit him to make a "covariance analysis," the lay attributor still uses it in a reasonable and unbiased manner.

We then encounter some important exceptions, in which the available information is used in systematically biased and even erroneous ways. Our problem becomes one of trying to make sense of this total pattern of results—the combination of rational and unbiased processes and biased ones. It is proposed that our theory of attribution must be grounded in a view of the layman as an "applied scientist," that is, as a person concerned about applying his knowledge of causal relations in order to *exercise control* of his world. This proposal is made in the belief that the person's motivation to control has consequences for his attributions and, further, that the process by which attributions are made and the nature of both the accuracies and errors they exhibit can be explained by the problems of control he commonly faces.

Covariation over Time

The first class of cases to be considered consists of those in which the attributor has relevant information from successive points in time. This is typically the case, of course, in social interactions. The *covariation principle* that attributors seem to follow is this: *An effect is attributed to the one of its possible causes with which, over time, it covaries.*

A simple experimental illustration of this principle is provided by an experiment on mutual fate control [Kelley, Thibaut, Radloff & Mundy 1962]. Two subjects were brought to separate rooms in the laboratory and placed before identical pieces of apparatus. Each person was afforded two responses, a left button and a right button, and was asked to press one of these each time a certain signal was given. He was also told that after each response he would receive one of two outcomes, a gain or a loss. The apparatus for the two subjects was interconnected so that each one's responses controlled the other's gains and losses. Thus each had total control over the other's fate. This experimental paradigm was developed primarily to study the "minimal social situation," in which the two subjects have no knowledge of each other nor of their interdependence. Our present interest, however, is in the case where (1) the relation was fully explained to each one *except* he was not told which response had which effect, and (2) the subjects were required to interact (each with the goal of making as many gains as possible) without any explicit communication.

The reader will understand the causal analysis problem that this situation poses for a subject. If he knew which of his responses had which effect, he could use this knowledge to provide the other person with gains and perhaps to induce the other to reciprocate. Results presented by Kelley, Thibaut, Radloff, and Mundy suggest that subjects are able to solve this problem. Over a series of successive trials, twenty-six of thirty-four pairs managed to reach a stable sequence of giving each other nothing but gains. As to how they accomplished this, a sizable number (twenty-nine) of the sixty-eight subjects reported using a simple covariation rule, namely, that if one of their responses was associated with trial-to-trial stability in their partner's behavior, this indicated the response yielded him gains, but if the response was associated with variability in the other's behavior, this meant it caused him losses. That this assumption played an important role in "solving" the interdependency problem is indicated by the fact that it

was mentioned in more of the dyads attaining a stable exchange of gains than in those not able to do so.

While the evidence from this study does not document the details of what happened, it is plausible to assume that a subject who was fully cognizant of the attribution problem proceeded as follows: He arbitrarily chose one of his responses and repeated it over a series of trials and observed the other person's behavior (as evidenced by his own gains and losses). Then he did the same for the other response and again observed the effect. From the temporal covariation between responses and effects, their causal properties were inferred. Specifically, the response accompanied by the greater stability in the partner's behavior was inferred to be the one causing a gain for the partner.

Several aspects of this procedure are to be noted.

1. The person's interpretation of the covariance analysis is based on a prior cause-effect assumption, namely, that loss leads to variation in behavior and gain to stabilization of behavior. Without this assumption, the subject might have inferred that one response caused behavioral variability and the other stability, without being able to interpret this difference in terms of gain or loss effects. (It so happens that the added assumption is not only a part of naive psychology but is a basic notion in scientific psychology—the "law of effect"—and was employed by Kelley and his colleagues in making their predictions about various developments in the mutual fate control situation.) This causal assumption could itself be tested by an appropriate covariation analysis, as by an "experiment" in which, with knowledge of whether losses or gains are impinging on a person at various times, the corresponding variability in his behavior is observed. It was not possible for subjects to make such analysis in the situation considered here. The general attributional point illustrated here is that the *interpretation of a given covariance analysis often depends upon the person's prior causal attributions.* Another way of putting this point is that the attributor often has to devise "indicators" of the effects he assumes he produces. Without direct knowledge of his gain or loss effects, the subject in the experiment described above improvised such indicators on the basis of attributional assumptions about *their* effects. This situation has its obvious parallels in experimental science where, in addition to manipulating the independent variables, the investigator must often identify appropriate indirect indicators of dependent variables to which he has no direct access.

2. The attribution strategy described above re-

quires a person temporarily to set aside his concern with gains and losses and to adopt an information-acquisition role in which he views the pattern of consequences simply in terms of what they tell him about his partner. He thus suspends his own tendency to be stable following gain and variable following loss, but in doing so he assumes and hopes that the partner will continue to exhibit this tendency. An obvious problem arises if both persons adopt the attribution strategy at the same time. By temporarily stabilizing his behavior in order to test its effects, one could easily mislead the other into thinking that that particular behavior was the one providing him with gain. The general point is that problems may arise if both interactors simultaneously assume the role of "attributors." The pattern of behavior appropriate for gaining information about cause and effect relations within the relationship is probably generally misleading if interpreted as reflecting those very relations. Veridical information about how one's behavior affects others can be gained only if those others express the effects in their own behavior and not if their behavior is itself under the control of some information-search strategy. For example, a young man who breaks off with his girl friend in order to test her dependence on him (that is, to test his efficacy in providing her with rewards) runs the risk she will interpret the action as reflecting her own failure to provide him with a satisfactory relationship. A different example concerns assessing the mutual effects of a common external cause. When a husband and wife are trying to decide whether to buy a particular new house, the guardedly favorable comments each one makes while trying to figure out how the other one feels about it (that is, the effect the house has on the other person) may lead each one to believe the other favors the purchase when in fact neither does.

In the situation just considered, the attributor was able to conduct "experiments" by varying the causes in question (his two responses) and observing the covariation in effects. Let us now consider another common type of situation, that in which the attributor is merely a powerless observer, processing information regarding covariation as it is presented by the natural flow of social interaction. A simple example is provided by Kelley and Stahelski [1970]. Subjects were observers of a brief bit of interaction between two players in the prisoner's dilemma game. They had first been carefully instructed in the game. They were shown that the game permits each person to make only one of two responses on each trial and that the outcomes to each player then depend on the

responses they have independently selected. Response C enables both players to make a small gain if both choose it, but if one chooses it and the other chooses D, the former suffers a large loss and the latter enjoys a large gain. Response D has the advantage described above if the other person has chosen C, but if both players choose D, both suffer modest losses. The rules of the game require the two players independently to make their response choices and these are then made known and the appropriate gains and/or losses are distributed. It can be seen that C is a relatively cooperative response, the principal reason for its choice being a desire to enable both players to receive small gains. In contrast, D is a relatively competitive action, enabling a person to exploit to his own advantage the other's C choice. D may also, of course, be a defensive choice, to protect oneself from the other's anticipated exploitation.

Kelley and Stahelski told their subjects that the players whose responses they would see had each been asked before the start of the game to decide whether his intention in the game would be to establish a cooperative or a competitive relationship. They were then shown brief sequences of the interaction between pairs of (hypothetical) players and were asked in each case to judge what they would infer one particular player's intention to be and their confidence in that judgment. For example, they were told that player A made response C on a given trial while, at the same time, B made response D. Then on the next trial, A again made response C. (We can summarize this pattern as C–D, C, the C–D referring to A's and B's respective responses on the first trial and the last term, C, to A's response on the second trial.) The subjects were always asked to judge A's intention.

From an attributional viewpoint, the subject's problem in judging A's intention can be considered that of inferring the cause of A's behavior. If we apply the principle of covariation over time to the various patterns of information (and it is appropriate inasmuch as we have instances of A's behavior on two successive trials), we note that there are two features of these patterns relevant to inferring the causes of A's behavior: A's behavior is stable or variable, and the stability or change stands in different covariance relations to B's behavior.

The *first* cue has the following relevance to the covariation principle. If the assumed cause is stable over time, so should be its presumed effect. In the present case, the intention the players set themselves for the relationship is presumably stable. This being so, a stable pattern of behavior provided a better cue to that cause than a variable one. And not surprisingly, this is what the data indicated, that A's consistent C (or D) response leads to a more confident attribution (and one made with more consensus among subjects) that A's intention is cooperative (or competitive) than does A's inconsistent response. This is a simple and obvious result presumably applicable to the inference of any cause assumed to be stable over time and not to causes of a more variable or evanescent variety.

The *second* cue implies that the observer is considering two possible causal factors relevant to A's behavior, his intention and the social context as defined by B's behavior. A logical way for the subject to allocate A's behavior to these two causes is to determine the degree to which A's behavior covaries with B's and to assume that the greater this covariance, the more the behavior is to be attributed to the social context and discounted as a reflection of A's intention.

If we consider only the patterns in which A's second response is D, we find that the two stable patterns (D–C, D and D–D, D) represent two degrees of apparent covariance between A's behavior and B's. In the first case, there is a rather clear independent or noncovariant relation between the two, there being no change in A's behavior even though he has an opportunity to be influenced by the example of B's different behavior. In the second case, the degree of covariance is indeterminant or ambiguous: A may have simply persisted in his preferred behavior or he may have persisted partly because of B's supporting example. Given these different degrees of relationship between A's behavior and its social context (B's behavior), clear independence versus an ambiguous degree of independence, we would expect the former to be taken as more informative about the intention than the latter. This is what the data showed, that there is more consensus in the former case that A is competitive and the pattern is rated as providing more information and supporting a more confident judgment about A's intention.

When we consider the two unstable patterns in which the second response is D (C–C, D and C–D, D), we find that they too entail different degrees of covariance between A's and B's behavior. In the case of the C–D, D pattern, there is a positive covariation between A's and B's behaviors, there being a change in A's behavior such that it corresponds to what B has done. This would suggest that the attributor would tend to discount the second behavior and, faced with the inconsistency in A's behavior (the

first cue), be uncertain about what intention to assign him. The results are consistent with this, there being little consensus and confidence as to A's intention in this case. In contrast, the C–C, D pattern provides a case of "negative" covariation inasmuch as A's behavior changes so that it is different from what B has done. In other words, A seems to "initiate" a competitive move in the face of B's cooperative example. This negative association between A's second behavior and its social context suggests that it can be attributed to him and affords a basis for inferring his intention. The result is high consensus and confidence among subjects that A indeed has a competitive intention.

Locus of Effect of the Covariant Cause

Several puzzling and unanticipated results from the Kelley and Stahelski study force us to broaden our view of the role of the covariant factor. The findings summarized above were not replicated for the patterns in which A's second behavior was C. When A's response was consistently C, he was more often judged to be cooperative than when he changed from D to C, but the effect of information as to what B was doing meanwhile seemed to have an effect opposite from the predicted one. This reversal was not significant in the original data but a recent unpublished study by Wayne Osgood suggests that the reversal is a stable effect, at least for the comparison between the C–C, C and C–D, C patterns. That is to say, judgments that A has a cooperative intention are more frequent in the first case than in the second.

Of the possible explanations for this reversal, a highly plausible one is that B's cooperative move in the first pattern is seen as encouraging or strengthening A's cooperative intention and that B's competitive move in the second case as discouraging or weakening it. This interpretation suggests that the context factor may play a quite different role in the inference process than the one we have been assuming. Rather than constituting a covariant causal factor acting upon A's behavior and thus affecting its significance as an indicator of his intention, in the present case it seems that the covarying factor is seen to operate directly upon the intention itself, either strengthening or weakening it. Thus, *the perceived locus of effect of B's behavior is not on A's behavior but on A's intention.*

This effect of B's behavior is relevant in the Kelley and Stahelski study only for the patterns where A is seen as rather cooperative, which in practice are the cases where his second response is the cooperative one. In these cases, B's cooperative response is probably seen to strengthen or encourage A's cooperative intention and his competitive response to weaken it. In contrast, if A's intention is a competitive one, there is probably no perceived difference between B's cooperative and competitive response in their effect on the intention; the one response encourages it as much as the other. The weak reversal from the expected trend noted above (and the ambiguous results for the comparison between D–C, C and D–D, C) may indicate the counterposition of the two interpretations of the locus of effect of B's behavior. Thus, in the comparison between C–C, C and C–D, C, interpreting B's behavior as acting upon A's behavior leads to a stronger inference of cooperative intention for the second pattern (A is cooperative despite B's provocation) but interpreting B's behavior as affecting A's intention leads to a stronger inference of cooperative intention for the first pattern (A's cooperative action strengthens B's own resolve to be cooperative). The opposite effects of these two interpretations may nearly cancel out each other.

If the reader can tolerate one further complication, it is perhaps important to report that when the subjects were asked a different question, the results for the C–C, C versus C–D, C comparison were as originally expected. Specifically, the latter pattern resulted in a higher frequency of judging A as having acted "on principle," the subjects more often choosing the first alternative when asked whether A established his intention for the relationship because he felt it was what he should always try to do and what one ought to do, *or* because it was the most rational and efficient way to maximize his score. In the light of the discussion above of the two causal roles that B's behavior can be assumed to play for the A who appears generally cooperative, this result suggests that the nature of the inquiry to the attributor can shift the emphasis he gives the two roles. When asked whether the evidence indicates a stable personal property, the attributor does not consider the covariant factor as possible cause of the *property* but rather merely as a possible cause of the *behavior*. Accordingly, in the C–C, C pattern the possible effect of B's cooperative move on A's disposition is suppressed and B's competitive move in the C–D, C pattern is taken as an influence on A's behavior that he resists, the pattern therefore being indicative of a principle-based disposition to cooperate.

Space does not permit full consideration of the dual role of the covariant factor. The problem is

raised here because in the remainder of this paper, the assumption is made that the attributor views extraneous (external, covariant, etc.) factors only in terms of their effect upon behavior. This is obviously too simple a view. Personal properties are not fixed forever but are subject to change, and external factors sometimes act to change them. As many social psychologists have observed [French & Raven 1959], certain external social influences affect only the target's behavior whereas others affect his dispositions (attitudes, intention, beliefs). This difference in locus of effect being an "objective" fact, it is highly probable that it is also a "subjective" fact, that is, that lay attributors are aware of the difference and take account of it in making their judgments (though not necessarily accurately so).

Assuming that external causal factors are sometimes seen as directly changing the relevant personal properties also provides one possible explanation for various other deviant results not otherwise intelligible in terms of the attribution principles emphasized in this paper. These are the several other instances in which the presence of a covariant factor or alternative causal explanation for the behavior results in a stronger attribution of the correspondent personal property. For example, Alexander and Knight [1971] report on interpersonal simulation of the Carlsmith, Collins, and Helmreich study [1966] of forced compliance. In one of their conditions in which the behavior of the target person is writing an essay expressing a view generally contrary to his attitudes, he is judged to have attitudes more consistent with the behavior the greater the inducement provided for writing the essay. In other words, instead of the essay-writing being discounted as indicative of his beliefs when elicited by a stronger external cause, the attitude is judged as being more in line with the essay. Here is it possible that the inducement is seen primarily as changing the attitude rather than as affecting only the behavior. Similarly, Kruglanski [1970, described more fully later] conducted a replication of Strickland's study of the relative trustworthiness attributed to two workers depending on how closely their prior work had been supervised. When the attributor was left unsure of the quality of the two men's production, he judged the one who had been more closely supervised to be more trustworthy. Kruglanski suggests that this result might be interpreted in terms of the perceived effect of the different degrees of supervision upon the workers' respective expectations about how closely they may be supervised in the future. In a sense, this implies that the close supervision was seen to change a disposition of the worker (though a rather transient one) relevant to his dependability on later occasions. (The interpretation also implies that the question put to the attributors permitted them to think in terms of a less than permanent personal property.) This result is the opposite of Strickland's original finding, which Kruglanski was able to replicate, that with known and equal productivity for the two men, the one who had been less closely supervised was judged the more trustworthy of the two.

Jae-Ho Cha [1971] has just completed a series of attributional studies in which he attempted to discover what conditions produce a "discounting" of the behavior in the light of covariant causal factors (and a stronger personal-property attribution the weaker are these factors) versus an "assimilation" of the personal property to the covariant factors (with a stronger attribution the stronger these factors). While he tested a specific theory as to the differentiating conditions, his informal conclusion is that the assimilation effects (equivalent to the "reversals" we have been discussing here) probably occur under a variety of different conditions. The data we have reviewed above suggest that one such condition may be that in which the covariant causes are seen directly to affect the relevant personal disposition.

Temporal Relations between Cause and Effect

The covariation principle is based on the assumption that effects covary over time with their causes. The "with" in this statement conceals the important and little-studied problem of the exact temporal relations between cause and effect. The effect must not, of course, precede a possible cause if that cause is to be perceived as the effective one. More interesting is the question of the optimal interval between the cause and the subsequent effect. This question is of particular importance in natural social interaction, which flows without regular or sharp time demarcations and in which psychological time is a very elastic dimension. For example, when I attempt to compliment a student on his work, how long am I to wait to see an effect from which I can infer my remark's casual properties? Or, to what earlier events am I to attribute the recent comment by my boss that "Things seem to be going very well in your part of the organization"?

At the level of perceived physical causality, Michotte demonstrated the remarkable importance of timing of successive events [1963]. His well-known demonstration consisted of two squares, the first, A, moving across the field to make contact with the second, B, which then also began to move. When the movement of B followed immediately upon the time of contact, the observer's impression was a clear one of causation, the movement of A giving rise to the movement of B. In sharp contrast, a brief interval (one-fifth of a second) between A's joining B and the onset of B's movement totally eliminated the impression of causality.

A social interaction counterpart to Michotte's demonstration could be provided by use of the procedure devised by Bavelas, Hastorf, Gross, and Kite [1965]. In the course of spontaneous group discussions, they found that rewards delivered immediately after the comments of one particular member (a green light displayed to him privately) and punishments delivered after the actions of the other members (red lights displayed to each of them) increased the frequency of the former's participation in the discussion, and he (as well as the other members) evaluated his contributions more highly than on earlier occasions. A close analogue of Michotte's result could probably be produced in this situation by simply introducing a standard time delay between each designated comment and its reward feedback. In fact, Bavelas and his colleagues destroyed altogether any systematic temporal relation between behavior and its effect. This was done by delivering the rewards at randomly designated *times* during the interaction rather than immediately after the designated member's comments. Presumably, as in Michotte's experiment, the perceived causal link between the person's actions and the rewards was broken. It is likely that as the rewarded member examined the covariance between his actions and the green lights, the evidence suggested that rewards were as likely to occur with his silences as with his vocalizations.

Under certain conditions of social interaction, the cue of temporal contiguity can be a misleading one, not related to true causation. For example, in many experimental interactions (as in the procedure typically used with the prisoner's dilemma game, described above) subjects are required to make behavioral choices simultaneously and independently on each trial. Only afterward are the consequences of their choices made known to them. This has the effect that the feedback a person receives immediately after his behavior could not possibly have been influenced by that behavior. If there is any degree of interpersonal influence under these conditions, it occurs with a time lag of one trial. While we might expect the individual to take account of this fact, he may not do so completely. At least this seems to be an implication of Swinth's study on the establishment of trust [1967]. A programmed player tried to establish a cooperative exchange in the prisoner's dilemma game after both he and the subject, on simultaneous first choices, had acted competitively. In a *sequential* procedure, this first event was followed by a series of alternating plays during which, when it came his turn to go first, the programmed player always made a cooperative move. In a contrasting *simultaneous* procedure, the first exchange was followed by further simultaneous moves, on the first of which the programmed player always made a cooperative move. A small sample renders the results inconclusive but they are consistent with the idea that the simultaneous response procedure makes ambiguous the programmed player's cooperative initiative. We might assume that under the sequential procedure, the programmed player's responsibility for the initiative is clear, but with the simultaneous procedure, because the subject learns about it *after* his own move, he may attribute the cooperative move to his own actions rather than to the other's good intentions.

The attributional consequences of the simultaneous response procedure, with its potentially misleading temporal cues, beg for careful experimental analysis. Such analysis is important because the experimental procedure undoubtedly has its analogues in spontaneous social interaction. Interdependent persons often have occasion independently and simultaneously to plan and commit themselves to actions having mutual consequences. Even in conversation where there is a superficial give and take in an alternating pattern, a person often formulates his next comment before he has fully heard out his partner's ongoing comment. Failing to take account of these temporal patterns, persons may seriously misinterpret the effects their actions have on others.

Multiple Plausible Causes:
The Discounting Effect

We turn now to what has been the most frequently investigated attribution problem in social interaction research. In this situation the attributor does not possess cause and effect information for successive points in time. Rather, he has information about a given effect and one or more possible causes. His problem is to attribute the effect to one or more of these causes. Being limited to this information and unable to make covariance tests to decide among the various causal candidates, the attributor does pretty much what a good scientist would do. If he is aware of several plausible causes, he attributes the effect less to any one of them than if he is aware only of one as a plausible cause. In other words, he makes his attributions according to a *discounting principle: the role of a given cause in producing a given effect is discounted if other plausible causes are also present.* This discounting is reflected in various ways. The attributor is less confident that the observed effect reflects the given cause. He is less willing to infer that the magnitude of the given cause is as great as might otherwise be indicated by the magnitude of the observed effect. In cases where the cause in question is a personal attribute, the attributor will make more neutral ratings of the attribute than he would in the absence of the other causes.

The progenitor of the long line of investigations of causal discounting is the well-known study by Thibaut and Riecken [1955]. It illustrates the genre as well as any study we might review here. The undergraduate subject worked with two other subjects (both actually the experimenter's confederates), one of whom was revealed to be of higher status than the subject and the other of lower status. (In one of two parallel experiments, status was defined in terms of educational level and position in the university, and in the other, it was defined in terms of social class, leadership experience, and age.) As the experiment proceeded, the true subject found it necessary to attempt to induce the two confederates to help him. Eventually and at the same time, both agreed to do so. This compliance constituted the effect for which the subject had available various plausible causal explanations. Specifically, he was asked whether each person complied because he wanted to (internal cause) or because he had been forced or pressured to (external cause). The results were quite clear. A large majority of the subjects attributed the high-status person's compliance to an internal cause and the low-status person's compliance to an external cause. They also increased more in their liking for the high-status person than for the low, but we will consider this aspect of this kind of experiment more fully below.

These results are consistent with applications of the discounting principle to the two instances of compliance each attributor was required to explain. The *possible* causes in each case are the internal and external ones, the latter being the subject's power with respect to the other two persons. In the case of the higher status person, the subject's power is not a *plausible* cause for the compliance, so the compliance is attributed solely (or to some high degree) to the internal cause, the actor's own preferences in the matter. On the other hand, the subject's power *is* a plausible cause for the low-status person's compliance, as also is that person's own desire. Given the two plausible causes, the role of the internal cause is discounted, with the result that, relative to the case of the high-status person with a single plausible cause, the low man's behavior is attributed more to external pressure. We would expect greater uncertainty in the latter case inasmuch as both the internal and external reasons are plausible, but Thibaut and Riecken's data do not bear on this point. They did document the differential plausibility of the subject's power in relation to the high- and low-power persons by means of evidence that subjects generally regarded the latter as less able to resist external influence.

Many variations have been played on this basic theme. Another well-known study, that of Jones, Davis, and Gergen, illustrates one of the other possible ways of demonstrating the discounting principle [1961]. Each subject-attributor heard a single recorded job interview in which the applicant was supposedly trying to make a good impression on the interviewer in order to qualify for the job. For some subjects the job was portrayed as that of a member of a submarine crew and for others as that of an astronaut. Considering only the former case, the subjects heard the interviewer describe the ideal job candidate as one who is obedient, cooperative, and friendly — in short, other-directed. As the interview proceeded, half of the subjects heard the candidate respond to questions with statements indicating he was indeed other-directed, and the other half of the subjects heard him indicate that he was inner-directed—independent and with little need for social contact. In a similar manner, the subjects listening to the interview for the job of astronaut heard the interviewer describe the ideal candidate as inner-directed, and then the applicant was heard, by different subjects, to present himself as either inner-directed or other-directed. In all cases, the subjects were finally asked to report their attributions of the applicant's behavior. These reports were not direct causal explanations for the behavior but rather were statements of what they thought he was *really* like as a person and of their confidence in these judgments. Of course, the subject's problem in this case is to

account for the behavior and, in light of the cause(s) to which he attributes it, to draw an inference about the candidate's characteristics. In each case the possible causal factors are internal to the candidate (his "personality traits") or external to him (demand characteristics of the job interview situation). However, the plausibility of the external cause depends upon the nature of the behavior. The interview situation is not plausible as a cause for behavior inconsistent with it. Thus, of the four conditions of the experiment there are two in which the attributor has only one plausible cause for the observed effect: that in which the applicant portrays himself as inner-directed even though the interview situation requires other-directedness and that in which he portrays himself as other-directed even though inner-directed behavior is called for. In these cases, the behavior should be attributed to the person himself and from it his properties should be inferred. The results show this to be true. In the first case he is described as truly inner-directed and in the second case as truly other-directed. In the remaining two conditions, the behavior has two plausible causes and therefore it should be attributed less to the person and taken to be less indicative of his properties. The ratings of both applicants who conform to the specified job requirements are rather neutral, do not differ from one another, and are made with low confidence. Thus, the dual plausible reasons present in these cases clearly reduce the attribution of the behavior to the internal cause (the person).

In a later paper, Jones and Davis interpret the earlier experiment, according to their theory of correspondent inferences, in the following terms [1965]: "In-role behavior does not lead to confident, correspondent inferences because such behavior has multiple consequences and many of these are high in cultural desirability. Most people want to avoid embarrassing others by not meeting their expectations, most people want to gain the rewards implicit in approval from authority figures, most people want to manifest their intelligence by showing that they understand what is required of them, and so on. Each of these effects is a 'plausible reason' for in-role behavior in the experiment just described. On the other hand, plausible reasons for out-of-role behavior (i.e., those with a reasonable degree of assumed social desirability) are comparatively scarce. One of the few noncommon effects of behavior at variance with role demands is the satisfaction of expressing one's true nature. This effect is also a possible accompaniment of in-role behavior, but in that case it exists . . . along with many other effects. Since there are fewer noncommon effects in the astronaut-other and submariner-inner choices, the effect of 'being oneself' forms the basis of a more correspondent inference in these conditions and the interviewee's behavior tends to be taken at face value" [p. 236].

From this statement it will be seen how much the present formulation of the discounting principle owes to Jones and Davis. They have clearly stated the key idea of several versus one (many versus few) plausible reasons and have asserted that the case of one or few reasons permits more confident inference from behavior to person properties. They rely heavily, as does the present formulation, on the vague term "plausible." They do, however, provide one conception of what it means, namely, a reason of high assumed social desirability, which is to say, a reason that would be effective for most people. At present there seems no more specific or systematic way to define the relevant causes. Operationally, we might define a plausible cause as one that any member of the same culture and time period as the experimenter would be likely to mention as a probable cause for the behavior if we describe it in its setting and ask, "Why did it occur?" This undoubtedly renders us too dependent on our subjects' introspections and verbal reports, but as a first approximation it seems appropriate.

In its divergences from the Thibaut and Riecken experiment, the Jones, Davis, and Gergen study illustrates some of the major variations in problem and procedure that have characterized this type of research. For example, the attributor may be an "observer" to the interaction or an actual participant. As was noted earlier, in the latter case the attributor's own causal role is often at issue. Studies of social interaction have not often involved systematic comparisons of the attributions made by actors and observers. In view of the important possible divergences suggested by Jones and Nisbett in their essay "The Actor and the Observer," this seems to be an area in which research is sorely needed. Such comparisons are also essential if we are to reach an informed evaluation of the attempts—most notably that of Daryl Bem [1967]—to reinterpret certain cognitive dissonance effects in attributional terms. These effects involve an actor's self-perceptions after having responded to social influence, and it has been proposed that the same processes are at work here as when an observer makes interpretations of the actor's behavior under similar circumstances.

The two studies we have reviewed also illustrate the fact that the external cause relevant to the behavior in question may be of many different sorts. In Thibaut and Riecken, it was the attributor's power vis-à-vis the actor. In Jones, Davis, and Gergen, it was the pressure of the social situation as defined by the job interviewer. In other studies, the external cause has been defined by such things as a dependency relationship between the actor and some other person, surveillance by a supervisor, the experimenter's instructions, a job assignment given a student by his instructor or coach, the importance placed on demonstrating one's compatibility with another person, and even the individual's own ability [". . . the sources of competence are in a sense external to the sphere of individual autonomy and responsibility" (Jones & deCharms 1957, p. 79)].

Our two examples reveal only some of the great variations among attribution studies in the kinds of dependent variables they employ and the degree to which attributions are explicitly measured. Thibaut and Riecken asked their subjects fairly direct questions as to causal imputations. Jones, Davis, and Gergen queried their subjects about the "real" properties of the stimulus person, these presumably being internal causal factors accounting for his behavior. As we will see below, many studies rely entirely on reports of liking, evidences of trusting behavior, or even behavioral choices having consequences for the actor (helping or hurting him). This fact creates the problems mentioned at the outset of this paper, as to what exactly are the mediating attributions and as to the relation between the attribution process and other processes, for example, those relating to reciprocity or attraction.

In both experiments we have considered, the comparison is between inferences made from two conditions: *internal only* and *internal + external*. The discounting principle is not, of course, limited to this type of comparison. It applies also to other possible comparisons, such as those of $internal_1$ *only* versus $internal_1 + internal_2$, and *external only* versus *external + internal*. The former would include cases of attributing performance to skill versus skill + effort. The latter relates to the problem of inferring the existence or potency of external causes. Thus, an experiment might compare interpretations made of behavior that occurs when the only plausible reason is an external cause (for example, influence from a powerful person) with the same behavior occurring under circumstances where there is both the same plausible external cause and an additional plausible internal one (the actor may have his own

10

reasons for the behavior). For this paradigm, the now familiar principle that behavior is discounted as being informative about a person if a plausible external cause is present would have its parallel in the principle that behavior is discounted as to its information value about the efficacy of an external cause if a plausible internal cause is also present. This latter principle bears on the problem of determining whether you have power over another person. The strategy suggested by the discounting principle is to attempt to induce the other person to do something he could have no internal reason to do, in which case his compliance will indicate clearly the external causal efficacy you exercise. (Better yet is the strategy suggested by our later discussion of inhibitory causes, which is to attempt to induce him to do something he has reason not to do.)

We may now consider in more detail some of the issues and problems arising in connection with the discounting principle and its use.

Constancy of Effect

The discounting principle assumes that the attributor faced with two or more plausible causes is attempting to explain the *same effect* as is the attributor faced with only one plausible causal hypothesis. In a within-subject design, the requirement is that the subject see the same effect, in the one case with two (or more) plausible causes and in the other case with only one. If he cannot assume the effect to be the same, he has no basis for applying the principle. For example, in the Thibaut and Riecken study, a greater (earlier, more vigorous) degree of compliance on the part of the low-status person might well have afforded a basis for inferring as much internal causation (own enthusiasm) for the act as a lesser degree of compliance would have for the high-status person. This possibility was precluded, of course, by the fact that the attributor saw the two stimulus persons comply at the same time and in the same manner.

The importance of information indicating that the effect is constant is shown by Kruglanski's replication [1970] of Strickland's experiment on surveillance and trust [1958]. In this procedure the subject serves as a supervisor for two other subjects, endeavoring to get them to maintain over trials a high level of output on a dull task. By experimental fiat, the subject is permitted to check on a specified worker's output each period and punish him if his output is found inadequate. The monitoring schedule permits the

subject to exercise this surveillance over worker A on more trials than worker B (nine versus two). At the end of the initial work periods, the subject learns that both workers have produced the same quantity of work whether monitored or not. The effect of this experience is then tested by allowing the subject to decide himself which worker to monitor on subsequent trials and to report his degree of trust in each and give his reasons for each one's performance. Strickland's results from this procedure were clear: the performance of the worker (A) for whose behavior there was available both plausible internal and external causes was attributed to him less than was the other worker's (B's) performance attributed to him. This differential attribution was clearly reflected in the tendency to choose more often to monitor A and to express less trust in him.

Kruglanski was able to replicate these results in his conditions comparable to Strickland's, but one of his variations completely eliminated the effect. This was a condition in which, although the subject knew that the volume of output was the same for the two subordinates, he did not know how their work compared in another important respect, namely, quality. (Quality was no consideration in Strickland's experiment.) The interpretation seems apparent. Only when the subject knows the nonmonitored subordinate has performed as well in every respect as the monitored one is he able to impute to the former a greater internal motivation to do the work.

To be tested in a between-subjects design, the discounting principle requires that a subject aware of two or more plausible causes see the same effect as the different subject who is cognizant of only one plausible cause. In other words, the perceived magnitude of the effect may not be affected by the information regarding the cause(s) or the application of the principle will be confounded. In the study by Jones, Davis, and Gergen described above, this meant that the inner-directed behavior had to appear equally inner-directed whether consistent with the situational demands or not. This condition would have been violated had there been either perceptual assimilation of the behavior to the role requirements (it appearing more inner-directed in the astronaut situation) or perceptual contrast in the out-of-role situation (it appearing more inner-directed in the submariner interview). In an analysis of the subject's recall of the applicant's behavior, the investigators found no evidence of either assimilation or contrast. They apparently had anchored the descriptions of the two types of behavior so firmly (as in the applicant's responses to a "choice test") that constancy of the perceived effect across conditions was assured.

Facilitative versus Inhibitory Causes

The relation of the external casual factors to the crucial behavior may be *facilitative* (as in the case of the subject's power in relation to the low-status person's compliance in Thibaut and Riecken) or *inhibitory* (as in the case of the astronaut's job demands in relation to other-directed behavior in Jones, Davis, and Gergen). In our interpretations so far, no note has been taken of this difference, but the distinction lends itself to different predictions.

When an effect (a behavior) occurs in the presence of a plausible inhibitory cause, a reverse version of the discounting principle, which might be called the augmentation principle, is required. This can be stated as follows: *if for a given effect, both a plausible inhibitory cause and a plausible facilitative cause are present, the role of the facilitative cause in producing the effect will be judged greater than if it alone were present as a plausible cause for the effect.* The central idea here is that the facilitative cause must have been effective, and potently so, if the effect occurred despite the opposing effect of the inhibitory cause. The difference in prediction, as compared with the discounting principle, is that a clear basis is provided for an inference as to the strength of the facilitative cause. In comparisons involving only facilitative causes, say between *external + internal* and *internal only*, the first case merely raises the possibility that the external cause was operative and therefore that the internal cause may not have been effective. Thus, the first case creates greater attributional ambiguity than the second. In certain comparisons involving inhibitory causes, say between *external (inhib) + internal (facil)* and *internal (facil) only*, the effect of the dual-cause condition is to increase the clarity of the efficacy of the internal cause and, thereby, to give the impression of its greater strength. (This is the basis for the special significance in the assessment or demonstration of inner strength and resources of pitting these internal causes against counterforces such as obstacles, temptations, problem difficulty, contrary social examples, etc.)

The comparison between *internal (inhib) + internal (facil)* and *internal facil only* is illustrated by Pruitt's study of reciprocity [1968]. In a resource exchange game, one player (actually following a programmed schedule) transferred larger or smaller amounts from his own resources to the subject (for whom the resources had greater monetary value). The subject then had an opportunity to reciprocate. Pruitt was able to show that holding constant the absolute value of what the first player gave, the smaller his total resources (that is, the larger the percentage of his total he had given) the more the subject gave him in return. While there are various possible explanations for this result, it is consistent with the hypothesis that the person who overcomes greater inhibitory factors in taking some action (represented here by the "costs" of the gift) demonstrates his stronger internal facilitative causes (his interests in cooperation, his confidence in the other's generosity, etc.). The recipient's attribution of the gift to these internal causes then presumably mediates his greater reciprocation. More direct evidence of the important role attributions play in the occurrence of reciprocity behavior is considered in a later section.

When certain experiments are examined in the light of both the discounting and augmentation principles, they are seen to be taking advantage of both processes at the same time. In the Jones, Davis, and Gergen study, the other-directed actor in the submariner interview represents an *external (facil) + internal (facil)* condition in the sense, noted earlier, that both the situation and his own personal traits constitute plausible causes for his behavior. The contrasting case of the other-directed actor in the astronaut interview probably represents not a simple *internal (facil)* condition, as implied in our earlier analysis, but rather an *external (inhib) + internal (facil)* condition. In that case, the situational pressures are likely to be seen as acting against the behavior being expressed. Thus, the experimental comparison is a "strong" one in the sense that there are two possible reasons for the difference between the two conditions: the more ambiguous causal role of the internal cause (the person's traits) in the first condition and the greater assumed strength of the same internal cause in the second. From this perspective, a meaningful intermediate or "control" condition would have been one in which the job interviewer gave no indication as to the ideal candidate for the position, this providing an *internal only* condition.

Another study of this type is that conducted by Mills and Jellison [1967]. A candidate for the state legislature was heard to argue that higher license fees should be imposed on truck trailers. Some subjects understood him to be addressing a friendly audience (the local union of railway men) and others, an unfriendly audience (the local union of truck drivers, who would be assumed to be strongly opposed to the message). As we might expect, the communicator was regarded as more sincere in the latter condition. It is not clear whether this opinion was due to the reduced attribution of the speech to the internal cause (his belief) in the friendly condition, to the increased attribution to the belief in the unfriendly condition, or to both. Consistent with earlier evidence from Steiner and Field [1960] that a less equivocal attribution of a persuasive communication to the communicator's belief increases its impact, the subjects in the Mills and Jellison study were found to be more favorable to increased truck license fees after hearing the message delivered to the unfriendly audience.

Ambiguity as to the Significance of External Causes

There seems to be a recurrent ambiguity in the role certain external causes play in attributions, and the ambiguity apparently concerns whether these causes are taken to be facilitative or inhibitory. In view of the importance of this distinction for the predictions made with the discounting principle, such ambiguity poses a central problem for attribution theory.

The problem can be illustrated by Ring's extension of the Thibaut and Riecken study [1964]. The earlier investigators had shown that when both a low- and high-status person complied with a given request, the latter's compliance was attributed to him (internal cause) and he was better liked. Ring investigated a similar situation, in which one person presents suggestions, opinions, and a request for a favor to another, and the other then responds favorably (accepting, agreeable, compliant), as in the Thibaut and Riecken study, or unfavorably. With the favorable reaction, Ring obtained results very similar to the earlier ones: if the responding person was higher in status (rather than lower) than the initiator, he was seen more as providing an honest evaluation and he was liked more. For the new condition, in which the response is an unfavorable one, Ring was faced with a question for which the earlier investigators had not provided a clear answer. Stated in discounting terms, the question is: if the effect is noncompliance (or negativity), does high or low status provide the more plausible external cause? In other words, does high status mean *all* the person's behavior is independent of external causation? Or does high status mean that *certain behaviors*, such as those specified or indicated by the role associated with the status,

are externally caused. Ring sensed the latter to be the case for noncompliant behavior. "Noncompliance in this situation is likely to be viewed as a perfunctory manifestation of B's power without regard to the worth of the statement to which he is meant to respond" [p. 651]. In other words, it is more or less a part of the high-status person's role to say "No."

(This role prescription might, in fact, afford the basis for the attribution to the high-status person of independence of external factors. Thus, a possible irony in the assumption is that there is external (role) control of behavior in the interests of establishing the appearance of its independence of external control! There is yet another attribution assumption implied by Ring's statement: the high-status person does not give the proposal as careful consideration as does the low-status person. Thus, his (negative) response can hardly be considered as causally related to the proposal itself, and the initiator gains no veridical information as to the properties of his proposal.)

Basing his prediction on the above assumption, Ring formulated the hypothesis for the noncompliance condition that the low-status noncomplier would be viewed as more sincere and more liked. His results confirm this hypothesis. Moral of the story: with regard to certain kinds of behaviors, high status provides stronger external determination than does low status. If we consider the original experiment in which agreement was the effect, we might now assume that high status is a plausible inhibitory external cause for this effect. When the high-status person agrees despite the presence of this cause, he is indeed demonstrating his strong internal reasons for agreement. We might then infer that the Thibaut and Riecken design involved a comparison between *external (inhib) + internal (facil)* and *internal (facil) only* (for the high- and low-status compliers, respectively) rather than a comparison between *internal (facil) only* and *external (facil) + internal (facil)*. Of course there may have been a combination of these effects, the high-status complier constituting an *external (inhib) + internal (facil)* condition and the low-status complier, an *external (facil) + internal (facil)* condition.

The ambiguity of facilitative versus inhibitory effect has also arisen in connection with monetary incentives as possible causal factors. When a person is offered a large amount of money to do something, is he provided with a plausible facilitative external cause for the behavior or a plausible inhibitory external cause? If he does the act and we consider the money to be a facilitative cause, the discounting principle indicates partial ascription of the behavior to the external cause and the actor is not held completely responsible for it. Thus, if it were a bad act, we might be less critical and more forgiving of him. On the other hand, if we consider the monetary incentive a plausible inhibitory external cause, the augmentation principle implies that we should attribute the behavior to the actor with more confidence and, perhaps, be more critical of him.

The few studies to date that bear on this problem yield inconsistent results [Kee 1969, unpublished research at UCLA by Kruglanski & Yinon] but include one instance in which the second hypothesis is supported, the person acting badly for larger gain being less liked than one doing so for smaller gain [Komorita & Mechling 1967]. This result calls our attention to the possibility that monetary incentive for certain kinds of behavior is perceived as an inhibitory external cause. If a monetary incentive does have this significance, the larger it is, the more the person should be deterred from the action. If he does it anyway, the evidence points to a powerful internal cause, which suggests he is truly a very bad person. This would be the case (as in coarse bribery) in which the perceived intention of the agent offering the reward is to induce violation of some social norm rather than merely to compensate the actor for legitimate work or services. The larger the proffered reward, the more serious will seem the desired violation of the norm and, therefore, the stronger should be the inhibition against the action.

Relevant here is the distinction that has been made between legitimate and illegitimate power [French & Raven 1959]. Brehm and Cohen [1962] have already noted the relevance of this distinction to attributional phenomena, specifically in its relation to perceived freedom of choice (internal causation). They suggested that compliance with legitimate forces implies low choice but compliance with illegitimate forces implies high choice. In general, we might say that social inducements may be appropriate for a given behavior (wage payments for productive work) or inappropriate (sexual favors for political support). If appropriate, such inducements constitute facilitative external causes and their presence reduces the attribution of the action to the person. If inappropriate (or perhaps only if highly so), they tend to be perceived as inhibitory external causes and their presence increases the attribution of the action to the person.

(There may be some question in cases of the type discussed above as to *constancy* of the effect. The nature of the cause, for example, the size or type of the offered reward, may change the meaning of the behavior itself, with the result that the effect in the presence of the large external reward appears to be much more extreme than that with a smaller reward. A somewhat more complete discussion, from an attributional viewpoint, of external incentives in relation to the evaluation of behavior is provided by Kelley, 1971.)

Reciprocation of Harm and Benefit

The tendency to reciprocate another person's behavior—to harm or dislike him if he has harmed you, or to help or like him if he has helped you—seems to depend strongly upon the attribution of causes for that behavior. At least this is the consistent conclusion of numerous laboratory studies. The result on reaction to harm dates back to Pastore's questionnaire study of students' reactions to arbitrary versus nonarbitrary frustration [1952]. The subjects' written responses to the various situations they read indicated a more aggressive reaction to the arbitrary than to the nonarbitrary instances. In terms of the discounting principle, the nonarbitrary cases are those in which there are two plausible reasons for the action of the frustrating agent, his own impulse and some external reason. Some examples: the guard on a boat prevents you from boarding but with a good justification; a bus driver passes you as you wait at a bus stop but you see that the bus is out of service and on its way to the garage; a person with whom you had an appointment calls to cancel it with the explanation that he is ill. In the arbitrary cases, the external justification is absent, so the attributor is pretty much reduced to attributing the behavior to the frustrating agent's own desires or whims.

The result of greater aggression in response to an arbitrary frustration has been obtained by many other investigators, including Cohen [1955] and Allison and Hunt [1959]. The plausible external cause for frustration may consist of such factors as the following:

A widely recognized physical cause.

A compelling institutional arrangement or rule.

A factor in the frustrator's psychological makeup, such as the mental illness of a person who attacks you. ("the derogator is not fully responsible for the act of judgment, being a victim of a traumatic past history" [Jones, Hester, Farina, & Davis 1959, p. 364].)

A lack of ability on the part of a person upon whose success one is dependent. ("Given information that the task is difficult and the subject incompetent, failure is attributed by the trainer to factors over which the trainee has no control . . ." [Lanzetta & Hannah 1969, p. 251].)

An inadequacy in the prior behavior of the person subjected to the frustration. ("If the perceiver believes he has done something to earn attack, insult, or rejection, he will presumably be less inclined to appraise his attacker negatively than if the attack was unreasonable or arbitrary" [Jones & Davis 1965, p. 249].)

An interesting recent study by Epstein and Taylor bears on the last point, the role of the attributor's own behavior as a causal factor in the counterpart's action [1967]. Each subject competed against another subject (actually programmed) in a series of speed of reaction contests. Before each trial, each contestant designated one of five levels of shock as the punishment his opponent should receive should the opponent be the slower of the two on that trial. Thanks to the programmed behavior of the opponent, as the true subject pitted himself against three successive "other subjects," he found himself to be consistently fast, medium, or slow in the contests. Thus, he was himself rarely, moderately often, or frequently shocked for having lost the successive contests. Whatever his success vis-à-vis these three opponents, however, he found them to be different in the shocks they chose for him should he be the loser. (Both contestants' settings were made public after each trial regardless of its outcome.) One opponent was minimally aggressive (MA), always setting the lowest possible shock level; another was rationally aggressive (RA), always matching the subject's own previous setting; and the third was unmitigatingly aggressive (UA), always setting the highest shock level. The research question was how the subject would react to these three opponents in terms of his own shock settings and his evaluations.

There being little external justification for the UA's behavior, he was of course rated most negatively and assigned high levels of punishment. However, there was a tendency for the aggression toward UA to depend upon the subject's own performance, the shocks given him being relatively lower if the subject was either a loser ("my losing justified his punishing me") or a winner ("my winning is making him angry"). Thus, the subject's own actions presumably provided a partial causal explanation for the aggression, reduced its perceived personal causation, and therefore reduced the amount of aggression reciprocated.

Epstein and Taylor's purpose was to demonstrate that although defeat involves frustration, it has no effect upon anger directed toward the opponent. Their results show this to be the case: averaging over all three types of opponents, the shocks set for him did not depend upon the frequency with which the subject lost. There is the interesting point here that, as the authors say "Instigation to aggression in a competitive aggressive interaction is determined largely by perception of aggressive intent of the opponent, whether or not the intent finds its mark" [p. 288]. Thus, the subject showed much aggression toward UA even when, because the subject usually beat him, UA was rarely able to follow through with his intention. It appears that we reciprocate the hostile intention and not the amount of injury or pain received. This applies, of course, to this type of competitive situation, in which the punishment actually received always has a plausible external cause, namely, one's poor performance.

Some studies by Worchel and his colleagues provide evidence that the effect of justification or non-arbitrariness in the reduction of aggressive behavior is due to the *inhibition* of aggression rather than to the reduced *instigation* to aggression [Rothaus & Worchel 1960, Burnstein & Worchel 1962]. This assertion is very difficult to prove, as these investigators acknowledge, but it seems to be entirely consistent with the attributional view that assumes that an interpretational process intervenes between the frustration and the behavioral or judgmental reactions to it. The injured person may feel quite angry, but because of social rules about retribution, he may constrain his overt reactions according to the perceived cause of the injury [Heider 1958, ch. 10].

Studies of causal attribution in relation to the reciprocation of benefit make much the same general point as those on reactions to harm. Thibaut and Riecken's study could be interpreted as showing that helping behavior attributed to the person leads to more reciprocation (in the form of liking) than helping behavior ambiguous as to its personal (internal) or external causation. The reciprocation is shown more explicitly by Goranson and Berkowitz [1966]. A fellow subject (a confederate) helped the (real) subject to complete his work on a dull task. The real subject then had an opportunity on the next task to return the help by working hard in the first subject's behalf. The original help was given either voluntarily or at the behest of the experimenter. As we would expect from assuming that the help is attributed more exclusively to the helper when voluntarily given (no plausible external cause being present), it was reciprocated more under those circumstances.

Several studies suggest an exception to the rule that helpful or affiliative behavior attributed to the person will elicit more liking than if attributed to the situation. These all seem to be cases in which, by virtue of the inappropriateness of the behavior, its attribution to the person suggests he may be peculiar, stupid, or not completely rational. In research using the prisoner's dilemma game, Solomon found that an opponent equal in power to the subject who played totally cooperatively (which would be difficult to attribute to the situation) was less well liked than a conditionally cooperative player (one whose cooperation was contingent upon—caused by—the subject's behavior) [1960]. Solomon suggests that the subject deals with this unusual behavior by attributing to the actor aberrations of motivation or understanding such that the cooperative choices do not have their usual meaning. A study by Schopler and Matthews provides another instance in which an apparently affiliative action (choosing to be dependent upon the subject), when attributed to the actor, raises sufficient questions about his good judgment that he is, relatively speaking, more rejected than if he had had no responsibility for the action [1965].

Sincerity, Veridicality, and Attribution of Causality

A person who presents himself in a favorable light (for example, the job applicant who emphasizes his independence and ability to tolerate social isolation in the interview for the position of astronaut) will often be described as insincere. This means his behavior is not caused by that by which it is presented as being caused, that is, by his own characteristics. He is not permitting his real properties to express themselves but is dissimulating, permitting other causes to affect his behavior.

Sincerity is also an issue with regard to informational states of the actor, such as his impressions about or feelings toward some event or object. A common case of this sort is flattery. Complimentary remarks about a person made under the guise of accurately reporting one's feelings about him (that is, supposedly caused by the speaker's true impressions or feelings) may be attributed to some other cause, such as the ambient social situation. For example, Jones, Gergen, and Jones report the relative

insincerity that is ascribed by a high-status colleague to a low-status person's complimentary ratings of him when the situation is one in which it is important for the low-status person to demonstrate his interpersonal compatibility [1963]. In the same situation, greater sincerity is attributed to a high-status person's complimentary ratings of his low-status partner. The point is much like that made by Thibaut and Riecken [1955]. In terms of the discounting principle, plausibility exists for both internal and external causes for the low-status person's compliments, but only for the internal cause (his true impressions) in the case of the high-status man. Consistent with this difference, whereas the low-status person is relatively sure that the high-status person is sincere (and rates him at a relatively extreme point on the sincerity scale), the high-status person is uncertain about the low-status person's sincerity and rates him near the center of the scale (and relatively lower). In this situation, then, sincerity means that the effect (the compliment) is attributed to the particular internal cause it is represented as reflecting, the speaker's true reactions to the person he is evaluating.

Sincerity plays a central role in the phenomenon of social influence by way of its relation to perceived veridicality of the source of influence. All persons are dependent upon others for information about certain aspects of their common world and must evaluate various features of others' behavior in terms of the degree to which it mediates accurate information about that world (that is, the degree to which it is caused by the properties of that world); see Kelley [1967] and Kelley and Thibaut [1969] for a fuller discussion of the attributional aspects of information dependence. A basic principle of information dependence is that a person is influenced by and accepts an informational report from another person only if he attributes the report to the particular aspect of their common environment to which it is purported to pertain. A veridical report about an entity is one "caused" by that entity. In most cases, however, informational reports are mediated by the reporter's perceptions of the entity; that is, the entity causes his perception that causes the report. As we have seen above, it is the latter link in this causal chain to which sincerity refers. The report has little chance of being veridical unless it is sincere. (An exception might perhaps occur by some quirk of compensating errors, in which an error in the first link is corrected by an error in the second.) The first link, the causal relationship between external entities and the person's perception, is usually referred to as "expertness," and the second one, here called sincerity, is often designated as "trustworthiness."

Walster, Aronson, and Abrahams have documented the detrimental effect on judged sincerity of the existence of external reasons for a communicator's saying what he does [1966]. A communicator who had something to gain from having others accept his view (for example, a criminal arguing that the power of the police and public prosecutor should be reduced) was judged less honest and less likely to be influential than a person advocating the same point of view when its acceptance was contrary to his own interests (one of the prosecutors himself).

Perhaps more impressive is the demonstration by Steiner and Field that the causal attribution of informal comments affects their persuasiveness [1960]. Trios of subjects discussed the question of social desegregation and one of them, a confederate of the experimenter, always expressed and argued for a prosegregation point of view. When this was done in compliance with the experimenter's assignment of roles, it had little effect upon the other (real) subjects' attitudes, but when apparently done more spontaneously, it had considerable influence. Auxiliary evidence indicated the subjects were more confident about what the confederate's true attitudes were in the latter condition. The attributional implication seems to be that in the single-cause condition (spontaneous discussion without role assignments) the confederate's remarks were taken as more sincere, and to the extent this assured them to be of higher veridicality (that is, true reflections of how the problem appeared to one thoughtful person), they were more influential. In contrast, in the role assignment condition the remarks could be at least partially attributed to the experimenter's instructions. Their quality of insincerity undoubtedly compromised them as informationally useful observations about the real facts of the matter.

Attributions as Mediating Variables

As we have seen, investigations relevant to attribution theory have often been primarily concerned with other matters, such as conditions favoring the expression of aggression, the bases of interpersonal attraction, reciprocity in helping, etc. While these latter behaviors are in part mediated by attributions of causality, there seem to be many exceptions. These exceptions call our attention to the perhaps obvious but nonetheless important fact that attribution theory encompasses only a limited domain of social percep-

tion and cognitive functioning and must not be evaluated in terms of how well it affords predictions for various other domains relating to social evaluation and interaction. The theory should be able eventually to predict causal interpretations, attributed characteristics and intentions, perceived trustworthiness or sincerity, and such, but will never constitute more than a partial basis for predicting such other phenomena as liking and evaluations, monitoring behavior, and the administration of sanctions.

As an illustration, consider moral judgments. We might expect these to be rendered when the target is judged to be responsible for his actions, and this is generally what the relevant research shows [Schmitt 1964, Shaw & Sulzer 1964]. There is strong intuitive appeal, however, in the notion advanced by Stevenson that ". . . ethical judgments look mainly to the future. Even when they are made of past or imaginary acts, they still serve a dynamic purpose—that of discouraging (or encouraging) similar acts later on" [1967, p. 142]. This statement implies that these judgments are guided by estimates of future responsibility rather than present or past responsibility, or by considerations of inducing the person to be responsible (to exercise a more effective causal role) in the future. Thus, criticism might be quite harsh after an immoral act, even if it were one for which the person's causal responsibility was quite unclear: "He should at least have *tried* to behave better." In brief, the moral evaluations of, say, a bad act may be guided partially by the attribution of that act but also partially by its future "avoidability."

Many of the attribution studies find it necessary to consider other than attributional determinants of their dependent variables. In his follow-up to Thibaut and Riecken, Ring assumed liking to be complexly determined [1964]. Thus, a person seeking another person's compliance with his suggestions will like the target person who gives him a sincere reaction to the suggestions (satisfying his information needs). But he will also like the target person who complies (satisfying whatever other needs the inducer had for making the suggestions). The first source of satisfaction (and liking) is mediated by the causal attribution for the compliance but the latter is independent of any such attribution.

Another example is afforded by Kruglanski's replication of Strickland's study of monitoring in relation to amount of prior surveillance [1970]. In the condition similar to Strickland's, Kruglanski's subjects monitored the subordinate worker for the purpose of *punishing* him if he failed to fulfill a given production criterion. Under these conditions Kruglanski found, just as Strickland had, that the more frequently monitored worker was subsequently trusted less and monitored more often. However, in a *reward* condition in which the monitoring served the purpose of rewarding the worker if he surpassed a given production level, although the less often monitored person was more trusted, he was also more often monitored. Kruglanski suggests that monitoring behavior can be governed by considerations other than trust. In the reward condition, a supervisor may monitor the more trusted worker in order to give him a chance to earn the reward and, thereby, as an acknowledgment of his very dependability.

Less Rational Attribution Tendencies

The attributional principles we have reviewed are obviously very sensible, affording reasonable ways to draw inferences from cause and effect information that is more or less limited. We now consider several less rational attributional tendencies—they might be called biases or errors—that have been documented in social contexts. There are several different ways in which the evidence relevant to an attribution is treated in a biased or partial manner, depending upon such factors as the type of information and its relevance to the actor's interests. After some of these less rational tendencies (no claim is made as to the exhaustiveness of this list) have been reviewed, an attempt will be made to interpret both the more and the less reasonable from a single theoretical viewpoint.

Too little account is taken of external causes (contextual factors) in judgments of other persons' behavior. This phenomenon is treated in detail by Jones and Nisbett. The possibility is suggested by a number of different studies in which the variation in behavior accounts for a larger portion of the variance in the observer's judgments than does any contextual factor (or, in the statistical analysis, the Context X Behavior interaction term in the ANOVA). For example, Jones and Harris found the attitude attributed to the debater to depend more on the position he espoused than on the circumstances (choice versus no choice) surrounding his coming to espouse that position [1967]. Similarly, in their unpublished study of resistance versus compliance in response to temptation, Kruglanski and Yinon found that evaluation and attribution of responsibility were more sharply affected by which action the person took than by the situational factors relating to his choice to resist or comply.

The point has been made by several investigators as follows: Heider: "behavior . . . has such salient properties it tends to engulf the total field rather than be confined to its proper position as a local stimulus whose interpretation requires the additional data of a surrounding field" [1958, p. 54]. Jones and Harris: "A striking feature of the results in each experiment was the powerful effect on attribution of the content of the opinions expressed" [1967, p. 22]. Pepitone and Sherberg, finding that an aggressive act carried out with what objectively were good intentions was often perceived as motivated by a bad intention, refer to a "general cognitive tendency to match motives with acts" [1957, p. 761].

It must be admitted that the results bearing on this generalization are subject to many alternative interpretations. The experimental comparison of the relative efficacy of different independent variables is a tricky one. It may well be that existing evidence simply indicates that the context factors have not been manipulated as strongly or as clearly as has the behavior itself. Thus, even though the perpetrator of a wrong act does it under high external pressure, he may be perceived to have had a meaningful degree of freedom not to comply with that pressure. It is difficult to charge the attributor with "error" or "bias" when this ambiguity exists as to the "real" nature of the contextual factors.

One kind of study bearing on the point does seem to enable us to describe the attributions as involving systematic "errors." These are experiments in which two subjects bargain and negotiate a contract with each other. The experimenter sets the bargaining *problem*, specifying for each subject a level of value he must obtain in the contract if he is to make any profit from it. However, neither subject is told the value that has been specified for his opponent. This assigned value constitutes the main external cause of each bargainer's behavior—how much he demands, how tough he is, etc. Two experiments have found (in both cases, serendipitously) that when subjects are asked at the end of the interaction to estimate their opponent's value, they consistently *underestimate* it [Pruitt & Drews 1969, Kelley, Shure, et al. 1970]. That is, they underestimate the amount that the opponent has been *required* to gain from the contract. A similar result was found by Shure and Meeker for a game in which two persons were required to work out a division of a set of territories, some of them having been privately designated to each person as being especially valuable to him [1969]. Again, postgame questions revealed that each player tended to underestimate the number of areas that had been specified as of high value for the other person. The gist of all three studies is that interacting persons in conflict tend to underestimate the degree to which the conflict they experience is due to the common external situation (the assigned values, the designated territories). In these studies there is an objective criterion as to the degree of external constraint acting upon each person's bargaining behavior. The evidence indicates that the magnitude of this external causal factor is systematically underestimated.

In and of themselves, the above results do not prove that in bargaining situations the opponent's personal contribution to the experienced difficulty (via his obdurate behavior) is *over*estimated. There are indications in other bargaining studies, however, that this is so. In an unpublished study from the Louvain Summer School, there is evidence that with an increase in objective difficulty of the bargaining problem (that is, with a narrowing of the bargaining range) there is a tendency to see the partner as seeking more profit and as having become less conciliatory [Kelley, Helus, et al. 1967]. The authors note that ". . . as long as the two interacting persons perceive themselves free to make a cooperative or competitive choice, any failures and shortcomings in the relationship would be presumably attributed to the partner or self and the more distant source of problems would not affect deeply the relationship. In summary, the proximal cause of experienced difficulty in interpersonal relationship would usually overshadow the more distal one in the causality chain . . ." [p. 29]. Similarly, unpublished data from a bargaining study by Dorris, Gentry, and Kelley show that with a narrower bargaining range (which is shown independently to be an external cause of conflict between the players) cooperative players are more often attributed competitive intentions and the partner is seen as trying to earn a larger share of the total possible profit. It appears that as the bargaining problem becomes more "difficult," attitudes toward the partner become more negative and, at least in part, the increasing difficulty is attributed to him. The external cause of conflict within the relationship is underestimated as to its importance and the causal role of the opponent is overestimated.

The generalization proposed here, that the contribution of contextual factors to the other person's behavior is underestimated, is supported largely by instances in which his behavior is bad or counter to the attributor's interests. Included here are cases in which he is in direct conflict with the attributor, as in a bargaining situation, or in which he expresses an opinion sharply divergent from that of the attributor. Perhaps, then, the generalization should be limited to that particular case and stated in terms of overattribution to the actor rather than underattribution to the context, as follows: those actions of another person that are in conflict with the attributor's interests tend to be attributed, more than they should be, to that person. We now examine the counterpart of this last proposition, namely, the tendency for the attributor himself to take credit for the other person's favorable behaviors.

In interdependent interaction with another person, the attributor tends to attribute to himself those actions of the other person that are consistent with the attributor's own interests. One investigation that bears on this point is the teaching experiment by Johnson, Feigenbaum, and Weiby [1964]. Women taking educational psychology classes participated in an experimental study of teaching mathematical skills to fourth-grade boys. Each teacher explained to two pupils how to multiply by ten and then saw that pupil A had done well but B had done poorly. She then taught them how to multiply by twenty. On receiving their subsequent work sheets, she learned (by virtue of the "programmed" nature of the boys' work) that A had continued to do well and B had (for half the subjects) continued to do badly or (for the other half) improved to do as well as A. On being asked to account for the performance of the two pupils, the teachers tended to attribute B's improved performance to themselves but to blame his continued low performance on B himself. (The latter tendency is, in fact, the clearer of the two.) Moreover, consistent with the self-evaluative effect reported by Bavelas, Hastorf, Gross, and Kite, the teachers evaluated their second presentations more highly when B improved than when he did not.

An important qualification must be entered at this early point regarding an interpretation of this or any similar experiment that implies the teachers have made some gross attributional error by failing to see that they were not responsible for the improvement. As has been noted elsewhere, insofar as the teacher tried harder or varied her instructional method after B's poor initial performance, the information pattern available to her would show a strong positive covariation between her own behavior and that of the improving student, but negative or noncovariance between her own behavior and that of the consistently poor performer [Kelley 1967]. By the covariation principle (see earlier), the former would warrant a self-attribution and the latter, not. Much needed in this regard are experimental procedures in which the degree of covariance of this sort is varied independently of the trend in the other person's behavior. Consistent with a covariance interpretation are Beckman's results that "observers" do not attribute the student's improvement to the teacher [1970]. Mrs. Beckman repeated the Johnson, Feigenbaum, and Weiby experiment and found, as did the earlier investigators, that the teachers tended to attribute the improving performance to their teaching. However, other subjects, to whom the teaching situation and its outcomes were described but who were not themselves involved as teachers, did not make this attribution. This result might be explained by assuming that the latter subjects, not having concrete evidence of variations in the teacher's manner or intensity of effort, did not have the covariance data that the teacher herself had.

The tendency described here probably applies to interactions between groups as well as to those between individuals. Streufert and Streufert studied pairs of subjects in an internation simulation, presumably playing against other similar pairs [1969] Each team was given a schedule either of increasing success (expert evaluations of their successive decisions improved) or of increasing failure. In post-experimental estimates of the reasons for the outcome, subjects attributed more causal effect to their own team under success but more causal effect to the other team under failure. This result has the highly significant implication, of course, that the attributional biases examined here may play an important role in the evolution of the intergroup relations.

A number of different experimental paradigms involve a comparison of different trends in the behavior of another person with whom the subject is in interaction. In the research on the "gain-loss" hypothesis of interpersonal attraction, a person making evaluations of the subject begins negatively but becomes positive (NP), or begins and continues to be positive (PP) [Aronson & Linder 1965, Sigall & Aronson 1967, Landy & Aronson 1968, and Mettee & Taylor]. The dependent variable is the evaluation the subject makes of this evaluator. The relevant result here is that in the final evaluations the NP evaluator is liked as much as or more than the PP evaluator, despite the fact that NP has made some highly negative comments about the subject in the early period of the interaction. The interpretation

of this result is not entirely clear at present. Certainly one possibility is that the subject attributes NP's change to himself, perceiving himself as having succeeded in exercising influence over the evaluator, and this self-attribution somehow results in liking for the evaluator. This corresponds approximately to the "competence" interpretation various investigators have suggested for the gain-loss effect. Consistent with such a perceived influence interpretation is Mettee and Taylor's result that the NP evaluator is as well liked as the PP evaluator only when the later positive evaluations represent "changes of mind" about the properties that had earlier been evaluated negatively.

A different interpretation, but also an attributional one, is in terms of "discernment." The NP evaluator demonstrates his discernment, that is, that his evaluation is not a property of himself (he's not *always* favorable) and is probably caused by (by virtue of its covariance with) the stimulus person's properties. Therefore, the final positive evaluation is more credible as a veridical reflection of the stimulus person and he is, then, more favorably impressed with it.

In experiments on bargaining and gaming, there has been frequent use of different schedules of concessions or of cooperative-competitive play. These have included comparisons similar to that between NP and PP, that is, between an opponent who begins negatively but becomes more positive and one who consistently acts positively. Benton, Kelley, and Liebling report that a bargaining opponent who begins with extreme demands and gradually moves to more moderate ones is evaluated more positively than one who begins with the moderate ones at the outset and persists with them (unpublished). With the former opponent, the subject also feels greater responsibility for the outcome and greater success in changing the partner. In his fine review of the use of programmed strategies with the prisoner's dilemma game, Oskamp summarizes the consistent findings that a change from a low to a high rate of cooperation is more effective in inducing subjects to cooperate than is a consistently high rate of cooperation [1971]. A highly plausible interpretation for this result is that the consistently cooperative partner is seen as a "sucker" and is exploited [Scodel 1962]. Still, one contribution to the more favorable effect of the increasingly cooperative schedule may be the sense of control the subject derives from attributing to himself the positive trends in the opponent's behavior.

The various sets of evidence pertaining to the present point are, unfortunately, quite ambiguous as to the interpretations they warrant. The results from a variety of experimental contexts show that a person who begins with behavior counter to the attributor's interests and then shifts to a more favorable behavior is responded to as favorably as or even more so than is a person who exhibits positive behavior from the outset. One possible interpretation of this result is in terms of a *control* effect: being in his own interests, the change in behavior is treated by the attributor as his own doing.

The subsequent positive consequences of this attribution (liking, cooperation) perhaps require some explanation. Is it reasonable to assume that the individual tends to like and to reciprocate benefits to people who respond to his control attempts? On the face of it, this proposal contradicts an earlier conclusion (suggested, for example, by Thibaut and Riecken's experiment) that a person responsible for his helpful behavior is more liked and more the object of reciprocation than the person whose helpfulness is externally caused. However, there is no real contradiction here. Thibaut and Riecken anticipated the point perfectly: "When an individual is confronted by a controllable and an uncontrollable other, he will tend to accept or prefer the controllable other, because of the relevance of control to goalward locomotion. On the other hand, when both (or all) others show compliance, discriminations in acceptance will be made on some basis other than the instrumental capacities of the other for satisfying the individual's needs" [p. 115]. The other basis to which these authors refer is, of course, the degree to which there is a spontaneous display of good will.

Another aspect of this problem is the social context in which the helpful behavior occurs. If interaction has a competitive component or involves a question of gauging one's own control or efficacy (as in bargaining or even in teaching), evidence of one's control is satisfying. By documenting your competence, the tractable opponent comes to deserve your positive regard and reciprocation of favors. If the relationship is a more purely cooperative one, however, the spontaneous, inner-caused expression of help is more fitting and serves to maintain the definition of the situation as one whose course can be predicted without reference to personal power.

More responsibility is attributed to the person for his actions taken for gain than for similar actions to prevent loss or to avoid punishment. In a study that bears on this point, deCharms, Carpenter, and Kuperman gave their subjects a series of stories in each

of which a hero was being persuaded to do something not ordinarily expected of him in his job [1965]. For example, an army private was asked by his commanding officer to stand extra guard duty in return for which he would be given a special three-day pass. Without specifying whether the hero complied, the questionnaire asked the subjects to state how much freedom he probably felt in deciding what to do. When the agent making the request was described as someone the hero liked, greater felt freedom was attributed to the hero than when the agent was disliked.

In interpreting this experiment, Bramel states the asymmetry being considered here: "Possibly subjects assume some implicit threat of punishment is present when A dislikes B, whereas A may be perceived simply as wanting to please a liked B. It is interesting that even though incentives for compliance can be readily imagined in both situations, the person potentially seen as wanting to please is considered more free than the one who possibly wants to avoid threatened punishment . . . . Further research might fruitfully explore this possibility—that a sense of subjective freedom is attributed more to people seeking positive incentives than to those seeking to avoid punishment" [1969, p. 94].

Kruglanski and Yinon in some unpublished research have found evidence partially consistent with Bramel's hypothesis. An athlete was portrayed as considering violating, under various conditions, the ethical standards appropriate to his amateur standing. In some cases, the reason for violation was to enable him to *improve* his economic circumstances, and in other cases, to enable him to *prevent* a deterioration in those circumstances. When the hero was then portrayed as succumbing to the temptation, his action was less negatively evaluated in the *prevent* than in the *improve* condition, and when he resisted the temptation, his action was more favorably evaluated in the *prevent* than in the *improve* condition. Both effects are consistent with a tendency to consider the person to be under strong external pressure when he is threatened with loss. He is, then, criticized less for bad behavior undertaken to forestall the loss, or if he shows an unwillingness to comply with the external pressure, he is more warmly approved. Unfortunately, questions inquiring directly about the hero's responsibility for the action did not yield entirely consistent results. Male subjects evaluated his responsibility pretty much as we would expect here. They attributed greater responsibility to the actor under the *improve* condition. The reverse, however, was true for the female subjects. On the other hand, a question concerning what most people could be expected to do if they were in the hero's place yielded data consistent with our general statement for both sexes. Most individuals were expected to act unethically in order to prevent loss, but most were expected to *resist* the temptation if gain were involved.

The present point reminds us of a problem discussed earlier, that the meaning of the behavior is undoubtedly influenced by the type of external incentives available for its performance. A salient example is the widely accepted legal principle that murder in *defense* of one's family or other personal interests is more tolerable than murder in the pursuit of *gain*.

The asymmetry suggested here has its parallel in the scientific analysis of approach versus avoidance behavior. The fact that avoidance tendencies decrease more sharply with increasing distance from the goal (the point of danger) than do approach tendencies (the latter with respect to the location of some positive incentive) has been interpreted by Miller in terms of differential cue dependence [1944]. Ordinarily, the avoidance tendency is more dependent upon external cues, usually ones near the goal, and the approach tendency is more dependent upon internal cues, such as drive states, which do not vary greatly with distance from the goal. This analysis is consistent with the observation here that the man in the street tends to ascribe avoidance behavior to external causes and approach behavior to internal causes. This example raises the fascinating question of how much of the scientific knowledge about the causes of behavior is incorporated in the lay attributor's intuitive understandings and assumptions.

Attribution and Control

As summarized in the foregoing sections, the attribution phenomena that have been documented in experimental studies of interpersonal relations seem to include processes that conform rather well to the logic of causal inference but also processes that involve systematic biases and asymmetries in the use of available information. This is not presented as an original observation. The more and the less rational aspects of attribution have been described by earlier observers such as Heider in 1958 and Jones and Davis in 1965.

I am not entirely convinced as to the "existence" of the less rational tendencies. Further, more carefully conducted research may well provide "rational" explanations for some or all of the "biases." This was suggested for the tendency to attribute the other person's increasingly favorable behavior to one's own efforts. Similarly, the asymmetry between gain and loss avoidance may appear more reasonable to us after more analytical investigation of the effect of incentive type upon the meaning of behavior. The "constancy of effect" requirement of the discounting principle may be seriously violated in certain such incentive comparisons.

These reservations will now be put aside in order to consider another approach to encompassing both the more and the less rational tendencies within the same theoretical perspective. We might simply leave our analysis at the point to which we have brought it—with the recognition that attributions are often reasonable but that they are also often influenced by personal interest, emotional considerations, and such. It seems worthwhile, however, to at least make an attempt to view attribution in a way that lends meaning to both kinds of phenomena.

The view here proposed is that attribution processes are to be understood, not only as a means of providing the individual with a veridical view of his world, but as a means of encouraging and maintaining his effective exercise of control in that world. The purpose of causal analysis—the function it serves for the species and the individual—is effective control. The attributor is not simply an attributor, a seeker after knowledge. His latent goal in gaining knowledge is that of effective management of himself and his environment. He is not a pure "scientist," then, but an applied one.

If this view is correct, a consideration of control, and especially of the particular problems of control that face the socially interdependent human, should afford a basis from which to "deduce" the various aspects of the attribution process, both the more and the less rational. Only the general outlines of how this analysis might proceed can be offered here. The central implication of this proposal is that the attributional process can be well understood only in the context of a comprehensive analysis of the exercise of control. Such an analysis is beyond the present reviewer's resources, but perhaps some indications can be given of what it might reveal.

Control of one's environment undoubtedly involves some sort of balance between controlling the *controllable* and controlling the *important*. Thus, on the one hand, control tendencies will persist only if a person has some success in exercising control. So it is essential that his control efforts be directed toward realms in which he has some chance of being effective. On the other hand, what is controllable is not always what is most important. To persist in attempting control with respect to important but intractable conditions is to experience repeated failure and, usually, to dampen one's control efforts. But *not to attempt* to exert control in relation to such circumstances is unnecessarily to delimit the quality of one's life. Thus, some sort of compromise must be reached between limiting and extending one's control attempts—a compromise between, so to speak, a philosophy of external and internal locus of control.

Some of the "biases" we noted earlier may be viewed in relation to the reinforcement of control attempts. The attribution to self of success and the attribution to external factors of failure provides the basis for the continuation of control attempts. If attributed to the self, success is a reason to exercise one's own causal powers again. Thus, these attributional biases may reflect a system partially in support of an internal locus of control orientation. It would be surprising, however, to find these biases with respect to realms of the environment in which one's true power is extremely low.

In the case of social interaction, the tension between the feasible and the important is often focused on the problem of where to direct one's attempts in order to improve another person's behavior. Should we attempt to change the person or should we rather try to change his circumstances? Are we to change his behavior, or his intentions and attitudes, or his inner urges and dispositions? In each of these cases, the choice is between more proximal and more distal causes of his behavior. The more proximal tend to be more readily changed but the more distal tend to be more important (more permanent and more ramifying).

From our assumption that the attributional processes are closely linked to the effective exercise of control, the tension between the feasible and the important becomes a tension in regard to the focus or level of the attributional analysis. On the one hand, controllable factors will have a high salience as candidates for causal explanation. In cases of ambiguity or doubt, the causal analysis will be biased in its outcome toward controllable factors. This might be the generalization at the basis of the tendency to attribute behavior to the individual at the expense of the context, contexts generally being more fixed

than some of the more "proximal" causes within the individual (such as attitudes and intentions). For example, in bargaining it is usually easier to change the opponent's attitudes toward you and his intentions as to the outcome of your negotiations than to change the break-even point defined for him by such external factors as his costs, the state of the market, and his alternative contractors. The bias toward the controllable may also explain the asymmetric causal significance of action for gain versus action to avoid loss. With the extreme versions of the two types of incentives, this asymmetry becomes the assertion that fear is regarded as less controllable than greed, so actions motivated by fear are less attributed to the person than actions motivated by greed.

On the other hand, bias toward the more important causes may shift the attributional focus toward causes that are not highly controllable but that, if affected, have important consequences. An example of this may be the logically unwarranted rendering of person attributions in certain cases of bad moral behavior for the purpose of correcting that behavior. Schmitt's interesting study, concerning the use of moral appeals, has a suggestive result bearing on this point [1964]. He found, as one would expect on "logical" grounds, that a moral norm is invoked most frequently (and presumably, most strongly) for an actor who refuses to fulfill an obligation but without benefit of a good external reason—he is able but simply not willing. However, Schmitt also found a tendency to direct the moral appeal to the person who has an external excuse (he is not able) *if he is also unwilling*. In other words, there appears to be a tendency to attempt to correct an important attitude (potentially important in many *other* situations) even though it cannot plausibly be considered as controlling the present or recent behavioral emissions.

For the important purpose of maintenance of the "moral system," people must *try* to act properly. To facilitate applying pressure on them to do so, causal attributions of their behavior may systematically involve the assignment of more personal responsibility than is warranted on more logical grounds. Suggestive evidence on this point is provided by Walster, who found that the worse the consequences of an apparent accident, the greater the responsibility assigned the person possibly responsible for it [1966]. Other investigators have not been able to replicate this study [Shaver 1970, Shaw & Skolnick, in press], but from the present argument we would expect the effect to be a subtle one. Thus, it would occur only when the *importance* of preventing such accidents (through responsibility assignment) is somehow more salient than the *infeasibility* of such control efforts.

Another example of the relation between attribution and moral control may be provided by the tendency, not yet well documented, to attribute responsibility to a person who complies with illegitimate power. The insistence that illegitimate power be resisted serves the interests of control by legitimate authorities, and this insistence may itself be supported by the tendency to hold a person responsible for his actions in the face of illegitimate power. The point of these last several examples is that the attributor is not only an agent of control in relation to his own immediate interests but is also an agent of moral control, and this fact is reflected in his attributional biases and tendencies.

The more rational attributional tendencies can probably be assimilated within the suggested viewpoint as readily as can the less rational ones. In responding to another person's negative actions, there is no corrective gain to come from blaming him if his physical or mental incompetence was involved, but there is considerable possibility for effective control if it was a matter of his intention, attitude, or motivation. On this point, the argument follows fairly closely the proposals of various moral philosophers, for example, Stevenson [1967]. In bargaining with another person with uncertainty as to the causal locus for the experienced conflict, inasmuch as one's own actions best assure control of the other, attributions tend to be biased in a manner that supports such actions. His past concessions are attributed to oneself, with the result that one is inspired to continue to seek further concessions. Also, as noted above, his resistance is attributed to him rather than to the less influenceable external framework within which the bargaining occurs. Reciprocity reactions guided by perceived intentions can also be understood as control behaviors, designed to reinforce and strengthen the other's tendencies to help one but to deter his tendency to hurt one.

In short, it is proposed that the perception of cause is intimately linked to the exercise of control. It contains within it systematic tendencies and biases such that the domain of attempted control is extended, delimited, shaped, and otherwise affected by the control problems of the individual and his social system.

BIBLIOGRAPHY

C. Norman Alexander and Gordon W. Knight, "Situated Identities and Social Psychological Experimentation." *Sociometry*, 1971, 34:65–82.

Joel Allison and David E. Hunt, "Social Desirability and Expression of Aggression Under Varying Conditions of Frustration." *Journal of Consulting Psychology*, 1959, 23:528–532.

Eliot Aronson and Darwyn Linder, "Gain and Loss of Esteem as Determinants of Interpersonal Attractiveness." *Journal of Experimental Social Psychology*, 1965, 1:156–171.

Alex Bavelas, Albert H. Hastorf, Alan E. Gross, and W. Richard Kite, "Experiments on the Alteration of Group Structure." *Journal of Experimental Social Psychology*, 1965, 1:55–70.

Linda Beckman, "Effects of Students' Performance on Teachers' and Observers' Attributions of Causality." *Journal of Educational Psychology*, 1970, 61:76–82.

Daryl J. Bem, "Self-Perception: An Alternative Interpretation of Cognitive Dissonance Phenomena." *Psychological Review*, 1967, 74:183–200.

Alan A. Benton, Harold H. Kelley, and Barry A. Liebling, "The Effects of Extremity of Offers and Concession Rate on the Outcomes of. Bargaining." Unpublished.

Dana Bramel, "Determinants of Beliefs About Other People." In Judson Mills, ed., *Experimental Social Psychology*. Macmillan, 1969.

Jack W. Brehm and Arthur R. Cohen, *Explorations in Cognitive Dissonance*. Wiley, 1962.

Eugene Burnstein and Philip Worchel, "Arbitrariness of Frustration and Its Consequences for Aggression in a Social Situation." *Journal of Personality*, 1962, 30:528–541.

J. Merrill Carlsmith, Barry E. Collins, and Robert L. Helmreich, "Studies in Forced Compliance: I. The Effect of Pressure for Compliance on Attitude Change Produced by Face-to-Face Role Playing and Anonymous Essay Writing." *Journal of Personality and Social Psychology*, 1966, 4:1–13.

Jae-Ho Cha, "Clarity of the Focal Stimulus Cue and the Mediation of Two Opposing Social Perceptual Effects." Ph.D. thesis, University of California, Los Angeles, 1971.

Arthur R. Cohen, "Social Norms, Arbitrariness of Frustration, and Status of the Agent of Frustration in the Frustration-Aggression Hypothesis." *Journal of Abnormal and Social Psychology*, 1955, 51:222–226.

Richard deCharms, Virginia Carpenter, and Aharon Kuperman, "The 'Origin-Pawn' Variable in Person Perception." *Sociometry*, 1965, 28:241–258.

Seymour Epstein and Stuart P. Taylor, "Instigation to Aggression as a Function of Degree of Defeat and Perceived Aggressive Intent of the Opponent." *Journal of Personality*, 1967, 35:265–289.

John R. P. French, Jr., and Bertram H. Raven, "The Bases of Social Power." In Dorwin P. Cartwright, ed., *Studies in Social Power*. University of Michigan, 1959.

Richard E. Goranson and Leonard Berkowitz, "Reciprocity and Responsibility Reactions to Prior Help." *Journal of Personality and Social Psychology*, 1966, 3:227–232.

Fritz Heider, *The Psychology of Interpersonal Relations*. Wiley, 1958.

Thomas J. Johnson, Rhoda Feigenbaum, and Marcia Weiby, "Some Determinants and Consequences of the Teacher's Perception of Causation." *Journal of Educational Psychology*, 1964, 55:237–246.

Edward E. Jones and Keith E. Davis, "From Acts to Dispositions: The Attribution Process in Person Perception." In Leonard Berkowitz, ed., *Advances in Experimental Social Psychology*, vol. 2. Academic, 1965.

Edward E. Jones, Keith E. Davis, and Kenneth J. Gergen, "Role Playing Variations and Their Informational Value for Person Perception." *Journal of Abnormal and Social Psychology*, 1961, 63:302–310.

Edward E. Jones and Richard deCharms, "Changes in Social Perception as a Function of the Personal Relevance of Behavior." *Sociometry*, 1957, 20:75–85.

Edward E. Jones, Kenneth J. Gergen, and Robert G. Jones, "Tactics of Ingratiation Among Leaders and Subordinates in a Status Hierarchy." *Psychological Monographs*, 1963, 77(566).

Edward E. Jones and Victor A. Harris, "The Attribution of Attitudes." *Journal of Experimental Social Psychology*, 1967, 3:1-24.

Edward E. Jones, Stephen L. Hester, Amerigo Farina, and Keith E. Davis, "Reactions to Unfavorable Personal Evaluation as a Function of the Evaluator's Perceived Adjustment." *Journal of Abnormal and Social Psychology*, 1959, 59:363–370.

Edward E. Jones and Richard E. Nisbett, "The Actor and the Observer: Divergent Perceptions of the Causes of Behavior." General Learning Press, 1971.

Herbert W. Kee, "The Development, and the Effects upon Bargaining, of Trust and Suspicion." Ph.D. thesis, University of British Columbia, 1969.

Harold H. Kelley, "Attribution Theory in Social Psychology." In David Levine, ed., *Nebraska Symposium on Motivation, 1967*. University of Nebraska Press, 1967.

Harold H. Kelley, "Moral Evaluation." *American Psychologist*, 1971, 26:293–300.

Harold H. Kelley, Zdenek Helus, Helmut Lamm, Marc Servais, Peter Veen, Maryla Zaleska, and Karel Wouters, "Direction of Change in Problem Difficulty and Perceived Source of Change as Independent Variables in a Negotiation Game." Working paper of the European Research Training Seminar in Experimental Social Psychology, University of Louvain, 1967.

Harold H. Kelley, Gerald H. Shure, Morton Deutsch, Claude Faucheux, John L. Lanzetta, Serge Moscovici, Jozef M. Nuttin, Jr., Jaap M. Rabbie, and John W. Thibaut, "A Comparative Experimental Study of Negotiation Behavior." *Journal of Personality and Social Psychology*, 1970, 16:411–438.

Harold H. Kelley and Anthony J. Stahelski, "The Inference of Intention from Moves in the Prisoner's Dilemma Game." *Journal of Experimental Social Psychology*, 1970, 6:401–419.

Harold H. Kelley and John W. Thibaut, "Group Problem Solving." In Gardner Lindzey and Elliot Aronson, eds., *The Handbook of Social Psychology*, vol. 4. Addison-Wesley, 1969.

Harold H. Kelley, John W. Thibaut, Roland Radloff, and David Mundy, "The Development of Cooperation in the 'Minimal Social Situation.'" *Psychological Monographs*, 1962, 76(19) (whole no. 538).

S. S. Komorita and John Mechling, "Betrayal and Reconciliation in a Two-Person Game." *Journal of Personality and Social Psychology*, 1967, 6:349–352.

Arie W. Kruglanski, "Attributing Trustworthiness in Supervisor-Worker Relations." *Journal of Experimental Social Psychology*, 1970, 6:214–232.

David Landy and Elliot Aronson, "Liking for an Evaluator as a Function of His Discernment." *Journal of Personality and Social Psychology*, 1968, 9:133–141.

John T. Lanzetta and T. E. Hannah, "Reinforcing Behavior of 'Naive' Trainers." *Journal of Personality and Social Psychology*, 1969, 11:245–252.

David R. Mettee and Shelley E. Taylor, "Affect Conversion vs. Affect Change as Determinants of the Gain-Loss Liking Effect." Unpublished.

A. Michotte, *The Perception of Causality*. Basic, 1963.

Neal E. Miller, "Experimental Studies of Conflict." In J. McV. Hunt, ed., *Personality and the Behavior Disorders*, vol. 1, Ronald, 1944.

Judson Mills and Jerald M. Jellison, "Effect on Opinion Change of How Desirable the Communication Is to the Audience the Communicator Addressed." *Journal of Personality and Social Psychology*, 1967, 6:98–101.

Stuart Oskamp, "Effects of Programmed Strategies on Cooperation in the Prisoner's Dilemma and Other Mixed-Motive Games." In Lawrence Wrightsman, ed., *Cooperation and Exploitation in Mixed-Motive Games*. Brooks/Cole, 1971.

Nicholas N. Pastore, "The Role of Arbitrariness in the Frustrations-Aggression Hypothesis." *Journal of Abnormal and Social Psychology*, 1952, 47:728–731.

Albert Pepitone and Janet Sherberg, "Intentionality, Responsibility, and Interpersonal Attraction." *Journal of Personality*, 1957, 25:757–766.

Dean G. Pruitt, "Reciprocity and Credit Building in a Laboratory Dyad." *Journal of Personality and Social Psychology*, 1968, 8:143–147.

Dean G. Pruitt and Julie Latané Drews, "The Effect of Time Pressure, Time Elapsed, and the Opponent's Concession Rate on Behavior in Negotiation." *Journal of Experimental Psychology*, 1969, 5:43–60.

Kenneth Ring, "Some Determinants of Interpersonal Attraction in Hierarchical Relationships: A Motivational Analysis." *Journal of Personality*, 1964, 32:651–665.

Paul Rothaus and Philip Worchel, "The Inhibition of Aggression Under Non-Arbitrary Frustration." *Journal of Personality*, 1960, 28:108–117.

David R. Schmitt, "The Invocation of Moral Obligation." *Sociometry*, 1964, 27:299–310.

John Schopler and Marjorie Wall Matthews, "The Influence of the Perceived Locus of Partner's Dependence on the Use of Interpersonal Power." *Journal of Personality and Social Psychology*, 1965, 2:609–612.

Alvin Scodel, "Induced Collaboration in Some Non-Zero-Sum Games." *Behavioral Science*, 1962, 6:335–340.

Vello Sermat, "The Effect of an Initial Cooperative or Competitive Treatment upon a Subject's Response to Conditional Cooperation." *Behavioral Science*, 1967, 12:301–313.

Kelly G. Shaver, "Defensive Attribution: Effects of Severity and Relevance on the Responsibility Assigned for an Accident." *Journal of Personality and Social Psychology*, 1970, 14:101–113.

Jerry I. Shaw and Paul Skolnick, "Attribution of Responsibility for a Happy Accident." *Journal of Personality and Social Psychology*, June 1971.

Marvin E. Shaw and Jefferson L. Sulzer, "An Empirical Test of Heider's Levels in Attribution of Responsibility." *Journal of Abnormal and Social Psychology*, 1964, 69:39–46.

Gerald H. Shure and Robert J. Meeker, "Bargaining Processes in Experimental Territorial Conflict Situations." *Peace Research Society: Papers*, 1969, 11:109–122.

Harold Sigall and Elliot Aronson, "Opinion Change and the Gain-Loss Model of Interpersonal Attraction." *Journal of Experimental Social Psychology*, 1967, 3:178–189.

Leonard Solomon, "The Influence of Some Types of Power Relationships and Game Strategies on the Development of Interpersonal Trust." *Journal of Abnormal and Social Psychology*, 1960, 61:223–230.

Ivan D. Steiner and William L. Field, "Role Assignment and Interpersonal Influence." *Journal of Abnormal and Social Psychology*, 1960, 61:239–246.

Charles L. Stevenson, *Facts and Values: Studies in Ethical Analysis*. Yale University Press, 1967.

Siegfried Streufert and Susan C. Streufert, "Effects of Conceptual Structure, Failure, and Success on Attribution of Causality and Interpersonal Attitudes." *Journal of Personality and Social Psychology*, 1969, 11:138–147.

Lloyd H. Strickland, "Surveillance and Trust." *Journal of Personality*," 1958, 26:200–215.

Robert L. Swinth, "The Establishment of the Trust Relationship." *Journal of Conflict Resolution*, 1967, 11:335–344.

John W. Thibaut and Henry W. Riecken, "Some Determinants and Consequences of the Perception of Social Causality." *Journal of Personality*, 1955, 24:113–133.

Elaine Walster, "Assignment of Responsibility for an Accident." *Journal of Personality and Social Psychology*, 1966, 3:73–79.

Elaine Walster, Elliot Aronson, and Darcy Abrahams, "On Increasing the Persuasiveness of a Low Prestige Communicator." *Journal of Experimental Social Psychology*, 1966, 2:325–342.

[Preparation of this paper grew out of a workshop on attribution theory held at UCLA in August 1969, supported by Grant GS-2613 from the National Science Foundation, and was also made possible by NSF Grant GS-1121X.]

2 · Order Effects in Impression Formation: Attribution Context and the Nature of the Entity

EDWARD E. JONES
Duke University

GEORGE R. GOETHALS
Williams College

The attribution process substitutes inferred structure for observed flux. Acts, appearances, and all manner of manifestations are potentially grist for the process. Such observable events are organized by the attributor into a conception of the underlying entities to which they appear to refer. In the interpersonal realm, a basic task of the attributor is to allocate the determinants of observed action to the person or to the environment. Does an act reflect some distinctive characteristic of the actor, and thus help us to identify the nature of his particular dispositions, or does it primarily reflect the evocative power of the environment?

A programmatic essay by Jones and Davis [1965] considers a rational strategy for making personal versus environmental attributions. When attributions are made to the person, we may speak of "correspondent inferences," since the inferred disposition corresponds to the act observed and the former is seen to have caused the latter. The Jones and Davis paper restricts itself, however, to the frozen moment in time when one unit of information, one act, is the input of the attribution process. The question of how behavioral data are combined is obviously a next step in the inquiry. There are many ways to approach the analysis of how inputs are combined in the inference process; this study considers what might be learned from a fresh look at an old and convenient comparative design, the order effect paradigm.

The order effect paradigm can be simply described as comparing responses to one sequence of information with responses to the same information presented in reverse order. It is clear that information within an interpersonal episode is neither produced nor perceived all at once. Since this is the case, it is reasonable to ask whether the attribution process is in systematic ways affected by the order in which information is received.

Reasonable to ask, that is, if one does not expect a simple answer. When information occurs in a particular temporal sequence, an attributor may organize it in such a way as to yield primacy, recency, or something in between. These crude outcome categories are like large earthenware vessels into which hard-to-identify and ill-assorted determinants may be poured. To change the metaphor, the order effect paradigm is an overcrowded crossroads where a variety of theoretical principles converge from a variety of angles. Since both primacy and recency are multiply determined, it is possible to get either effect for several reinforcing reasons, or it is possible that the competition between primacy determinants and recency determinants results in a neutralizing stand-off.

The study of order effects has moved from the question of primacy versus recency to a more sophisticated inquiry into the conditions under which one or the other effect may be expected. But the search for determining conditions has favored the easily controlled and varied over the more naturalistic and context-relevant determinants. Especially in the able hands of Norman Anderson, the order effect inquiry has become increasingly precise and increasingly detached from the problems actually confronting an attributor in a natural interpersonal setting. Anderson's contributions have been important, as we shall see, but it is time to look carefully at the boundary conditions within which they were produced.

Primacy versus recency is not a gripping theoretical issue in its own right. Information order, like time, age, and number of siblings, is not a conceptually unitary psychological variable. The appropriate justification for studying order effects is that sequence transformation experiments can provide occasions for observing the attribution process at work. In the impression formation realm, the order effect paradigm typically presents information about a target person in such a sequence that the implications of the early information are very different from the implications of the later information. There is built in information conflict, and the interest is in how it is resolved by attributional processes. If time or order do not enter into the resolving process, there will be neither primacy nor recency. When primacy or recency obtain, any one of a number of factors may be operating, ranging from cognitive tendencies "wired into" the human organism to hypotheses developed by the perceiver from his particular experiences with different sequential event orders. In an effort to redress the bias of the literature, we shall emphasize the latter portion of this range, focusing on some of the principles that may give rise to sequence-related hypotheses in forming an impression of an actor. The discussion will enter a realm of greater confusion and complexity than the traditional primacy-recency literature, but hopefully with the compensating gain of viewing the order effect paradigm in terms more appropriate to naturalistic predictions.

The major proposition we shall attempt to document is that *the information conveyed by the order of events itself is contingent on the context in which these events unfold and on the nature of the entity being considered as an attributional target.* The role of primacy versus recency has been investigated under different guises in many different content domains. There are at present several nonintersecting subliteratures dealing with order effects, and it is our hope that by examining the implications of the above proposition for these various problem areas certain general conclusions about order and attribution can be reached. Before embarking on such a review, however, some attention should be given to the general problems of comparability when evaluating different experiments dealing with the effects of order. In the following section, therefore, we consider several potentially important distinctions of method that should be kept in mind during the subsequent comparative review.

Some Useful Distinctions

We have stated that the order effect paradigm can be simply described as comparing one sequence of information with the same information presented in reverse order. In the analysis of specific empirical studies, however, this simplicity breaks down both with respect to the information items being compared and the response measures used in making the comparison. We assume at the outset that different kinds of information will produce different kinds of order effects. Even restricting ourselves to the impression formation domain, one would intuitively hesitate to predict the same effects of order from trait-adjective sequences [Anderson 1965], paragraphs describing inconsistent behavior [Luchins 1957], and the direct observation of the behavior itself [Jones, Rock, Shaver, Goethals, & Ward 1968]. These different kinds of materials certainly present the observer with different inference problems [see Anderson & Norman 1964]. At the very least, the observer of unfolding behavior is faced with an additional problem of moving from observed acts to inferred dispositions, and therefore of assessing the role of the environment at each point in the ordered sequence of acts.

Attending to these distinctions between different types of information suggests a more fundamental difference between the sequence in which information is generated by a target person and the sequence in which it is received by a perceiver. While it sometimes happens, of course, that we learn about someone's recent exploits before we learn about his past, the natural sequence of behavior observation coincides with the sequence of behavior production: in the typical acquaintance process, where one person observes another's actions over time, the order of generating and receiving information is confounded. What happened first in time is perceived first in time. To our knowledge there are no published studies that have explored the consequences of this confounding, but it should make some difference in those temporally extended settings where orderly changes in performance are expected from the effects of practice, warm-up, fatigue, or indeed in any setting where changes in the stimulus environment may be inferred. We shall subsequently describe an experiment comparing behavior sequences that explicitly preserve or scramble the order in which the behaviors occurred. For the moment it will suffice to bear in mind the distinction between confounding and separating orders of producing and receiving information.

In addition to these important potential differences in the nature and context of entity manifestations, the effects of information order may be measured in several different ways. We are primarily interested in measures of attributed personal characteristics, but this does not move us very far toward a clear understanding of the most appropriate measure on any experimental occasion. The most straightforward measure of attribution would presumably involve ratings of the entity on dimensions relevant to the axis of change in the stimulus sequence. Depending on the dimension, of course, we may be asking "how warm?" or "how intelligent?" or "how liberal?" is the person. Subtle differences in how these questions are asked may have implications for the fate of primacy versus recency. An important issue is whether order effect differences in attribution ratings represent shifts in the meaning of the judgmental language used or true differences in the perception of the entity being judged. As Campbell, Lewis, and Hunt [1958] have shown, it makes a difference whether the judgments obtained are in relativistic terms (heavy versus light, sweet versus salty) or in absolute terms that are extensive and have some anchorage outside the particular experimental situation (ounces, inches, degrees temperature in Fahrenheit).

The fact that there are no all-purpose, interchangeable, attribution measures makes it difficult to make all but the crudest comparisons across attributional domains. A partial solution to this problem is available as long as the investigator sticks to dimensions that have clear evaluative implications, and compares good-to-bad with bad-to-good sequential orders. Under such conditions, *general evaluative ratings* can serve as useful measures of the effect of order. Much of the work with positive and negative trait-adjectives has used evaluative ratings as a dependent variable, and with notable success as judged by the criterion of cumulative and comparable results. Such judgments, however, hardly meet the test of being couched in a language that is absolute and extra-experimentally anchored.

Presumably, various *behavior prediction measures* should be correlated with both the direct attributive and the evaluative measure of order effects. If the investigator has doubts about the reliability and validity of simple ratings of, say, intelligence, he can ask the subject to predict the target person's performance on a relevant subsequent task. The more intelligence is attributed to the target person, in all probability, the higher will be the predicted performance. A variant of this kind of measure is concurrent subjective probability estimation. As subjects are exposed to a series of events, they can be asked to estimate the probability after each event that the next will be an X or a non-X (a good trait or a bad trait, a success or a failure). Insensitivity to objectively shifting probabilities can then become a measure of primacy [see Peterson & DuCharme 1967].

Finally, it would seem almost mandatory to insert somewhere in the design a *measure of recall*. The chances are that a person who recalls more of the positive adjectives than the negative ones will have a more favorable view of the person being described than the person remembering more of the negative traits. One recalled as solving many problems will be seen as more intelligent than one recalled as solving just a few. Distortions in memory in a primacy or recency direction can obviously affect attribution when, as is usually the case in the order effect paradigm, items are systematically arranged to convey different information at the beginning than at the end. Though one should not accept a simple measure of recall as a direct measure of attribution, recall distortions may be sufficient explanation for any primacy-recency effects observed. (It is also quite possible, of course, that recall distortions can be an *effect* of prior attributional decisions.)

Unfortunately, we are presently in no position to distinguish clearly among these various measures or to predict their differential sensitivity to order. It may be, however, that order affects evaluation differently than it does descriptive attribution, and that behavior predictions perform differently than either. One would expect these various measures to be highly intercorrelated, but the fact that they might not be is reason enough to raise the dependent variable issue before embarking on the following review. The reader should be warned also that no attempt will be made to provide a comprehensive survey of the voluminous order effect literature in the different content areas in which it has been generated. Those examples that raise issues and provoke speculation will be featured.

The Order Effect Paradigm Family: Variations in Judgmental Contexts and Their Distinctive Implications

Adjective Combinations

In 1946 S. E. Asch described a series of studies in which subjects were asked to make summary impression ratings of a person allegedly described by a series of traits. In one group of these studies, some subjects were exposed to a list of traits and others to the same list in reverse order. An example: intelligent —industrious—impulsive—critical—stubborn—envious. Comparison of impressions suggested by the two sequences revealed a primacy effect. Asch explained his primacy findings in terms of the directional implications of item content. "It is not the sheer temporal position of the items which is important as much as the functional relation of its content to the contents of the items following it [p. 272]. With these studies the order effect paradigm was born, and the effects of order were given a structural interpretation in terms of meaningful interactions among trait meanings, with the earlier traits exerting a directional force on the later ones.

The interpretation suggested by Asch seemed so reasonable, apparently, that no one readily perceived the seeds of controversy in any relevant alternative explanations of the primacy effects obtained. Asch was essentially arguing that no particular trait-adjective has a fixed meaning and the overlapping connotations of adjectives appearing late in a series are selectively processed in terms of the connotative implications of earlier adjectives. Bruner, Shapiro, and Tagiuri [1958] presented some data to show that impressions inferred from lists of traits could be very reliably predicted from an arithmetic averaging of

their independent meanings, but their report was an isolated addendum to Asch, rather than a systematic re-examination of his suggested interpretation.

Some fifteen years after Asch's classic study, Anderson and his colleagues published the first in a series of studies exploring the effects of the order of evaluative adjectives on the favorability of resulting impressions. Working with traits selected for their valence on the basis of judges' ratings, Anderson and Barrios [1961] presented over sixty sets of six adjectives to each subject and asked him to rate his impression of the person being described by each set on a scale ranging from $+4$ (highly favorable) to -4 (highly unfavorable). The sets were composed of adjectives that either abruptly or gradually changed from positive to negative or vice versa. Strong primacy effects were observed across all sets, and though these effects declined with repeated judgment trials, they did not disappear. Furthermore, it did not seem to make any difference whether the transition of valence within the set was abrupt or gradual.

Anderson's subsequent studies have used the order effect paradigm in an effort to discriminate between different models of information processing. The main conclusion of the most relevant studies [Anderson 1962, Anderson 1968] is that adjectives presented in this manner do not interact to form a new gestalt structure. The connotation of one adjective does not depend on the other adjectives in the set, as Asch had argued. If one assigns a given favorability value to each adjective (based either on the consensus of judges or on the subject's own preratings), the resulting impression of the set can be closely approximated by calculating the arithmetic mean of the values. When the set is so arranged that there is a systematic shift in valence, primacy effects arise because subjects assign differential weights to early and late adjectives: "the net influence of an adjective decreases linearly with its ordinal position in the set" [Anderson 1965].

The implications of Anderson's weighted average model are similar to the implications of Asch's "change in meaning" interpretation and it is not immediately obvious how one could crucially test their relative power of prediction. Anderson's weighted average model might be preferred on the grounds of parsimony alone—it requires fewer individualized, content-specific assumptions. In addition, however, the weighted average, linear-decrease model implies that subjects "tune out," or even if they remain attentive late in the series, they discount inconsistent information in other ways. Support for an attention decrement explanation of primacy is seen in studies by

Anderson and Hubert [1963], Stewart [1965], and Hendrick and Costantini [1970], where instructions designed to equalize attention over the entire list appear to wipe out primacy. One could not have predicted these differences from a change-in-meaning position.

In general, Anderson should be commended for introducing elegant refinements into the design and analysis of order effects and for his sensitivity to qualifications and alternative explanations. Nevertheless, several cautionary words are in order before we rush to apply the weighted average, linear decrease model to the general case of impressional attribution. It is quite clear that the test of any information processing model requires data, and these data have to be generated in a particular judgmental context with particular kinds of informational content. Anderson has chosen to work with the impression formation context as a convenience, but in the interests of precision and elegance he may have worked himself away from a number of significant variables that affect the natural attribution process in the domain of interpersonal judgment.

First of all, the strategy of using elaborate counterbalanced designs in which each subject responds to numerous trait-adjective lists creates important difficulties that limit the generality of his conclusions about averaging and interaction among the traits used. Since the kind of interaction effects suggested by Asch may or may not result in primacy, the averaging across adjective lists may obscure the kinds of strong interactions that might be expected with certain trait combinations only. One might describe the typical primacy effects of an Anderson experiment as the residual of various operations designed to rule out the vagaries of *particular* trait interactions.

Anderson and Jacobson [1965] did compare impressions formed from trait combinations involving antonyms (honest–deceitful) with those formed from traits that are merely of different affective value (honest–reckless). Because the traits were read by the subject in both regular and reversed orders, however, the implications of this variation for order effects was explicitly ruled out. Different conditions were established in which instructions either encouraged or suppressed discounting. When discounting was encouraged by suggesting that all traits might not be equally valid, the antonym-inconsistency lists departed more from the weighted average model than the affective-inconsistency lists. In attempting to track down the particular patterns of differential weighting that resulted from the discounting tendency, Anderson and Jacobson were led to

modify their earlier attacks on the interactive argument: "even though the averaging formulation shows promise in accounting for the impression response data per se, it cannot completely account for [the form of differential weighting observed]. In this respect it would appear that the adjectives do interact in forming the impression, a conclusion in harmony with the views of Asch (1946)" [p. 539]. The best conclusion would seem to be that the effects of trait interactions have not been properly tested in relation to order of presentation, and any final choice among inferential models seems premature at this point.

Possible effects of instructions. Problems may arise not only by commitments to particular items of information in the trait lists, but also by commitments to particular instructions that provide the judgmental context. Anderson has not been entirely consistent in how he presents the adjectives to be combined, but in no instance has he made an effort to convince the subjects that the traits refer to real persons. In the typical case the subject is to think of the adjectives as having been given by different persons who knew the target person well. The lists are either explicitly or implicitly hypothetical. Except in the Anderson and Jacobson [1965] study, furthermore, the instructions typically have indicated that all adjectives of a set should be considered as having equal importance. Perhaps it is not surprising that the combination of a hypothetical judgment setting and instructions about equal weighting should lead to confirmation of a weighted average model. One might contend that the subjects are simply following the direct implications of experimental instructions, or being responsive to "experimenter demand." It is true, however, as Anderson and Jacobson argue, that this is not completely preordained by the circumstances, since the meaning of the traits is not fixed and assimilation and contrast effects could occur. Such effects, of course, imply interactions among trait meanings.

A related observation is that only in the Anderson [1968] study is any mention made to the subjects about the meaning of order. Here "the serial presentation procedure was explained by analogy to real life in which one customarily gets to know a person step by step" [p. 365]. This seems a halfhearted effort in the direction of the earlier described natural confounding of information generated and received. It is perhaps not incidental that this most recent Anderson study is the only one in which the results show more recency than primacy in the various order effect comparisons. In none of the other studies in this

31

program is anything said about order, but this does not mean that subjects are oblivious to various shared and idiosyncratic connotations of presentational order. A subject might conceivably assume that the experimenter put the most important adjective first, or the most useful, or the most generic. Otherwise, why not simply put the terms in alphabetical order? This may appear to be dangerously close to nit-picking, but such a hypothesis, even if entertained by only a minority of the subjects, could contribute to the typical primacy effects observed when adjectives are presented in a sequence presumably determined by the experimenter.

Have Anderson and his colleagues ever discovered how to produce recency effects in the impression formation domain? In a study especially designed to distinguish between the applicability of averaging and additivity models, Anderson [1968] employed adjective lists involving less affective contrast than in all the previous studies of presentational order. The affective transitions ran from extremely favorable traits to moderately favorable traits, or from extremely unfavorable to moderately so. In this study, as we have noted above, explicit mention was made of the natural meaning of order in the acquaintance process. The results came out in favor of the averaging versus the additive formula. In brief, the moderate traits pushed the impression toward neutrality rather than toward the even more extreme judgments that would be predicted if the favorability values of the traits were simply added. The results also showed a general tendency toward recency.

Anderson attributes the prevalence of recency to the lack of affective inconsistency in the trait lists. The discounting mechanism, which he favors as an explanation of primacy, is not brought into play because there is insufficient affective inconsistency among the traits. He does not consider the possibility that the explicitly serial presentation might have contributed to recency. In our view this remains a possibility even though the lack-of-inconsistency explanation may have more inherent plausibility.

To say that Anderson favors the discounting hypothesis does not necessarily imply that he rejects the hypothesis of attention decrement. His weighted average model is compatible with either process, and both are preferred to a "new gestalt," change-of-meaning explanation. In his 1965 paper with Jacobson, Anderson attempted to relate the discounting and attention decrement explanations by suggesting that decreased weights for the later adjectives might be *caused* at least in part by decreased attention [p. 539]. Hendrick and Costantini [1970] have proposed

that discounting should vary with the degree of inconsistency between traits, whereas 'attention decrement should be independent of inconsistency and perhaps dependent only on the length of the series. If this assumption is granted, their results support an attention decrement hypothesis in that instruction to pronounce each trait (an attention-equalizing manipulation) converts primacy into recency. There is no support for discounting in their data, however, since the effects of order were unrelated to the degree of discrepancy among the traits.

Reference Scale Anchors and Judgmental Contrast

While we have emphasized the Anderson research program because of its quality and coherence, there are a host of other studies employing trait-adjective combinations in an impression formation context. If one were to have a run-off of primacy versus recency conclusions, primacy effects would win hands down. But another important research literature suggests that recency should be the predicted outcome under a wide range of conditions and is not just an anomolous exception to the primacy law. This derives from the tradition of research on psychophysical scale construction and the judgment of weight, brightness, pitch, numerosity, opinion extremity, and so on. It is appropriate to ask how this line of research relates to that featuring the combination of adjectives.

Anderson makes an interesting stab at bringing the two sets of data together. In an attempt to account for the findings of recency obtained in his 1968 experiment discussed above, he concludes that recency is the generally expected outcome when information is presented in a sequence, and a "necessary though not sufficient condition for primacy would be inconsistency among the stimulus items. Whether this view has any generality is difficult to say since the primacy-recency area is especially marked by conflicting results. . . . However, since most work in this area has in fact used stimuli of mixed polarity, conflicting results might be expected on the present view. With such stimuli, tendencies toward primacy and toward recency could be operating together and the net resultant would depend heavily on experimental details" [p. 361].

The conclusion that recency is the generally expected outcome derives partly from the serial-position learning literature, and partly from the literature on contrast effects in the judgment of stimuli in a series. From the former we can extract the common sense principle that recent events are more easily remembered than more remote ones, though the serial learning data show primacy effects as well as recency effects, with the items in the middle being most subject to retention difficulty because of retroactive and proactive inhibition. Miller and Campbell [1959] contend that recency will tend to win out over primacy when the measure of memory or impression occurs immediately after the end of the sequence, but their argument refers to longer time spans than those with which we shall be concerned.

The literature on assimilation and contrast in the psychophysical tradition seems more directly relevant to our problem than the nonsense-syllable learning and retention literature. In the typical psychophysical judgment task, a subject is confronted with a series of objects that can be arrayed along the same attributive dimension. By any of a variety of methods (paired comparison, single stimuli, and the like) he is asked to locate specific objects along this dimension. There is some objective way to measure the true intensity value of each stimulus being judged—either by physical measurement in the classical psychophysical case or consensual judgment in the case of "goodness" or attitudinal extremity. Since this is so, it is possible to plot relations between the objective stimulus values presented and the subjective judgments given.

One of the conditions known to affect these relations is the item context preceding the particular item being judged. The preceding items serve as an "anchor" in terms of which a given item is judged. If the preceding items do produce anchoring effects, these may be either in the direction of contrast or assimilation—the judged item can either appear less like the items preceding it (contrast) or more like these items (assimilation) as judged against some objective criterion. The next step is to realize that assimilation is a sufficient condition for a primacy effect when the task is to summarize the characteristics or nature of the entire series, and contrast is a sufficient condition for recency. Thus in a series of trait adjectives that are ordered from positive to negative, the later, negative adjectives might be judged more negative because of the anchoring effect of the earlier positive items. This would be a contrast effect and it would lead to recency when the subject attempted to rate his impression of the person described by the adjectives.

Restricting our consideration to sequences of changing information about a person, there are several theoretical positions that would expect contrast and therefore recency to characterize summarizing judgments in such a case [Johnson 1944, Helson 1947, Volkmann 1951]. The basic contention of each of

these theorists is that earlier stimuli are in one way or another integrated into an expectancy or adaptation level in terms of which later stimuli are judged. No particular provision is made for assimilation in these theoretical statements. A more complicated position is taken by Sherif and Hovland [1961] and Sherif, Sherif, and Nebergall [1965], who propose that either contrast or assimilation can occur, depending on the discrepancy between the value of the stimulus being judged and the anchor. When the stimulus is close in value to the anchor it will be assimilated to the anchor. Beyond some critical discrepancy value, however, the stimulus will be contrasted with the anchor and the discrepancy between the two will be magnified. Where this critical point is that separates assimilation from contrast depends on a number of factors discussed in detail by Sherif and Hovland. In general, the width of the assimilation range depends on the breadth and ambiguity of the cognitive categories involved. If a new stimulus falls near but within the defining boundary of the category defined by the anchoring stimuli preceding it, it will be assimilated to the typical instance of that category [Bruner 1957]. If it falls outside the defining category boundary, contrast formation should occur [see Jones & Gerard 1967, Berkowitz 1960].

What are the implications of the Sherif and Hovland argument for the analysis of order effects in impression formation? We have said that assimilation and contrast provide sufficient conditions for primacy and recency. Obviously, however, primacy and recency can occur without any implied distortion of the value of early- or late-appearing stimuli. In fact, Anderson's weighted average formula does not take assimilation or contrast into account; such factors would imply shifts in the meaning or scale value of at least some of the traits being assessed and would thus fall outside Anderson's model. If we accept the possibility of assimilation and contrast effects, however, then we can draw some interesting inferences about the relation of such effects to primacy-recency as a function of the entity being judged and the context of judgment.

In order to understand what might be involved, assume once again that we confront subjects with items of information in a sequence. If we insist to the subject that these items definitely refer to, describe, are manifestations of, the entity, such an insistence would presumably set up pressures toward assimilation—that is, toward judging each item as more similar to early (or modal) items than if the items were in isolation. If there is some reason to believe that different entities are being described together, or that the manifestations are not equally valid or reliable, the effects of assimilation in this sense should be much weaker and contrast, in fact, could result. As an example of contrast effects where different entities are being judged in sequence, consider an experiment by Bieri, Orcutt, and Leaman [1963]. These investigators presented sequences of contrived clinical cases in such a way that a case of moderate pathology was preceded by two cases of high or low pathology. As predicted, moderate cases preceded by high cases were judged less pathological than moderate cases preceded by low cases—the third case in the sequence was contrasted with the preceding two, anchoring, cases.

Actually, most cases of psychophysical judgment emphasize the relative or absolute evaluation of individual stimulus items and the subject is not asked to view the items as manifestations of some underlying entity. If items x, y, z are being independently judged as entities X, Y, Z, we should expect contrast. If items x, y, z are presented as manifestations of the same entity, however, there should be more pressures toward assimilation. It is the latter circumstance that characterizes the typical impression formation situation, and studies by Anderson and Lampel [1963] and Anderson [1966] clearly indicate the effects of viewing discrepant information samples as manifestations of the same entity. Subjects were told to rate each of three adjectives in terms of "how much you like the traits implied by the adjective." In some cases, they made these ratings after initially being told that the adjectives described a certain person and having rated their liking for that person. Subjects who made these initial ratings showed a "positive context effect" in their subsequent individual trait ratings. In other words, a favorable trait in combination with two unfavorable traits was judged as less favorable only when the traits were allegedly descriptive of the same person. We would venture to substitute the word "assimilation" for "positive context effect," though it is true that the results do not prove that the traits actually changed their meaning. The assimilation may be, then, more like a composite rating of the person and the trait—even though the instructions point only to the trait.

As we have already noted, assimilation (or a "positive context effect") is not automatically guaranteed in single entity situations because the manifestations to be judged may be differentially valid or referrable to causal factors besides the entity itself. This is quite possible when the task is to form an impression from samples of behavior over time, because behavior may be attributed either to the person or the evoking situation. In the Anderson paradigm the traits being evaluated may be seen as a joint function of the person being described and the person who (hypothetically) gave the description. Any suggestion that the traits are not equally valid should break up the tendency toward assimilation. Primacy effects may still occur for other reasons, however, since the chances are good that the later traits will be discounted entirely (rather than distorted through assimilation) if they are in conflict with the earlier traits.

A recent experiment by Thibaut and Ross [1969] is of special interest because it bears on these issues and introduces still another consideration, namely the extent to which the subject is *committed* to his initial impression—in this case, an impression of an artist's ability. An experimental manipulation committing the subject to an initially good or bad impression of the artist should promote assimilation of subsequent disconfirming information. In order to study the effects of commitment in comparison to appropriate control conditions, identical sequences of information were presented with different cover stories. The investigators presented twenty 16×16 matrixes containing varying proportions of 0's and 1's. Subjects were exposed either to an ascending series with a generally increasing proposition of 1's in the successive matrixes or to a descending series in which the proportion of 1's decreased. There were three conditions of judgment to which different subjects were assigned. In the *preference* condition each matrix was said to represent the ratings of a particular painting by sixteen nontrained judges assessing sixteen esthetic attributes as good ("1") or bad ("0"). Each matrix in the series of twenty was alleged to refer to a different painting by the same artist. The subject's task was to announce how good he thought each picture was after seeing the judges' ratings using a preference scale ranging from 0/16 to 16/16. After observing the entire series of slides, each subject also evaluated the artist himself on a number of bipolar adjective scales. It may be noted that the trial-by-trial rating task is similar to the typical psychophysical judgment of individual stimuli, whereas the second rating task is more like the typical impression judgment.

In the *commitment* condition subjects initially ranked a series of seventeen reproductions of "representative" paintings by different artists. They then proceeded exactly as in the preference conditions except that the ascending series of matrix ratings was said to be of paintings by the artist whom the subject had ranked second from the worst and the descending series by the artist ranked third from the best.

In the *attribute* condition, subjects were merely

asked to estimate for each slide the proportion of 1's in the matrix from 0/16 to 16/16. Since the subjects in the other two conditions were asked to express their own judgments of the goodness of the painting in these same proportional terms, the dependent variable was comparable in all conditions. In all conditions subjects were then exposed to a second series of slides that were actually the same twenty in reverse order. Thus subjects went from an ascending to a descending series or vice versa. A separate control group of subjects was exposed to a random series of matrixes (neither ascending nor descending) in the attribute condition.

The main results were presented in terms of the average value assigned to each judgment over the twenty matrixes in a series. On the first series of twenty slides contrast effects were obtained in the preference and attribute conditions, as predicted, and a slight but nonsignificant assimilation effect occurred in the commitment condition. In the second series (presumably judgments of another group of twenty paintings by a different artist) there was a strong assimilation effect in the commitment conditions, but the contrast effect was no longer observed in the preference and attribute conditions. This is quite in line with previous findings [Bieri, Orcutt, & Leaman 1963, Campbell, Lewis, & Hunt 1958] that practice with alternating anchors reduces contrast. In the Thibaut and Ross study apparently the joint effects of practice and commitment were necessary to produce a full assimilation effect.

Results on the final ratings of the artist paralleled in almost every way the results summarizing the subjects' ratings of individual painting matrixes. Thus, in the present case at least, judgments of the individual paintings seem to be remembered when it comes to making an overall appraisal of the artist. Or to put it in another way, the summary judgment of the artist seems to have been affected by assimilation and contrast effects in the preceding judgment of his work.

The Thibaut and Ross study makes several points that are congenial to our main proposition. First of all, the context of judgment is obviously important. The more strongly the subject is committed to his initial judgment, the more he will tend to assimilate subsequent discrepant information. Secondly, without special manipulations of commitment, contrast appears to be facilitated by successive judgment instructions. Although the subjects in the preference condition are encouraged to think they are judging appraisals of productions by the same artist, they are also making successive stimulus judgments comparable to those of psychophysical rating tasks where

contrast is a typical finding. Finally, it is of interest to note that overall judgments of the artist summarize the preceding individual matrix judgments, thus converting contrast into recency.

It is not at all clear that the results would have been the same if the procedures had asked *only* for a final summarizing judgment. Given such a procedure, Anderson and others [such as Hendrick & Costantini 1970] might argue that the early matrixes would be more salient and the later ones affected by attention decrement. Perhaps the successive matrix judgments, in other words, prevent attention decrement and therefore primacy—except when the power of commitment to an initial impression is sufficiently strong.

Unfolding Behavior Sequences

In the introduction to this paper we drew attention to the confounding that typically exists in the natural environment between the order in which information is generated by a target person and the order in which the information is received for processing by an attributor. As an example of what might be involved in such confounded sequences, let us consider a study in which we put together a video tape consisting of twenty-one brief conversational vignettes involving two undergraduate students. Each vignette featured the same student expressing his views about other people in general and certain acquaintances in particular. These vignettes showed the student as either very accepting and benevolent or as rejecting and pessimistic about human nature. In one condition (the accept–reject sequence) the early statements by and large extolled the charity of human nature whereas the later statements were more generally cynical and malevolent. A few transitional statements were placed in the middle to enhance credibility. In another condition the sequence was reversed (reject–accept). Cross-cutting these sequence variations were instructions designed to vary whether the student's actions were seen in the natural order in which they occurred. Half the subjects were told that the original sequence of these comments had been preserved on the tapes—they occurred at various points during the semester when these two students met once a week as part of a "get acquainted experiment." Thus the subjects given these instructions could imagine that the target person changed in his outlook over the semester, or perhaps that his initial uneasiness in the relationship wore off, revealing his true personality, or that he changed the expression of his outlook when he found out about the beliefs of his conversational partner. The remaining subjects were told that the vignettes were scrambled and arranged in random order. All subjects were subsequently asked to fill out the same impression rating scale, designed to measure attributed benevolence–malevolence, and to write a paragraph describing their overall impression of the target person.

Did the instructions about order have any effect? First of all, there were some marginal differences between the summed benevolence–malevolence ratings. The random arrangements yielded a significant primacy effect: the target person was seen as more benevolent after the accept–reject sequence than after the reject–accept sequence. In the "sequence-preserved" conditions neither primacy nor recency was observed. What is of particular interest is that few of the subjects in the random condition were able to develop reasonable hypotheses to explain the variation in expressed views. The free-impression paragraphs were analyzed to determine whether subjects had entertained any hypotheses to account for the behavior shift and, if so, what these hypotheses were. In the random conditions, nearly 80 per cent of the subjects did not develop any resolving hypotheses about the dispositional characteristics of the target person. They either wrote matter-of-fact descriptions of the behavior they had observed (70 per cent) or presented polarized impressions that ignored half of the information received (10 per cent). The remaining random condition subjects recorded what might be called *diagnostic* impressions, most of which had a pejorative twist ("he's very confused in his values," "he strikes me as very insecure," ". . . muddle-headed").

In the sequence-preserved condition, on the other hand, almost 60 per cent of the subjects developed hypotheses to account for the inconsistency of the student's opinions and 40 per cent of the total number (as opposed to zero per cent in the random conditions) made references to external events or the setting of the taped interaction. Fourteen out of the seventeen subjects who developed these hypotheses gave greater weight to the later information, manifesting a recency effect. They either supposed that the target person's outlook was changed by something that had happened during the semester in which the conversations took place—that there was a real change in the target person—or they felt that he was cautious or defensive at first and as he became more relaxed his true self was more clearly expressed. Three of the sequence-preserved subjects saw the target person as a chameleon, a hypothesis suggesting a weak primacy effect, since the target person

would presumably start out being himself and later change to whatever position was being advocated by his partner. These conflicting hypotheses, plus the number of subjects who gave purely descriptive (25 per cent) or polarized (18 per cent) impressions, produced a wide range of responses to the benevolence–malevolence rating task in the sequence-preserved conditions. Thus there was no overall tendency toward primacy or recency, as we noted above.

A final point of interest in the data is that it made some difference in the choice of hypotheses whether the sequence was accepting–rejecting or rejecting–accepting. Somewhat surprisingly perhaps, subjects observing the rejecting–accepting sequence were more prone to conclude that the target person was initially nervous and defensive than subjects in the accepting–rejecting sequence. There were not enough subjects in any such refined hypothesis subcategory to confirm a definite "interaction effect," but it seems highly plausible that the effects of confounding the sequence generated with the sequence received should vary as a function of the particular content and particular sequential direction involved.

The results of this study provide support for our basic proposition by showing that subjects do relate the changing manifestations of an entity to imagined external events when this possibility is made salient by instructions. It is important to realize that not all subjects do this, and some in fact seem curiously insensitive to the role of order in the sequence-preserved condition. But it seems self-evident that more clear-cut differences between random and sequence-preserved conditions could be obtained by more clearly structuring the interaction context (suggesting, for example, that the target person was undergoing intensive psychotherapy during the time span of the observed interviews). Thus more pains could have been taken to specify the influence potential of the particular program of conversations.

In addition, sharper differences might have emerged if the dimension of behavioral variation had been more salient conceptually, and perhaps more clearly exemplified by the observed episodes. The malevolence–benevolence continuum may be organized into very different cognitive structures by different subjects. Also, the kinds of comments presented in the video-taped conversations were necessarily noisy, imperfect indicators of one's position on the continuum. In order to maintain credibility, the comments had to be varied, concrete, and not blatantly self-contradictory. For example, in one of the "benevolent" segments the target person made an appreciative remark about someone who had stopped and helped him with a flat tire. Such a reminiscence might reflect benevolence, by the logic of salience and selective recall, but it is also a response determined by the characteristics of an external entity, the helper himself.

Finally, and of broader theoretical interest, the malevolence–benevolence disposition is a rather unstable one in most persons. We all have good moods and bad moods, and charity can rapidly give way to cynicism. It may be that the more unstable the attribute that supposedly underlies an unfolding behavior sequence the less pressure there will be toward assimilation and primacy.

For this reason it is appropriate to review the results of a series of experiments on the attribution of ability [Jones, Rock, Shaver, Goethals, & Ward 1968]. Ability as a dispositional construct obviously differs from benevolence–malevolence in many respects. One of the most crucial differences is that ability is a more stable attribute and its manifestations may be somewhat more reliable and diagnostic. Ability does not come and go like our moods of optimism and pessimism; only the conditions favorable to its manifestations come and go. One implication of this fact is that a reliable glimpse of talent may assure us that the person "has it in him," even though we may never see him perform as capably again. Once high ability is attributed, therefore, subsequent declines in performance may be explained away in terms of motivational variations, outside distractions, neurotic problems, and so on. The person who performs well after we have decided he is low in ability may cause us to revise our estimate of his talents. It is also common, however, to find excuses for his belated excellent performance and attribute it to luck, the help of others, or dogged perseverance. There is some reason to believe that the "late bloomer" never gets the fair shake he may deserve, while the one who starts off on the right performance foot may gain a lasting impressional edge.

Let us consider the experimental situation designed by Jones et al. [1968]. Subjects observed a stimulus person attempting to solve a series of thirty multiple-choice progressions and analogies. All items were described as of equal difficulty level (in terms of college norms) and they were varied and discrete like most intellectual aptitude test items, so that practice and learning effects would not be expected. The stimulus person always solved fifteen correctly, but in some cases he solved more of the later items (ascending series). In all cases, the subjects then predicted his success on a second series of unfolding items much like the first series. After this, subjects

were asked to rate the intelligence of the stimulus person and to recall the number of correct answers given in the first series of thirty problems. A final questionnaire included ratings of attributed motivation, perception of item-difficulty level, and other relevant probes.

In four separate experiments along these general procedural lines, primacy effects were obtained. Although some experiments showed stronger effects on one measure of order effects than on another, in general subjects confronting a descending performer predicted that he would solve more on the second series, and judged him to be more intelligent. These indications of primacy were maintained whether or not the subject himself solved the problems along with the stimulus person (and thus might be motivated to belittle the latter's performance) and whether or not the subjects made successive item-by-item estimates of the subjective probability of success on the next item.

How might this primacy effect in ability attribution be explained? We may begin by ruling out a few likely alternatives. One possibility is that subjects judging the descending stimulus person assumed that he lost interest in the task after an early display of mastery. If such were the case, the subjects might conclude that the stimulus person did poorly toward the end of the series almost *because* he was so bright, and therefore bored. The items were very difficult, however, and it is hard to imagine highly selected college students not being motivated to do their best in such a situation of public intellectual evaluation— and in fact the subjects rated the descending performer and the ascending performer as equally (and highly) motivated.

Another possibility is that the subjects got bored and ceased to pay attention to the performer's changing fortunes. This would be the *attention decrement* explanation of primacy, an explanation receiving some support in the adjective combination literature. If such "tuning out" actually occurred, however, one would surely expect the primacy effect to be reduced in a condition where subjects are asked to make subjective probability estimates of success before each trial. In fact, the addition of such a condition led to an increase rather than a decrease in primacy. Furthermore, as judged by the accuracy with which they were able to track changes in the objective probability of success, subjects in the probability estimation condition clearly maintained their attention throughout. A simple inattention explanation is hard to defend in the face of these data.

It is possible that subjects related the different patterns of performance to changes in the difficulty level of the items—in spite of instructions to the contrary. In fact, however, subjects in each of the experiments judged the items to be of equal difficulty level throughout the series.

The explanation of *discounting* proposed by Anderson and Jacobson [1965] is distinct from that of attention decrement, and would suggest that in some ways subjects view later performance successes as unreliable or invalid indicators of ability. Such an explanation is perhaps plausible when subjects are trying to integrate discrepant traits ascribed by different acquaintances of the target person—it is easy to assume that some acquaintances knew the person better or were more discerning judges. It is more difficult to see how the discounting hypothesis might apply in performance evaluation when there is no evidence for motivation decrement or variations in problem difficulty.

The explanation for primacy that seems most convincing to us is one that stresses the phenomenal status of ability as a stable disposition and the information assuring that the items were of equal difficulty. The equal difficulty instructions should imply to the subjects that initial performance would be a valid indicator of performance to come—unless there was some change in the performer's motivation or ability. No change in motivation was perceived and ability is assumed to be a stable personal attribute. We posit, for these reasons, an initial expectancy that successes will be equally distributed over the thirty trials. Such an expectancy should bias the recall of performance in the direction of a more equal spread of successes. A final assumption of assimilation to the initially observed proportion of successes would be sufficient to account for the observed primacy effect. In short, the subjects expect the early trials to tell them what the later ones will be like and, in spite of their attention to the evidence of these later trials, there is some assimilation in memory to bring this evidence more in line with the projected forecast.

The best evidence for this interpretation is in the recall data. After predicting trial-by-trial success over the second series of thirty items (viewed as a behavioral measure of attributed ability), subjects were asked to recall how many of the *first* thirty items the stimulus person had correctly solved. This measure showed consistent distortion of recall in favor of a greater number of successes for the descending stimulus person. In one experiment—which, incidentally, asked for successive probability judgments during the first series—the average subject recalled that the descending performer was correct on 20.6 of the 30

initial trials whereas the ascending performer was recalled as solving 12.5. In both cases, of course, the true number was 15. The magnitude of distortion is rather remarkable, and such distortion provides a sufficient explanation for the primacy effect in ability attribution. It is possible that an attributional decision about ability leads to subsequent distortion of recall, but it seems much more likely that recall distortion leads to differential attribution. It might be noted, along these lines, that the recall data make even less plausible the interpretation of perceived motivational decline in the descending case. If the descending stimulus person were seen to fail on the later items because he was not trying, there would be no reason to see him as solving many more items than he in fact did.

Our favored explanation, then, is that of short-term memory assimilation to the expected proportion of successes and failures. This expectancy is jointly a function of the phenomenal stability of intelligence, an equal distribution assumption, and forecast data from the early trials. The evidence rules out a number of alternative interpretations and is consistent with the one we are offering; nevertheless, the evidence hardly makes an airtight case.

The memory assimilation interpretation does not rest on any quality peculiar to the attribute of intelligence aside from its relative stability. We hope we can make experimental predictions on the basis of variations in such general attributes as entity stability and do not have to construct new functional relations for each new entity being studied. The present interpretation should, then, apply in any judgmental setting where the subject is led to expect an equal distribution of the manifestations of a stable entity. Our next step was to conduct a follow-up experiment that imported these features into a setting of impersonal judgment.

Jones, Goethals, Kennington, and Severance tried to design the experiment as a close analogue of the ability study. It was introduced to the subjects as a study in information processing, "to see how well people can predict subsequent events on the basis of earlier information." The subjects' specific task was to turn over thirty cards, one at a time, after predicting in each case whether the card would be an ace or a non-ace. To set the stage for this task, subjects were shown an array of thirty-card decks and told that the decks had been doctored so as to contain anywhere frem three to twenty-seven aces. The subject was asked to choose one of these decks at random and to shuffle the deck several times, being careful not to look at the card values while doing so. After the deck was shuffled, a previously prepared deck was surreptitiously substituted just before the prediction task was to begin. This contained fifteen aces in the same ascending or descending order as successes in the ability studies.

After the subject went through this prearranged deck attempting to predict ace versus non-ace before each turnover, he was given an interpolated task consistent with the experimental rationale of forecasting events in a series. The specific task was to predict whether the next checker taken from a large cannister would be red or black. After this interpolated task, the subject was asked to recall how many aces there had been in the deck of cards he had exposed and to indicate the distribution of these aces across thirty trials.

The result was a primacy effect: more aces were recalled in the descending than in the ascending condition. Furthermore, it was clear from the distributional memory data that subjects tended to exaggerate the number of late-appearing aces in the descending condition and to underestimate the number of late aces in the ascending condition. The estimates over the first ten trials were quite accurate. In short, there was fairly clear evidence of assimilation of late-appearing to early information.

Is this really an apt analogy to the ability situation? In arguing the affirmative, we would point out two crucial features of the setting and procedure. First of all, the attribute of "aceyness" is indeed stable in the sense that we intend to use that term. The number of aces in the chosen deck is fixed—like the ability of the performer in the earlier studies—and there is no apparent way that the number could change in the course of the experiment. Second, the shuffling procedure is similar to the equal-difficulty instructions of the ability studies in assuring the subjects that, except for random fluctuations, the distribution of aces should be equal. The actual distribution, of course, departed considerably from randomness, but as long as the subject retained the equal distribution expectancy he should have recalled the series as less lopsided than it actually was, adjusting primarily the later trial data to the earlier established expectancy about the probable proportion of aces in the deck.

A next step would be to manipulate directly the stability of the entity, to see if increasing instability leads to decreasing primacy. Alternatively, one might manipulate the expectancy of an equal-distribution of positive manifestations of the entity. The benevolence–malevolence experiment was one effort in this direction, but for several acknowledged reasons that

study does not make clearly the point we seek to establish. Another alternative would be to stay within the framework of ace prediction while attempting to manipulate expectations concerning the stability of aceyness and the distribution of aces. Specifically, a deck could be created so that it would be difficult to predict "aceyness" from an initial sample of turned-up cards. This was attempted in an experiment also reported in Jones, Goethals, Kennington, and Severance. The procedure in the crucial condition involved having the subject choose a red-backed deck and a blue-backed deck from large arrays of both. Each deck contained twenty cards and (allegedly) anywhere from zero to twenty aces. After the subject shuffled each deck carefully several times, the decks were rather casually combined into one by the experimenter and handed back to the subject with instructions to predict whether the next card would be an ace or a non-ace. Again, the experimenter substituted a prepared deck containing either an ascending or descending series of aces. The backs of the cards showed, furthermore, that the two subdecks were unevenly distributed throughout the pack and the subject could see that more red (or blue) cards appeared early in the series. The cards were arranged in such a way, then, that there was a correlation between color of back and "aceyness."

This changing or unstable entity condition was compared to two control conditions, each featuring stacked decks with the same patterns of ascending and descending aces. In the first, the subjects chose one from among several large (forty-card) single-color decks, each allegedly containing anywhere from zero to forty aces. In the second, decks of two colors were again combined but there was no correlation between card color and probability of being an ace. Unlike the changing entity deck, therefore, the red and blue backs were evenly distributed over the entire series. In all conditions subjects engaged in the same task of turning over each card in turn and predicting the probability that the next one would be an ace.

The results of this final card-monitoring study showed that significant primacy in recalling the total number of aces occurred in both control conditions. As predicted, there was no primacy in the crucial condition in which card color provided a clue to the changing frequency of aces. Such clues make salient the fact that there is no reason to expect the later cards exposed to replicate the early cards in terms of the predominance of aces. If the entity is unstable or changing, in other words, strong expectancies should not form on the basis of early instances, and without such expectancies primacy by the assimilation route would not be expected.

A major difference between our assimilation to expectancy proposal and the hypotheses of discounting or attention decrement is that the focus is on memory rather than initial information input. Evidence from both the ability and the card studies shows that subjects' memories are distorted in the direction of primacy even after they have made successive probability judgments that show sensitivity to the cumulative impact of preceding trials. What happens, we propose, is that the data across trials are equally attended to, but in the five- to ten-minute delay between exposure to the final item and questions about "how many aces?" the subject has made subtle adjustments to bring data in line with expectancy. (Perhaps it is appropriate to recall here that Miller and Campbell [1959] would predict the increase of primacy with an increasing delay between the event and its measurement—at least up to some point.) The extent to which assimilation and thus primacy will occur depends jointly on the stability of the entity and on cues suggesting how entity manifestations will be distributed. Finally, once these assimilative memory distortions have occurred, a variety of other attributional consequences can follow. The fact that the drift of memory toward expectancy is the culprit does not make the phenomena of primacy trivial or uninteresting since the attributional consequences that follow may be significant indeed. It often makes a great difference whether we judge someone to be intelligent or even, especially when the stakes are high, whether we feel we are dealing with a truly acey deck.

There are a few additional studies of the effects of order on the interpretation of unfolding behavior, but most of these are studies in which one person comments on his increasing or decreasing attraction for another. These studies will be briefly discussed because they bring up an important consideration that we have thus far ignored, the extent to which the information contained in later behavior replaces or subsumes the information contained in earlier behavior.

The Replacement Information Case

Aronson and Linder [1965] designed an experiment in which subjects were exposed to different patterns of sequential feedback reflecting the attitudes of a target person toward them. The procedures involved an elaborate but plausible scenario wherein one female subject overheard another female subject, actually an experimental accomplice, making remarks about her to the experimenter. The subject heard these remarks from an adjacent room while she was busy at the task of recording the number of plural nouns in the accomplice's remarks. This activity fit the cover story presenting the experiment as one involving an attempt to increase the use of plural nouns through reinforcement from the experimenter. Between each of seven sets of remarks, the subject entered the accomplice's room and engaged her in conversation for three minutes. The subject believed she was doing this to see whether the increased use of plural nouns would generalize to someone other than the reinforcer. Actually, this periodic contact was a crucial feature of the experiment because it gave the accomplice a pretext for changing her mind and presumably endowed the evaluative remarks with greater personal significance for the subject.

There were four experimental conditions in the main study. As subjects listened to the accomplice's remarks about them, they learned that she (a) thought highly of them throughout the experiment (steady positive treatment), (b) started out negatively disposed but became increasingly favorable (gain treatment), (c) thought highly of them initially but became increasingly cool (loss treatment), or (d) remained unfavorable throughout (steady negative treatment). At the end of the seven conversational and monitoring episodes, the subject was led to the office of a final interviewer, who asked several questions to assess the subject's evaluation and final impression of the accomplice.

The results of the major assessment question showed that the subject liked best the accomplice in the gain treatment, next most the accomplice who gave steady positive feedback, next the steady negative accomplice, and least the accomplice in the loss treatment. The accomplice in the gain treatment was liked significantly better than the accomplice in the steady positive treatment. The steady negative and the loss conditions were not significantly different. Aronson [1969] interprets these results in the framework of "gain-loss theory," and suggests that the subject's attraction for the accomplice is a function of the latter's responsibility for *changes* in the subject's self-esteem. He proposes that the accomplice in the gain treatment may be better liked because she first upsets the subject, raising her uncertainty level, and then reduces uncertainty. Some alternatives to this anxiety reduction hypothesis are (a) that the gain accomplice establishes greater credibility through her discrimination, (b) that the subject feels rewarded for her strivings to secure a more favorable impression after a bad start (an efficacy reward explanation), and (*c*) that the final feedback values are seen in contrast to the expectancies established by the initial values (a contrast effect explanation).

A study by Landy and Aronson [1968] at least reduces the likelihood that a discrimination hypothesis is sufficient to account for the Aronson and Linder results. They found that a discriminator was liked better than a nondiscriminator and a positive evaluator was liked better than a negative evaluator. There was no interaction effect, as the discrimination hypothesis would require. A recent study by Mettee [1971b], however, suggests that Landy and Aronson may have manipulated judgmental variability under the guise of "discrimination" without affecting perceived credibility, supposedly a main component of the term's meaning. Cognitive contrast may contribute in a small way to the effects observed, but it seems insufficient in view of the explicit nature of the evaluative remarks and the fact that such remarks should be fairly clearly anchored within the range of feedback received and observed in everyday life. The efficacy interpretation could be evaluated by a replication in which the subject's own remarks were prerecorded and played episodically to the stimulus person. Thus the subject could not vary his behavior in response to early negative feedback. Regardless of the specific hypothesis preferred, and several processes may be operating in various combinations in the situation, the fact remains that the Aronson and Linder results give a recency effect in both change conditions. This is especially clear when we note that the gain and loss conditions were maximally discrepant on the dependent variable liking measure.

Mettee [1971a] conducted a follow-up experiment to investigate the effects of varying the *importance* of the internally changing evaluations received by a subject. In the general setting of an experiment on the effects of knowledge of results upon group decision-making processes, subjects were exposed to two successive evaluations of their responses to the legendary Johnny Rocco case. Half of the subjects were asked first to comment on a very specific aspect of the case and then received highly favorable or unfavorable written comments from the leader. The remaining subjects were asked to comment more generally on the decision that should be made and to base their decision on a general philosophy regarding love and punishment as disciplinary methods. These subjects also received either favorable or unfavorable evaluations of their responses. Following this initial feedback stage, each half of the sample was then given the instructions the others had received initially and

these always received feedback opposite to that initially given. Mettee's intent was to expose each subject to a combination of positive and negative feedback, and to endow one feedback message with more significance than the other because it was based on a more important sample of behavior and concerned with more general and more personal issues. After exposure to one of four information combinations (defined by the fourfold table of major-minor, gain-loss feedback), all subjects were asked to rate the leader in terms of their liking for him as a person.

Table 1. Final Liking Ratings of the Evaluator.

Group	Mean	SD
Small Loss ++/−	3.29	1.16
Large Gain −/++	2.20	1.45
Large Loss +/−−	1.10	1.55
Small Gain −−/+	.62	1.38

Source: D. R. Mettee, 1971a.

Unlike the Aronson and Linder study, Mettee asked his subjects to rate the target person after each feedback message received. It is not clear, therefore, whether the final ratings on the two experiments can be meaningfully compared because of the commitment possibilities inherent in making the intervening rating. However, as the table above shows, the results are very different indeed from those obtained by the Aronson and Linder procedure. Some aspects of these results are trivial and do little more than validate the manipulations of feedback importance and order. What is interesting is the evidence for a primacy effect. The appropriate comparisons are those conditions in which exactly the same information is conveyed, but in opposite sequences. Thus the experimenter in the "small loss" condition is better liked than the "large gain" experimenter.

Why should these results be essentially the opposite of the Aronson and Linder results? Rather than focus on the differential importance of the information units per se, Mettee suggests that his feedback units were essentially independent of each other and contributed to an additive resolution of the evaluational conflict. The positive evaluation had to be looked at *in conjunction with* the negative evaluation, and vice versa, in order for the subject to determine the experimenter's overall opinion of him. In contrast, the gain and loss sequence of the Aronson and Linder experiment involved successive information units that *replaced* the preceding units. To an important extent, the accomplice's expression of liking for the subject after seven conversational episodes subsumed his report of liking after six, five, four, and so on episodes. Rather than seeing these as an added bit of information that needed to be integrated by the subject, he was dealing with the latest word in a pattern of cumulative readings of the accomplice's attitude toward him.

In a more recent experiment Mettee and Taylor attempted to compare reactions to replacement information with reactions to independent information. The procedure involved two-part interviews with female subjects; the interviews were punctuated by prerecorded evaluative remarks allegedly delivered by a male experienced in evaluating female "datability." In the replacement conditions the second half of the interview dealt with expansions of topics covered during the first half. In the independent conditions the second half of the interview covered entirely new topics. Gain, loss, steady positive, and steady negative feedback patterns were presented in both replacement and independent contexts. The main measure of the subject's final liking for his evaluator showed primacy in the independent information conditions and recency (replicating Aronson and Linder's results) in the replacement conditions.

Unfortunately, the Mettee and Taylor experiment is not conclusive because, in the interests of plausibility, the second-half feedback remarks were noticeably different in content (and possibly in affective intensity) in the two contexts. Nevertheless, the results certainly encourage belief in the hypothesis, and the hypothesis is itself very plausible. It is not difficult to see, for example, that the adjective lists used by Anderson and others are typically combinations of independent information units. This is implied, at least, by the instructions stating that the adjectives each come from a different person who is well-acquainted with the person being judged. If the ability attribution studies had dealt with a skill that was susceptible to rapid improvement with practice, this would have certainly implied a replacement unit judgmental set—the one who was doing well at the end should be judged as the most capable, or at least should be expected to continue to do well on the next series of trials. Certain equivocal results in the order effect literature may reflect the fact that a mixture of independent and replacement unit cues have been combined in the same experiment. Perhaps this was one of the difficulties with the benevolence-malevolence experiment. Some subjects treated the sequential information as independent and additive, whereas others saw the later information as growing out of and replacing the earlier impression. The replacement unit concept is important to bear in mind in any ongoing interpersonal situation to the extent that any comment or reaction builds on or subsumes previous behavior.

Underlying Processes: A Speculative Résumé

It is not an easy task to summarize the foregoing remarks, much less embed them in a coherent account of the principles involved in order effects. At least the reader has been forewarned that primacy, recency, and the absence of either can come about as the resultant product of a variety of processes. Hopefully, we have teased out some of these processes by commenting on the antecedent conditions that appear to produce order effects and by attempting to juxtapose experimental traditions that have heretofore only touched each other gently in passing. About all we can do now is identify the major processes that seem to be involved in determining primacy or recency and make a few common sense remarks about each. Perhaps this hurried Cook's Tour will serve as an interim substitute for the more extensive journey that awaits additional comparative research.

Toward Primacy

The three major processes involved in primacy effects are *attention decrement, discounting,* and *assimilation.* Attention decrement may result from distraction or from the increase of fatigue in processing sequential information, or it may be a more active process protecting against the disturbing implications of incongruity. The subject, in other words, may actively block out or ignore incompatible information.

More commonly, one would imagine, selective attention favoring early events probably occurs to the extent that there is cognitive overload—too much to remember. If the subject has to make a decision about holding on to one impression at the expense of another, it is not surprising that the initial impression has an advantage in the competition. This may be especially true when the subject is bored and has no particular incentive to do the best job he can with the complex information presented to him.

Presumably, the impetus for discounting depends unequivocally on the extent to which the information really is incompatible. At least this is Anderson's suggestion, and it has been exploited experimentally by Hendrick and Costantini [1970]. Our assumption has been that while incongruity may provide the impetus for discounting, its likelihood of occurrence should be enhanced by any factors in the context that permit judgments of differential reliability or validity. Anderson's instructions—that not all traits are equally valid—facilitated discounting. One could imagine other cues that operate in a first-impression setting, causing the receiver to attribute early actions to the person and later, incompatible ones to the situation. This presumably is a common attributional tendency and it clearly may operate to preserve an initial impression of ability, attitude, or personality.

Primacy effects that result from attention decrement are not of theoretical interest, if all they show is that subjects become inattentive during an experimental series. Discounting maneuvers may also be theoretically trivial if the judging context is such that subjects can easily explain away recent information as unreliable. Assimilation is a more mysterious and pervasive phenomenon. We have tried to relate assimilation in the order effects domain to the general notion of cognitive assimilation. This general notion, going back to Bartlett and beyond, assumes that information creates or finds its way into pre-existing categories. These categories are like hypotheses about the nature of reality being confronted. Once a categorical decision is made, subsequent evidence is distorted to fit the category or to confirm the hypothesis—as long as it is not too discrepant from the category's typical instance. Unlike discounting or attention decrement interpretations, assimilation implies that the value, intensity, or frequency of later units are shaped by the categories (expectancies) established by early information. Primacy is more than a function of assigning lower weights to more recent events.

Any factor that contributes to the speed with which a category can be formed and to the degree of confidence with which it is held should increase the tendency toward assimilation. As we have seen, this includes a variety of procedures designed to increase the subject's commitment to his initial judgment. Commitment puts the subject in a postdecisional phase in which consistency is of greater importance than accuracy [Festinger 1964, Jones & Gerard 1967].

Cognitive categories are more readily formed when the entity being judged is stable and its manifestations are assumed to be equally distributed over time. Unstable entities with capricious, cyclical, or aperiodic manifestations should contribute to the suspension of conclusive attributional judgments and the avoidance of the kind of premature closure on which assimilation apparently depends. Such consid-erations have intriguing implications for the question of which kinds of personal attributes are most likely to be prematurely judged in a developing relationship and what are the consequences of such selective distortion for interpersonal harmony and disharmony.

As indicated above, assimilation probably depends in a critical way on the discrepancy between items of unfolding information. All who make some attempt to deal with the concept of assimilation recognize that there is some point of information discrepancy beyond which assimilation cannot take place. Considerably more research is needed to determine the effects of discrepancy size and even to develop measures of discrepancy when dealing with semantic interactions among traits. One might propose, for example, a curvilinear hypothesis relating discrepancy magnitude to primacy. If later manifestations are only slightly different from earlier manifestations in their entity implications, they should be readily assimilated in value. The later manifestations should, in effect, be seen as more like the earlier manifestations than in fact is the case, giving rise to a primacy effect. With slightly greater discrepancies, however, we might expect contrast to occur. Later items should exert a disproportionate influence on the category (entity, expectancy?) being formed and should bring about recency. But beyond some point of moderate discrepancy, the processes of incredulity, denial, and discounting should give rise to primacy again.

Toward Recency

Three major kinds of processes seem to favor recency. First there are those processes that appear to be a simple and direct reflection of *recall readiness*. There is abundant evidence that immediate past events are better remembered than more remote events. The extent to which this is true depends on how remote the early events are that we want to use for comparison and how close the recent events are to the point at which the impression is being measured. One would expect natural sequences of events occurring over long periods of time to lend themselves more to recency than to primacy.

When short, circumscribed time spans are involved, the more relevant process may be that of judgmental *contrast*. Early information creates anchoring expectancies in terms of which later experiences are judged. The extent of contrast can vary with the pattern and range of information presented, the nature of the judgmental language being used, the amount of practice with other sequences in the same domain, and so on. The typical setting for attaining contrast effects is one in which the subject is required to make independent judgments of items in terms of an attribute scale. Contrast arises under circumstances where those items are presented in a systematically biased rather than a random or counter balanced order. To the extent that the later-appearing items are contrasted with the earlier, anchoring, items, one might expect a resultant impression of the series to show recency. This requires that the judgment of the earlier anchors does not change in retrospect before the summarizing, impressional judgment is made—that the contrast is irreversible.

A number of *content-* and *context-related hypotheses* are also potential preconditions for recency. If the entity is known to be capable of progressive changes or development, its later manifestations are obviously more significant than earlier manifestations for interactions with the entity. Maturation, growth, learning and practice effects, profiting from experience in general—each of these factors can contribute to a tendency to attribute greater significance to more recent entity manifestations. Alternatively, the content and context of judgment may trigger off hypotheses that discredit early information for different reasons. If there are warm-up effects, if the individual is shy and unrevealing at first, early manifestations should be relatively ignored. Finally, the ordered content may be presented in a form that suggests that early information is being superseded by later information. We have noted this when information about liking is involved, but there may be other instances in which later behavioral data explain or subsume earlier evidence.

Swing Factors

When one considers the role of content and context, as this essay is recommending, the problem of order effects becomes more relevant to interpersonal behavior and much more complicated to analyze. Within the confines of an experimental design, information value can be manipulated with a fair amount of precision. For example, some attempt can be made to equalize the importance and level of information while systematically varying favorability. In the natural information environment, however, the person is exposed to considerably more chaotic data patterns that vary simultaneously on a number of different dimensions. If we listen to one person inform us about another, he is likely to range from behavior description through evaluation to inferences about motives and back again to description. Mixtures of positive and negative information can also take infinite forms and assume a great variety of intensity values.

There is certainly no question that some items of information assume priority over others or, to use Asch's term, some traits have a dominant centrality in the formation of an impression. Primacy or recency can obviously be affected by the position at which such central determinants fall. There are many reasons—plus some data [Ritchie, McClelland, & Shimkunas 1967]—supporting the likelihood that unfavorable information is given greater weight than favorable information when units of different value are being combined. The centrality of an item, furthermore, may interact with its position in a sequence.

The possibilities for running into trouble when attempting to predict the effects of order in a complex natural setting are thus real ones. Our present effort has been less concerned with developing prescriptions for prediction than with using the order effect paradigm to suggest some of the processes underlying impression formation. There is much more to be understood, but our review points up enough consistencies across different traditions of research to suggest that some progress has been made and more is in the offing. At the very least, it is a kind of progress to realize that things are not as simple as they seem and to identify some of the reasons why.

BIBLIOGRAPHY

Norman H. Anderson, "Application of an Additive Model to Impression Formation." *Science*. 1962, 138:817–818.

Norman H. Anderson, "Primacy Effects in Personality Impression Formation Using a Generalized Order Effect Paradigm." *Journal of Personality and Social Psychology*, 1965, 2:1–9.

Norman H. Anderson, "Component Ratings in Impression Formation." *Psychonomic Science*, 1966, 6:279–280.

Norman H. Anderson, "Application of a Linear-Serial Model to a Personality-Impression Task Using Serial Presentation." *Journal of Personality and Social Psychology*, 1968, 10:354–362.

Norman H. Anderson and Alfred A. Barrios, "Primacy Effects in Personality Impression Formation." *Journal of Abnormal and Social Psychology*, 1961, 63:346–350.

Norman H. Anderson and Stephen Hubert, "Effects of Concomitant Verbal Recall on Order Effects in Personality Impression Formation." *Journal of Verbal Learning and Verbal Behavior*, 1963, 2:379–391.

Norman H. Anderson and Ann Jacobson, "Effect of Stimulus Inconsistency and Discounting Instructions in Personality Impression Formation." *Journal of Personality and Social Psychology*, 1965, 2:531–539.

Norman H. Anderson and Anita K. Lampel, "Effect of Context on Ratings of Personality Traits." *Psychonomic Science*, 1965, 3:433–434.

Norman H. Anderson and Ann Norman, "Order Effects in Impression Formation in Four Classes of Stimuli." *Journal of Abnormal and Social Psychology*, 1964, 69:467–471.

Elliot Aronson, "Some Antecedents of Interpersonal Attraction." In William J. Arnold and David Levine, eds., *Nebraska Symposium on Motivation*. University of Nebraska Press, 1969.

Elliot Aronson and Darwyn Linder, "Gain and Loss of Esteem as Determinants of Interpersonal Attractiveness." *Journal of Experimental Social Psychology*, 1965, 1:156–172.

Solomon E. Asch, "Forming Impressions of Personality." *Journal of Abnormal and Social Psychology*, 1946, 41:258–290.

Leonard Berkowitz, "The Judgmental Process in Personality Functioning." *Psychological Review*, 1960, 67:130–142.

James Bieri, Ben A. Orcutt, and Robin Leaman, "Anchoring Effects in Sequential Clinical Judgments." *Journal of Abnormal and Social Psychology*, 1963, 67:616–623.

Jerome S. Bruner, "On Perceptual Readiness." *Psychological Review*, 1957, 64:123–152.

Jerome S. Bruner, David Shapiro, and Renato Tagiuri, "The Meaning of Traits in Isolation and in Combination." In Renato Tagiuri and Luigi Petrullo, eds., *Person Perception and Interpersonal Behavior*. Stanford University Press, 1958.

Donald T. Campbell, N. A. Lewis, and William A. Hunt, "Context Effects with Judgmental Language that is Absolute, Extensive, and Extra-Experimentally Anchored." *Journal of Experimental Psychology*, 1958, 55:220–228.

Leon Festinger, *A Theory of Cognitive Dissonance*. Row Peterson, 1967.

Harry Helson, "Adaptation Level as a Frame of Reference for Prediction of Psychophysical Data." *American Journal of Psychology*, 1947, 60:1–29.

Clyde Hendrick and Arthur F. Costantini, "Effects of Varying Trait Inconsistency and Response Requirements on the Primacy Effect in Impression Formation." *Journal of Personality and Social Psychology*, 1970, 15:158–164.

Donald M. Johnson, "Generalization of a Scale of Values by the Averaging of Practice Effects." *Journal of Experimental Psychology*, 1944, 34:425–436.

Edward E. Jones and Keith E. Davis, "From Acts to Dispositions: The Attribution Process in Person Perception." In Leonard Berkowitz, ed., *Advances in Experimental Social Psychology*, Vol. 2. Academic Press, 1965.

Edward E. Jones and Harold B. Gerard, *Foundations of Social Psychology*. Wiley, 1967.

Edward E. Jones, George R. Goethals, Gregory E. Kennington, and Laurence J. Severance, "Primacy and Assimilation in the Attribution Process: The Stable Entity Proposition." Unpublished.

Edward E. Jones, Leslie Rock, Kelly G. Shaver, George R. Goethals, and Lawrence M. Ward, "Pattern of Performance and Ability Attribution: An Unexpected Primacy Effect." *Journal of Personality and Social Psychology*, 1968, 10:317–340.

David Landy and Elliot Aronson, "Liking for an Evaluator as a Function of his Discernment." *Journal of Personality and Social Psychology*, 1968, 9:133–141.

Abraham S. Luchins, "Primacy-Recency in Impression Formation." In Carl I. Hovland, ed., *The Order of Presentation and Persuasion*. Yale University Press, 1957.

David R. Mettee, "Changes in Liking as a Function of the Magnitude and Affect of Sequential Evaluations." *Journal of Experimental Social Psychology*, 1971, 7:157–172. (a)

David R. Mettee, "The True Discerner as a Potent Source of Positive Affect." *Journal of Experimental Social Psychology*, 1971, in press. (b)

David R. Mettee and Shelley E. Taylor, "Affect Conversion versus Affect Change as Determinants of the Gain-Loss Liking Effect." Unpublished.

Norman Miller and Donald T. Campbell, "Recency and Primacy in Persuasion as a Function of the Timing of Speeches and Measurements." *Journal of Abnormal and Social Psychology*, 1959, 59:1–9.

Cameron R. Peterson and W. M. DuCharme, "A Primacy Effect in Subjective Probability Revision." *Journal of Experimental Psychology*, 1967, 73:61–65.

Marjorie H. Richey, Lucille McClelland, and Algimantas M. Shimkunas, "Relative Influence of Positive and

Negative Information in Impression Formation and Persistence." *Journal of Personality and Social Psychology,* 1967, 6:322–327.

Carolyn W. Sherif, Muzafer Sherif, and Melda S. Nebergall, *Attitude and Attitude Change.* Saunders, 1965.

Muzafer Sherif and Carl I. Hovland, *Social Judgment: Assimilation and Contrast Effects in Communication and Attitude Change.* Yale University Press, 1961.

Ralph H. Stewart, "Effect of Continuous Responding on the Order Effect in Personality Impression Formation." *Journal of Personality and Social Psychology,* 1965, 1:161–165.

John Thibaut and Michael Ross, "Commitment and Experience as Determinants of Assimilation and Contrast." *Journal of Personality and Social Psychology,* 1969, 13:322–329.

John Volkmann, "Scales of Judgment and Their Implications for Social Psychology." In J. H. Rohrer and Muzafer Sherif, eds., *Social Psychology at the Crossroads.* Harper, 1951.

[*Preparation of this paper grew out of a workshop on attribution theory held at UCLA in August 1969 supported by Grant GS-2613 from the National Science Foundation. Some of the research described herein was supported by NSF Grant 8857 to Edward E. Jones.*]

3 · Negativity in Evaluations

DAVID E. KANOUSE
University of California, Los Angeles

L. REID HANSON, JR.
University of California, Los Angeles

Attribution theory is usually described as the process by which people form causal interpretations of the events around them. The theory applies more generally, however, to the process whereby people attribute characteristics, intentions, feelings, and traits to the objects in their social world. The attribution process seems to serve the individual's need to make sense of the world around him. While he frequently makes use of causal inferences in so doing, he also uses descriptive constructs. To form a meaningful picture of the world, he must answer questions not only about the "whyness" of things, but about their "whatness" as well. Interestingly enough, most constructs fit equally well into a descriptive or causal context. The traits we use on some occasions to describe people serve on other occasions as causal explanations for their behavior. The process of attributing constructs such as traits serves a dual function: it aids us in building models of the essential nature of the entities around us and in explaining the causal nature of events and actions involving those entities.

This discussion is concerned with how the individual assesses information about the diverse aspects of an object in order to form an overall evaluation of it. In other words, we are concerned with the attribution of *value*, a construct underlying many traits and characteristics used in both a descriptive and a causal context.

We shall examine the proposition that people are generally cost oriented in forming overall evaluations—they weigh negative aspects of an object more heavily than positive ones. We first consider several areas of the research literature that bear on this issue, and then we discuss a number of relevant theoretical perspectives.

Negativity Biases in Impression Formation

The study of impression formation has generated the most extensive social-psychological evidence about how people combine diverse information into an overall evaluation. In the standard impression formation paradigm, subjects are presented with a set of trait adjectives describing various attributes of a hypothetical stimulus person (for example, "intelligent, loyal, and quarrelsome"). Their task is to combine this information about isolated traits into an overall evaluation of the stimulus person. The major goal of researchers investigating impression formation has been to find a simple, parsimonious rule that adequately describes the relationship between the overall evaluation of a stimulus person and separate evaluations of his attributes. Two prominent candidates for such a rule have received extensive attention: an "adding" rule and an "averaging" rule. Models of impression formation based on an adding rule propose that the individual, in effect, "adds up" the values of the separate traits possessed by a stimulus person and reaches something approximating the *sum* of these trait values in his overall evaluation. Models based on an averaging rule propose that the individual, again in effect, averages the separate trait values in making his overall evaluation. Luckily, the empirical battles fought over this issue provide detailed evidence about the differential impact of positive and negative traits on the overall evaluation of a stimulus person.

In one of the earlier averaging-versus-adding papers, Anderson had subjects rate how much they personally would like a person characterized by a set of personality-trait adjectives. The particular adjectives used were chosen from among 555 personality-trait adjectives that "had been previously rated from 0 to 6" [1965, p. 395]. Using these ratings, Anderson made up lists of four kinds of adjectives, fortunately chosen so that the positive and negative adjectives were equidistant from the neutral point of the scale: highly positive adjectives (designated H), moderately positive (M+), moderately negative (M−), and highly negative (L). Anderson then constructed sets of adjectives from each of these four scale ranges. Combinations of two adjectives were of the form HH, M+M+, M−M−, and LL. Similarly, combinations of four adjectives from each scale range yielded the sets HHHH, M+M+M+M+, M−M−M−M−, and LLLL. Finally, there were two "mixed" combinations of the form HHM+M+ and LLM−M−, in which highly polarized adjectives were combined with less polarized adjectives of the same sign.

The subjects were told to read the adjectives slowly to themselves and then "to use 50 to rate a person they would neither like nor dislike, to use lower numbers for persons they would dislike, and to use higher numbers for persons they would like. Except for centering the scale at 50, subjects were told they could use any numbers they wished" [p. 396].

The mean ratings for each of the ten set types are shown in table 1. Assuming that 50 is indeed the neutral point, the mean ratings of the negative sets, with the one exception of the M+++++ and M−−−− comparison, are further from the neutral point than the mean ratings of the corresponding positive sets. Negative adjectives thus seem more powerful than positive adjectives in affecting the overall evaluation.

Table 1. Mean Response to Each Type of Set.

Set Type	Mean Response
HH	72.85
M+M+	57.56
M−M−	42.18
LL	23.70
HHHH	79.39
M+M+M+M+	63.20
M−M−M−M−	39.50
LLLL	17.64
HHM+M+	71.11
LLM−M−	25.67

SOURCE: Anderson [1965].

This finding of course is not very convincing in itself. No statistical comparisons are reported that allow us to determine the reliability of the differential positive-negative impact; nor can we be certain that the real neutral point was not less than 50. There is, however, one other pertinent aspect of the results for which Anderson does provide statistical comparisons. For the two "mixed" sets of adjectives, HHM+M+ and LLM−M−, Anderson notes that both the averaging and the adding models predict that the mean evaluations should lie midway between the evaluations of the corresponding homogeneous sets. That is, HHM+M+ should be evaluated roughly midway between the sets HHHH and M+M+M+M+, and the evaluation of LLM−M− should fall midway between LLLL and M−M−M−M−. For positive adjectives this seems to be the case. The mean evaluation of 71.11 for the HHM+M+ set is only .19 scale points from the average of the HHHH and M+M+M+M+ sets.

However, the mixed negative set, LLM−M−, lies 2.90 scale points *below* its expected value ($F = 8.53$, $d.f. = 1,44$, $p < .01$). Thus, highly polarized negative adjectives appear to lower the overall evaluation more than would be predicted on the basis of either the adding or the averaging model. At the same time there is no indication that highly polarized positive adjectives exert a similar disproportionate influence. With respect to the adding-versus-averaging controversy, Anderson notes, "This significant discrepancy naturally raises some doubt that either formulation can give an exact, quantitative account of the data" [1965, pp. 398–399].

A similar phenomenon emerges in a study by Feldman [1966] on the modifying capacities of different adjectives. Feldman had subjects rate each of 25 adjectives in the standard context—"he is an [*adjective*] man"—on a 9-point *bad-good* scale. Each subject also rated 175 of the 625 possible two-adjective combinations in the same standard context. By comparing the ratings given when the adjectives were used alone with ratings given to pairs of adjectives, Feldman was able to obtain estimates of the "modifying capacities" (defined as the extent to which each adjective pulls toward itself the evaluation of pairs in which it appears) of each adjective. It is immediately apparent in table 2 that the most "powerful" adjectives are negative.

The correlation between evaluation and modifying capacity is −.69. Thus it again appears that the weight given to negative adjectives exceeds the weight given to positive adjectives when several adjectives must be combined into one overall evaluation.

A similar study is reported by Rokeach [1968]. In this study subjects responded to assertions linking two concepts they had evaluated separately. For example, they were asked to rate the concepts "athlete," "dishonest," and "a dishonest athlete." Altogether there were nine combinations in which a positive concept was linked with a negative concept. For eight of these nine combinations, the overall evaluation was substantially more negative than would be predicted by a simple averaging of the scale values of the two separate concepts.

A study by Birnbaum [1972] provides evidence for negativity in a different realm. Birnbaum asked subjects to provide moral evaluations of pairs of behavior items, such as "pocketing the tip the previous customer left for the waitress *and* poisoning your neighbor's dog whose barking bothers you." The separate behaviors had previously been judged on a morality dimension [Parducci 1968], thus allowing us

Table 2. *Evaluations and Modifying Capacities of Positive and Negative Adjectives.*

	Evaluation (9-point good-bad scale)	Modifying Capacity
Adjectives Positive		
Holy	7.34	.206
Sincere	7.58	.192
Wise	7.49	.261
Lovable	7.46	.474
Decent	7.34	.266
Nice	6.98	.486
Scholarly	6.80	.366
Clean	6.70	.230
Refined	6.66	.187
Moderate	6.44	.257
Interesting	6.39	.249
Normal	5.88	.279
Average	5.45	.396
Tolerable	5.14	.315
Mean		.297
Adjectives Negative		
Ignorant	4.28	.157
Crude	3.48	.420
Dirty	3.23	.186
Depraved	2.48	.439
Heartless	2.42	1.013
Unprincipled	2.37	.817
Immoral	2.16	.722
Unscrupulous	2.11	.906
Corrupt	1.98	.437
Horrid	1.88	.656
Cruel	1.74	.701
Mean		.587

SOURCE: adapted from Feldman [1966].

to determine whether moral evaluations of pairs of immoral deeds are more influenced by a severely immoral act than by a mildly immoral act. The results, shown in figure 1, indicate that the fouler of the two deeds is more important in determining the overall evaluation of the pair. This finding is supported by a significant interaction (F $(16,1584) = 15.08$, $p < .001$), indicating that the impact of the first scale value decreases as the second scale value becomes more negative.

At this point let us consider the major substantive interpretations of the data presented so far. The most obvious of these is straightforward: negative infor-

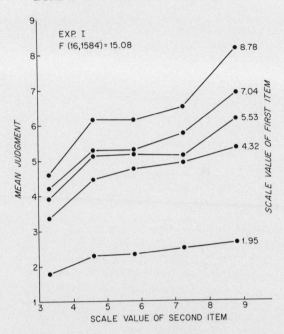

Figure 1. Moral evaluations of pairs of behavior items as a function of separate scale values.

mation carries greater weight than positive. It is also possible, however, to argue that the greater impact of negative adjectives and highly immoral deeds arises not so much from their negativity as from their greater surprisingness [Feldman 1966], infrequency of usage [Zajonc 1968], or infrequency of occurrence [Jones & Davis 1965]. In this view negative information carries greater weight because it typically flies in the face of expectation and therefore carries more information value. This view has some intuitive appeal, since it is hard to deny that positivity and frequency are highly correlated [Zajonc 1968]. Several of these factors, however, may be eliminated in Feldman's 1966 study through the use of partial correlations, and a strong negativity effect remains. Feldman reports that ratings on the bad-to-good scale correlate −.68 with ratings of "surprisingness" and −.24 with the common logarithm of Thorndike and Lorge's [1944] summary index of word frequency. But as Kinder notes [1971], by also considering the correlations with modifying capacity of surprisingness and log frequency (+.54 and −.50 respectively), the effects of surprisingness and log frequency may be partialed out of the evaluation-modifying capacity correlation. When surprisingness is partialed out the correlation between evaluation and modifying capacity is reduced only from −.69 to −.52. When log

frequency is eliminated the correlation is still −.60. Thus surprisingness and frequency of usage do not seem to be very important in determining the greater impact of negative traits in impression formation. Furthermore, a study by Abelson and Kanouse [1966] experimentally controls for factors intrinsic to particular adjectives, yet finds a very large negativity effect.

Negativity Biases in the Attribution of Evaluations to Others

In the relevant portion of their study Abelson and Kanouse presented their subjects with a task bearing many structural similarities to the standard impression formation task. Respondents were presented with a series of evidence sentences describing the actions or feelings of a class of actors toward the attributes of a particular object. On the basis of these statements, respondents were asked to form inferences about the actors' actions or feelings toward the object itself. The following item illustrates the task:

All Fung is a sweet, tuberous, pretty plant.
Candidates like sweet plants.
Candidates do not like tuberous plants.
Candidates like pretty plants.
Do candidates like Fung?

In our example, and indeed in all items of this type in the study, the respondents were asked to judge the orientation of the actors (in this case, candidates) toward an object (Fung) on the basis of information about the actors' orientation toward three attributes of the object. The particular objects, actors, and verbs were systematically varied. The task is similar to the impression formation task in that the respondent must combine information about attributes or traits into a judgment of an overall response toward the object. It differs primarily in two respects: the judgment concerns the response of a hypothetical class of actors, not the respondent's own; and the evaluative information is provided by the verb describing the actors' sentiments or actions, not by the content of the attributes themselves.

Indeed, attribute content and attribute evaluation in this study were independent. Candidates can as easily be said to like tuberous and pretty plants but not sweet ones as to like sweet and pretty plants but not tuberous ones. Because content and evaluation were independent, the positivity or negativity of the attributes was unconfounded with their frequency, surprisingness, or information value.

Thus it is particularly interesting to note that a very strong negativity effect emerged in this study. When the actor had a positive orientation toward two of the three attributes, respondents were willing to infer a positive orientation toward the object itself only 22 per cent of the time (table 3). But when the actors' orientation toward the attributes was predominantly negative, respondents inferred a simi-

lar negative orientation toward the object 67 per cent of the time. In sum, people are much more willing to make a deductive inference on the basis of evidence about *negative* orientations toward a set of attributes than on the basis of *positive* orientations toward a set of attributes, even when the content (and therefore the surprisingness, infrequency, and so on) of the attributes is held constant.

Negativity Biases in Risk Taking

A negativity bias is also found in studies on the evaluation of risks, in which the objects of evaluation are alternative courses of action having positive and negative attributes (rewards and costs). Here Kogan and Wallach have convincingly argued that "the deterrence value of costs for failure exceeds the attraction value of gains from success in affecting risk-taking" [1967, p. 133]. To support their position, Kogan and Wallach focus primarily on "life dilemmas," which are frequently used to study the risky-shift phenomenon, and on a series of studies of ethical risk taking performed by Rettig and his colleagues [Rettig & Rawson 1963, Rettig & Pasamanick 1964, Rettig & Sinha 1966].

The twelve standard life dilemmas require a choice between two alternatives. One of the alternatives is more rewarding if successful, but is more likely to result in failure. Subjects are asked to check the lowest probability of success that they would consider acceptable before they would choose the riskier alternative. A typical dilemma, condensed by Kogan and Wallach, is as follows: "Mr. A, an electrical engineer, has the choice of staying with his present job at a modest though adequate salary or of moving on to another job offering more money but no long-term security." Kogan and Wallach informally analyze these twelve situations in terms of the potential gains and costs involved and conclude that the potential costs are far more potent determinants of response than are potential gains. Thus, in the example of the engineer, Kogan and Wallach argue that subjects are more influenced by the possible costs (for example, the possibility that the new company will collapse) than by the possible gains (for example, a higher salary).

This "clinical judgment" about studies of life dilemmas is supported by Rettig and Rawson. They presented subjects with a paragraph about a stimulus person named Tom, who was faced with a decision about whether or not to steal some money. Each paragraph was constructed to be either high or low

Table 3. Percentage of Agreement with Positive and Negative Assertions When Evidence is Based on Attributes.

Positive Verbs		Negative Verbs	
Help	32%	Hate	85%
Love	31	Avoid	79
Recommend	31	Ignore	76
Use	27	Fear	73
Need	23	Fight	63
Steal	23	Harm	53
Approach	21	Destroy	40
Trust	21		
Be aware of	20		
Have	20		
Produce	17		
Like	13		
Understand	13		
Buy	11		

SOURCE: adapted from Abelson and Kanouse [1966].

on each of the following independent variables: (*a*) reinforcement value of gain; (*b*) expectancy of gain; (*c*) reinforcement value of censure; (*d*) expectancy of censure; (*e*) severity of offense. The task of the subject was to estimate the likelihood that Tom would decide to commit the unethical act. If costs are weighted more than gains, the reinforcement value and expectancy of censure should have more impact upon likelihood estimates than the reinforcement value and expectancy of gain. The analysis of variance table generally supports this expectation. While all of the independent variables above made significant contributions, the reinforcement value of censure accounted for fully 50 per cent of the explained variance. Surprisingly, the *expectancy* of censure (the chance of getting caught) was no more important than the expectancy of gain. This might reflect a tendency to underestimate the probability of an aversive event [Marks 1951, Irwin 1953]. Alternatively, it may represent a failure to differentiate different probabilities of loss. We have no data to support this possibility, but it seems reasonable that any possibility of serious loss leads to general avoidance. The commonness of such questions as "Yes, I know the stock market will probably go up, but what *if* there is another crash?" indicates that low probabilities of loss may be given considerable weight.

Thus Kogan and Wallach's informal judgment about the heavy emphasis placed on possible costs holds when potential gains and costs are varied in a more systematic fashion. There are, however, two major shortcomings in Rettig and Rawson's study. The first is that the subjects' predictions of behavior bear no necessary relationship to actual behavior. This shortcoming is remedied, however, by subsequent studies by Rettig and Pasamanick and Rettig and Sinha of actual unethical behavior, for example, cheating on a motor skill task or violating experimental instructions. Subjects were actually given the opportunity to transgress in situations that were either high or low on each of the following: (*a*) reinforcement value of gain; (*b*) expectancy of gain; (*c*) reinforcement value of censure; (*d*) expectancy of censure; and (*e*) severity of offense. Here the reinforcement value of censure was the major determinant of *actual* unethical behavior.

The second shortcoming, which also applies to life dilemmas, is that the costs involved in these examples may simply be more extreme than the rewards. It would be of little interest to us to find that subjects turned down a bet in which there was an equal chance of winning $10 or losing $1,000. It would not be fair to conclude from this that subjects give

greater *weight* to the value of the negative outcome. Therefore, as long as we are ignorant of the relative value of costs and gains, we are unable to draw strong conclusions about the weight given to costs and gains in risk taking. Unfortunately, it is a delicate matter to determine whether, say, "being expelled" is as bad as "getting out of debt" is good. For this reason we will turn our attention to laboratory studies of monetary gambling. Gambling studies lack the richness of ethical risks or life dilemmas, but because money follows the arithmetic rules of the real number system, it provides a convenient way to measure more precisely the scale values of costs and gains. Some might argue that any greater weighting of monetary costs than gains is also due "merely" to scaling differences; that, in units of utility, $-x¢$ is farther from zero than $+x¢$. But in fact this is an example of what we are trying to show: that, in general, utility curves are steeper for losses than for gains:

That potential costs are more heavily weighted than potential gains has become a truism within the experimental gambling literature. For example, Slovic and Lichtenstein discussing one aspect of their findings, state that their study "reproduces one of the most common findings in studies of risk taking—namely, that potential losses exert more influence on a gamble's attractiveness than potential gains of the same magnitude" [1968 pp. 9–10]. This view is echoed by almost every researcher in the area who mentions differential weighting of costs and gains. The reader can probably join the ranks of believers by considering whether he would be willing to flip a coin for any nontrivial amount of money or, as Kogan and Wallach [1967] suggest, by trying to recruit subjects for a study in which they will gamble with their own funds.

It is surprising then that only a few of the hundreds of experimental gambling studies in the literature present data relevant to the differential impact of costs and gains. Nonetheless, we agree with Slovic and Lichtenstein that potential costs are weighted more than potential gains. We shall therefore first describe a few studies that support this view, then examine some conflicting studies.

First let us consider an experiment performed by Atthowe [1960]. Atthowe offered his college subjects a series of "wagers" that were described as "mathematical reasoning problems taken from an advanced intelligence test." The subjects were asked to choose one of two wagers. Each alternative consisted of two equiprobable potential outcomes, as in the following example:

Wager A	Wager B	
[a] win 35¢	win 5¢	$P = \frac{1}{2}$
[b] lose 25¢	win 5¢	$P = \frac{1}{2}$

Thus, if the subject chose wager A, he would have an equal chance of winning 35¢ and of losing 25¢. In fact, no money changed hands, nor were any of the wagers actually decided.

Atthowe investigated six different types of conflict represented by pairs of wagers, but only the two types shown in table 4 need concern us here. In each of these "conflicts" three of the four outcome values remained constant throughout the experiment. The fourth value, x, was varied until the "point of indifference" was established by the method of constant stimuli. For instance, if x in subtype 3 of table 4 randomly assumed the values 10, 14, 16, 18, 20, and 24, and subjects' choices were A, A, A, B, B, and B, the point of indifference lies midway in the interval bounded by 16 and 18 (that is, 17).

Table 4. Two Types of Conflicts.[a]

	Subtype 3			Subtype 4	
	A	B		A	B
a	win 35¢	win 5¢	a	win 26¢	lose 5¢
b	lose x¢	win 5¢	b	lose x¢	lose 5¢

[a] A and B are alternative choices; a and b represent possible outcomes. The probability of occurrence of any a or b is equal to ½.

SOURCE: Atthowe [1960].

The point of indifference, x_1, allows us to determine the relative weights given to possible costs and gains. Consider subtype 3. If the subjects follow expected value, that is, weight the positive and negative values equally, x_1 should be 25¢ (that is, when x = 25¢, the two choices, A and B, are equal in expected value). If, on the other hand, costs are given more weight than gains, the subject should be more conservative and x_1 should be less than 25¢. Similarly, if gains are weighted more heavily than costs, the subject should be willing to risk more than a loss of 25¢ in order to get a chance at a gain of 35¢; that is, his indifference point should be greater than 25¢. The actual results, shown in table 5, reveal that 17 of Atthowe's 32 subjects were cost oriented, while only 6 were gain oriented. Ignoring the 9 "ties," Z = 2.11, $p < .04$. Similar results obtain for subtype 4 (table 4), where 20 subjects were cost oriented and 5 were gain oriented (Z = 2.80, $p < .01$). From Atthowe's results it appears that a majority of people place more em-

Table 5. Frequency of Gambling Strategies.[a]

Strategy	Subtype 3	Subtype 4
Cost oriented	17	20
Rational	9	7
Gain oriented	6	5

[a] Entries refer to the number of subjects whose indifference points indicated a given strategy.

SOURCE: Atthowe [1960].

phasis on the negative than on the positive aspects of bets in reaching an overall evaluation of the bet. This is especially impressive when it is remembered that the subjects were told that the task came from an advanced intelligence test (thus increasing the "demand" for rational solutions).

Myers and his colleagues [Myers, Reilly & Taub 1961, Myers & Suydam 1964, Myers, Suydam & Gambino 1965, Katz 1964] have conducted a series of gambling studies that are nearly perfect analogs to Rettig's studies on ethical risk taking [Rettig & Rawson 1963]. Though these studies do not provide as clear a test of our "negativity" effect as does Atthowe's, they are nonetheless suggestive.

The basic paradigm requires subjects to predict which of two events—E_1 or E_2—will occur on the next trial. The amount won for a correct prediction (gain) and the amount lost for an incorrect prediction (cost) are varied independently for the two events. Thus, in the study by Myers, Reilly, and Taub, subjects were given one hundred chips worth ½¢ each and were then placed in the following contingency situation:

Prediction		Outcome
E_1	E_1	Subject wins 1 chip in all conditions
	E_2	Subject loses 1, 2, or 4 chips
E_2	E_1	Subject loses 1 chip in all conditions
	E_2	Subject wins 1, 2, or 4 chips

In addition to varying the costs of "missing" and the gains for "hitting" independently, Myers and his colleagues also varied the actual probability of E_1 over three levels. Considering only the cases in which E_1 and E_2 were equiprobable, we have nine experimental conditions (three levels of cost for missing E_2 combined with three levels of gain for hitting E_2). Thus, as in Rettig's studies, the bettor must choose between two alternatives, both of which contain the possibility of gain and cost. This paradigm does not allow the same precision in determining the relative weights given to costs and gains that Atthowe's study does. However, it is possible to look at the relative effects of a *change* in cost and a mathematically equivalent change in gain. If costs are more potent determiners of behavior than gains, a change of x units in cost should produce a greater behavioral change than a change of x units in gain.

Since only the cost of missing and the gain for hitting E_2 are varied, each condition may be described by two values—one for cost of missing E_2 and one for hitting E_2. Thus we can use -2 and $+4$ to indicate the following contingency:

Prediction		Outcome
E_1	E_1	Subject wins 1 chip
	E_2	Subject loses 2 chips
E_2	E_1	Subject loses 1 chip
	E_2	Subject wins 4 chips

Our interest is in the effect of symmetrical changes in the negative and positive directions from a "base" contingency. Consider first the condition -1 and $+1$. In this condition E_1 and E_2 have identical contingencies—in each case there is an equal chance of winning and losing one chip. Despite this fact, subjects were not quite indifferent between E_1 and E_2 in this condition; during the last fifty trials (the only ones reported), they predicted E_1 55.2 per cent of the time. When the possible cost of predicting E_1 was increased by one chip (condition -2 and $+1$), subjects chose E_1 27.75 per cent of the time. Thus an increase of one chip in the potential cost of predicting E_1 reduced the percentage of E_1 choices from 55.25 per cent to 27.75 per cent. A symmetrical positive change (from condition -1 and $+1$ to condition -1 and $+2$), however, reduced the percentage of E_1 responses to only 35.25 per cent. Thus an increase of one chip in the cost associated with predicting E_1 had more effect on the subjects' behavior than an increase of one chip in the gain associated with predicting E_2.

The other two comparisons of symmetrical changes in table 6 produce stronger results. An increase over the base condition of three chips of potential cost (condition $[-4, +1]$) reduces E_1 choices to 11 per cent while a corresponding increase of three chips in potential gain (condition $[-1, +4]$) reduces E_1 responses only to 32.75 per cent. Similarly, condition $(-4, +2)$ reduces E_1 responses to 17.75 per cent

Table 6. Betting Choices as a Function of Rewards and Costs.

Condition	Expected Value of E_1	Expected Value of E_2	E_1 Choices (last 50 trials)
$-1, +1$	0.00	0.00	55.25
$-1, +2$	0.00	0.50	35.25
$-1, +4$	0.00	1.50	32.75
$-2, +1$	-0.50	0.00	27.75
$-2, +2$	-0.50	0.50	22.50
$-2, +4$	-0.50	1.50	33.75
$-4, +1$	-1.50	0.00	11.00
$-4, +2$	-1.50	0.50	17.75
$-4, +4$	-1.50	1.50	15.50

Source: Myers, Reilly, and Taub [1961].

while condition $(-2, +4)$ reduces E_1 responses only to 33.75 per cent. Indeed, this effect is so powerful that an increase in potential cost of only one chip over the base condition $(-1, +1)$ reduced E_1 responses more than an increase of three chips in potential gain. This study has since been replicated by Katz [1964] with exactly the same pattern of results.

Another series of studies [Slovic & Lichtenstein 1968, Slovic 1969, Lichtenstein 1965] has used a different kind of betting game to examine the relative importance of various betting dimensions, including possible amount to be won ($W), possible amount to be lost ($L), probability of winning (PW), and probability of losing (PL). By using "duplex bets" in which subjects choose one pair of bets rather than another pair, they are able to eliminate the confounding of $W, $L, PW, and PL with other variables such as variance and probability level, found to be important by Edwards [1953, 1954a, 1954b]. "A duplex gamble is represented by two large discs, each with a pointer on it. The left-hand disc is used for determining winnings. The right-hand disc is used for determining losses. To play, the subject must spin the pointers on both the winning and losing discs. This means that he can win and not lose; lose and not win; both win and lose; or neither win nor lose" [Slovic & Lichtenstein 1968, p. 6]. An example of duplex bets is shown in figure 2. If a subject were to choose to play the top row, he would be said to prefer maximizing $W over minimizing $L, while if he were to choose to play the bottom row, his preference would be the opposite. By using this and similar duplex bets, one can determine a preference matrix for $W, $L, PW, and PL. The results from Slovic and Lichtenstein shown in table 7 are strikingly similar to those found by Rettig and Rawson. Preferences for

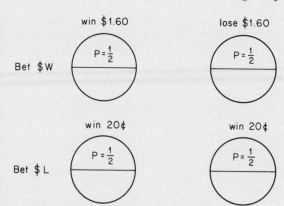

win $1.60   lose $1.60

Bet $W

win 20¢   win 20¢

Bet $L

Figure 2. A duplex bet.

Table 7. Betting Preferences as a Function of Rewards, Costs, and Probabilities.[a]

Preferences	Rating Group	Bidding Group
PW preferred over PL	60	80
PL preferred over PW	26	40
$W preferred over $L	27	37
$L preferred over $W	51	87

[a] Entries refer to the number of subjects whose choices between pairs of bets indicated a certain preference.

SOURCE: Slovic and Lichtenstein [1968].

the rating group were determined by ratings of the bets, while preferences for the bidding group were determined by how much was bid for a chance to play a particular bet. As we would expect, $L is more important than $W; that is, subjects minimize possible losses rather than maximize possible gains. However, as in Rettig and Rawson's study, the probability of loss is no more important than the probability of gain. In fact, the probability of gain is clearly more important than the probability of loss. For example, subjects would prefer a duplex pair with high probabilities of winning and losing over a pair with low probabilities of winning and losing. At first this seems inconsistent with a negativity bias. If costs are given more weight than gains, then subjects should choose a low probability because the possibility of loss would take precedence over the possibility of gain. But again a possible explanation for the preference for high probabilities is that people consider any possibility of loss "bad" without differentiating degrees of badness. If subjects were relatively indifferent to the difference between a .4 and a .8 probability of loss, then the loss disc would provide little basis for a choice between the two pairs of bets. But a .8 probability of winning might be much preferred to a .4 probability of winning. The subject would therefore chose the high probability pair of discs because both loss discs were pretty much the same while the .8 win disc was much better than the .4 win disc.

So far the literature on gambling is relatively clear and supportive. Unfortunately, the case for negativity in betting is not always so clear-cut. For example, Suydam [1965] repeated the procedure used by Myers et al [1961] but used a confidence rating as the dependent measure. Increases in potential gain

were somewhat more associated with an increase in confidence than equivalent increases in potential cost. However, this finding may have resulted simply because her subjects felt better (and therefore more confident) when they had a chance of winning than when they had merely avoided a possible loss.

A duplex betting study by Slovic [1969], however, is more troubling. Using a procedure almost identical to that used by Slovic and Lichtenstein, Slovic found the relative preferences for $W, $L, PW, and PL shown in table 8. There is clearly no support for any "negativity" tendency. Indeed, group H shows strong evidence of "positivity," 77 per cent of them preferring chances of winning and/or losing $1.60 to chances of winning and/or losing $.20. It is extremely interesting to note the differences between groups H and RP, however. "The Ss in Group H (N = 184) made hypothetical choices. They did not actually play any of their preferred gambles. The Ss in Group RP (N = 29), after making their choices, played a number of gambles to determine their salary" [p. 434]. Subjects were more conservative (that is, cost oriented) when gambling for real money than for imaginary money.

Table 8. Proportion of S's Who Weighted the Row Dimension More Heavily than the Column Dimension.[a]

Risk Dimension	Group H				Group RP			
	$W	PW	$L	PL	$W	PW	$L	PL
$W		.65	.77	.70		.41	.52	.55
PW	.35		.56	.67	.59		.34	.55
$L	.23	.44		.50	.48	.66		.48
PL	.30	.33	.49		.45	.45	.52	

[a] N = 184 in group H and 29 in group RP.

SOURCE: Slovic [1969].

These results raise interesting questions concerning possible limitations of the negativity phenomenon.

They suggest that negativity effects may occur only in situations possessing a degree of realism and importance for the subject. If so, the Slovic study presents unusual interpretive problems. The situation for group H subjects lacked realism and importance because their choices were hypothetical. Even for RP subjects, however, the situation would appear to be less than optimally realistic. The subjects in this condition "played" eighteen bets in a row before any of them were chosen by the experimenter for actual running. Furthermore, these subjects were instructed that they could expect to win about 30¢ from their bets over and above their initial $1.50 stakes. Inasmuch as the actual expected value of all of the bets was zero, the subjects may quite reasonably have assumed that the stated odds were phony, that is, that the experimenter would kindly rig things in their favor to provide them with the promised gain. Such reassuring instructions by the experimenter hardly provide the ideal conditions for a test of possible negativity effects.

Indeed, most laboratory studies of gambling contain this problem. Unless the experimenter is unusually clever in convincing subjects that potential losses are a real possibility, most subjects are quite likely to believe that nothing really bad will happen to them in a psychology experiment. Moreover, there is a potential danger of the intrusion of demand characteristics when the subjects know that the experimenter is studying gambling; quite understandably, they might feel that riskiness and "gambling" are called for in the situation. Furthermore, Marks [1951] and Irwin [1953] find that children and college students are more likely to express an expectation of a favorable event than a nonfavorable event, even when there is no rational reason for such optimism.

Despite such nettlesome problems, negativity is more commonly found than the opposite. Thus we feel justified in concluding that in general more weight is given to possible costs than gains in risk taking. Two important qualifications must be kept in mind, however. First, the *probability* of losing appears not to carry much weight in affecting the overall evaluation, and second, cost orientation appears to decrease as the risk becomes less realistic.

Before we examine possible reasons for the negativity bias, let us summarize the empirical findings. We find that negative personality traits outweigh equally polarized positive traits in determining an overall evaluation of a stimulus person; that moral evaluations of a pair of acts depend primarily on the worst of the two; that subjects readily infer a negative orientation on the part of an actor toward an object on the basis of a negative orientation toward two of three attributes of the object, while they generally do not infer a positive orientation on the basis of a positive orientation toward the same two attributes; and finally that people are, on the whole, cost oriented in risk taking.

Explanations for Negativity

In listing some possible explanations for negativity in evaluations, we have generally resisted the temptation to suggest different explanations for different subparts of the broad phenomenon. Rather, we have searched for explanations that might account for negativity in all realms.

Figure-Ground Explanations

The first class of explanations for the existence of negativity biases is based, ironically, on the existence of a complementary set of positivity biases. There is abundant evidence that people generally perceive most of their outcomes as good and that in the absence of evidence to the contrary they form generally positive expectations. For example, positive relationships are expected more often than negative ones [De Soto & Kuethe 1959]; positive words are used more frequently than negative words [Zajonc 1968]; and personal expectations and reports of personal happiness tend to be highly positive [Cantril 1965, Bradburn & Caplovitz 1965] (see Sears and Whitney [1972] for a more thorough review of the literature on positivity biases).

It seems that negativity biases occur against a backdrop of perceived bliss—indeed, perhaps because of it. Given that most people perceive the world as a predominantly positive place, there are a number of reasons why one might expect them to weight positive information rather more lightly than negative. First, there is the well-known judgmental anchoring, or contrast, effect. In a world of ointment, the fly seems bad indeed. Second, if most choices and behavior-relevant evaluations are made from a range of generally positive alternatives, it is simpler and less effortful to sort the alternatives on the basis of their few negative aspects rather than their many positive ones. This is so for much the same reason that one counts empty seats in a theater that is largely filled, and filled seats in a theater that is largely empty.

Both above notions suggest that the strength of negativity biases should depend on the positivity of the context in which the evaluation is made. Indeed, in a Hobsonian situation in which all the alternatives are predominantly negative, positive aspects might carry greater weight than negative ones.

Jones and Davis [1965] have suggested another line of explanation that, although it is less general than the two described above, still deserves discussion. They point out that because of the normatively positive informational environment, negative traits and behavior are likely to lead to a greater attribution of personal characteristics to the individual, and thus they provide more information than positive traits. If an individual believes that most people are sincere, he is likely to be relatively unimpressed with the information that person X is sincere. Given that sincerity is a norm, credit for it attaches to social pressure or to the simple fact of being human rather than to person X. Insincerity, however, is another matter. By standing in contrast to the norm, the insincere individual invites attributions of responsibility for this trait. These attributions in turn are likely to increase the importance and centrality of the trait in evaluations of him *qua* individual. The argument is a subtle one; while sincerity may be just as good as insincerity is bad, differential attributions of responsibility for the two traits may produce an asymmetry in evaluations of individuals possessing them.

The Range-Frequency Explanation

Parducci [1963, 1965, 1968] has examined a wide range of judgments ranging from judgments of weight, size, and numerosity to moral deeds and sat-

isfaction with monetary outcomes. He repeatedly finds that the psychological neutral point of a distribution of items varying along a given dimension seems to lie about halfway between the midpoint and the median of the distribution. For example, subjects given various distributions of monetary payoffs report satisfaction with those payoffs that fall above the average of the midpoint and the median and dissatisfaction with payoffs that fall below that point. The same point, about halfway between the median and midpoint, splits distributions of size judgments into small versus large, and so on.

To explore the implications of this finding, let us make two assumptions: (*a*) most outcomes are good; (*b*) extremely bad outcomes are more frequent than extremely good ones. These assumptions would suggest a distribution of life outcomes similar to the distribution shown in figure 3. Such a distribution strikes us as plausible. It seems likely that most of the time people are able to obtain fairly good outcomes, if for no other reason than that they are able to work their way into "suitable" environments and out of "unsuitable" ones. At the same time, extremely good outcomes, such as winning a sweepstakes, are less frequent in the experience of most individuals than extremely bad outcomes, such as the death of someone close.

Parducci's range-frequency compromise principle suggests that the psychological neutral point of the distribution should fall at about point MM (see figure 3). This suggestion implies that the majority of outcomes will be evaluated as positive, that is, above the psychological neutral point. As we have indicated, there is strong evidence that this is the case

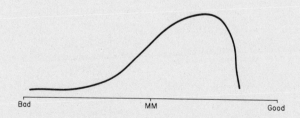

Figure 3. Hypothetical distribution of life outcomes.

[Sears & Whitney 1971]. Of more concern to us here, however, is the question of the relative effects that an extremely positive or negative outcome would have on the psychological neutral point. It can be seen from figure 3 that an extremely negative outcome would produce no change in the range and very little change in the median. Thus the neutral point should remain relatively unaffected. However, an extremely positive outcome would extend the range on the positive side, thereby moving the neutral point in the positive direction. This would have the unfortunate effect of shifting many outcomes previously labeled as positive into the negative zone. The hapless victim of such a scale shift would now be "spoiled." Thus a hidden drawback to very positive outcomes is that they may decrease the enjoyment of intermediate outcomes. Perhaps, then, individuals avoid negatives more than they approach positives because they have learned that the pursuit of highly positive outcomes is illusory. Thus it may be easier to obtain happiness by maximizing the *proportion* of nonnegative outcomes than by maximizing the positivity of individual outcomes.

The range-frequency explanation is ultimately teleological in nature, positing reasons why negativity biases might be adaptive and sensible rather than pointing to specific psychological processes that might be involved. We shall therefore turn our attention to explanations that are more suggestive both of process and of situational determinants of negativity biases.

Attribute Independence and Interference Effects

The presence of negative attributes within a complex stimulus may frequently have aversive consequences beyond the noxiousness of the attributes themselves. More specifically, the negative attributes of an object can frequently *interfere* with enjoyment of the positive aspects, while positive attributes seldom reduce our experience of negative aspects. Consider, for example, Kanouse's [1971] rancid soup example. The finest spices do little to alter our evaluation of rancid soup—the rancidness completely negates the positive characteristics of the spices. A similar argument can be made for financial risk taking. If he loses too much the gambler goes broke, and his opportunity for future gains is severely curtailed. However, his gains do not correspondingly prevent him from losing in the future.

Many implications of this interference theory can be tested. For example, cost orientation should decrease as the good and bad attributes of an object become increasingly independent and separable. To the extent that negative attributes are present only in and of themselves and do not reduce the consumability or enjoyability of positive attributes, they should receive less weight. The Abelson and Kanouse study [1966] supports this view. A strong negativity effect was found in the deductive form of evidence, in which actors had positive or negative orientations toward *characteristics* of an object. In the inductive form, in which actors had positive or negative orientations toward (separable) instances of a class of objects, no tendency for negativity appeared.

Inductive reasoning was investigated with items such as the following:

Altogether there are three kinds of magazines:
  Sports, News, Fashions
    Southern tribes do not have sports magazines
    Southern tribes do not have news magazines
    Southern tribes have fashion magazines
  Do Southern tribes have magazines?

Here subjects were asked to predict orientations toward a general class of objects on the basis of orientations toward some specific instances of that class. When presented with this form of evidence, subjects showed a *positivity* bias. A positive orientation toward two of three members of a class of objects led to the inference of positive orientation toward the class 79 per cent of the time, while a corresponding negative orientation toward two of three members of the class led to the inference of negative orientation toward the class only 57 per cent of the time. This reversal of the negative bias with inductive evidence strongly suggests that negative components of a complex object are overweighted only when the good and bad are found together in one object, when they are inseparable.

Many variables are likely to affect the separability of good and bad attributes, but probably one of the most important is to what extent the individual can control the duration and mode of his interaction with the object. When a mother-in-law who is delightful when sober but a terror when drunk comes for a brief visit, it may be possible to manipulate the situation in such a way that she is constantly surrounded by tea and ginger ale. On an extended visit, however, this effort becomes more difficult and one must take the drunk with the sober.

In general, it seems plausible to suggest that cost orientation should increase with the absolute magnitude, duration, and proximity of the outcome. With respect to magnitude, there is some support for this notion in Slovic's [1969] study: subjects making bets for real were more cost oriented than those making hypothetical bets. In much the same way, a set of mildly annoying mannerisms that might fail to deter us in selecting a casual date may become important deterrents indeed in selecting a spouse.

This speculation is reminiscent of Neal Miller's [1944, 1959] analysis of approach and avoidance gradients. Miller posited that as an animal approaches a goal having both positive and negative attributes, both the approach and avoidance tendencies increase, but the avoidance tendencies increase at a faster rate. We are suggesting that as the tangibility, importance, and proximity of an object or outcome increase, so does the salience of its negative attributes. To be sure, it is possible to explain Miller's animal data in terms of the differences between hunger and fear [1944], but the general notion as it applies to impression formation, risk taking, and evaluation is eminently testable. Indeed, Edward E. Jones has recently and independently arrived at a similar prediction on the basis of approach-avoidance theory.

Situational Determinants of the Salience of Rewards and Costs

While our general argument in this article is that most people weigh costs more heavily than rewards in forming overall evaluations, we do not wish to argue that a bias toward negativity exists as a universal propensity unqualified by individual differences. Indeed, theoretical treatments of relevant individual variables provide one convenient starting point for a theoretical analysis of the more general bias toward negativity.

Thibaut and Kelley [1959] and Canavan [1969] present theoretical analyses pertinent to individual differences. The former suggest that reward orientation (that is, the tendency to view rewards as more important than costs) is characteristic of individuals with a subjective sense of the power to control their own outcomes, while cost orientation is characteristic of individuals with a sense of powerlessness. Although this suggestion has considerable intuitive appeal, it leaves the question of *situational* determinants largely unanswered (but see the earlier discussion of the ability to control the mode and duration of interaction with the object).

Canavan offers a provocative analysis of possible situational determinants. She suggests that in an achievement situation an individual is likely to de-

velop a reward orientation if he is praised for success while his failures are ignored, and a cost orientation if he is criticized for failure while his successes are ignored. In an experimental study in which praise and criticism were varied (independently of feedback about absolute level of performance), she found strong support for this hypothesis.

Canavan's hypotheses and results raise a number of interesting questions. The first and most obvious concerns the nature of the mechanism underlying the differential effects of praise and criticism. There are at least three prominent possibilities. First, individuals may become cost oriented when criticized simply to avoid the aversive effects of criticism. Second, criticism may simply serve to make failures more salient than successes, independent of its aversive consequences. Finally, criticism may serve as a cue that the task is one in which it is more important to avoid doing badly than to try to do well. While these three alternative explanations are not mutually exclusive, they do have different implications.

The latter two explanations involve the general notion that cost orientation is likely to be increased by those situational cues that differentially increase the salience of costs, while reward orientation is likely to be increased by those situational cues that increase the salience of rewards. Many situational cues that should have this effect are obvious. In an achievement situation, criticism of failure while success is unrewarded should make failure differentially salient. In a gambling situation, the extension of credit to cover losses while winnings are paid in cash should increase the salience of rewards and decrease the salience of costs.

Other situational cues, however, may affect the differential salience of rewards and costs in a less obvious way. Of these, we suspect that one of the most important categories is provided by situational cues that implicitly define the nature of success and failure in a given task or, more generally, the nature of satisfactory versus unsatisfactory experience vis-à-vis a given object or situation. For example, consider our national pastime. The batting champion of the American or National League has the highest ratio of hits to at-bats. Thus the occasions on which he fails to get a hit lower his average. In contrast, the home run champion has the most home runs at the end of the year. Any particular occasion on which he fails to hit a home run does not detract from his record—it merely fails to enhance it. Thus it is interesting to note that one will occasionally find the leading candidate for a batting title sitting out the last few days of the season to avoid lowering his average, while the home run hitter is out swinging for the fences.

These championships, however, are defined by arbitrary convention. There is no real reason why the batting championship should not be determined on the basis of who has the greatest *number* of hits or that the home run championship should not be determined by who has the largest number of home runs per at-bat.

Cultures, institutions, and individuals often have considerable flexibility in how they choose to define standards of acceptability for outcomes. Which definition prevails may substantially affect the relative salience of rewards and costs, successes and failures. Our school systems, to take another example, usually define success or failure on the basis of average performance, when they might just as easily do so on the basis of maximum or cumulative performance; for example, a student must perform a certain amount of work at a certain level of quality, and it matters not how much unacceptable work he generates in the process. It seems possible that such "built-in" definitional cues might have profound effects on the evaluational biases of individuals operating within a given reward structure.

The Nature of Approach and Avoidance

An implicit assumption, underlying both adding and averaging models, is that there is a single good-bad dimension. There is reason to believe, however, that this assumption may be unwarranted. Thus Anderson [1962] has shown that different approach and avoidance gradients logically imply *independent* approach and avoidance tendencies. And from another vantage point, Stein [1964] and Cantril [1967] have argued that there are separate and relatively independent reward and punishment systems in the brain. If two distinct and independent systems are involved in the evaluation of compound stimuli, then it is hardly surprising that positive and negative aspects are not equally weighted. As Jordan argued with respect to liking and disliking: "The custom of finding an arithmetic average of attitude and opinion ratings that includes both positive and negative ratings . . . may literally be a mixing of apples and cabbages" [1965, p. 322].

One final explanation of negativity biases is little more than a Darwinian observation on the human condition. Ordinarily we construct our evaluational scales symmetrically, with the neutral point located at the middle of the scale. But as we noted in discussing range-frequency theory, the range of outcomes in real life is hardly symmetrical. The worst among all possible eventualities seem both more numerous and further removed from neutrality than do the best. There is even some indication of this asymmetry in the realm of word frequencies, which traditionally have been used to support the existence of biases toward positivity. In an informal word count of fifty randomly chosen pages of *Webster's New Collegiate Dictionary*, the present authors found roughly three times as many evaluatively negative nouns and transitive verbs as positive ones. (Trait adjectives, in contrast, appear to be equally divided between good and evil.) It appears that although we use positive words more frequently than negative ones, should we ever choose to change our minds, the English language has provided us with truly impressive resources.

In any case, ultimate negatives such as death and lifelong suffering do not seem to be balanced by ultimate positives such as immortality and perpetual nirvana. Viewed in this light, it is highly adaptive to weigh costs more heavily than gains.

Summary

Research in several different areas suggests that the overall evaluation of objects having both good and bad characteristics lies closer to the bad than to the good. A typical finding in the literature of impression formation is that ratings of people described by positive and negative adjectives are more negative than would be predicted by simply averaging the scale values of the adjectives when used alone. Similarly, Feldman [1966] found that the "modifying capacity" of negative adjectives is greater than that of positive adjectives. And Birnbaum [1972] found that evaluations of pairs of immoral deeds were closer to the worst of the two deeds.

An internal analysis of Feldman's data [Kinder 1971] and a study by Abelson and Kanouse [1966] suggest that the greater weight typically given to negative characteristics cannot be accounted for by such artifacts as the greater surprisingness or lesser frequency of negative characteristics. The relationship between scale value and modifying capacity in Feldman's data remains strong even when such factors as frequency and surprisingness are controlled through partial correlation techniques. Moreover, in Abelson and Kanouse's study, the specific content of the positive or negative characteristics was manipulated independently of their evaluative sign, yet a strong negativity effect emerged.

Similar negativity biases appear in the evaluation of risks, where integration of positive and negative information is often required. In a review of the risk-taking literature, Kogan and Wallach [1967] conclude that potential costs are more important in determining an overall evaluation than potential gains. Substantial support for this position is found in studies reported by Rettig, Myers, Atthowe, Slovic, and others. Typically, individuals in these studies seem more motivated to avoid potential costs than to seek potential gains.

Thus there seems to be substantial support for the proposition that negative information carries greater weight than positive information. Why might this be? There are several possible lines of explanation. First, negative information may outweigh positive because it stands in contrast to a predominantly positive set of norms and expectations. In a world which is perceived as predominantly positive, negative aspects are likely to be more salient. Moreover, evaluational strategies giving heavy weight to a few negatives are likely to be simpler and more manageable than strategies that require weighing and comparing many positives.

A somewhat different perspective on the negativity bias is provided by Parducci's [1963, 1965, 1968] finding that the psychological neutral point of a distribution of satisfactions lies about midway between the mean and the median of the distribution. One implication of this "range-frequency principle" is that overall satisfaction with one's outcomes can more easily be maximized by seeking a high *proportion* of positive outcomes than by seeking the best possible individual outcome. A simple behavioral strategy to avoid wherever possible the risk of a bad outcome would, of course, have this effect.

A third explanation for the negativity bias is based on the notion that negative attributes are more likely to cancel the benefits of positive attributes than vice versa. While there is little data supporting this notion, it is not difficult to think of compelling examples, and the idea is worth empirical pursuit.

It seems likely that the negativity bias can be accentuated by structural and situational factors that increase the salience of costs. As we have tried to indicate, many structural factors, such as cultural and subcultural definitions of success or failure, may have this effect in ways not readily apparent.

Finally, it is not unreasonable to suggest that life outcomes are themselves distributed asymmetrically,

with more extremely negative outcomes than extremely positive ones. If so, then the negativity bias could certainly be considered adaptive in the Darwinian sense.

Indeed, recent research on the brain suggests the existence of relatively separate and independent reward and punishment systems [Stein 1964]. Ultimately there is no reason to assume that these separate systems act so that approach and avoidance tendencies are equally strong.

It should be evident from the above that any theorist who attempts to find the "explanation" of negativity biases is confronted with an embarrassment of riches. Fortunately, to add to our knowledge of the phenomenon it is not necessary to design experiments in which all these various explanations are pitted against one another. The explanations themselves are not so much a set of mutually exclusive explanatory principles only one of which is useful as they are theoretical perspectives from which to view the problem, each suggesting a number of interesting theoretical and empirical questions.

BIBLIOGRAPHY

Robert P. Abelson and David E. Kanouse, "Subjective Acceptance of Verbal Generalizations." In Sheldon Feldman, ed., *Cognitive Consistency*. Academic, 1966.

Norman H. Anderson, "On the Quantification of Miller's Conflict Theory." *Psychological Review*, 1962, 69:400–414.

Norman H. Anderson, "Averaging Versus Adding as a Stimulus-Combination Rule in Impression Formation." *Journal of Personality and Social Psychology*, 1965, 2: 1–9.

Norman H. Anderson, "Likableness Ratings of 555 Personality-Trait Adjectives." *Journal of Personality and Social Psychology*, 1968, 9:272–279.

John M. Atthowe, Jr., "Types of Conflict and Their Resolution: A Reinterpretation." *Journal of Experimental Psychology*, 1960, 59:1–9.

Michael Birnbaum, "Morality Judgments: Tests of an Averaging Model." *Journal of Experimental Psychology*, 1972, 93:35–42.

Norman M. Bradburn and David Caplovitz, *Reports on Happiness*. Aldine, 1965.

Donnah Canavan, *The Development of Individual Differences in the Perception of Value and Risk-Taking Style*. Unpublished Ph.D. dissertation, Columbia University, 1969.

Hadley Cantril, *The Pattern of Human Concerns*. Rutgers University Press, 1965.

Hadley Cantril, "*Sentio, Ergo Sum:* 'Motivation' Reconsidered." *Journal of Psychology*, 1967, 65:91–107.

Clinton B. De Soto and James L. Kuethe, "Subjective Probabilities of Interpersonal Relations." *Journal of Abnormal and Social Psychology*, 1959, 59:290–294.

Ward Edwards, "Probability-Preferences in Gambling." *American Journal of Psychology*, 1953, 66:349–364.

Ward Edwards, "Probability-Preferences among Bets with Differing Expected Values." *American Journal of Psychology*, 1954a, 67:56–67.

Ward Edwards, "Variance Preferences in Gambling." *American Journal of Psychology*, 1954b, 67:441–442.

Sheldon Feldman, "Motivational Aspects of Attitudinal Elements and Their Place in Cognitive Interaction." In Sheldon Feldman, ed., *Cognitive Consistency*. Academic, 1966.

Francis W. Irwin, "Stated Expectations as Functions of Probability and Desirability of Outcomes." *Journal of Personality*, 1953, 21:329–335.

Edward E. Jones and Keith E. Davis, "From Acts to Dispositions: The Attribution Process in Person Perception." In Leonard Berkowitz, ed., *Advances in Experimental Social Psychology*, Academic, 1965, pp. 220–226.

Nehemiah Jordan, "The Asymmetry of Liking and Disliking: A Phenomenon Meriting Further Reflection and Research." *Public Opinion Quarterly*, 1965, 29:315–322.

David E. Kanouse, "Language, Labeling, and Attribution." General Learning Press, 1971.

Leonard Katz, "Effects of Differential Monetary Gain and Loss on Sequential Two-Choice Behavior." *Journal of Experimental Psychology*, 1964, 68:245–249.

Donald Kinder, "Implicative Information of Positive and Negative Trait Adjectives." Unpublished manuscript, University of California, Los Angeles, 1971.

Nathan Kogan and Michael A. Wallach, "Risk Taking as a Function of the Situation, the Person, and the Group." In *New Directions in Psychology III*. Holt, Rinehart and Winston, 1967.

Sarah Lichtenstein, "Bases for Preferences among Three-Outcome Bets." *Journal of Experimental Psychology*, 1965, 69:162–169.

Rose W. Marks, "The Effect of Probability, Desirability, and Privilege on the Stated Expectations of Children." *Journal of Personality*, 1951, 19:431–465.

Neal E. Miller, "Experimental Studies of Conflict." In J. Hunt, ed., *Personality and the Behavior Disorders*, vol. 1. Ronald, 1944.

Neal E. Miller, "Liberalization of Basic S-R Concepts: Extensions to Conflict, Behavior, Motivation, and Social Learning." In S. Koch, ed., *Psychology: A Study of a Science*, vol. 2. McGraw-Hill, 1959.

Jerome L. Myers, Raymond E. Reilly, and Harvey A. Taub, "Differential Cost, Gain, and Relative Frequency Reward in Sequential Choice Situation." *Journal of Experimental Psychology*, 1961, 62:357–360.

Jerome L. Myers and Mary M. Suydam, "Gain, Cost, and Event Probability as Determiners of Choice Behavior." *Psychonomic Science*, 1964, 1:39–40.

Jerome L. Myers, Mary M. Suydam, and Blase Gambino, "Contingent Gains and Losses in a Risk-Taking Situation." *Journal of Mathematical Psychology*, 1965, 2: 363–370.

Allen Parducci, "Range-Frequency Compromise in Judgment." *Psychological Monographs*, 1963, 77(2).

Allen Parducci, "Category Judgment: A Range-Frequency Model." *Psychological Review*, 1965, 72:407–418.

Allen Parducci, "The Relativism of Absolute Judgments." *Scientific American*, 1968, 219:84–90.

Soloman Rettig and Benjamin Pasamanick, "Differential Judgment of Ethical Risk by Cheaters and Non-cheaters." *Journal of Abnormal Social Psychology*, 1964, 69:109–113.

Soloman Rettig and Harve E. Rawson, "The Risk Hypothesis in Predictive Judgments of Unethical Behavior." *Journal of Abnormal Social Psychology*, 1963, 66:243–248.

Soloman Rettig and J. B. P. Sinha, "Bad Faith and Ethical Risk Sensitivity." *Journal of Personality*, 1966, 43:275–286.

Milton Rokeach, *Beliefs, Attitudes and Values*. Jossey-Bass, 1968.

David O. Sears and Richard E. Whitney, "Political Persuasion." To appear in I. de S. Pool, F. Frey, L. Fein, W. Schramm, N. Maccoby, and E. Parker, eds., *Handbook of Communications*, Rand-McNally, 1972.

Paul Slovic, "Differential Effects of Real versus Hypothetical Payoffs on Choices among Gambles." *Journal of Experimental Psychology*, 1969, 80:434–437.

Paul Slovic and Sarah Lichtenstein, "Relative Importance of Probabilities and Payoffs in Risk Taking." *Journal of Experimental Psychology*, 1968, 78: pt 2.

Larry Stein, "Reciprocal Action of Reward and Punishment Mechanisms." In R. G. Heath, ed., *The Role of Pleasure in Behavior*. Harper and Row, 1964.

Mary M. Suydam, "Effects of Cost and Gain Ratios, and Probability of Outcome on Ratings of Alternative Choices." *Journal of Mathematical Psychology*, 1965, 2:171–179.

John W. Thibaut and Harold H. Kelley, *The Social Psychology of Groups*. Wiley, 1959.

Edward L. Thorndike and Irving Lorge, *The Teacher's Word Book of 30,000 Words*. Teacher's College, Columbia University, 1944.

Robert B. Zajonc, "Attitudinal Effects of Mere Exposure." *Journal of Personality and Social Psychology*, 1968, 7: Monograph, 1–29.

[*Preparation of this paper grew out of a workshop on attribution theory held at U.C.L.A. in August 1969, supported by Grant GS-2613 from the National Science Foundation.*]

4 · Perceiving the Causes of One's Own Behavior

RICHARD E. NISBETT
University of Michigan

STUART VALINS
State University of New York at Stony Brook

Attribution theory, as it has evolved from the work of Heider, has been primarily concerned with the individual's perception of the causes of the behavior of other people. The emphasis has been on the rules governing a person's attribution of causes for the behavioral effects manifested by the people around him. Now we wish to examine the causal interpretations that the individual applies to himself—the individual's search for explanations of his own behavior. Some readers might be inclined to object at this early point, asking rhetorically, "Search for explanations of our own behavior? Don't we *know*, or think we know, why we do what we do?"

Daryl Bem [1967] has answered this "rhetorical" question in the negative. He has argued that, despite the human's reputation as a thoughtful animal, he often emits behaviors quite unself-consciously and then asks of himself, as he might of another person, "Why did I do that?" The answers are reached by the same kind of causal analysis that Jones and Davis [1965] and Kelley [1967] have suggested that we employ in our attempts to understand the behaviors of others. Just as we learn about the likely attitudes and dispositions of others from watching what they do, we learn about our own attitudes and dispositions from self-observation. Specifically, Bem has proposed that we often survey our behavior toward an entity and then infer that our attitudes toward the entity are consistent with our behavior toward it.

In discussing the perception of the causes of one's own behavior, we shall find it helpful to use Bem's proposition as the unifying theme. As we shall see, however, the topic of causal self-analysis is broader than the hypothesis that we learn what we think from watching what we do.

Bem introduced his proposition in the context of his reinterpretation of the body of evidence supporting dissonance theory. In the typical dissonance experiment, the subject is induced to perform some behavior for which there is insufficient justification. Dissonance theorists argue that this situation is painful to subjects and they are motivated to seek additional justification for their behavior—to find "added attractions" in the goal toward which the behavior was directed, as Lawrence and Festinger [1962] put it. Bem argues instead that subjects merely passively survey their behavior toward an object, taking into account the low extrinsic justification for the behavior, and infer that the intrinsic justification must have been high or else they would not have performed the behavior. Bem's view is thus an *information-processing* one that denies any motivational interpretation of the attitude change found in experiments on insufficient justification.

It is not our intention to dwell on the controversy surrounding Bem's reinterpretation of the phenomena uncovered by dissonance theorists. Instead, we wish to discuss research that is related to Bem's proposition but that is largely irrelevant to, or unexplained by, dissonance theory.

First, we shall review the available evidence that directly tests the proposition that we infer our attitudes from our overt behavior. Most of the data Bem has presented in support of this proposition consist of "interpersonal simulations" [1965, 1967]. While suggestive, these studies are not very direct or very persuasive tests. Recent research by Bandler, Madaras, and Bem [1968] and others provide stronger support for Bem's proposition.

Second, we shall introduce the concept of "overly sufficient justification." Dissonance theory, dealing as it does only with situations where the individual presumably attempts to justify his behavior to himself, cannot make predictions about situations where the behavior is more than adequately justified. From the information-processing viewpoint of attribution theory, however, one can make the explicit prediction that if people are too heavily compensated for their behavior they should devalue the behavior. When extrinsic justification for behavior is very great, the behavior should be perceived as less desirable and valuable in its own right than when extrinsic justifications are slight.

Third, we wish to argue that there is substantial support for a modified version of Bem's proposition in the work by Schachter and his colleagues on emotion. Following Kelley, we shall argue that these data may be construed as support for the proposition that people infer their attitudes and feelings from observation of their autonomic behavior. Indeed, the data in support of this proposition are far more extensive than the data supporting Bem's proposition.

Fourth, we shall discuss behavioral consequences of belief inferences. If it is true that people infer their beliefs from their behavior, it would seem to follow that people would often want to check, validate, or confirm these inferred beliefs by initiating and observing their behavior in later situations that are relevant to the beliefs. These efforts to check belief inferences will sometimes result in confirmation and sometimes not. We wish to explore the implications of inference-checking processes for attribution theory and research.

Fifth, we wish to show how the research area of self-perception might be broadened beyond the confines of the experimentation to date. We shall propose that inferences are likely to result from new information about any aspect of behavior—its form and intensity, its causes, its consequences, and the context, including attitudinal context, in which it occurs.

Inference of Attitudes from Overt Behavior

Let us first consider Bem's original hypothesis and review the evidence in support of it. Do people infer their attitudes from their behavior? The chief direct evidence produced in support of this hypothesis is an ingenious study by Bandler, Madaras, and Bem [1968]. Subjects in that experiment were given a series of thirty shocks. Preceding ten of the shocks was a light that signaled to the subject that he could *escape* the shock by pressing a button. Subjects were told, in effect, that if they found the shock not at all uncomfortable they need not escape it, but the experimenter would really prefer it if they did. Virtually all the subjects did in fact choose to escape the shock on virtually all of the trials. But the experimenter's demand was rather subtle and it was expected that the subjects would interpret their escape behavior as self-produced: subjects should thus infer from this escape behavior that the shocks were indeed rather painful. The subjects' ratings of the shocks in this condition were compared to their ratings of identical shocks in a condition where a light preceding the shocks merely signaled a *reaction time* trial. Pressing the button under these circumstances was mandatory. As predicted, the shocks in the escape condition were rated as considerably more painful than the identical shocks in the reaction time condition. Escape behavior was thus used as a basis for inferring that the shocks were painful.

The results of a third condition, however, did not support Bem's proposition. Preceding the remaining ten shocks was a light that indicated that the experimenter wanted the subject to endure or *not to escape* the shock. Subjects were told that if they found the shock painful, they could escape it by pressing the button, but the experimenter preferred that they not escape. As in the escape condition, virtually all subjects complied with the experimenter's low-keyed request. It was anticipated that subjects would interpret their failure to escape as self-produced. They should have inferred from the fact that they did not escape that the shocks were not painful. Nevertheless, these shocks were not rated differently from the shocks in the reaction time condition. Subjects were willing to infer pain from escape behavior but not the absence of pain from no-escape behavior.

This asymmetry could be explained in the following way. Subjects may perceive themselves to have less freedom of action when they are asked not to do something they wish to do than when they are requested to do something they are inclined to do anyway. Requests to perform counterattitudinal behavior ("no-escape" behavior) may be perceived as more controlling than requests to perform proattitudinal behavior ("escape" behavior). When he perceives that his behavior is under external control, the individual may be less willing to make inferences from his behavior. If this is the explanation for the asymmetry, then it might be possible to persuade subjects to infer the absence of pain from "no-escape" behavior in other experimental contexts, where there is no counterattitudinal request.

Davison and Valins [1969] have performed an experiment that, while not designed to investigate this issue, is quite relevant to it and quite supportive of Bem's proposition. Davison and Valins asked their subjects to take a series of electric shocks of steadily increasing intensity and told them to report when the shocks first became painful and when they became too painful to tolerate. Following the shock series and threshold determination, subjects were asked to take a drug, actually a placebo, which, they were told, might have effects on "skin sensitivity." After a brief period of time supposedly sufficient to allow the pill to take effect, subjects were asked to take the shock series over again. The experimenter had meanwhile altered the intensity of the shock across the whole range of values in such a way that every shock was half as intense as it had been on the preceding series. The effect of this alteration was

to approximately double the number of shocks subjects took before they announced pain and before they asked the experimenter to terminate the series.

The experimental manipulation occurred at the end of the second series, which subjects believed to be the end of the experiment. Some subjects were merely thanked for their participation and told that in a few minutes, after the drug had worn off, they would participate in another, similar experiment. Subjects in a second group were told that they had not been given a drug at all, that instead they were in a control group and had simply been given a placebo. Thus, at this point in the experiment, the first group of subjects ("drug" subjects) presumably believed they had been able to take many more shocks on the second series because of the effect of a drug that was now wearing off. The second group of subjects ("placebo" subjects) could only assume they had taken more shocks because the shocks were now less painful to them. In other words, subjects had the same knowledge about their actual behavior on the second series but differing "knowledge" about the reasons for that behavior. Drug subjects would assume the behavior had an extrinsic origin, implying nothing about their actual ability to withstand shock. Placebo subjects would assume the behavior had a more personal origin, reflecting a new ability to withstand shock. The investigators reasoned that these differing inferences from the same behavior would lead to differential ability to withstand shock on a third shock series.

The third and final shock series was given under the auspices of an alleged second experiment conducted by a new experimenter. The new experimenter said that he was studying "intersensory stimulation" and would use the apparatus of the previous experiment to determine the subject's reaction to electric shock while being exposed to auditory stimulation. The subject was to be given a series of shocks, first without auditory stimulation, then with it. The auditory series was never given and instead subjects were given only the "preliminary" series, a duplication of the procedures and intensities of the very first threshold series.

Placebo subjects, who presumably believed they had been responsible for their improvement on the second shock series, took significantly more shock on the third series than they had on the first. Drug subjects, who presumably believed a drug had been responsible for their improvement on the second series, took trivially less shock on the third series than they had on the first. Thus, subjects who believed their pain-enduring behavior was a reflection of a new reaction to the shock apparently inferred that the shocks were less painful and were willing to tolerate more of them. Under some circumstances, then, pain-enduring behavior is used as the basis for an inference about the painfulness of a stimulus. Precisely why subjects chose to act on this inference, tolerating more shock than before, will be discussed in more detail below. For the moment, we simply suggest that an inference may function like a hypothesis and that perhaps placebo subjects took more shock on the last series because they were trying to test or confirm the inference that the shocks were now less painful.

A third experiment relevant to Bem's proposition has been performed by Kiesler, Nisbett, and Zanna [1969]. These investigators wanted to show that an inference about belief will occur when an individual commits himself to behavior relevant to that belief. They chose a behavior that was ambiguously relevant to subjects' beliefs and directly manipulated the perceived relevance of behavior to belief. Subjects were asked to persuade passersby on a New Haven street corner to sign a petition urging action against air pollution. The experimenter explained that he was studying the optimum number of arguments that should be employed in persuasive communications and wanted large numbers of experimenters—Yale students, like the subject—to present communications with varying numbers of arguments. A confederate, who was presumably going to deliver a persuasive communication to passersby about auto safety, was present at each session. Also present was another naive subject who believed that he was to participate in a later phase of the experiment. This subject, the "witness," observed everything that occurred and differed from the participant subject only in that he did not expect to have to deliver any persuasive communication himself.

After explaining the procedure and the alleged purpose of the experiment, the experimenter asked the participant if he had any objections to delivering persuasive communications about air pollution. The participant invariably did not. The experimenter then asked the confederate if he had any objections to delivering persuasive communications about auto safety. At this point, the confederate delivered the experimental manipulation, saying either (*a*) that he wouldn't mind convincing people about something he really believed in and he guessed that that was the important thing or (*b*) that the topic seemed a good one for the experimenter's purpose and that he would be quite willing because he guessed the important thing was to be in an experiment that really showed

something. The confederate's statements thus made salient one of two very different reasons for the behavior the subject was about to perform, defining the behavior in one case as genuine proselytizing for a strongly held conviction and in the other as mere assistance in a scientific investigation. The investigators reasoned that subjects for whom the proselytizing definition was made salient would accept this as an explanation of their own behavior and consequently infer that they believed very strongly in the importance of combating air pollution. Apparently this was the case. Subjects were asked to give their opinions on a variety of social issues, including air pollution, just prior to performing the persuasion task (which never actually took place). Subjects for whom the proselytizing motive was made salient reported that they were considerably more opposed to air pollution than did subjects for whom the scientific motive was made salient. The experimental manipulation had no effect on the opinions of the witnesses, who did not expect to perform the behavior. Nor did the manipulation have any effect on either the witnesses' or the participants' attitudes toward auto safety.

The belief relevance manipulation apparently also produced differences in motivation to perform the persuasion task. "Proselytizing" subjects reported that they intended to work harder at their task than did "scientific" subjects. This enhanced motivation probably was a consequence of the subjects' inference that they held strong convictions on the topic of air pollution. In the "proselytizing" condition there was a correlation of .69 between opposition to air pollution and intention to work hard at the task. In the "scientific" condition there was a correlation of only .14 between those variables.

These three experiments provide the clearest support available for the proposition that we infer our beliefs from our behavior. Escape from shock was used to infer pain; toleration of increased intensities of shock was used to infer diminished pain; and commitment to proselytizing behavior was used to infer a stronger belief. Each of the experiments also points to an obvious but important qualification of the proposition: people seem to infer their beliefs from their behavior only when they have good reason to believe that their behavior toward a stimulus is produced primarily by their feelings about the stimulus. When subjects had reason to believe that their behavior was produced in large part by circumstantial factors extrinsic to the stimulus—the experimenter's requirements, a drug, a request to help in a scientific investigation—a belief inference did not take place.

This distinction between causal factors intrinsic to the stimulus and those extrinsic or circumstantial is a central one for self-perception research. It will be helpful to discuss this distinction in relation to allocational distinctions made by others. The distinction should not be confused with the "external-internal" dimension used by Kelley [1971] and others or with the similar "situational vs. dispositional" dimension discussed by Jones and Nisbett [1971]. Both these latter dimensions are concerned with establishing the causal role of the environment in contrast to the causal role of the person. If the behavior is seen as having been caused by the person, then causal factors are "internal" in Kelley's terms and "dispositional" in Jones and Nisbett's terms. If the behavior is seen as having been caused by the environment, then causal factors are "external" or "situational."

In contrast, the stimulus-circumstance distinction is concerned with the allocation of cause between various aspects of the environment. Thus, electric shock is a constant stimulus across all the conditions of the Bandler et al. experiment. In one of the conditions (escape condition), subjects attributed their behavior toward the shock stimulus to their reactions to the shock itself, while in other conditions behavior was attributed to the particular circumstances under which they were exposed to the shock, that is, to the instructions to behave in a particular way toward the shock. Both causes are "external" or "situational," but it makes a great deal of difference just which external, situational factor is perceived as causal.

It may be noted that Skinner's [1957] mand-tact distinction, employed by Bem in his analyses of dissonance experiments, may be easily translated into the present terms. From the present viewpoint, tacts are statements about a stimulus that are elicited by the person's intrinsic feelings about the stimulus. Mands are statements about a stimulus that are elicited by the person's desire to gain a particular reinforcement from the environment, that is, statements elicited by an aspect of the circumstances other than the individual's intrinsic feelings about the stimulus.

Insufficient Justification and Overly Sufficient Justification

It is useful to discuss dissonance or "insufficient justification" experiments in terms of the distinction between stimulus factors and circumstance factors. In the typical insufficient justification experiment,

subjects are induced to perform some behavior under conditions in which the properties of the stimulus toward which behavior is directed do not justify the behavior and in which no other aspect of the circumstances serves to adequately justify the behavior. For example, in the Festinger and Carlsmith study some subjects were offered $1 to tell another person that a dull task they had just completed had been interesting. Neither the stimulus (the inherent interest of the task) nor the circumstances (the amount of money offered) was sufficient to justify the behavior. (For readers who are tempted to ask why subjects ever perform the behavior in the first place, when the causes are so inadequate, Kelley [1967] has provided a satisfying answer. They do so because of well-concealed but often massive social pressure from experimenters. In other words, because of a relatively invisible aspect of the circumstances.) In the view of dissonance theorists, $1 subjects find the inadequate justification painful. They then change their minds about the inherent interest of the task, thereby cognitively rendering stimulus factors sufficient to justify the behavior. Subjects offered $20 to say the task is interesting already have sufficient justification for their behavior and thus have no need to tamper with their cognitions about the stimulus.

To this point, the analysis does not differ much in substance from that offered by dissonance theorists. The only difference, and it is not a central one, is that the $20 subject is portrayed not merely in negative terms, as lacking dissonant cognitions, but instead is portrayed as possessing a cognition that requires him to attribute his behavior to stimulus-irrelevant circumstances. This concept has by now a place in the modified dissonance theory of Brehm and Cohen [1962], which singles out perceived volition as an essential preconditon for the experience of dissonance. In the present terms, lack of perceived volition or choice means causal attribution to some compelling extra-stimulus feature of the situation. This may be the experimenter's demand, as in the "low choice" control condition of a host of dissonance experiments, or a large monetary inducement, as in the Festinger and Carlsmith experiment. The present analysis, in other words, provides a common construct for operationally quite distinct "low dissonance" manipulations, while doing no violence to the core notions of dissonance theory.

Violence aplenty, however, is wreaked by Bem's information-processing reinterpretation of dissonance theory, which may be crudely described as throwing the motivational baby out of the cognitive bath. Again, we may use the present terminology to paraphrase Bem's account of insufficient justification experiments.

Bem's reinterpretation of dissonance phenomena avoids the use of any motivational concept, maintaining that when subjects perceive that the circumstances do not provide adequate justification for behavior, they *infer* that factors intrinsic to the stimulus must have been adequate. Thus, the subject offered $1 realizes that (*a*) he doesn't like to tell lies, (*b*) he had no particular reason to do so (only $1 was offered), and therefore (*c*) he must not have particularly disliked the experimental task and must not have told a lie when he said it was interesting. The subject offered $20 does not re-evaluate the task because, while he knows he does not like to tell lies, he also knows that he is willing to tell them for adequate compensation. Bem therefore argues that the re-evaluation of the stimulus exhibited by subjects in the insufficient justification conditions of dissonance experiments does not occur because of an unconscious, motivated effort to justify behavior. Instead, he argues, their evaluations are the result of an honest information-processing error. In attempting to understand why they behaved as they did, such subjects mistakenly infer that their attitudes toward the stimulus are more in line with their behavior than they really are.

While our sympathies lie with Bem, we shall avoid reviewing the arguments and counterarguments concerning Bem's nonmotivational reinterpretation of the dissonance experiments and simply express the opinion that the two positions seem to be at a logical impasse. So long as the behavior in question is insufficiently justified, the dissonance theorist may claim that this knowledge is painful and that any resulting attitude change is a motivated process rather than a passive, inferential process. We believe it is possible to apply Bem's proposition to new territory, so we will not remain on an old battleground.

An information-processing analysis may be brought to bear on the mirror image of the insufficient justification paradigm—situations where behavior is justified both by stimulus factors and by the circumstances. Here there can be no dissonance because there is no discomfort. Information processing can go on, however, and an information-processing view can make predictions about attitude change. Consider, for example, the case of an individual who is asked to read a speech that is *consonant* with his opinion. What would be the effect on his opinion if he were paid $5 to do so as opposed to $1? The information-processing view would lead us to expect that subjects who are highly paid merely for reading a brief speech

that is consistent with their beliefs might infer that there was less justification for the behavior on stimulus grounds than subjects who were paid $1. The behavior of subjects paid $5 is amply justified by the circumstances, and such subjects might therefore consider their behavior to be less motivated by the stimulus, that is, less prompted by their convictions. Just as the information-processing view maintains that subjects in the insufficient justification conditions of dissonance experiments *discover* stimulus causes for their behavior, it can predict that subjects in "overly sufficient" conditions of "consonance" experiments will *ignore* the stimulus causes for their behavior.

Kiesler and Sakumura [1966], under the guise of a study of regional speech accents, have conducted an experiment similar to the one described. Their results are consistent with the information-processing view. Subjects paid $5 for reading a speech consistent with their opinions on lowering the voting age to eighteen were subsequently more persuaded by a communication arguing against their beliefs on the voting age than subjects paid only $1. The opinions of the $5 subjects were held to less tenaciously, in other words, indicating that their beliefs were undercut by the high reward. When subjects were *not* presented with a countercommunication, however, Kiesler and Sakamura found that payment did not have a differential effect on their opinions. The information-processing view would predict a payment effect even in the absence of a countercommunication, but the failure to find such an effect may be due to the fact that the behavior required of the subjects was rather inconsequential. Kiesler, Nisbett, and Zanna [1969] have suggested that "speech reading behavior . . . does not necessarily imply adherence to the contents of the speech. It may be that many behaviors are of this latter neutral sort, suggesting nothing about belief except when situational cues intervene with an implication that the behavior is relevant to belief [p. 322]." The Kiesler, Nisbett, and Zanna experiment was in part a test of this notion and provided support for it. Commitment to proselytizing behavior affected beliefs only when the link between behavior and belief was made salient. Perhaps, then, Kiesler and Sakamura's countercommunication served the essential function of rendering salient the link between speech reading behavior and the subjects' beliefs.

Carlsmith and Lepper [personal communication] have performed an experiment that is a virtual replication of the Kiesler and Sakamura experiment. In Carlsmith and Lepper's experiment, high-school students were paid either $.50 or $2.50 to write a brief essay in support of their view that the legal driving age should not be raised. The payment variable had no effect on opinions. Other subjects did not write essays but were paid either $.50 or $2.50 to read a countercommunication arguing that the driving age should be increased to eighteen. The payment variable had no effect on opinions under these circumstances either, nor was there any evidence that the countercommunication had any effect on opinions. A third group of subjects was paid either $.50 or $2.50 to read the countercommunication and *then* write their essays. Here the payment variable had a powerful effect. Subjects paid $.50 held more strongly to their initial opinions than did subjects paid $2.50. The investigators thus repeated both the overjustification effect found by Kiesler and Sakumura together with the qualification that a countercommunication was essential to produce the effect.

A very provocative experiment, from the present standpoint, has been performed by Bogart, Loeb, and Rutman [1969]. These investigators attempted to change the work attitudes of clients in Horizon House, a postpsychiatric rehabilitation center in Philadelphia, by instituting a program of rewards for attendance and punctuality. Rewards ranged up to a maximum of about $8 (in prize value) for perfect attendance throughout the month during which rewards were offered. The present line of reasoning would suggest that, while such rewards might or might not be successful in improving attendance during the period while they are in effect (and might actually produce a decrement in attendance), they should definitely have deleterious effects on attendance once the reward program is discontinued. The client should develop the belief that he is attending the workshop in part to obtain the reward. To the extent that this is true, attendance should drop, perhaps immediately, and at any rate when rewards are no longer obtainable by attendance.

The pattern of results was quite consistent with this notion. Attendance did rise from about 90 per cent to 95 per cent during the reward period, but decreased to about 75 per cent when rewards were withdrawn. In another condition of the experiment, much smaller rewards were offered for attendance—up to a maximum of about $2 in prize value for a month of perfect attendance. The present line of reasoning would lead us to expect that withdrawal of a relatively modest program of rewards would have less deleterious effects on performance. This was the case. Attendance did not drop when rewards were removed for the low reward group. Interpreta-

tion of the results for this group is somewhat confounded by the fact that attendance rates were initially slightly lower than for the high reward group. (The base rate for the low reward group was about 82 per cent, the rate during the reward period 88 per cent, and the rate after the reward period 90 per cent.) The investigators replicated the basic pattern of results, however, on a second population that was exposed to both of the reward treatments in succession: base period, low reward, withdrawal, second base period, high reward, second withdrawal. High reward had deleterious effects *both* during its maintenance and after its withdrawal, and low reward had beneficial effects during both maintenance and withdrawal.

It should be noted that the experiment by Bogart et al. was conducted as a test of dissonance theory, and that its design allows for a dissonance interpretation if the assumption is made that the introduction of low rewards serves to generate dissonance that may be reduced by changing attitudes toward the workshop in a more favorable direction. Furthermore, neither the Kiesler and Sakumura [1966] nor the Carlsmith and Lepper experiments were conducted as tests of anything like the present notion. In order directly to test the hypothesis that overly sufficient reward for behavior produces a decrement in the value placed on the behavior, Lepper, Greene and Nisbett [1971] performed the following experiment.[1]

Nursery school children were asked to draw pictures for an experimenter, using distinctive drawing materials: felt-tipped "magic marker" pens, and white, artist's quality, paper. One group of children, the Expected Reward group, was asked to draw the pictures in order to obtain a "Good Player" award, a

---

[1] At least one other investigator, however, has pursued this hypothesis intentionally, and independently. After this essay was written, Edward Deci [*Journal of Personality and Social Psychology*, 1971, *18,* pp. 105–115] reported an experiment conceptually similar to that of Bogart *et al.* Subjects were asked to solve puzzles for an experimenter. One group of subjects was paid on one occasion and not paid on a later occasion for solving the puzzles. Another group was never paid. During a "break" in each session, subjects were "left alone" for a few minutes to do whatever they wished, including continuing to work on the puzzles. The experimenter watched and recorded their behavior from behind a one-way mirror. Formerly paid subjects, at the final session, tended to spend less time working on the puzzles during the break than never-paid subjects. Deci ascribed this result to an undermining of the intrinsic motivation to solve the puzzles, as a consequence of having previously attempted to solve them in order to obtain an extrinsic reward.

certificate with a gold seal and ribbons and space to write the child's name and school. Other groups, the Unexpected Reward and Control groups, were offered no extrinsic reward for drawing the pictures. At the end of the drawing session, the experimenter praised the work of all children and gave a Good Player award to each child in the Expected Reward and Unexpected Reward conditions, writing the child's name on the award with a flourish and allowing the child to pin the award to an "Honor Roll" bulletin board. Several days later, all children were given several opportunities to use the distinctive drawing materials in the free-play situation of the nursery school. The drawing materials were made available by the nursery school teachers, and the children could either use them or work on a variety of other activities standard in the school. Observers watched the activity of each child from behind one-way mirrors. The dependent variable of interest was the percentage of time that children would spend drawing with the materials as a function of experimental condition.

It was anticipated that Expected Reward children would be less motivated to work with the drawing materials than other children. During the session with the experimenter, they should have had the cognition that they were drawing with these materials in order to obtain the extrinsic reward of the Good Player certificate. To the extent that this cognition was salient, it should have obscured intrinsic reasons for drawing. Unexpected Reward and Control subjects would have lacked this competing explanation and, when later offered the opportunity to use the materials, should not view them merely as "something to work with in order to get rewards." This anticipation was supported. Expected Reward children worked with the drawing materials in the test situation only about half as much as children in the other two groups. Apparently it is possible, at a very tender age, to undermine intrinsic motivation by extrinsic rewards.

If further work supports the overjustification hypothesis, it will cast doubt on traditional reinforcement theories in the same way that the dissonance-generated research on insufficient justification has. For example, the long-established tradition of rewarding school children with grades for scholastic performance and the newly established "token economies" for prisons, mental institutions, and schools might both become suspect if it could be shown that rewards often serve to undermine rather than "reinforce" attitudes. Of course, it is not likely that support for the overjustification hypothesis would require psychologists universally to condemn the ancient and widespread practice of giving rewards for desirable behavior. Overjustification research is likely to support only the limited hypothesis that rewards may undermine values in situations where it is possible to elicit behavior without resort to promises of large or arbitrary extrinsic rewards—i.e., where the intrinsic value of behavior is relatively high.

The similarity of the overjustification notion to the personal causation ideas of de Charms [1968] should be explicitly acknowledged. De Charms has proposed that it is of great importance whether the individual views himself as the origin of his behavior or as a pawn of the environment. The individual is likely to place little value on a given behavior if he perceives himself to be performing the behavior in order to receive some reward from the environment. The same behavior may be pleasurable and valuable, if the individual perceives himself to be performing it as an end in itself. The overjustification notion also overlaps somewhat with Zimbardo's [1966, 1969] notions of cognitive control. Zimbardo has argued that attitudes shift into line with behavior when the individual perceives himself to have chosen the behavior and fail to do so when the individual feels that the behavior is under the control of environmental contingencies and constraints.

In summary, it may be seen that three disparate research areas—the research on belief inference discussed in the first section, the entire body of insufficient justification research, and the foregoing "overly sufficient justification" research—can all be subsumed under one principle. *A belief inference may result from the observation of one's behavior if the behavior is perceived to have been elicited by one's intrinsic reaction to the stimulus toward which behavior was directed, but a belief inference will not result if the behavior is perceived to have been elicited by some aspect of the circumstances extrinsic to the stimulus.* In the next section we shall see that the principle can be extended to the case of autonomic behavior.

Inference of Feelings from Autonomic Behavior

Recent work on emotions by Schachter and his colleagues may profitably be viewed as evidence for a variant of Bem's basic proposition—to wit, that we infer our feelings from our autonomic behavior. This corollary of Bem's proposition has an intuitive appeal that is lacking in the original proposition. The corollary is implicit in such common observations as "I knew I was in love because my heart skipped a beat" or "I could tell I was angry because my face was flushed." The corollary also has considerable empirical support, as will be seen.

Information about Source of Arousal

The distinction between behavior perceived to be produced by the stimulus and that perceived to be produced by circumstances extrinsic to the stimulus is as crucial for autonomic behavior as for overt behavior. Whether an individual confronted with a given stimulus and a given level of arousal will be emotional or not depends on the degree to which he believes his arousal is produced by the stimulus. If the individual believes that his arousal is produced by the stimulus, he infers that he feels strongly about the stimulus and displays emotion toward it. If the individual believes that his arousal is produced by circumstances unrelated to the stimulus, he does not infer that he feels strongly about the stimulus, and is not likely to be emotional.

Schachter and Singer [1962], in their classic experiment, exposed subjects to one of two emotion-provoking stimulus situations. In one of the situations subjects were asked to fill out a questionnaire that asked insulting questions. An experimental confederate took the questionnaire at the same time, pacing himself to the subject's rate of answering items, and expressed outrage at appropriate points. In the other situation subjects were asked to wait in a room filled with potential playthings. An experimental confederate feigned a euphoric state and played with the objects, encouraging the subject to join in the fun. Prior to being placed in these situations, subjects were given one of three experimental treatments. Some of the subjects were given epinephrine (adrenalin), a drug that produces autonomic arousal. Other subjects were also given epinephrine but were informed that the drug would produce arousal symptoms. Finally, control subjects were injected only with a placebo.

The chief finding of the study was that subjects in the first group, the uninformed, epinephrine-injected group, tended to be more emotional than subjects exposed to either of the other treatments. The former subjects tended to be angrier in the anger-inducing situation and more euphoric in the euphoria-inducing conditions. In terms of Bem's proposition, the uninformed subjects given epinephrine may be said to have inferred from the fact that they were highly aroused that they were very angry at the experimenter or very amused by the confederate. The subjects injected with epinephrine but informed of this fact might be said to have failed to infer anything about their feelings toward social stimuli because they already had a satisfactory explanation of their arousal in terms that had nothing to do with those stimuli.

Put another way, the Schachter-Singer experiment shows that if two people have identical stimulus inputs and identical levels of arousal but differ in their belief about the degree to which the stimulus has produced the arousal, they will also differ in their evaluation of the stimulus. It is perhaps not too surprising that when arousal is exogenously produced, by a drug, and subjects are informed of this fact, they fail to infer that they are emotionally affected by the stimulus situation. It is less obvious that subjects might fail to infer that they are affected by a stimulus if they were exposed to a stimulus that *genuinely* produces arousal but were incorrectly informed that their arousal was produced by an extrinsic agent. In order to determine whether subjects could be led erroneously to attribute stimulus-produced arousal to an external source, Nisbett and Schachter [1966] attempted to persuade subjects that the autonomic arousal produced by electric shock was actually produced by a drug.

Nisbett and Schachter asked subjects to take a series of electric shocks of steadily increasing intensity, telling them to report when the shocks became painful and when they became too painful to tolerate. Just prior to the shock series, subjects were given a placebo pill. Some subjects were told that the pill would cause hand tremor, palpitations, and other autonomic arousal symptoms. Other subjects were told that the pill would cause a variety of physical symptoms not autonomic in nature. The investigators anticipated that, to a degree, subjects would judge the painfulness and tolerability of the shocks on the basis of the autonomic arousal the shocks produced. If so, then the subjects who were told they would experience autonomic arousal from the pill should have found the shocks more tolerable than other subjects, who could only assume their arousal was produced exclusively by the shock. This was the case. Subjects who thought their arousal was produced by the pill were willing to tolerate four times the shock amperage tolerated by other subjects.

The finding that subjects can be persuaded to attribute stimulus-produced arousal to an external source has been repeated several times. Using a technique similar to the Nisbett and Schachter manipulation, Ross, Rodin, and Zimbardo [1969] have produced a reduction in fear of anticipated electric shock. Their subjects were persuaded to attribute arousal accompanying fear of impending electric shock to a loud noise. Such subjects were found to work less hard at avoiding the shock than subjects who were not led to reattribute their arousal symptoms. A number of other investigators have produced re-evaluations of stimuli by cognitively shifting perceived causal origin of arousal [Dienstbier & Munter 1971, Hanson & Blechman 1970, O'Neal 1970, and Weiner & Valins 1970]. Emotions affected by such re-evaluations have ranged from the fear of being caught cheating on an exam to the enjoyableness of sexual intercourse.

Ross et al. suggested that the reattribution technique might have therapeutic uses. An experiment by Storms and Nisbett [1970] indicates that this suggestion is feasible. They asked subjects, all of whom were insomniacs, to take a pill before bedtime. Subjects were told that the pill (actually a placebo) would cause alertness, palpitation, and high body temperature—arousal symptoms that pretest subjects reported as characteristic of a night with insomnia. The investigators reasoned that insomnia is due in part to arousal caused by rehearsing emotional thoughts. The perception of arousal, in terms of the present line of reasoning, should lead to the inference that the emotional cognitions are quite powerful. This inference should in turn heighten emotionality. If the subject believes his arousal is caused by a pill, however, the perception of arousal should not result in an inference of emotionality, the cycle might be broken, and sleep should ensue. It was found that such subjects did in fact report getting to sleep more quickly on the nights when they took the pills. This and other possible therapeutic applications of the reattribution technique are discussed by Valins and Nisbett [1971].

The experiment by Storms and Nisbett also afforded a test of a second reattribution hypothesis, namely that a belief that arousal has been artificially reduced will lead to an inference that emotional cognitions are unusually powerful. They reasoned that if insomniac subjects believed themselves to be under the influence of a drug that was capable of *reducing* arousal, any arousal felt at bedtime might be taken as evidence that the emotional thoughts that were present were quite intense. Subjects would be expected to infer, in effect, "If I'm as aroused as this when a pill is supposed to be keeping me calm, then I must be very worked up." Some of their subjects were accordingly given placebos that they were told would serve to reduce alertness, body temperature, and heart rate. As expected, it took such subjects longer to get to sleep on the nights they took the pills than it had previously taken them. Apparently, it is

as easy for experimenters to strengthen attribution of arousal to the stimulus situation as it is to weaken such attributions.

The evidence is good then that people infer their feelings and attitudes from knowledge of their autonomic behavior. When subjects are artificially aroused, they infer that they have strong feelings about the salient stimulus, unless they are informed of the extrinsic origin of their arousal. When the stimulus is the actual source of arousal, subjects will fail to infer that they are strongly affected by it if they are led to believe that the arousal has an extrinsic origin. When subjects are led to believe that their arousal has been reduced by an extrinsic agent, and arousal level remains high, they infer that they are affected in a particularly strong way by the stimulus. Information and misinformation about the source of arousal can thus play a critical role in attitude inference and emotionality. As we shall see in the next section, misinformation about *degree* of arousal also affects attitudes and emotion.

Information about Degree of Arousal

In a series of studies Valins and his colleagues have explored the possibility that people will change their attitudes toward a stimulus on the basis of purely cognitive information about the arousal produced by the stimulus. Their work clearly supports this supposition. The research is also of value in helping to elucidate the process by which a belief inference takes place. It strongly indicates that the process is not by any means necessarily passive, but instead may involve quite active hypothesis-testing behavior as the individual attempts to understand and confirm new information about his behavior.

In the first study of the series, Valins [1966] showed slides of nude females to male college students. Dummy electrodes, which allegedly measured heart rate, were placed on the subjects and they were allowed to "overhear" their heart rates while they looked at the nudes. The heartbeats subjects heard were programmed so as to make it appear that heart rate altered radically in response to some slides and was unaffected by others. For some of the subjects the alteration was an increased heart rate and for others a decreased heart rate. Both groups rated the nudes more attractive when they heard a heart rate change than when they did not. At the end of the experiment, subjects were told that they could take some of the slides home with them. Most of the slides they chose had been accompanied by a heart rate change. Subjects apparently inferred that they were strongly attracted to the nudes they believed caused autonomic changes.

Some anecdotal data reported by Valins help to clarify the process by which attitude change toward the nudes takes place. Apparently, the changes reflect something more than the inference process that Bem has proposed and we have endorsed. When subjects heard the altered heart rate, they appeared to entertain the hypothesis (make the inference) that the nude was unusually attractive. Since the nudes were in fact quite attractive, it was usually possible for subjects to confirm this hypothesis: "Closer inspection simply showed them what their 'subconscious' knew all the time. The girl's breasts or buttocks were indeed nicer than they had thought" [p. 407]. When subjects could not confirm the hypothesis that the nude was unusually attractive, they sought other, nonemotional explanations of the heart rate change. They were likely to attribute their reactions to being startled out of a daydream, to a sudden fit of coughing, or to a slight resemblance of the nude to a former girl friend. Subjects appeared to accept the false arousal feedback as valid, in other words, but to infer that the nude was highly attractive to them only when this seemed plausible in view of the evidence. The validity of the inference was thus checked before it was completely accepted.

Subsequent studies of this phenomenon support the idea that there is a sequence of hypothesis formation and hypothesis confirmation that results in a changed feeling state. Valins [1972] examined the effect of debriefing on subjects' rating of nudes. After putting subjects through the slide presentation and false feedback procedure, Valins simply told subjects the truth —that they had not been listening to their heart rate at all, but to a preprogrammed tape recording. If changed attractiveness ratings in the original experiment were due to nothing more than a passive inference process, then debriefing might be expected to reverse the inference and thus destroy the difference in ratings. If, on the other hand, arousal information results in the inference or hypothesis that the nude is in fact highly attractive and this inference leads to testing behavior—looking for positive features of nudes—then one would not expect debriefing to have much effect on later ratings. The debriefing would not in itself undo the confirmatory results of the searching process. The actual findings were that debriefing had very little effect. Subjects who were told that the feedback was false still rated the nudes differentially as a function of feedback.

Another implication of the hypothesis-confirmation notion is that attractiveness ratings should be af-

fected by feedback only when there is ample opportunity to scan the nudes and therefore to confirm the hypothesis. If subjects do not have time to validate the inference that they are unusually attracted to the nude, then attractiveness ratings should be unaffected by feedback. Barefoot and Straub [1971] examined this possibility. Subjects were shown a series of ten slides and allowed to view each slide for thirty seconds. Subjects were then presented with five of the original ten slides and told that they consisted of "those slides which caused the greatest heart rate reaction during the first presentation." Some of the subjects were allowed to view each of these slides for a total of twenty-five seconds on two subsequent presentations and some for only ten seconds. If only a passive inference process were at work, the authors reasoned, the two exposure times would produce equal differences in ratings. If a relatively time-consuming, hypothesis-testing process were at work, on the other hand, the longer exposure time should produce a greater effect on evaluations. The results favored the hypothesis-testing view. Subjects given twenty-five seconds to view the slides rated "heart rate reaction" slides as more attractive than control slides. Subjects given only ten seconds rated such slides as no more attractive than control slides. The longer search time was therefore essential to changing the subjects' feelings toward the slides.

Other work indicates that similar inference processes operate when subjects are given information that their arousal level is *unaffected* by a stimulus. Valins and Ray [1967] asked subjects who were frightened of snakes to look at slides picturing various snakes. Interspersed among the snake slides were slides imprinted with the word "SHOCK." Seven seconds after presentation of shock slides, subjects received a mild electric shock to the fingers. Throughout this procedure subjects believed themselves to be hearing their own heart rate. In fact, they were listening to a prerecorded tape that made it sound as though heart rate were increasing when shock slides were flashed and not increasing when snake slides were flashed. The authors reasoned that subjects might infer from this arousal information that, while they were afraid of shocks, they were not afraid of snakes. After the slide presentation, subjects were asked to approach a thirty-inch boa constrictor. Experimental subjects were able to approach the snake more closely than control subjects who had gone through the same preliminary procedure but who did not believe the sounds they heard were produced by their own heartbeats. One would assume from this that experimental subjects had inferred that they were not as frightened of snakes as they had thought.

On the other hand, it is important to note that subjects were asked to report on their fear of snakes at the end of the slide exposure treatment, immediately before the approach task. Experimental subjects did not report themselves to be any less frightened of snakes than did control subjects. This fact suggests that something like an opportunity for hypothesis-confirmation is necessary for subjects in this feedback situation also. The "knowledge" that heart rate does not increase when viewing snake slides may have led subjects to the hypothesis "Maybe I am not as afraid of snakes as I thought." They then needed to test this hypothesis and thus approached the snake more closely. They may have failed to rate themselves as being less frightened of snakes because the ratings were obtained before they could test their hypothesis.

In summary, it appears that we infer our feelings about stimuli from information about the degree and source of autonomic arousal, even when that information is verbally supplied by an experimenter and even when it is false. There is evidence to suggest, however, that such inferences are not necessarily passive or immediately accepted. Instead, subjects may actively attempt to validate their inferences before encoding them as truth.

Behavioral Validation of Belief Inferences

The proposition that we infer our beliefs from our behavior assumes that behavior is an important source of information for the evaluative process. It may often be the case, however, that a brief sample of behavior will not provide *sufficient* information to produce an inference that will be accepted with any degree of confidence or persistence. In Kelley and Thibaut's [1971] terms, a brief sample of behavior may serve chiefly to introduce attributional instability and consequent information-seeking. It is an important consideration, then, whether an inference should be considered a statement of fact, "I enjoyed that task," or a statement that is more tentative and more like a hypothesis, "I must have enjoyed that task." The previous section reflects our view that an inference should often be considered as a hypothesis rather than a conclusion.

If we accept the view that inferences often function like hypotheses, there are some interesting implications for theory and research. First, the overt behavior of our subjects may not be a simple reflec-

tion of the internal state that we intended to manipulate but rather a reflection of the subjects' attempt to validate inferences about that state. This appears to have been the case in the Valins and Ray [1967] experiment on snake approach. Their subjects approached the snakes more closely after arousal feedback that indicated to them that they were not frightened of snakes. The subjects did not *report* themselves to be less frightened of snakes immediately after hearing the feedback, however. It therefore seems likely that the snake approach behavior was a validation attempt and not a reflection of a changed attitude.

A second implication of the view that inferences often function like hypotheses is that subjects may often need an opportunity to test their inferences before their inferences are translated into attitudes, beliefs, or feelings. This implication is essentially the view expressed by Weick that "behavior is more than an incidental accompaniment of attitudes. Behavior that occurs in close proximity to belief change or that is relevant to beliefs can validate, confirm, commit, disconfirm, stabilize or immunize. Behavior, in other words, is presumed to be an important determinant of the success of any attempt to change attitudes" [1966, p. 244]. That validation behavior may be essential to produce attitude change is indicated by the series of studies on manipulated attractiveness of nudes. In the absence of sufficient opportunity to scan the nudes [Barefoot & Straub 1971], heart rate feedback was ineffective in producing re-evaluation. The opportunity to adequately test the inference was apparently essential.

A third implication of the hypothesis-confirmation notion is that, as Weick proposes, behavior may often *disconfirm* inferences. There is some evidence that such a disconfirmation took place in the Davison and Valins [1969] experiment on shock toleration. In that experiment subjects who thought their increased shock toleration on the second series was self-produced (placebo subjects) were expected to infer that the shocks were now less painful to them. Such subjects did subsequently take more shock before announcing pain and before stopping than did control (drug) subjects. The hypothesis-confirmation notion leads us to believe that this increased shock-taking behavior was not an indication of diminished pain but rather an indication that subjects were taking more shock in an attempt to test the inference that the shocks had become less painful to them. That this test served to disconfirm their inferences is indicated by their subsequent ratings of sample shocks. Experimental subjects rated them no differently than did control subjects. It is easy to understand why the hypothesis held by these subjects should have been disconfirmed. On the first threshold test they had tolerated an average of about twenty-one shocks; on the second (while presumably under the influence of nothing but a placebo and while the intensities had been surreptitiously halved) they had tolerated forty-eight shocks; and on the third threshold they tolerated twenty-five shocks. Since their third threshold performance was considerably closer to their first than to their second, it is likely that any inference that they were more able to tolerate shock than they had thought would have been disconfirmed.

We would like to acknowledge that there are undoubtedly circumstances in which the observation of one's own behavior results in immediate and confident attitude change. This might be expected to occur when the behavior is dramatic and the link between belief and behavior direct and vivid. As experimenters, however, we are not always going to know when this is true, and the present considerations have some rather clear methodological implications. Where an attitude inference is held weakly, as a hypothesis, the individual would need an opportunity to test his inference and, once tested and confirmed, this inference would be reflected in attitudinal statements. Under these conditions, however, behavior change would not be a direct indicator of the individual's attitude but rather a measure of his attempt to validate his inference about his attitude. It should be clear, moreover, that the results of this testing behavior might be disconfirming. If so, we could be left with a situation, as in the Davison and Valins experiment, in which the behavior seems to reflect the predicted attitude yet the attitudinal statement does not.

A still more paradoxical situation is possible. We can conceive of conditions under which weak manipulations of attitude change might produce greater indications of behavior change than strong manipulations of attitude change. If the behavior under examination is more amenable to hypothesis-testing than it is to the expression of genuinely changed attitudes, then subjects who hold this attitude with little confidence might manifest more of the behavior than subjects who hold the attitude with much confidence. It is quite possible that if the attitude of the low confidence subject is confirmed by his behavioral test, then he might subsequently express attitudes equal in strength to those of the subject who initially held the attitude with much confidence. If the behavior

validation attempt disconfirms the hypothesis, then the most paradoxical pattern of all would result: subjects who are most likely to display the behavior would be least likely to express attitudes in line with the behavior. An important task facing investigators in this area is to determine those conditions where hypothesis-testing behavior will occur and to differentiate such behavior from behavior that expresses attitudes that are more firmly held.

The Scope of Self-Perception Phenomena

Thus far we have dealt with the question of self-perception in arbitrarily restricted ways. We have dealt exclusively with errors in self-perception and we have spoken primarily in terms of Bem's proposition that we infer our beliefs from our behavior. Our exclusive concern with error has occurred because (1) most of the research has used manipulations designed to produce errors; (2) such experimentally produced errors are an excellent way of discovering the way attribution processes work—one of the best techniques for understanding a process is to systematically interfere with its operation; and (3) failures in self-perception are perhaps inherently more interesting than successes. There is less justification for our narrow theoretical concern, however, and in this section we shall take steps to broaden the theoretical base of the topic of self-perception.

A little thought reveals that Bem's proposition rests on two assumptions: (1) we do not have fixed or completely independent knowledge of our attitudes and feelings; (2) we do not have infallible or direct knowledge of the causes of our behavior. If we knew our feelings about objects independently of our behavior toward them, observation of our behavior could not influence our feelings. If we knew exactly why we behaved as we do, we would by definition know the role played by our beliefs, and our beliefs would be uninfluenced by observation of our behavior.

This starting point makes it somewhat easier to broaden the scope of inquiry into self-perception. It should be clear that there are at least two other elements in the attitude-behavior cycle where knowledge is sometimes lacking and where errors can be introduced. These are beliefs about the behavior itself (what was done, or with what intensity) and the consequences of behavior (what were the environmental effects—success or failure, reaction of the

recipient of the action, and so on). We would propose that *knowledge about any one of these elements
—the behavior, its causes, its consequences, and feelings about the object toward which behavior was
directed—can influence the perception of any of the
others.*

It is relatively easy to classify the research to date
in terms of these four elements. None of the studies
measured effects on the perception of any of our four
elements other than feelings about the object toward
which behavior was directed. The bulk of the research has involved manipulations only of the perceived *cause* of behavior. Thus, Bandler, Madaras,
and Bem manipulated the perceived cause of escape
behavior (either experimenter's request plus subject's own desire to escape shocks or the experimenter's demand) and Davison and Valins manipulated
the perceived cause of increased ability to tolerate
shock (either a drug or the subject's own new-found
reaction to shock). Nisbett and Schachter, and
Storms and Nisbett, similarly manipulated the perceived cause of autonomic behavior (either a drug
or the subject's intrinsic response to the salient stimulus). The rest of the research has involved manipulation of the perceived *intensity* or *meaning of
behavior.* Thus, Schachter and Singer's experiment
and Valins' series of feedback studies employed a
manipulation of the perceived intensity of autonomic
behavior. Kiesler, Nisbett, and Zanna's "sidewalk persuasion" study employed a manipulation of the perceived meaning of behavior: the stooge defined the
behavior either as proselytizing or as assistance in a
scientific investigation.

The failure to measure changes in anything but
feelings about the object toward which behavior was
directed leaves serious gaps in the literature on self-
perception. The failure to manipulate anything but
the perceived cause and perceived intensity or meaning of behavior leaves additional gaps. There are
several indications from the literature on perception
of others that manipulation and measurement of other
elements would yield interesting payoffs. For example, Walster [1966] has shown that manipulation
of the perceived consequences of behavior (serious
versus minor harm to another) results in differential
perception of the causes of behavior (criminal negli-
gence versus forgivable thoughtlessness). It seems
likely that such demonstrations will turn out to have
parallels in self-perception.

To illustrate the mutual influence that the various
elements of self-perception might be expected to have
on one another, it will be helpful to draw on the

simple event used by Abelson [1968] to elucidate his
theory of psychological implication. "Jim gave flowers
to Amy. Amy was pleased." Let us say that shortly
before Jim leaves to visit Amy his sister sees him with
the flowers and says, "Oh, I see you're trying to make
up to Amy for forgetting to ask her to the prom." It
is possible that this manipulation of perceived cause
might affect Jim's beliefs about the meaning of his
behavior, the consequences of it, and his attitudes
toward Amy. Rather than thinking of his behavior as
a token of his affection he might think of it as a peace
offering; rather than perceiving Amy as being
touched by his gesture he might perceive her as mol-
lified by it; and rather than inferring greater love
for Amy from his behavior he might infer greater fear
of her wrath.

Similarly, if Jim overhears Amy's mother whisper
to a neighbor, "My, my, Jim gave her roses. Tom only
gave her carnations," we might expect this manipulation of the perceived intensity or meaning of behavior
to have effects on Jim's perception of the causes (he
may perceive his desire to please as greater) and
consequences of behavior (Amy may be perceived
as more thrilled), and on his perception of his attitudes toward Amy (he may infer greater love for
Amy).

Or, if Amy were to show the greatest delight over
the gift that Jim had ever seen her express, this
manipulation of perceived consequences might be
expected to affect Jim's perceptions of the cause and
intensity of his own behavior (it was a love offering
instead of a token of esteem) and to affect his perception of his feelings toward Amy (she is not merely
esteemed but beloved).

Finally, if Amy were to wear a subtle and intoxi-
cating perfume and look particularly attractive on
the evening of the flowers, this manipulation of attitude toward Amy might be expected to affect Jim's
beliefs about the cause and intensity of his behavior
(his gesture was as chivalrous as her form is fair) as
well as its consequences (Amy's radiance was perhaps produced by the gift).

While the foregoing paints a slightly terrifying and
admittedly exaggerated picture of man at the mercy
of overheard conversations, our point is hopefully
made. Research in the area of self-perception has
been arbitrarily restricted up to the present. In terms
of the present analysis, the research has been concerned exclusively with the effects on attitudes of
manipulations of the perceived causes of behavior
and manipulations of the perceived intensity and
meaning of behavior. The analysis of the act sequence

into cause, behavior, consequences, and attitudes is itself arbitrary (see the somewhat different analysis of Jones and Nisbett [1971]), but it serves to show that research to date has been unnecessarily narrow and that there are undoubtedly some interesting self-perception phenomena waiting in the wings.

Summary and Conclusions

People appear to infer their beliefs and feelings from observations both of their own overt behavior and their own autonomic behavior. Purely cognitive information about behavior, supplied by an experimenter, is sufficient to produce an attitude inference. The inference resulting from observation of behavior may apparently take the form of a hypothesis that the individual attempts to confirm. These attempts at confirmation may or may not be successful, resulting sometimes in a changed attitude and sometimes in a retrenchment of the prior attitude.

The individual's perception of the causal origin of his behavior appears to be crucial. If he considers his behavior toward a stimulus to be produced chiefly by his attitude toward it, a belief inference is likely to result from observation of that behavior. If he perceives his behavior to be produced by circumstantial factors extrinsic to the stimulus, a belief inference is not likely. It was proposed that the more an individual perceives his behavior to be produced or justified by factors extrinsic to the stimulus, the less likely he will be to infer that his attitudes toward the stimulus are congruent with his behavior. One implication of this proposal is that it is possible to overly justify behavior, thereby undercutting attitudes toward an object by overrewarding behavior toward it.

Finally, it was suggested that the phenomena of self-perception have been explored only very sketchily. It seems plausible that any new information about an element in the attitude-behavior cycle might affect perceptions of every other element in the cycle.

BIBLIOGRAPHY

Robert P. Abelson, "Psychological implication." In R. P. Abelson, E. Aronson, W. J. McGuire, T. M. Newcomb, M. J. Rosenberg, and P. H. Tannenbaum, eds., *Theories of Cognitive Consistency: A Sourcebook*. Rand McNally, 1968.

Eliot Aronson and J. Merrill Carlsmith, "Effect of the Severity of Threat on the Devaluation of Forbidden Behavior." *Journal of Personality and Social Psychology*, 1963, 66:584–588.

Richard J. Bandler, George R. Madaras, and Daryl J. Bem, "Self-Observation as a Source of Pain Perception." *Journal of Personality and Social Psychology*, 1968, 9:205–209.

John C. Barefoot and Ronald B. Straub, "Opportunity for Information Search and the Effect of False Heart Rate Feedback." *Journal of Personality and Social Psychology*, 1971, 17:154–157.

Daryl J. Bem, "An Experimental Analysis of Self-Persuasion." *Journal of Experimental Social Psychology*, 1965, 1:199–218.

Daryl J. Bem, "Self-Perception: An Alternative Interpretation of Cognitive Dissonance Phenomena." *Psychological Review*, 1967, 74:183–200.

Karen Bogart, Armin Loeb, and Irvin D. Rutman, "Behavioral Consequences of Cognitive Dissonance." Paper read at Eastern Psychological Association meeting, 1969.

Jack W. Brehm and Arthur R. Cohen, *Explorations in Cognitive Dissonance*. Wiley, 1962.

Gerald G. Davison and Stuart Valins, "Maintenance of Self-Attributed and Drug-Attributed Behavior Change." *Journal of Personality and Social Psychology*, 1969, 11:25–33.

Richard de Charms, *Personal Causation: The Internal Affective Determinants of Behavior*. Academic Press, 1968.

Richard A. Dienstbier and Pamela O. Munter, "Cheating as a Function of the Labeling of Natural Arousal." *Journal of Personality and Social Psychology*, 1971, 17:208–213.

Leon Festinger and J. Merrill Carlsmith, "Cognitive Consequences of Forced Compliance." *Journal of Abnormal and Social Psychology*, 1956, 52:384–389.

L. Reid Hanson and Elaine Blechman, "The Labeling Process During Sexual Intercourse." Unpublished manuscript, U.C.L.A., 1970.

Fritz Heider, *The Psychology of Interpersonal Relations*. Wiley, 1958.

Edward E. Jones and Kenneth E. Davis, "From Acts to Dispositions: The Attribution Process in Person Perception." In L. Berkowitz, ed., *Advances in Experimental Social Psychology*, Vol. 2. Academic Press, 1965.

Edward E. Jones and Richard E. Nisbett, "The Actor and the Observer: Divergent Perceptions of the Causes of Behavior." General Learning Press, 1971. Also in E. E.

Jones, D. E. Kanouse, H. H. Kelley, R. E. Nisbett, S. Valins, and B. Weiner, *Attribution: Perceiving the Causes of Behavior*. General Learning Press, 1971.

Harold H. Kelley, "Attribution in Social Interaction." General Learning Press, 1971. Also in E. E. Jones, D. E. Kanouse, H. H. Kelley, R. E. Nisbett, S. Valins, and B. Weiner, *Attribution: Perceiving the Causes of Behavior*, General Learning Press, 1971.

Harold H. Kelley, "Attribution Theory in Social Psychology." *Nebraska Symposium on Motivation*, 1967, 14: 192–241.

Harold H. Kelley and John W. Thibaut, "Group Problem Solving." In G. Lindzey and E. Aronson, eds., *Handbook of Social Psychology*. Addison-Wesley, 1971.

Charles A. Kiesler, Richard E. Nisbett, and Mark P. Zanna, "On Inferring One's Beliefs from One's Behavior." *Journal of Personality and Social Psychology*, 1969, 11:321–327.

Charles A. Kiesler and Joseph Sakamura, "A Test of a Model for Commitment." *Journal of Personality and Social Psychology*, 1966, 3:349–353.

Douglas H. Lawrence and Leon Festinger, *Deterrents and Reinforcements*. Stanford University Press, 1962.

Mark R. Lepper, David Greene, and Richard E. Nisbett, "How to Undermine Intrinsic Motivation by Extrinsic Rewards." Unpublished manuscript, Stanford University, 1971.

Richard E. Nisbett and Stanley Schachter, "Cognitive Manipulation of Pain." *Journal of Experimental Social Psychology*, 1966, 2:227–236.

Edgar O'Neal, "The Influence of Future Choice Importance and Arousal upon the Halo Effect." In H. London and R. Nisbett, eds., *The Cognitive Alteration of Feeling States*. Aldine, in press.

Lee D. Ross, Judith Rodin, and Philip G. Zimbardo, "Toward an Attribution Therapy: The Reduction of Fear Through Induced Cognitive-Emotional Misattribution." *Journal of Personality and Social Psychology*, 1969, 12:279–288.

Stanley Schachter and Jerome E. Singer, "Cognitive, Social and Physiological Determinants of Emotional State." *Psychological Review*, 1962, 69:379–399.

B. F. Skinner, *Verbal Behavior*. Appleton-Century-Crofts, 1957.

Michael D. Storms and Richard E. Nisbett, "Insomnia and the Attribution Process." *Journal of Personality and Social Psychology*, 1970, 16:319–328.

Stuart Valins, "Cognitive Effects of False Heart-Rate Feed-back." *Journal of Personality and Social Psychology*, 1966, 4:400–408.

Stuart Valins, "Persistent Effects of Information about Internal Reactions: Ineffectiveness of Debriefing." In H. London and R. E. Nisbett, eds., *The Cognitive Alteration of Feeling States*. Aldine, in press.

Stuart Valins and Richard E. Nisbett, "Attribution Processes in the Development and Treatment of Emotional Disorders." General Learning Press, 1971. Also in E. E. Jones, D. E. Kanouse, H. H. Kelley, R. E. Nisbett, S. Valins, and B. Weiner, *Attribution: Perceiving the Causes of Behavior*. General Learning Press, 1971.

Stuart Valins and Alice A. Ray, "Effects of Cognitive Desensitization on Avoidance Behavior." *Journal of Personality and Social Psychology*, 1967, 7:345–350.

Elaine Walster, "Assignment of Responsibility for an Accident." *Journal of Personality and Social Psychology*, 1966, 3:73–79.

Karl E. Weick, "Task Acceptance Dilemmas: A Site for Research on Cognition." In S. Feldman, ed., *Cognitive Consistency*. Academic Press, 1966.

M. J. Weiner and Stuart Valins, "Misattribution of Physiological and Psychological Arousal." Unpublished manuscript, 1970.

Philip G. Zimbardo, "The Cognitive Control of Motivation." *Transactions of the New York Academy of Sciences*, 1966, 28:902–922.

Philip G. Zimbardo, ed., *The Cognitive Control of Motivation*. Scott, Foresman, 1969.

[*This paper grew out of a workshop on attribution theory held at UCLA in August 1969, supported by Grant GS-2613 from the National Science Foundation. The paper was written while Richard Nisbett was supported by a Morse Faculty Fellowship from Yale University and a National Science Foundation postdoctoral fellowship. The writing of the paper and some of the research reviewed was facilitated by NSF Grant 2587 to Nisbett and by NIMH Grant 14557 to Valins.*]

5 · The Actor and the Observer: Divergent Perceptions of the Causes of Behavior

EDWARD E. JONES
Duke University

RICHARD E. NISBETT
University of Michigan

When a student who is doing poorly in school discusses his problem with a faculty adviser, there is often a fundamental difference of opinion between the two. The student, in attempting to understand and explain his inadequate performance, is usually able to point to environmental obstacles such as a particularly onerous course load, to temporary emotional stress such as worry about his draft status, or to a transitory confusion about life goals that is now resolved. The faculty adviser may nod and may wish to believe, but in his heart of hearts he usually disagrees. The adviser is convinced that the poor performance is due neither to the student's environment nor to transient emotional states. He believes instead that the failure is due to enduring qualities of the student—to lack of ability, to irremediable laziness, to neurotic ineptitude.

When Kitty Genovese was murdered in view of thirty-nine witnesses in Queens, social scientists, the press, and the public marveled at the apathy of the residents of New York and, by extension, of urban America. Yet it seems unlikely that the witnesses themselves felt that their failure to intercede on the woman's behalf was due to apathy. At any rate, interviewers were unable to elicit comments from the witnesses on the order of "I really didn't care if she lived or died." Instead, the eyewitnesses reported that they had been upset, but felt that there was nothing they could or needed to do about a situation that in any case was ambiguous to them.

In their autobiographies, former political leaders often report a different perspective on their past acts from that commonly held by the public. Acts perceived by the public to have been wise, planful, courageous, and imaginative on the one hand, or unwise, haphazard, cowardly, or pedestrian on the other, are often seen in quite a different light by the autobiographer. He is likely to emphasize the situational constraints at the time of the action—the role limitations, the conflicting pressures brought to bear, the alternative paths of action that were never open or that were momentarily closed—and to perceive his actions as having been inevitable. "Wise moves" and "blunders" alike are often viewed by the leader as largely inescapable under the circumstances. The public is more inclined to personalize causation for success and failure. There are good leaders who can cope with what the situation brings and bad leaders who cannot.

In each of these instances, the actor's perceptions of the causes of his behavior are at variance with those held by outside observers. The actor's view of his behavior emphasizes the role of environmental conditions at the moment of action. The observer's view emphasizes the causal role of stable dispositional properties of the actor. We wish to argue that *there is a pervasive tendency for actors to attribute their actions to situational requirements, whereas observers tend to attribute the same actions to stable personal dispositions.* This tendency often stems in part from the actor's need to justify blameworthy action, but may also reflect a variety of other factors having nothing to do with the maintenance of self-esteem. We shall emphasize these other, more cognitive factors but include also a consideration of the role of self-justification.

The proposition that actors attribute their behavior to situational constraints while observers attribute the behavior to dispositions of the actor is best characterized, perhaps, as an actuarial proposition. We acknowledge at the outset that there are undoubtedly many exceptions. In our opinion, though, there are good theoretical reasons for believing that the proposition is generally correct. We wish to explore what we believe to be powerful cognitive forces impelling actors to attribute their behavior to the environment and observers to attribute that same behavior to characteristics of the actor. The proposition has not been fully tested, but there are a few experiments that provide data consistent with it. We will now describe these experiments in order to supplement our selected anecdotes.

Experimental Evidence Consistent with the Proposition

Jones, Rock, Shaver, Goethals, and Ward [1968] compared the attributions made by actor-subjects with those made by observer-subjects in a rigged IQ testing situation. To collect their observer data, Jones et al. asked each subject and an accomplice to take an IQ test "designed to discriminate at the very highest levels of intelligence." The items were quite difficult and some were insoluble. Success and failure feedback for both the accomplice and the subject was reported after each item. The items were ambiguous enough to permit feedback that bore no necessary relation to the performance of the subject. The pattern of "successes" was such that at the end of the series the subject believed he had solved ten of the thirty items, with success scattered randomly throughout the test. In one of the experimental conditions, it was made to appear that the accomplice had solved fifteen randomly scattered problems. In another condition, it was also made to appear that the accomplice solved fifteen problems, but many more of the initial problems were solved than final problems. In a third condition, the accomplice again solved fifteen problems, but he had many more successes at the end than at the beginning. Special pains were taken to assure the subjects that the items were of equal difficulty, and the evidence suggests these assurances were accepted.

Whether the accomplice solved more problems at the beginning of the series (descending condition) or at the end (ascending condition) had a pronounced influence on (*a*) the subject's recall of the accomplice's performance, (*b*) the subject's prediction about the number of problems the accomplice would solve on a later, similar series, and (*c*) the subject's estimate of the accomplice's intelligence. If the accomplice solved a great many problems at the beginning of the series, the subject perceived him as more intelligent, distorted his overall performance on the test in a more favorable direction, and predicted that he would do better on the later series than if the accomplice solved few problems at the beginning. For most of the measures, in most of the variations of the experiment reported by Jones et al., the randomly successful accomplice was judged to be intermediate between the descending and ascending accomplices.

Jones et al. interpreted their data as evidence of a strong primacy effect in the attribution of ability: early information was weighted heavily and later evidence was essentially ignored [see Jones & Goethals 1971]. For our purposes, the important point is that ability attributions were made at all. This fact serves as the background against which to evaluate the results of a variation in which the tables were turned and the accomplice randomly solved the ten problems while the subject solved fifteen problems, either in random order, in descending order, or in ascending order.

When the feedback patterns were thus reassigned, the results were markedly different. In the descending and ascending conditions it was apparently impossible for the subjects to resist the conclusion, despite the experimenter's initial disclaimer, that the item difficulty had changed over the series. Descending subjects believed that the items got more difficult and ascending subjects believed they got less difficult. These beliefs apparently affected subjects' expectations about their performance on a future series. Ascending subjects predicted they would do better on the later series than did descending subjects, completely reversing the direction of observers' predictions. As would be expected, subjects' judgments about their own intellectual ability were unaffected by the experimental manipulations.

The pattern of attributions is therefore quite different for actor and observer. In identical situations, the actor attributes performance to variations in task difficulty, the observer to variations in ability.

The experiments by Jones et al. present data for actors and observers in identical situations. Another set of experiments, while lacking data on actors themselves, indicates that observers are remarkably inclined to see behavior in dispositional terms. Three experiments were conducted by Jones and Harris [1967]. In the first of these they asked their college student subjects to read essays or listen to speeches presumably written by fellow students. Subjects were asked to give their estimates of the communicator's real opinions. They were told either that the communicator had been assigned one side of the issue or that he had been completely free to choose a side. It is the "no choice" conditions that are of most interest to us here. In one case the impression of no choice was created by telling subjects they were reading essays written for a political science course in which the instructor had required the students to write, for example, a "short cogent defense of Castro's Cuba." In another experiment subjects believed they were reading the opening statement by a college debater whose adviser had directed him to argue a specified side of the Castro topic. In a third experiment subjects believed they were hearing a tape recording of a subject in a psychology experiment who had been instructed to give a speech favoring or opposing segregation. Questionnaire responses showed that subjects easily distinguished between choice and no choice conditions in the degree of choice available to the communicator.

Despite the fact that the subjects seem to have clearly perceived the heavy constraints on the communicator in the no choice conditions, their estimates of the true opinions of the communicator were markedly affected by the particular position espoused. When subjects read an essay or speech supporting Castro's Cuba, they inferred that the communicator was pro-Castro. If the communication opposed Castro's Cuba, they inferred that the communicator was anti-Castro. Across the three experiments, the effect of taking a pro versus anti stand was a highly significant determinant of attributed attitude in no choice conditions, though the effect of position taken was roughly twice as great when the communicator had complete choice.

These results are extremely interesting if they may be taken as evidence that observers attach insufficient weight to the situational determinants of behavior and attribute it, on slim evidence, to a disposition of the actor. It may be, however, that something about the content of the speeches caused the subjects to infer that the communicator actually held the opinion he was advocating. If the communications were quite eloquent and drew on esoteric sources of knowledge, it would not be surprising to learn that observers inferred that the communicator held the opinion he was delivering. This does not seem to be the proper explanation of the results, however, in view of the following facts: (*a*) the communications were designed to be "neither polished nor crude;" "of a C+ quality" in the case of the political science essay; (*b*) in each experiment it was made clear that subjects had access to study materials to help them formulate their arguments; (*c*) in a later series of experiments, Snyder (unpublished data) found that when the communications used were the actual products of students under no choice conditions, the same effects found by Jones and Harris were obtained. A crucial feature of Snyder's experiments was that each subject wrote a no choice essay himself, to be delivered to another subject. Thus the subjects should have been clearly aware of the constraints involved and of the ease or difficulty of generating arguments for a position opposite to that privately held.

The Jones and Harris experiment provides evidence, then, that observers are willing to take behavior more or less at "face value," as reflecting a stable disposition, even when it is made clear that the actor's behavior is under severe external constraints. These results have been replicated both by Snyder and more recently by Jones, Worchel, Goethals, and Grumet [1971] with "legalization of marijuana" as the issue.

A second study providing data for observers only has been performed by McArthur [1970]. Her study is quite relevant to our proposition if one is willing to lean heavily on intuitions about the causal attributions that would be expected of actors. Subjects were given a simple, one-sentence description of an action, such as "George translates the sentence incorrectly,"

"While dancing, Ralph trips over Jane's feet," "Steve puts a bumper sticker advocating improved automobile safety on his car." They were then asked why this action probably occurred: Whether it was something about the *person* that caused him to act this way ("Something about *George* probably caused him to translate the sentence incorrectly"), or something about the *stimulus* ("Something about the *sentence* probably caused George to translate it incorrectly"), or something about the *situation* ("Something about the *particular circumstances* probably caused George to translate it incorrectly"). If subjects found none of these simple explanations to be the likely one, they were allowed to give whatever explanation they thought necessary to account for the behavior. These were then coded into complex explanations involving both person and stimulus, both person and circumstances, both stimulus and circumstances, or all three. (As it happened, only the person-stimulus combination was resorted to with very great frequency.)

It seems likely that if one were to ask a random sample of people who had mistranslated sentences, tripped over feet, or placed bumper stickers on their cars why they had performed their various actions, a rather high fraction of explanations would be pure stimulus attributions or mixed stimulus-circumstance attributions. We would expect answers such as "That sentence was difficult to translate," "It was dark and Jane doesn't cha-cha the way I do," "The AAA sent me this catchy bumper sticker in the mail." For McArthur's vicarious observers, however, such reasons were extremely infrequent, amounting to only 4 per cent of the total attributions. By far the greatest proportion of reasons given—44 per cent for each of these particular actions—were pure *person* attributions: George translates the sentence incorrectly because he is rather poor at translating sentences and Steve is the sort who puts bumper stickers on his car.

McArthur also presented her subjects with statements about emotional experiences, such as "John laughs at the comedian," "Sue is afraid of the dog," "Tom is enthralled by the painting." One would expect that in a random sample of people found laughing at comedians, being frightened by dogs, or being enthralled by paintings, most of the actors would explain their experiences in pure stimulus terms: The comedian is funny; the dog is scary; the painting is beautiful. For McArthur's observers, however, only 19 per cent of the attributions were pure stimulus attributions and the most frequent attributions (45 per cent of the total) were *person-stimulus interactions:* "Sue tends to be afraid of dogs and this is a very large one." Interestingly, one of the emotion items did produce a very high proportion (52 per cent) of pure stimulus attributions: "Mary is angered

by the psychology experiment." Since subjects were at that moment participating in a psychology experiment, it is tempting to conclude that they were responding as actors rather than as observers.

It is possible that some unintended feature of McArthur's highly artificial situation forced attributions away from the stimulus and toward the person. Perhaps a different sample of statements or a more extended account of the behavior would yield different results. Nevertheless, the willingness of her subjects to invoke explanations involving dispositions of the person seems striking. One's strong intuition is that the actors themselves in real-life situations of the type described to McArthur's subjects would rarely interpret their behavior in dispositional terms.

McArthur [1970] completed a second experiment that is less open to criticism on methodological grounds. Subjects were induced to perform a particular act and a written account of the actor and the surrounding circumstances was presented to observers. It was then possible to compare the attributions made by the actor subjects with the later attributions made by observer subjects. McArthur obtained the consent of subjects to participate in a survey concerning interpersonal relationships and then asked the subjects why they had agreed to participate. As we would expect, subjects were inclined to attribute their participation to the importance of the survey and were not likely to attribute their participation to a general disposition to take part in such surveys. Observers exactly reversed this pattern, attributing subjects' participation primarily to a personal inclination to take part in surveys and only secondarily to the value of the survey.

McArthur's study comes very close to being a direct test of the proposition that actors attribute cause to situations while observers attribute cause to dispositions. It suffers, however, from the interpretive difficulty that information about the actor's behavior was given to observers only in printed, verbal form. Two studies by Nisbett and his colleagues avoided this problem by examining situations where more nearly equivalent forms of information were available to actors and observers.

In the first of these studies, Nisbett and Caputo [1971] asked college students to write a brief paragraph stating why they had chosen their major field of concentration and why they liked the girl they dated most frequently. Subjects were asked to write similar brief paragraphs explaining why their best friends had chosen their majors and girl friends. It proved possible to code all of the answers, à la McArthur, into either stimulus attributions ("Chemistry is a high-paying field," "She's a very warm person") or person attributions ("I want to make a lot of money," "I like warm girls"). When answering for himself, the average subject listed roughly the same number of stimulus and person reasons for choosing his major and twice as many stimulus as person reasons for choosing his girl friend. When answering for his best friend, subjects listed approximately three times as many person as stimulus reasons for choosing the major and roughly the same number of stimulus as person reasons for choosing the girl friend. Thus, when describing either choice of a major or choice of a girl friend, subjects were more likely to use dispositional language for their best friends than for themselves.

In a final study, Nisbett, Legant, and Marecek [1971] allowed observer subjects to watch actor subjects in a controlled laboratory setting. Subjects were Yale coeds. Those designated as actors believed they were to participate in a study on decision making. Subjects designated as observers believed their task would be to watch the subject make decisions and then make judgments about the subject's reasons for making her decisions. Prior to the fictitious decision-making study, the experimenter met with the actor and two confederates who presumably also were going to be subjects in the decision-making study. The observer sat in the background, with instructions simply to observe the (real) target subject. The experimenter, after some introductions and throat-clearing, said, "Before we begin the study, I happen to have sort of a real decision for you to make." The experimenter explained that the "Human Development Institute" at Yale would be sponsoring a weekend for the corporate board and some of their prospective financial backers. The wives of these men would need entertainment and campus tours for the weekend. As a consequence, the Institute had asked the psychology department to recruit students to help with this chore. After elaborating on details of time, place, and specific activities, the experimenter solicited the help of the two confederates and the actor. The confederates were always asked first, and, in order to boost compliance rates on the part of actors, always willingly volunteered.

The amount of money offered to volunteers was manipulated—either $.50 per hour or $1.50 per hour—with very large effects on compliance rates. Only about a fifth of the low-payment actors volunteered, while two-thirds of the high-payment actors volunteered. Volunteers' rates were thus determined in a major way by a purely extrinsic factor: the amount of money offered for compliance.

Actor and observer were then led to separate rooms where they were asked detailed questions concerning the actor's reasons for volunteering or not volunteering. The questions included an item designed to tap the extent to which the actor's behavior was considered an expression of a general disposition to volunteer or not volunteer for worthy activities: "How likely do you think it is that you (or the subject) would also volunteer to canvass for the United Fund?" Observers of volunteering actors thought that the actors would be more likely to volunteer for the United Fund than observers of nonvolunteering actors. Actors themselves did not think they were any more likely to help the United Fund if they were volunteers than if they were nonvolunteers. Thus, in this experimental situation, observers infer dispositions from observation of the actor's behavior, while actors themselves do not.

This last experiment is useful in pointing out the relationship between our proposition and the proposal by Bem [1965, 1967] emphasizing the *convergent* perceptions of actors and observers. In all important respects, according to Bem, people use the same kinds of evidence and follow the same logic whether they are making self-attributions or deciding about the characteristics of others. Actors are self-observers, viewing their own behavior in terms of the surrounding context and inferring what their attitudes and feelings must have been. We agree that actors often reflect on their own actions to check on the direction and intensity of their attitudes and feelings, but contend that actors are much more likely than observers to see those actions as constrained by the situations. We feel it is frequently the case that, as in the experiment just described, observers make dispositional inferences from behavior that is interpreted quite differently by actors. To support this contention we shall now examine what we believe to be differences in the information available to actor and observer and differences between the two in the processing of the available information.

The Information Available to Actor and Observer

It is a truism that the meaning of an action can be judged only in relation to its context. It is central to our argument that the context data are often quite different for actor and observer and that these differing data prompt differing attributions. The kinds of data available for the attribution process may be conveniently broken down into effect data and cause data. Effect data are of three broad types: data about the nature of the act itself (what was done), data about the environmental outcomes of the act (success or failure, reaction of the recipient of action, and so on), and data about the actor's experiences (pleasure, anger, embarrassment). Cause data are of two broad types: environmental causes (incentives, task difficulty) and intention data (what the actor meant to do, how hard he was working to do it). This categorization is useful for pinpointing the areas where discrepancies are likely to occur in the information available to actor and observer.

Effect Data

Under the category of effect data, it seems clear that actor and observer can have equivalent information about the nature of the act and about environmental outcomes. The observer may know that the actor has delivered an insult and that the recipient is angered. The observer can, however, have no direct knowledge of the experiential accompaniments of the act for the actor. The observer's knowledge about the actor's feelings is limited to inferences of two types: attempts to read inner experience from physiognomic and gestural cues, and judgments based on the observer's knowledge of what others and he himself have felt in similar situations. The observer may infer from the actor's flushed face that he spoke in anger, or he may guess that an insult of the type delivered would probably only be spoken by someone in a great rage. Of course, expressive behavior may not be witnessed by the observer at all. If it is not, then he simply has no information on this score. If it is, his knowledge of the experience of the actor may range from superior in rare cases—a parent may know better than his child that the child is disappointed over a failure or frightened of moving to a strange city—to quite inferior or utterly wrong. In many circumstances actors are motivated to conceal their inner feelings. In others, misperceptions derive from unrecognized individual differences in expressive style. Knowledge of the actor's feeling states is therefore never direct, usually sketchy, and sometimes wrong.

Cause Data

Under the category of perceived causes, it seems clear that there can be equal or nearly equal knowledge of the proximal environmental stimuli operating on the actor. The observer, for example, may know that the recipient of the actor's insult had previously taunted the actor. In principle such knowledge can be as complete for the observer as for the actor. In practice such completeness is probably rarely approximated, if only because of the likelihood that the actor is responding to events more extended in time than those available to the observer. The particular taunt that triggered the actor's outburst may have been the straw that broke the camel's back—the latest in a series of frustrations. The observer is more likely to work instead with the data from one slice of time.

Even so, the discrepancy in information about the causal role of the environment is probably rarely as great as the discrepancy in knowledge about the experiential accompaniments of the action. Nor is the discrepancy as great as it is with the second type of data concerning causality—the intentions of the actor.

Like the actor's feeling states, his intentions can never be directly known to the observer. In attempting to determine whether the insult was a spontaneous outburst produced by rage or a calculated move to embarrass and motivate the recipient, the observer may infer intentions from the actor's expressive behavior or from the "logic" of the situation. But, as with feeling states, knowledge of intentions is indirect, usually quite inferior, and highly subject to error.

Historical Data

As the previous section indicates, it is never really possible to divorce a given act from a broader temporal context. Much of the discrepancy between the perspectives of observer and actor arises from the difference between the observer's inferred history of everyman and the concrete individualized history of the actor himself. The actor has been exposed to a sequence of experiences that are to a degree unique, but the observer is constrained to work with the blunt conceptual tools of modal or normative experience.

Kelley [1967] has proposed that naive causal inference resembles the scientist's analysis of variance. The attributor possesses three different kinds of information that correspond to different causal possibilities: consensus information (do other actors behave in the same way to a given stimulus?); distinctiveness information (does the actor, and do other actors, behave in the same way to other stimuli?); and consistency information (does the actor, and do other actors, behave in the same way to the given stimulus across time and situational contexts?). The attributor then makes use of whatever information he has available in the "analysis of variance cube" formed by these three dimensions and makes the best causal inference he can. In Kelley's terms, the observer always lacks some of the distinctiveness and consistency information the actor possesses by virtue of knowing his own history. The observer may approach the actor's knowledge of these dimensions if he knows the actor well, but he cannot reach it. If the actor is unfamiliar to him, he knows nothing at all of this data set.

Because the actor knows his past, he is often diverted from making a dispositional attribution. If the actor insults someone, an observer, who may assume that this is a typical sample of behavior, may infer that the actor is hostile. The actor, on the other hand, may believe that the sample is anything but typical. He may recall very few other instances when he insulted anyone and may believe that in most of these instances he was sharply provoked. The actor's knowledge about the variability of his previous conduct—associated, in his mind, with different situational requirements—often preempts the possibility of a dispositional attribution. We suspect that because of the differences in the availability of personal history data, actors and observers evaluate each act along a different scale of comparison. The observer is characteristically normative and nomothetic: He compares the actor with other actors and judges his attributes accordingly. The actor, on the other hand, is more inclined to use an ipsative or idiographic reference scale: This action is judged with reference to his other previous actions rather than the acts of other actors.

There is, in summary, good reason to believe that actors and observers often bring different information to bear on their inferences about the actor and his environment. Typically, the actor has more, and more precise, information than the observer about his own emotional state and his intentions. (We say "typically" rather than "obviously" because there are occasions when the actor might be defensively unaware of his own motives, motives that are readily discernible to the observer.) Moreover, in the absence of precise knowledge of the actor's history, the observer is compelled to deal with him as a modal case and to ignore his unique history and orientation.

The difference in information available to actor and observer probably plays an important role in producing differential attributions, but this is not the whole story. There are good reasons for believing that the same information is differentially processed by actors and observers.

Differences in Information Processing

While it hardly seems debatable that actors and observers operate much of the time with different background data, the contention that actors and observers differ fundamentally in the *processing* of available data is bound to be more controversial. We believe that important information-processing differences do exist for the basic reason that *different aspects of the available information are salient for actors and observers and this differential salience affects the course and outcome of the attribution process.*

The actor and the observer are both reaching for interpretations of behavior that are sufficient for their own decision-making purposes. With unlimited time, and using the kinds of probes that emphasize a full deterministic picture of an action sequence, observers can probably reach attributional conclusions very similar to those of the actor. In the heat of the interaction moment, however, the purposes of actor and observer are apt to be different enough to start the inference process along distinctive tracks. Conceptualization of this problem depends to some extent on the kind of action-observation situation we are considering. Two extreme cases are the mutual contingency interaction [Jones & Gerard 1967], where each actor observes and is affected by the other, and the asymmetrical case of passive observation, where running behavioral decisions are thrust exclusively upon the actor while the observer's only task is to record and interpret—as if from behind a one-way screen.

We shall later examine the differences between these two situations, but a very important feature is common to both: the action itself—its topography, rhythm, style, and content—is more salient to the observer than to the actor. In establishing the reasons for this we may begin with the observation that action involves perceptible movement and change (by definition) and it is always to some extent unpredictable. While the environment is stable and contextual from the observer's point of view, action is figural and dynamic. The actor, however, is less likely to focus his attention on his behavior than on the environmental cues that evoke and shape it. In part this is because the actor's receptors are poorly located for recording the nuances of his own behavior. Many response sequences are preprogrammed and prepackaged, as it were, and do not require careful monitoring. The actor need not concern himself with his response repertory until there is conflict among the demands of the environment. Even then he will resolve the conflict in terms of perceived stimulus requirements. In short, the actor need not and in some ways cannot observe his behavior very closely. Instead, his attention is directed outward, toward the environment with its constantly shifting demands and opportunities.

These attentional differences should result in differences in causal perception. The actor should perceive his behavior to be a response to environmental cues that trigger, guide, and terminate it. But for the observer the focal, commanding stimulus is the actor's behavior, and situational cues are to a degree ignored. This leaves the actor as the likely causal candidate, and the observer will account for the actor's responses in terms of attributed dispositions.

The effect of these differential attribution tendencies is amplified by bias from another source, the tendency to regard one's reactions to entities as based on accurate perceptions of them. Rather than humbly regarding our impressions of the world as interpretations of it, we see them as understandings or correct apprehensions of it. The nature of this bias is perhaps easiest to see with young children, where it is much more extensive and profound than for adults. Philosophers and other adults make a distinction between the properties of entities that a three-year-old child does not make. The distinction is between those properties that have an existence apart from the transaction of a human being with the object and those properties that are the result of such a transaction. Properties of the former type include the bulk, shape, mass, and motion of an object. Most philosophers and almost all scientists and laymen would agree that such properties have an existence apart from the perception of them. Philosophers since the seventeenth century have designated these as primary qualities and have distinguished them from what are called secondary qualities, including taste, odor, sound, and color, which have no existence apart from the interaction of a sense organ with the object. The layman, it is important to note, does not ordinarily distinguish between primary and secondary qualities unless corrected by a philosopher. He does, however, distinguish in principle between the primary and secondary qualities on the one hand and what may be called evaluations on the other. Evaluations include judgments such as those concerning the goodness, beauty, or propriety of an object or action. Adults realize, at least intellectually, that evaluations do not have the status of perceptions, but are only interpretations or reactions.

How is it that a three-year-old correctly learns the distinction between evaluations and primary qualities and incorrectly learns to group the secondary qualities with primary qualities instead of with evaluations? The answer seems to be that the child learns that certain of his reactions to objects meet invariably with consensual validation while others do not. Once he learns the designation "blue," his judgment that an object is blue is almost never contradicted. He eventually learns, however, that not everyone agrees with his evaluations of objects as pretty, funny, or good. In terms of Kelley's [1967] analysis of variance analogy, the child comes to learn that certain of his reactions to entities are shared by all others and that he himself has those same reactions at all times and under all circumstances. Simultaneously, he learns that there are certain other types of reactions that may or may not be shared by others and that he himself does not invariably have. Before the analysis of variance cubes begin to fill in, however, the child

believes that clowns are funny in the same way that balls are round. Funniness is experienced as a property of the clown.

It seems clear that the distinction between evaluations and primary qualities is never fully made. We never quite get over our initial belief that funniness is a property of the clown and beauty is in the object. The probable reason for this is the fact that there remains a considerable degree of consensus even for our most subjective evaluations. Almost always at least some people agree with our evaluations, and sometimes almost everyone agrees with our evaluations. Phenomenologically, the distinction between evaluations and primary qualities is merely a quantitative one, just as the initial basis for learning the distinction—the degree of consensus—is quantitative. Just as we erroneously feel that secondary qualities are primary, we continue to feel that our subjective evaluations are in some sense perceptions.

This confusion between what is inherent in the object and what is a reaction elicited by it comes close to what Heider labels "egocentric attribution":

> Attribution to the object . . . means more than the dependence of *p*'s pleasure on the object. It also means that there is something enjoyable about the object. The attractiveness is a quality of the object, just as is the sweetness of a fruit or the roughness of a terrain. Consequently, *p*'s expectations, and therefore beliefs, refer not only to his own reactions to *x* on future occasions, but also the reactions of other people. The basic scheme is as follows: "Since my pleasure was aroused by *x*, *x* is positive, and therefore everyone will like it." An expectation of similarity between the reactions of others and the self is thus egocentrically determined" [1958, p. 158].

Our responses to immediately impinging stimuli are therefore biased in two ways: they are too salient and they are too "real." These biases should have a pronounced effect on the interpretations given by an actor and an observer to the actor's behavior. The actor will experience his behavior as proceeding naturally from the attractions, compulsions, and restraints in his environment. For the observer, it is not the stimuli impinging on the actor that are salient, but the behavior of the actor. The observer will therefore tend to see the actor's behavior as a manifestation of the actor, as an instance of a quality possessed by him. For the actor to interpret his behavior as the result of a disposition, he would have to weight the impact of the immediate environment less heavily, regard his knowledge about the environment as mere evaluations that may or may not be shared, and recognize that others might not respond as he does to this particular environment. For the observer to interpret the actor's behavior as a response to his environment, he would have to weight the vivid, sense-impression data of the behavior itself less heavily and strain his empathic abilities to allow himself to imagine the vividness for the actor of the environmental cues he confronts. To the extent that actor and observer fail to accomplish these tasks, the actor will overattribute his behavior to the environment and the observer will overattribute the behavior to qualities of the actor.

The quotation from Heider is but one reflection of our debt to him, but we wish to demur from the tone of Heider's analysis. The term "egocentric attribution" and Heider's discussion of the concept make the process sound willful and motivated, or at best the result of self-satisfied laziness. We hold that the individual comes by "egocentric attribution" honestly for the most part. All of our evaluations would be "egocentric attributions" were it not for the fact that we occasionally learn that our evaluations are not shared. The illusion that our reactions are perceptions is sustained in part by the apparent consensus accompanying most of our reactions, a consensus that may rest as much on transmitted cultural norms as on the compelling features of objective "reality."

Another of Heider's observations is closely related to our present discussion:

> It seems that behavior . . . has such salient properties that it tends to engulf the field rather than be confined to its proper position as a local stimulus whose interpretation requires the additional data of a surrounding field—the situation in social perception [1958, p. 54].

What we have said about the observer's perspective on the actor's behavior clearly echoes Heider's idea. Again, however, we differ with Heider about the explanation for this phenomenon. Heider appears to believe that behavior engulfs the field because the observer often cannot see all the environmental stimuli operating on the actor and because the observer often has not seen that the actor displays different behavior in other circumstances. We have already seconded this opinion in the section dealing with differences in available information, but we also believe that behavior engulfs the field in part because the salient, vivid stimulus for the observer is the actor's behavior. Even when the stimuli influencing the actor's behavior are visible to the observer, he ignores them to an extent.

Our differences with Heider are clearly minor and involve primarily subtleties of emphasis. It should be noted, however, that our analyses have different starting points. We prefer to derive the notion that behavior engulfs the field from the assumption that, for the observer, behavior is figural against the ground of the situation. And we prefer to derive the concept of egocentric attribution from the assumption that

the primitive belief in evaluations as perceptions is never outgrown.

It is now time to return to the distinction between passive and active observers, and to consider the implications of this distinction for our discussion. By definition the passive observer is not in a position to respond to the actor and the actor is unaware of his specific presence. The observer may be affected by the actor, but the actor cannot be affected by the observer—there is asymmetrical contingency. This is the situation of the moviegoer, the TV watcher, and the concealed observer behind a one-way screen. The passive observer may have any of a number of purposes that make him more attentive to certain kinds of information than others. As Lazarus [1966] and Aderman and Berkowitz [1970] have shown, it is possible to affect the amount of empathy shown by the observer for the actor by simple variations in observational instructions. Presumably, the more the observer is set to empathize with the actor, the more similar their attributional perspectives will be. Unless the observer has a strong empathy set, however, we would expect him to show the general observer tendency to underestimate the role of the environment, if only because of the differential salience of behavioral and situational information.

For the observer who is at the same time an actor, the tendency toward heightened salience of action should become more pronounced for several reasons. The fact that the observer is also caught up in action suggests that he will not be in a position to make leisurely appraisals of the setting and its contributions to unfolding behavior. Rather than being in a set to understand and evaluate the relative contributions of person and environment, the actor-observer will be tuned to process those cues that are particularly pertinent for his own next responses. Short-run behavior prediction is of paramount importance to the observer who is preparing his next act, and we suggest that the actor's behavior is more likely to seem pertinent for such predictions than the situational context evoking it. The acting organism probably does not operate at the peak of potential cognitive complexity, but it is likely to be attracted to convenient simplifying assumptions about the environment. One such simplifying assumption is that action implies a disposition to continue acting in the same manner and to act in such a manner in other situations as well.

A second consideration arises from the fact that the observer's presence and behavior may affect the actor's responses in ways not discerned by the observer. It is difficult for the active observer to evaluate the significance of his own presence because he is not often afforded clear comparative tests—tests that pit the stimulus contributions he generally makes against the stimulus contributions of others. In the situation we are now considering, where the observer is also an actor, the observer is likely to exaggerate the uniqueness and emphasize the dispositional origin of the other's responses to his own actions, actions the observer assumes to be perfectly standard, unexceptional, and unprovocative.

A final feature of the mutual contingency interaction is that the surrounding environment is roughly the same for each actor-observer. Therefore, the extent to which each actor behaves differently in the same situation should cause *each* to attribute the other's actions to internal, dispositional factors. If actor A is attuned to the reality of the situation and sees himself as behaving accordingly, any variations in B's behavior will be attributed to B's idiosyncratic interpretations of that reality.

In summary, the observer and the actor are likely to take different perspectives toward the same information. For the observer, the actor's behavior is the figural stimulus against the ground of the situation. The actor's attention is focused outward toward situational cues rather than inward on his own behavior, and moreover, those situational cues are endowed with intrinsic properties that are seen to cause the actor's behavior toward them. Thus, for the observer the proximal cause of action is the actor; for the actor the proximal cause lies in the compelling qualities of the environment. Finally, the tendency for the observer to attribute action to the actor is probably increased to the extent that the observer is also an actor and to the extent that both the observing and the observed actor are tied together in a mutually contingent interaction.

The Naive Psychology of Observers and Actors

The preceding discussion is likely to raise in the reader's mind a question as to who is correct, the actor or the observer. In the typical case, is behavior really caused by the actor or elicited by the environment? Put in these simplified terms, the question is of course unanswerable. All behavior is in one sense caused or produced by the actor. Except perhaps in acts such as the patellar reflex, all action involves some form of explicit or implicit decision process suggesting volition or personal causation.

The more pertinent and answerable question concerns the extent to which a particular setting is likely to evoke the same response across many persons. According to either the logic of Kelley's [1967] analysis of variance cube or of Jones and Davis' [1965] correspondent inference theory, a situation that evokes a response common to many persons is likely to be

seen as causing the behavior. Situations that evoke varied or unique responses are much less likely to be seen as causal. Obversely, when a person acts in a similar fashion on many different occasions, the act is seen to reflect a personal disposition.

It is obviously safer to talk about *phenomenal* causality than to raise any questions concerning accuracy or objective causality. Nevertheless, it is interesting to consider the many occasions on which the observer appears to violate the rules set up for him by Kelley and by Jones and Davis—to make a dispositional inference when the data do not allow it. Without insisting that the actor is usually right, we can point to many instances where the observer's interpretation of behavior is simply wrong. The observer is wrong when he infers that an attitude is consistent with an essay written in response to a legitimate request. He is wrong when he thinks the nonintervening bystander is apathetic, or infers that the subject who agrees to help out for a handsome fee is a chronic volunteer. In each of these cases the observer seems to underestimate the power of the situation and to overestimate the uniqueness of the (in fact modal) response.

The Observer's View: Personality as a Trait Package

It is interesting to speculate on the possible implications of the observer's bias for the conception of personality structure held by most people in our society and indeed by most personality psychologists. At bottom this conception is an Aristotelian view of personality as a collection of traits, that is, the most general kind of dispositions. Does this conception err by overemphasizing individual differences at the trait level and slighting the impact of situational variance?

Mischel [1968] argues persuasively that such overemphasis is common. He reviews the evidence on the existence of several dimensions of behavior usually presumed to be manifestations of a trait—honesty, dependency, attitudes toward authority, rigidity or intolerance for ambiguity, persuasability, and so on. Using the restricted empirical criterion of predictability from one behavior that is presumed to reflect the trait to another such behavior, Mischel finds little evidence that traits exist anywhere but in the cognitive structure of observers. For example, in the early but very sophisticated and ambitious honesty study of Hartshorne and May [1928], children were exposed to a variety of temptations in a variety of settings, including the opportunity to cheat on a test, steal money, and lie to save face. Despite the fact that there was some reliability of behavior (for example, the correlation between cheating by copying the answer key on one test in school and copying the answer key on another test was .70), there was very little generality of honesty across settings. It was rare for correlations across different behaviors, and especially for different behaviors across different settings, to exceed .30. This means, of course, that the improvement in predicting dishonesty in one situation by virtue of knowing about behavior in another situation is negligible. Mischel reviewed many other studies attempting to find behavioral generality across settings usually presumed to reflect a given trait. With the rather clear exception of abilities and ability-related traits, no disposition was found to be immune from the indictment of low generality.

The trait concept fares no better when it is examined in terms of attempts to predict behavior from paper and pencil trait measurements. When trait scores are obtained from questionnaire self-reports, they rarely predict with any accuracy behavior that is presumed to tap the trait dimension. Mischel facetiously proposes that the term "personality coefficient" might be used to describe "the correlation between .20 and .30 that is found persistently when virtually any personality dimension inferred from a questionnaire is related to almost any conceivable external criterion involving responses sampled in a *different* medium—that is, not by another questionnaire" [p. 78]. Thus, when we ask a person what his position is on a trait or when we infer it from his response to questionnaire items, we learn almost nothing about his actual behavior.

What Sustains the Belief in Traits?

Mischel therefore contends that there is little evidence for the existence of the broad trait concepts that have been such a standard part of our psychological vocabulary for centuries. From our position of lesser expertise, we agree that a conception of personality emphasizing behavior generality is inadequate and misleading. How does it happen, then, that students of personality have persistently embraced a trait construction of behavior? Why has it taken forty years of negative findings on the question for anyone to propose seriously in a textbook on personality that these trait dimensions may not exist? One answer is that the conclusion is based on inadequate data, another, that the traits have not been measured properly, or still a third, that the wrong traits have been examined. Another answer, and this is a conclusion that Mischel and the present writers prefer, is that traits exist more in the eye of the beholder than in the psyche of the actor.

If we are to uphold the position that personality traits are overattributed, then it is incumbent upon

us to account for the widespread belief in their existence. Beliefs in a trait psychology are especially perplexing when held by personality psychologists who have worked in the area and watched the negative evidence accumulate. If the belief in traits is mistaken, there would have to be very strong forces operating to sustain it. We believe there are such forces and have already dealt with two of them: (1) the information-processing biases that conspire to make behavior appear as a manifestation or quality of the actor and (2) the informational deficit of the observer, which prevents disconfirmation of the trait inference. We believe there are still other important reasons for the illusion. In discussing these reasons, it will be helpful to categorize them into sources of informational bias, sources of information-processing bias, and sources of linguistic bias. The discussion draws heavily on similar arguments made by Mischel [1968, 1969] and to a lesser extent on ideas expressed by Heider [1958] and Icheiser [1949].

Informational bias. Apart from the general ignorance one has about the range of behaviors that another person can exhibit, and apart from one's general ignorance of the environmental forces operating on him, there are some quite specific and systematic information deficits that help to turn ignorance into error. As Mischel [1968] notes, most of the people we observe are seen only in a very few roles. Within those already narrow confines, we are likely to see them in a biased sample of situations: when they are at their best or at their worst, when they are at their most harassed or their most relaxed, in their work moods or their play moods, in the morning or in the evening, in the company of people they like or with people they dislike. Those of us who are embedded in a bureaucracy may be especially prone to confuse responses to role requirements with personality dispositions. Bank presidents are usually surprised when the drab, black-suited teller absconds with the funds and is found living it up in Tahiti. To the extent that role and situational factors produce behavior that can be labeled as conforming, hostile, thrifty, brave, clean, or reverent, observers are likely to see the individual as being a conforming, hostile, thrifty, brave, clean, or reverent person.

Beyond the sampling bias produced by roles and situations, one carries with him into a relationship with others a bias in the form of oneself. To the extent that one's own behavior is a restricted sample of possible behaviors, it will evoke a restricted sample from the other person in turn. This point has been anticipated in our previous discussion of the "active observer" and is similar to one made by Kelley and Stahelski [1970]. They point out that one's own behavior may evoke complementary responses in another that one then mistakenly perceives as a manifestation of the other's personality. One may unwittingly shape the other's behavior in a variety of ways: by one's own role- and situation-determined behaviors toward the other, by implicitly communicated expectations and hopes about his behavior, and by a host of personal characteristics such as one's abilities, physical appearance, mannerisms, or social status.

Information-processing bias. Much has been written about the human tendency toward cognitive balance or consistency. Surely the tendency toward consistency must play some role in the observer's assignment of traits. A person who is aggressive in one setting should, to be "consistent," be aggressive in other settings. To see dependence and independence in the same actor may lead to greater subtleties of categorization, or it may lead to misperception of the evidence so that it becomes more consistent. In short, all the cognitive mechanisms of inconsistency reduction can be put to work in the service of dispositional accounts of action. It is not surprising that personal consistency is exaggerated in the eye of the beholder.

The tendencies toward primacy and assimilation discussed by Jones and Goethals [1971] also operate to create illusions of consistency. Out of his needs to impose structure on the environment, the observer often makes premature commitments to the nature of those entities he is observing. Within certain limits of discrepancy, therefore, inconsistent information will be seen as more consistent than it deserves to be. Even beyond these limits, contradictory data can be treated as anomalous, even as the exception that proves the rule.

Mischel [1968] points to still another factor that may encourage us to see people as being more of a piece than they are. The simple fact that another person is physically continuous, always looks more or less the same, and has the same mannerisms, may encourage the impression that there is continuity in his behavior as well. The fact of physical constancy may produce the illusion of behavioral and therefore dispositional consistency.

Linguistic distortions. Language probably facilitates the inference of traits in several ways. Once we have labeled an action as hostile, it is very easy to move to the inference that the perpetrator is a hostile person. Our language allows the same term to be applied to behavior and to the underlying disposition it reflects. It is possible to imagine that we all have little syllogistic subroutines through which we constantly generate trait inferences from act labels: "*lo* has behaved *x*-ly; people who have the *x* trait behave *x*-ly; *o* has the *x* trait." The application of the syllogism

will lead to an erroneous trait inference whenever we overlook the fact that there are other reasons for behaving *x*-ly besides having the trait of *x*. Which is to say, often.

It may also be noted that our vocabulary is rich in dispositional or trait terms (the Allport-Ogbert list includes over 18,000 terms) and quite impoverished when it comes to describing the situation. Among personality theorists H. A. Murray [1938] has shown as much sensitivity to this problem as anyone, but his list of environmental "presses" is merely adapted from a complementary list of needs. In social psychology Roger Barker [1968] has stood almost alone in attempting to develop a descriptive taxonomy for behavior settings. His important effort is undoubtedly much impeded by the inadequate resources placed at his disposal by the English language.

The momentum of our linguistic machinery undoubtedly does not stop with the inference of a single trait. Passini and Norman [1966] have shown that the same factor structure is obtained for trait ascriptions to total strangers as for trait ascriptions to well-known acquaintances. This would seem to indicate that we carry trait-intercorrelation matrices around in our heads, or to put it in a more traditional way, that we have implicit personality theories [Jones 1954, Cronbach 1955]. We tend to assume that trait *x* is, in general, associated with trait *y*. This means that we may pass from observation of an act that we label as *x*-like to the inference of an *x* trait to the inference of a *y* trait because of our assumption that traits *x* and *y* are correlated.

The rarity of disconfirmation. Informational bias, processing bias, and linguistic bias all operate, therefore, in such a way as to generate trait inferences where there may be no traits. Are there no mechanisms that can curtail and reverse the errors? There probably are. Certainly the better we know someone, the more restraints there are against facile trait ascription. There are probably sharp limits, however, to the power of additional information to disconfirm a trait ascription. Once we have decided that a person is hostile or dependent, a wide variety of behaviors can be construed as support for this supposition, including even behaviors commonly taken as implying the opposite of the trait ascription. A kind behavior on the part of a "hostile" person may be perceived as insincere, manipulative, or condescending. We are probably all rather adept at the maintenance of a trait inference in the face of disconfirmatory evidence. When practiced by some psychoanalytic writers, the maneuvering can be truly breathtaking.

It might be argued that discussion with others provides ample opportunity for disconfirmation of a trait inference. The individual may find in such discussion that his trait inferences are not shared. This is undoubtedly true. We can all think of instances where our beliefs about another person have been altered by hearing about someone else's experiences with that person. There are good reasons to expect that our erroneous trait inferences will more often receive consensual validation, however. To the extent that another person resembles oneself in role, status, personal and physical characteristics, he is likely to have the same sorts of experiences with a given person that one has had oneself, and therefore to have made the same trait inferences. It seems likely, moreover, that the more similar two people are the more probable it is that they will discuss the personality of someone they know mutually. The chairman of a department does not often exchange opinions with graduate students on the intelligence or warmth of assistant professors. Finally, when one's trait inferences are flatly contradicted by another person, everything we have said implies that one is likely to explain the contradiction in terms of the dispositions of the person who is contradicting him: "I wonder why John is unable to see the essential kindness of Mary."

In summary, the observer, even when he is a professional psychologist, is apt to conceive of the personalities of others as a collection of broad dispositions or traits, despite the scant empirical evidence for their existence. This conception appears to result from deficits and biases in the information available to the observer and to a variety of biases in the processing of information at the perceptual, cognitive, and linguistic levels. It should be noted, however, that the low empirical validity of the trait concept may be of importance only to the psychologist. The observer, in his daily life, may achieve fairly high predictability using trait inferences that the psychologist can show to be erroneous. If the observer is habitually insulted by a given actor, it may make little difference to the observer whether the reason for this consistent behavior is the hostility of the actor, the actor's dislike of the observer, or the fact that the observer sees the actor only in the early morning when the actor is always grouchy.

The Actor's View: Personality as a Value Matrix

There has been relatively little research on the actor's view of his own personality structure. The individual's implicit theory of his own personality has not usually been singled out for study by personality theorists, probably because it is generally assumed that actors regard themselves only as "instances" of personalities generally. Much that we have said about the actor's perspective on his own behavior prompts the suggestion that this assumption may not be correct.

Mischel has noted that "Dispositional theories try to categorize behaviors in terms of the hypothesized historical psychic forces that diverse behaviors supposedly serve; but it is also possible to categorize the behaviors in terms of the unifying, evoking, and maintaining conditions that they jointly share" [1969, p. 1016]. Mischel, of course, prefers the latter conception of individual differences as the more nearly accurate account.

We would suggest that the actor's view of his own personality is close to the conception preferred by Mischel. Consistent with the actor's strong preference for assigning causal significance to the situation, he tends to focus on Mischel's "evoking and maintaining conditions" as the stimuli guiding his own behavior. Whereas observers operate as trait psychologists, actors may operate as contingent reinforcement theorists, mapping their behavioral plans in terms of perceived reinforcement potentials. The observer, we have argued, processes actions in a nomothetic, taxonomic way, and is thus likely to construe behavior on what Allport [1937] would call a common trait basis. The actor, if he thinks of himself as having traits at all, is likely to see an "individual trait" (the term again is Allport's), expressing the congruity of interrelated purposes. When the actor steps back to view himself, he is probably inclined to emphasize not the superficial topography of behavior but the underlying purposes mediated by the behavior. The actor is consequently more likely to conceive of his personality as a configuration of values and strategies than as a collection of response dispositions. When the actor compares himself to others, we might expect him to believe that he differs chiefly in the priorities that he assigns to his goals and in the particular means he has devised to achieve them.

We have criticized the observer harshly for his errors, and to be fair we should note that the actor is also likely to make some mistakes. We have already observed that people fail to distinguish between primary and secondary qualities and tend to blur the distinction between perceptions and evaluations. The actor probably consistently errs by ignoring the role of his own biases in responding to situations. In Lewinian terms the actor locates the valence in the object rather than the need in himself. If the observer assumes that people are more different than they are, the actor probably assumes that he is too much like everyone else—that the qualities he sees in the environment are really there, and not a product of his own motives and expectancies.

In quite another sense, however, the actor is likely to conceive of himself as more unique than he is. Each actor lacks knowledge of the population base rates for various experiences, beliefs, and motives. There may exist, in effect, a sort of pluralistic ignorance of the human condition. If so, it might account for what Meehl [1956] has called the "P. T. Barnum effect," the readiness of the client to accept as uniquely applicable a clinician's assessment of himself that could in fact apply to almost everyone. Stagner [1958] and Ulrich, Stachnick, and Stainton [1963] have capitalized on this kind of egocentric attribution in clever demonstrations of the susceptibility of businessmen and college students, respectively, to allegedly tailor-made diagnoses of their personality. Each subject was given an identical personality description ("Some of your aspirations tend to be pretty unrealistic"; "Sexual adjustment has presented some difficulties for you") and asked to comment on its accuracy. The great majority of the subjects were impressed by what they perceived as a penetrating analysis, with some expressing the view that they had been helped by these insights into their characters.

Personality Traits Are Things Other People Have

If it is true that actors and observers have different conceptions of personality structure along the lines we have discussed, then it should be the case that each individual perceives every other individual to have more stable personality traits than he himself possesses. He should view others as having generalized response dispositions but himself as acting in accord with the demands and opportunities inherent in each new situation. In order to test this proposition, Nisbett and Caputo [1971] constructed a variant of the standard trait description questionnaire. A list of twenty polar adjectives ("reserved–emotionally expressive;" "lenient–firm") was presented to subjects, along with the option, for each dimension, "depends on the situation." Each of the male college student subjects was asked to check one of the three alternatives for each trait dimension for each of five people: himself, his best friend, an age peer whom the subject liked but did not know well, his father, and (to fill in the remaining cell of the young–old, familiar–unfamiliar matrix) the television commentator Walter Cronkite. In line with anticipations, subjects were likely to use the "depends on the situation" category for themselves but quite willing to assign traits to the other stimulus persons. Neither degree of acquaintance nor similarity in age was a very potent

determinant of the willingness to ascribe traits to others: subjects assigned traits in about equal numbers to each of the other stimulus persons.

We have already discussed a large number of cognitive factors that would be expected to produce Nisbett and Caputo's findings. Perhaps we should add to the list the individual's desire for control over his environment. Brehm [1966] has written at some length on the strength of man's desire to see himself as free in varied ways and the "reactance" created by threats to behavioral freedom. The perception of freedom is probably best maintained by simultaneously ascribing traits to others and denying them in oneself. When the observer infers the existence of a trait, this gives him the happy, if sometimes illusory, feeling of predictability of behavior and therefore of control over the environment. On the other hand, the individual would lose the sense of freedom to the extent that he acknowledged powerful dispositions in himself, traits that imperiously cause him to behave consistently across situations.

The reader may have noticed that this last paragraph represents virtually our only consideration of traditional motivational concepts. In the final section, we will discuss in some detail the role of motives that are perhaps even more powerful than reactance.

Motivational Influences on Attribution Processes

Perhaps we have gone as far as we can go by acting as though man's motives are exclusively cognitive —that all he wants is to test and structure reality so that he can respond appropriately to it. There are many other motives that affect information processing, the most obtrusive of which is probably the motive to maintain or enhance one's self-esteem. Our examples of actor-observer differences in processing information have more frequently involved blameworthy than praiseworthy acts. Is it possible that most of the facts may be explained by merely invoking the notion that actors try to excuse their reprehensible actions by blaming them on circumstances, whereas observers are coldly, perhaps gleefully, ready to put the shoe of blame on the actor's foot? Have we perhaps erected a fanciful cognitive edifice to surround and obscure this simple principle of human pettiness?

Our answer is a qualified no. We have emphasized —perhaps overemphasized—the role of cognitive and perceptual factors in developing our major theme. We have argued that both actors and observers are concerned with processing useful information and suggested that action cues and situation cues are utilized differentially by them. We would now like to acknowledge that motivational factors may often serve to exaggerate the broad tendencies that we have tried to describe. At the same time, however, we would also like to express the opinion that motivational factors may often mute those tendencies.

Perhaps the simplest way of describing what we believe to be the relationship between the divergent biases of actor and observer and motivational factors such as the desire to maintain self-esteem is to suggest that the biases are generally found even when the act in question is neutral affectively and morally and when the observer holds a neutral opinion toward the actor. If the action is reprehensible, the tendency of actors to attribute to the situation is undoubtedly enhanced ("You would have done the same in my shoes."). If the action is praiseworthy, on the other hand, this tendency is probably muted and perhaps often reversed ("Class will tell."). We also readily grant that, when the observer has a favorable opinion of the actor who performs a praiseworthy act, a dispositional inference is more likely. (Alan Jay Lerner's father is supposed to have responded to an opening night patron's comment that his son was a lucky man, "Yes, and I've noticed that the harder he works, the luckier he gets.") The tendency to infer dispositional causes is undoubtedly also enhanced when the observer dislikes the actor who performs a blameworthy act. ("What can you expect from people like that?") Again, however, the observer's bias can just as easily be reversed, as when the observer likes the perpetrator of bad acts ("The other boys made him do it") or dislikes the performer of good acts ("You must have caught him in a good mood").

Whether it is ecologically more frequent that our proposition is set back or given a boost by motivational factors depends on parameters we are not likely ever to know, such as the relative frequency of blameworthy and praiseworthy acts and the probability of liking actors versus disliking them. The more answerable question is whether or not the attributional biases exist when there is no reason to assume that motivational purposes are served by them. As should be clear, we strongly believe this to be so. As Leventhal has pointed out, a set of stimuli may give rise to both motivational and cognitive processes. It is unwarranted to assume in such an instance that one set of processes determines or even affects the other. In fact, we suspect that the attributional biases often hold even when motivational purposes are thwarted by them. The accidental hero seems often to be quite convinced that others would have been heroic in the same spot. The selfless missionary and the Nobel scientist are probably well aware of external incentives and ulterior motives that cloud the picture of virtue conveyed by their actions.

However powerful motivational factors may be, it should be noted that here, as in other psychological contexts, there is an inherent conflict between the "pleasure principle" and the "reality principle." Jones and Gerard [1967] have discussed the general conflict between these two orientations under the heading of the "basic antimony," and suggest that the pleasure principle is dominant in the postdecisional phase, whereas the reality principle is dominant when action and choice are still possible. We may want to believe that we are responsible for our good acts, always and exclusively, but such a belief is not very adaptive in the long run.

It should be emphasized, finally, that we have dealt with only a few of the motives that interact with attribution processes. The individual, whether he is an actor or an observer, is a self-esteem enhancer, a balance maintainer, a dissonance reducer, a reactance reliever, a seeker after truth, and more. The relative strength of these motives, in competition with one another and with more purely cognitive processes, is a problem best pursued empirically.

Summary and Conclusions

Actors tend to attribute the causes of their behavior to stimuli inherent in the situation, while observers tend to attribute behavior to stable dispositions of the actor. This is due in part to the actor's more detailed knowledge of his circumstances, history, motives, and experiences. Perhaps more importantly, the tendency is a result of the differential salience of the information available to both actor and observer. For the observer behavior is figural against the ground of the situation. For the actor it is the situational cues that are figural and that are seen to elicit behavior. Moreover, the actor is inclined to think of his judgments about the situational cues as being perceptions or accurate readings of them. These cues are therefore more "real" as well as more salient than they are for the observer. Behavior is thus seen by the observer to be a manifestation of the actor and seen by the actor to be a response to the situation.

The observer often errs by overattributing dispositions, including the broadest kind of dispositions—personality traits. The evidence for personality traits as commonly conceived is sparse. The widespread belief in their existence appears to be due to the observer's failure to realize that the samples of behavior that he sees are not random, as well as to the observer's tendency to see behavior as a manifestation of the actor rather than a response to situational cues. A variety of additional perceptual, cognitive, and linguistic processes help to sustain the belief in traits.

It is suggested that the individual's view of his own personality differs from his view of the personalities of others. The individual may be inclined to view his own personality as consisting of "individual traits," values, goal priorities, and means of attaining goals. The actor may simultaneously view his own personality as being more unique than it is and his own behavior as being more appropriate to given situations than is the behavior of others.

BIBLIOGRAPHY

David Aderman and Leonard Berkowitz, "Observational Set, Empathy, and Helping." *Journal of Personality and Social Psychology,* 1970, 14:141–148.

Gordon W. Allport, *Personality: A Psychological Interpretation.* Holt, 1937.

Roger G. Barker, "Explorations in Ecological Psychology." *American Psychologist,* 1965, 20:1–14.

Daryl J. Bem, "An Experimental Analysis of Self-Persuasion." *Journal of Experimental Social Psychology,* 1965, 1:199–218.

Daryl J. Bem, "Self-Perception: An Alternative Interpretation of Cognitive Dissonance Phenomena." *Psychological Review,* 1967, 74:183–200.

Jack Brehm, *A Theory of Psychological Reactance.* Academic Press, 1966.

Lee J. Cronbach, "Processes Affecting Scores on Understanding of Others and Assumed Similarity." *Psychological Bulletin,* 1955, 52:177–193.

H. Hartshorne and Mark A. May, *Studies in the Nature of Character,* Vol. I. *Studies in Deceit.* Macmillan, 1928.

Fritz Heider, *The Psychology of Interpersonal Relations.* Wiley, 1958.

Gustav Icheiser, "Misunderstanding in Human Relations: A Study in False Social Perception." *American Journal of Sociology,* 1949, 55: part 2, 1–70.

Edward E. Jones, "Authoritarianism as a Determinant of First Impression Formation." *Journal of Personality,* 1954, 23:107–127.

Edward E. Jones and Keith E. Davis, "From Acts to Dispositions: The Attribution Process in Person Perception." In Leonard Berkowitz, ed., *Advances in Experimental Social Psychology,* Vol. 2. Academic Press, 1965.

Edward E. Jones and Harold B. Gerard, *Foundations of Social Psychology.* Wiley, 1967.

Edward E. Jones and George R. Goethals, "Order Effects in Impression Formation: Attribution Context and the Nature of the Entity." General Learning Press, 1971. (Also ch. 3 in Edward E. Jones, David Kanouse, Harold H. Kelley, Richard E. Nisbett, Stuart Valins, and Bernard Weiner. *Attribution: Perceiving the Causes of Behavior.* General Learning Press, 1971.)

Edward E. Jones and Victor A. Harris, "The Attribution of Attitudes." *Journal of Experimental Social Psychology,* 1967, 3:1–24.

Edward E. Jones, Leslie Rock, Kelly G. Shaver, George R. Goethals, and Lawrence M. Ward, "Pattern of Performance and Ability Attribution: An Unexpected Primacy Effect." *Journal of Personality and Social Psychology,* 1968, 10:317–340.

Edward E. Jones, Stephen Worchel, George R. Goethals, and Judy Grumet, "Prior Expectancy and Behavioral Extremity as Determinants of Attitude Attribution." *Journal of Experimental Social Psychology,* 1971, 7: 59–80.

Harold H. Kelley, "Attribution Theory in Social Psychology." *Nebraska Symposium on Motivation,* 1967, 14: 192–241.

Harold H. Kelley, "Attribution in Social Interaction." General Learning Press, 1971. (Also ch. 2 in Edward E. Jones, David Kanouse, Harold H. Kelley, Richard E. Nisbett, Stuart Valins, and Bernard Weiner, *Attribution: Perceiving the Causes of Behavior.* General Learning Press, 1971.)

Harold H. Kelley and Anthony J. Stahelski, "The Social Interaction Basis of Cooperators' and Competitors' Beliefs About Others." *Journal of Personality and Social Psychology,* 1970, 16:66–91.

Richard S. Lazarus, *Psychological Stress and the Coping Process.* McGraw-Hill, 1966.

Howard Leventhal, "Findings and Theory in the Study of Fear Communications." In Leonard Berkowitz, ed., *Advances in Experimental Social Psychology,* Vol. 5. Academic Press, 1970.

Leslie Z. McArthur, "The How and What of Why: Some Determinants and Consequences of Causal Attribution." Unpublished Ph.D. dissertation, Yale University, 1970.

Paul E. Meehl, "Wanted—A Good Cookbook." *American Psychologist,* 1956, 11:263–272.

Walter Mischel, *Personality and Assessment.* Wiley, 1968.

Walter Mischel, "Continuity and Change in Personality." *American Psychologist,* 1969, 11:1012–1018.

Henry A. Murray, *Explorations in Personality.* Oxford, 1938.

Richard E. Nisbett and G. Craig Caputo, "Personality Traits: Why Other People Do the Things They Do." Unpublished manuscript. Yale University, 1971.

Richard E. Nisbett, Patricia Legant, and Jeanne Marecek, "The Causes of Behavior as Seen by Actor and Observer." Unpublished manuscript, Yale University, 1971.

Frank T. Passini and Warren T. Norman, "A Universal Conception of Personality Structure?" *Journal of Personality and Social Psychology,* 1966, 4:44–49.

Ross Stagner, "The Gullibility of Personnel Managers." *Personnel Psychology,* 1958, 11:347–352.

Roger E. Ulrich, Thomas J. Stachnick, and N. Ransdell Stainton, "Student Acceptance of Generalized Personality Interpretations." *Psychological Reports,* 1963, 13: 831–834.

[Preparation of this paper grew out of a workshop on attribution theory held at UCLA in August 1969, supported by Grant GS-2613 from the National Science Foundation. Some of the research described herein was supported by NSF Grant 8857 to Edward E. Jones. The paper was prepared while Richard E. Nisbett was supported by an NSF postdoctoral fellowship and a Morse Faculty Fellowship (Yale University).]

6 · Perceiving the Causes of Success and Failure

BERNARD WEINER
IRENE FRIEZE
ANDY KUKLA
LINDA REED
STANLEY REST
ROBERT M. ROSENBAUM

University of California, Los Angeles

Motivational theorists have generally set two goals for themselves: to identify the contemporary determinants of action and to specify the mathematical relationships between the components in their theories. Such an approach frequently is identified with Clark Hull and his programmatic statement that behavior is a function of Drive X Habit, although many other major contributors in the area of motivation have favored this type of pursuit [Kurt Lewin, Kenneth Spence, Edward C. Tolman].

Motivational theories emerging from the analysis of behavior can be broadly subsumed within either of two opposing camps, often labeled mechanistic [Hull 1943, Spence 1956] and cognitive [Atkinson 1964, Lewin 1938, Tolman 1938]. The major differences between these two approaches are the degree to which the experiential variable in the formulated models is explicable without referring to higher mental processes and the extent to which the goal object is represented mentally ("anticipated") during the instrumental response sequence (consider the habit versus expectancy controversy). Clearly, greater importance is placed upon mediating cognitive processes in the works of Atkinson, Lewin, and Tolman than in the writings of Hull and Spence. Yet in many respects the so-called cognitive conceptions of motivation are little concerned with mental events—expectancy of goal attainment is the only intervening mental process in the formulated models. For the most part, the conceptions formulated by Atkinson, Lewin, and Tolman disregard cognitive operations such as information processing, formulations of beliefs concerning the causes of events, and the influence of appraisal on affect and action.

The general format of a cognitive model of motivation is: S → cognition → R. That is, an incoming stimulus, viewed as a source of information, is encoded into a belief system that gives it "meaning." The subsequent response is then guided by the intervening structure of thought. Thus, a cognitive model of motivation requires a two-stage analysis. First, there must be the rudiments of a theory of thought, and second, laws that relate thought to action must be specified [Baldwin 1969].

This paper presents an attributional model of achievement motivation, guided by the general cognitive approach outlined above. The model is based upon the assumption that beliefs about the causes of success and failure mediate between antecedent stimulus-organism transactions and ensuing achievement behavior. The general outline of the paper is as follows. First, an attributional model of achievement behavior is presented, with a summary of evidence indicating the need to distinguish between the model's components. Attention is then turned to the leading contemporary theory of achievement motivation [Atkinson 1964], and the data accumulated to support Atkinson's conception are reinterpreted in the language of the attributional model. In this discussion a number of experiments generated by ideas concerning causal ascriptions for success and failure are reported. The model subsequently is employed in the analysis of experimental extinction. Here again, previously unreported research is presented to demonstrate the role played by casual inferences in the extinction process. The research highlights inadequacies in the locus of control literature. Finally, some educational implications of this motivational approach are examined.

An Attribution Model of Motivation

Our model is greatly influenced by the pioneering ideas of Fritz Heider [1958] and guided by research in the area of locus of control [Crandall, Katkovsky, & Crandall 1965, Rotter 1966]. We postulate that individuals utilize four elements of ascription both to postdict (interpret) and to predict the outcome (O) of an achievement-related event. The four causal elements are ability (A), effort (E), task difficulty (T), and luck (L):

$$O = f(A, E, T, L)$$

That is, in attempting to explain the prior outcome (success or failure) of an achievement-related event, the individual assesses his own or the performer's ability level, the amount of effort that was expended, the difficulty of the task, and the magnitude and direction of experienced luck. It is assumed that values

are assigned to these elements and the task outcome differentially ascribed to the four causal sources. Similarly, future expectations of success and failure are based upon the assumed level of ability in relation to perceived task difficulty (labeled by Heider as "can"), as well as an estimation of intended effort and anticipated luck.

The mathematical relationship between the elements in the model is not specified. It is proposed that the components combine either conjunctively or disjunctively, with as yet undetermined distributive rules. Heider [1958] contends that both "can" and "try" are necessary for an action to be completed successfully. At times, however, ability and effort are perceived as compensatory or disjunctive (for example, "I am bright enough to receive a good grade in this course without studying"). It is also conceivable that a positive outcome might be perceived as determined entirely by good luck. At this time it is somewhat premature to specify the quantitative properties of the model, although this problem is touched upon in subsequent pages.

A Scheme for Classifying Causal Dimensions

Two of the four components in the model (ability and effort) describe qualities of the person undertaking the activity, while the two remaining components (task difficulty and luck) can be considered properties external to the person, or environmental factors. Further, two of the elements (ability and task difficulty) have somewhat enduring characteristics, whereas the magnitudes of the two remaining components (effort and luck) are relatively variable. Thus, the four elements in the model can be comprised within two basic dimensions: locus of control (internal versus external) and degree of stability (fixed versus variable). This analysis is summarized in table 1.

The locus of control and stability dimensions have frequently been confounded in past research. For example, investigations in the locus of control area examine expectancy changes in skill (ability) versus chance (luck) situations. Thus, the effects of an

Table 1. Classification Scheme for the Perceived Determinants of Achievement Behavior.

Stability	Locus of Control	
	Internal	External
Stable	Ability	Task difficulty
Unstable	Effort	Luck

internal, stable attribute are compared with those of an external, unstable attribute. It is therefore not possible to examine independently the motivational consequences of ascriptions to these two dimensions of causality. We now turn briefly to evidence justifying the distinction between the two attributional dimensions and the ability-effort differentiation outlined in table 1.

Evidence Supporting the Proposed Causal Distinctions

Internal versus External Control. Studies in the area of locus of control are concerned either with performance generated in situations that give rise to internal versus external ascriptions about causality (for example, skill or internal versus chance or external task structures), or with the behavioral effects of individual differences in perceived internal versus external control of reinforcements. The empirical findings reveal that disparities in ability versus luck attributions of causality are responsible for variations in expectancy, aspiration, and information seeking, as well as affecting a number of other behavioral indexes; see extensive reviews by Lefcourt [1966] and Rotter [1966]. Detailed discussion of some of this work is presented later in this paper.

Stability versus Instability. The differentiation between fixed versus variable factors has not been fully examined in experimental settings. A number of investigations, however, do bear upon this issue. It is instructive to consider the dimension of stability within the context of a representative level of aspiration paradigm. Level of aspiration may be defined as "the level of future performance in a familiar task which an individual, knowing his past performance in that task, explicitly expects to undertake" [Frank 1935, p. 119]. If past behavior at a task is attributed by the actor to the fixed factors of ability or task difficulty, there should be fewer atypical aspiration shifts (increasing aspiration after failure or decreasing aspiration following success) than if the outcome of the prior performance was ascribed to the variable elements of luck or effort. For example, Phares [1957] found stronger tendencies toward atypical shifts given luck rather than ability task structures. Similarly, the negative recency effect that is frequently reported in gambling situations [the "gambler's fallacy": an increase in expectancy of success after a loss, or a decrease after a gain (Cohen 1960)] further indicates that in games determined by luck inconsistent outcomes are anticipated (although in

this particular case the consequences are misconceived as being dependent). There are also indications that individuals display an unusual number of atypical responses in situations of failure; see Atkinson [1964]. Merton [1946] argues that belief in chance enables an unsuccessful individual to preserve self-esteem; attribution to luck therefore may be a defense that one is prone to employ following failure.

The logic of the prior analysis also leads to the hypothesis that atypical responses will be relatively frequent if outcomes are ascribed by the performer to heightened or depressed effort. Hence, if one believes that a positive result occurred because of "superhuman" effort or that an undesired failure came about because of a lack of trying, atypical responses should be observed in future aspiration settings. This is an apparently obvious prediction. Yet in prior discussions of level of aspiration, atypical shifts are expected when attributions are external (luck) and typical shifts anticipated when ascriptions are internal; for example, see Rotter. Effort, however, is an internal attribute that has characteristics in common with luck; that is, neither is a subjectively fixed factor, and self-ascriptions to these factors should produce atypical responses. One implication of this analysis, which is explored in detail later in the paper, is that expectancy shifts are primarily determined by the stability, rather than the locus of control, of the attributional element. This contradicts the position held by Rotter and other psychologists working in the locus of control area.

Ability versus Effort. Moral evaluations rest upon the distinction between ability (can) and effort (try); see Maselli and Altrocchi [1969]. An experiment by Schmitt [1964] nicely illustrates this point. Schmitt established hypothetical situations in which an act was not committed either because of the actor's lack of willingness or because of the absence of ability. For example, a situation was described in which an individual did not repay a debt either because he did not have the money (can) or because he was unwilling (try). Subjects then disclosed the degree to which the borrower was morally obligated to return the money. The data clearly demonstrate that the invocation of moral sanctions is expressed primarily when the individual is unwilling to repay the debt. That is, moral judgments are linked to the attribution of intentionality, rather than with ability.

The evaluative consequences of ability versus effort attributions also have been examined in achievement-oriented contexts. Jones and deCharms [1957] established an experimental "common fate" condition in which group rewards required that each member of the group individually succeed at a task. A confederate in this group then failed. [When that failure was perceived as due to insufficient effort, the confederate received a lower personal evaluation from the group members (less dependable, likable, competent) than when the failure was assumed to be due to a lack of ability.] These differences did not emerge when the rewards for the individuals in the group were not linked with the actions of the other group members.

A number of studies concerning the evaluative consequences of ability versus effort attributions in achievement contexts have also been undertaken by Weiner and Kukla [1970]. In those studies subjects are asked to assume that they are grade school teachers. They are given information concerning their students' ability (present or absent), effort (present or absent), and exam performance (excellent, fair, borderline, moderate failure, or clear failure). The subjects then are required to dispense performance feedback to the pupils, which is conveyed by placing "stars" on their exam papers. From 1 to 5 gold stars (reward) or 1 to 5 red stars (punishment) can be allotted to each student. Each subject evaluates all 20 hypothetical conditions (2 levels of ability × 2 levels of motivation × 5 levels of outcome). Thus, for example, the subjects have to provide feedback to a pupil who has ability, did not expend effort, and has a borderline test result, and so forth.

Figure 1 illustrates the results of one such experiment in which male college students served as subjects. The figure reveals that ability and motivation (effort) attributions differentially influence rewards and punishments. Among pupils either with or without ability, those who are perceived as having expended effort are rewarded more and punished less than pupils believed not to have tried. Conversely, given either effort or no effort, *low* ability pupils are rewarded more and punished less than pupils believed to possess ability [see also Lanzetta and Hannah 1969]. In addition, the figure indicates that effort is a more salient determinant of rewards and punishments than is ability.

Although at first glance rewarding lack of ability seems shocking, it is readily understandable. We are especially likely to praise individuals who overcome personal handicaps and succeed (effort and no ability) and are particularly prone to punish those who do not utilize their potential and fail (ability and no effort). Figure 1 indicates that these two

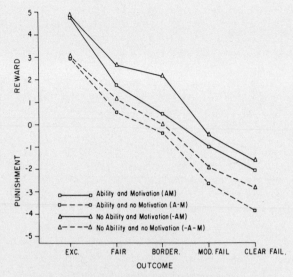

Figure 1. Evaluation (reward and punishment) as a function of pupil ability, motivation, and examination outcome (relatively upper class college sample). [From Weiner & Kukla 1970.]

groups do differ most in the magnitude of rewards and punishments.

Perhaps it is reasonable to reward and punish effort more than ability. As previously contended, ability is perceived as a dispositional or relatively invariant property of the person. Hence, it cannot be "controlled" by appropriate reinforcement techniques. On the other hand, as implied by table 1, effort presumably can be altered and therefore may be influenced by contingent rewards and punishments.

These findings have been generally substantiated in other investigations using subject populations of lower class high school males and female student-teachers [Weiner & Kukla]. In addition, the general pattern of results has been replicated in Germany by Heckhausen (unpublished study), using experienced teachers as subjects. A similar experiment reported by Weiner and Kukla, in which student-teachers were asked to introspect about their personal feelings of pride and shame in the twenty experimental conditions, yields the same general conclusions as when reward and punishment are dispensed to others.

Antecedent Conditions Affecting Causal Attribution

The review in the preceding pages established that dimensions and distinctions comprised within the model—internal versus external control, stable versus unstable elements, and ability versus effort—can be coordinated with established empirical findings. How does the individual use available information then to explain the outcome of a previous achievement action or to specify future expectations about success? For example, given a personal success experience, what cues give rise to the interpretation that "I was just lucky" or "I will do even better next time"? Similarly, what information allows an observer to conclude that "he has ability" or that "he will do worse next time"? For ease of presentation the following discussion of antecedent conditions generally assumes that equivalent information is employed and identical inferences reached when making judgments about oneself or others.

Ability. It is postulated that perceived ability at a given task is a function of the degree of past success at that and similar tasks. Thus, consistency and generality of performance are salient cues for ability attributions; see Kelley [1967]. The temporal pattern of past outcomes also influences attributions about ability. Jones, Rock, Shaver, Goethals, and Ward [1968] found, for example, that subjects performing well on early trials of a problem-solving task are perceived as more intelligent than those receiving a random pattern of success or performing well on later trials. Thus, a primacy effect apparently operates in ability inferences. Maximum performance on prior occasions also affects ability attributions, presumably because an individual who does well on one occasion has the capacity to do well again. Rosenbaum, in an unpublished study, found that ability ratings were significantly related to the previous maximum performance level, although over all trials the mean performance scores of the comparison groups were equated.

Task difficulty. It is assumed that task difficulty is inferred from social norms indicating the performance of others at the task. If the norms convey that many others succeed, the task is perceived as "easy"; if few others in the comparison group solve the problem, it is "difficult." Of course, characteristics of the task, such as length and complexity, can also influence initial judgments of difficulty. It is postulated, however, that information concerning outcome primarily determines final task appraisal. Indeed, in many studies of achievement motivation, level of difficulty is conveyed by merely telling subjects, "Our norms indicate that ____% of the other subjects have been able to solve this task"; see Feather [1961] and Weiner [1970].

Knowledge of social norms must be considered in conjunction with personal performance to reach conclusions concerning outcome causality. If performance is consistent with the norms, that is, success when others succeed or failure when others fail, the outcome is attributed to the external factor of task difficulty, and insufficient information is provided for self-evaluation. On the other hand, performance at variance with social norms—success when others fail or failure when others succeed—is likely to give rise to internal attributions and self-evaluative judgments [see Weiner & Kukla 1970, Frieze & Weiner in press].

Luck. In the prior paragraphs information relevant for the formulation of ascriptions to the two stable behavioral determinants was outlined. Concerning the unstable elements, it is postulated that luck is inferred from the pattern of prior reinforcements: the more random or variable the pattern of outcomes, the higher the probability that luck will be perceived as a causal influence. Bennion [1961] presents data supporting this contention. He demonstrated that expectancy changes given variable outcomes conform to those exhibited in luck situations, while expectancy fluctuations given relatively constant outcomes are similar to those displayed when performance is at a task perceived as skill determined. Of course, instructions indicating that the task is determined by chance also affect luck attributions. Such instructions, if accepted, will initially result in the perception of outcomes as predominantly externally caused. However, if future outcomes deviate from their expected variability, then ability and effort may come to be regarded as performance determinants. For example, a coin toss that constantly turns up heads is not likely to be regarded as a "fair" game. Many investigators have overlooked this intuitively obvious point (see the subsequent discussion of experiments conducted by Rotter and his associates).

Effort. The conditions necessary to attribute an outcome to effort are somewhat more difficult to determine. Covariation of performance with incentive value, or covariation with cues such as perceived muscular tension or task persistence, conceivably will lead to the inference that effort was a dominant behavioral determinant. Such covariations are also expected to minimize attributions of the outcome to luck. Further, one interesting and apparently reliable finding is that individuals employ outcome information to infer how hard they tried; that is, "effects often play the role of data through which we learn to know about origins" [Heider 1944, p. 365]. For example, Weiner and Kukla had subjects attempt to solve a digit-sequence task in which the numbers were actually arranged randomly (although this was unknown to the subjects). Subsequent ratings revealed that effort is judged greater after success than following failure. Jenkins and Ward [1965] previously reported a similar finding. It is probable that in one's life history performance covaries with effort; hence, success or failure results in effort attributions in situations in which effort may or may not be a behavioral determinant.

The pattern of performance also gives rise to effort attributions. For example, Jones et al. report that subjects who are led to believe their performance increases over trials perceive themselves as trying harder than those with apparently decreasing patterns of performance. This disparity in subjective effort was displayed despite the fact that the ascending and descending groups had identical overall performance levels, and the outcomes were entirely under experimental control. Judgments about others are also influenced by the temporal pattern of performance. Beckman [1970] found that students increasing their performance over trials are considered more motivated than pupils exhibiting performance decrements, although again the mean overall performance of the ascending and descending groups was identical.

An Investigation of Causal Judgments

Experiments were conducted by Frieze and Weiner to examine whether individuals can assemble and combine information from some of the diverse sources listed above and reach reliable conclusions about the causes of success and failure. In one experiment, the subjects were given information that specified the percentage of success a hypothetical person experienced at a task (100 per cent, 50 per cent, or 0 per cent), the percentage success that person encountered at similar tasks (100 per cent, 50 per cent, or 0 per cent), and the percentage of other individuals successful at the particular task (100 per cent, 50 per cent, or 0 per cent). These three sources of information were selected because they correspond to three attributional criteria discussed at length by Kelley [1967]: consistency over time (reliability), consistency over modality (generality), and consensus (social norms). The nature of the task was left ambiguous. Further, the subjects were told that the individual attempted the task again and either succeeded or failed. Thus, there were 54 combinations of information (3 × 3 × 3 levels of descrip-

tion × 2 levels of immediate outcome). The subjects then rated the degree to which the immediate success or failure was attributable to ability, effort, task difficulty, and luck. Ratings could range from 0 (not a cause) to 3 (very much a cause), with each of the four causal elements rated for every informational combination. These judgments were consistent with the outcome, for example, good luck was specified as a cause of success and bad luck a cause of failure.

Some of the findings in this study are intuitively obvious and conform to expectation, while others are exceedingly complex and not predictable. Only a small selected sample of the many results in the study is presented here. Figure 2 shows the magnitude of the attributions made to the four causal elements as a function of immediate performance outcome and the percentage of prior success. The figure indicates that attributions to luck and effort, the unstable variables, increase as a function of the discrepancy between the outcome and prior performance. That is, greatest attributions to luck and

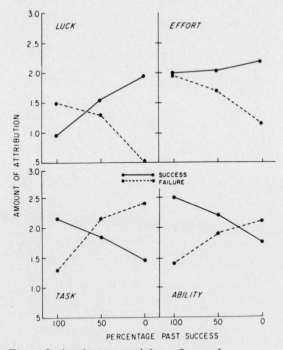

Figure 2. Attributions to ability, effort, task difficulty, and luck as a function of the percentage of prior success and the immediate task outcome (success or failure).

effort are reported when an individual succeeds after never succeeding in the past, or fails after having a history of repeated success; see Feather [1969]. The reverse pattern characterizes task difficulty and ability attributions. Greatest attributions to these stable components in the model occur when past behavior is consistent with current outcome. (All interactions are significant beyond the p < .001 level.) The findings illustrated in figure 2 have been replicated in two other experiments. A parallel pattern of results is observed when information is provided about performance on similar tasks, although the effects are somewhat modulated (interactions range between p <.01 and p <.05). These data support the supposition that ability and task difficulty are perceived as stable factors, while effort and luck are variable causal elements.

It should be noted that when attributions to the stable elements are high, ascriptions to the unstable elements are low, and vice versa. These attributions suggest the compensatory or disjunctive nature of inferences made concerning these components.

Figure 3 illustrates the interaction between the percentage of prior success and the percentage of others designated as having succeeded at the task. Figure 3 illustrates only a portion of the data given a *success* outcome; the left half of the figure portrays ability attributions, while the luck attributions are shown on the right. The figure indicates that the causal significance of ability varies as a function of the percentage of prior success, as is also shown in

figure 2. Further, ability attributions are also related to the percentage of others who are successful (p <.01). As expected, greatest judgment of ability as a causal factor occurs when the individual always succeeds while others consistently fail. Ability is least likely to be inferred as the cause of the immediate success when the individual has never succeeded in the past, while others have always been able to perform the task. Attributions concerning luck are somewhat more complex. In the right half of figure 3 it can be seen that, given no prior success, luck attributions for the immediate success experience do not covary with the performance of others. On the other hand, given consistent prior positive outcomes, attributions to luck vary monotonically with the performance of others (interaction p <.001).

One additional result, shown in figure 4, portrays the degree to which causal attributions to the four elements are a function of task outcome. Figure 4 indicates that greater absolute attributions to ability and effort (p < .005) and luck (n.s.) are made following a success than after a failure. Conversely, inferences about the difficulty of the task are greater following failure than success (p <.05). These findings have also been replicated by Frieze and Weiner.

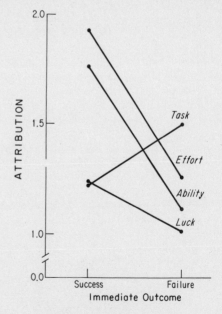

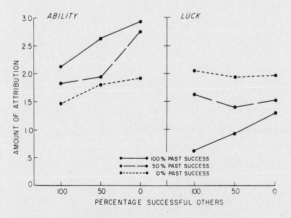

Figure 3. Attributions to ability (left) and luck (right), given a successful outcome, as a function of the percentages of prior success and the percentage of others successful at the task.

Figure 4. Attributions to ability, effort, task difficulty, and luck as a function of the immediate outcome (success or failure). [From Frieze & Weiner in press.]

The pattern of inferences suggests that success is more likely to be attributed to internal factors than is failure, while there is a tendency to attribute failure to external sources. This resembles the operation of ego-defensive factors observed when subjects make attributions about their own performance; see Hoppe [1931] and Weiner and Kukla [1970], though in this case judgments are not being made about the self. Perhaps, then, attributional judgments are a function of the positivity or negativity of an event and are not "motivated" or "ego-protective" errors.

In conclusion, it is evident from this experiment that individuals are able to form systematic causal judgments in complex achievement situations. That is, the postulated antecedent conditions give rise to ascriptions to the four causal categories. There appears to be ample evidence that the first stage of a general cognitive model of motivation (S $\longrightarrow$ cognition) is determinable in this specific attributional approach.

General Summary

It is contended that individuals are able to process a wealth and diversity of information to reach inferences about the causes of their own and others' behaviors, that the casual categories in achievement setttings include ability, effort, task difficulty, and luck, that the causal ascriptions are schematized into the dimensions of locus of control and stability, and that the attributions made have motivational significance. Thus, information processing, judgment and decision making, inferences about causality, and the role of appraisal in determining affect and action, that is, the mental processes previously listed as neglected by prior "cognitive" conceptions of motivation, are the central concerns in this analysis of behavior.

Achievement Motivation

To examine the stage 2 specification of a cognitive model of motivation (cognition $\longrightarrow$ R), we turn to the extant experimental findings in the area of achievement motivation. These data were accumulated primarily to provide evidence for a theory of achievement motivation developed principally by Atkinson [1957]. Therefore, it is instructive to discuss Atkinson's initial conception of achievement motivation and then to summarize some of the data

generated by that theory. More recent developments in achivement theory are generally neglected; see Atkinson [1964, 1969] and Weiner [1970]. Following this review, the hypotheses and data in these achivement studies are reconstrued in the language of attribution theory. Previously unreported experiments are also presented in support of the proposed attributional interpretation.

Atkinson's Theory of Achievement Motivation

Atkinson [1957] conceives achievement-oriented behavior to be the resultant of an approach-avoidance conflict. The achievement-oriented tendency (T_A) is conceptualized as:

$$T_A = M_s \times P_s \times I_s - (M_{AF} \times P_f \times I_f) \qquad [1]$$

Among the determinants of the approach tendency, defined by the first three factors in equation 1, M_s represents a relatively stable personality disposition to strive for success, which is conceived as a capacity to experience pride in accomplishment (the need for achievement). The probability of success, P_s, represents the likelihood that a given instrumental action will lead to the goal; P_s denotes a cognitive expectancy that a response made to a given stimulus will lead to the goal stimulus [Atkinson 1954]. I_s symbolizes the incentive value of success. Within Atkinson's model for achievement-oriented behavior, I_s does not have independent operational existence; I_s is determined by the magnitude of P_s: $I_s = 1 - P_s$. Atkinson reasons that the incentive value of success is an affect often labeled "pride." The amount of pride experienced following goal attainment is inversely related to the subjective difficulty of the task; that is, one experiences more pride following success at a task perceived as difficult than after success at a task perceived as easy. Because $I_s = 1 - P_s$, and I_s and P_s are multipicatively related, the greatest approach tendency is derived when $P_s = .50$. In that condition, $P_s \times I_s$ is maximum, or .25. As P_s increases or decreases from .50, approach motivation decreases.

The determinants of avoidance, the last three factors in equation 1, are analogous to those of the approach tendency. M_{AF} symbolizes a relatively stable personality disposition to avoid failure, and may be considered a capacity to experience shame in achievement-oriented contexts. Among the environmental determinants of avoidance behavior, P_f represents the subjective probability of failure, and I_f the incentive value of failure (it is assumed that $P_s + P_f$

=1). The negative affect associated with nonattainment of an achievement-related goal is considered to be shame. Atkinson reasons that the easier the task, the greater the shame experienced following failure. I_f, therefore, is conceived as $-(1-P_f)$. Inasmuch as $I_f = -(1-P_f)$, and I_f and P_f are multiplicative, the maximum avoidance tendency is derived when $P_f = .50$, and decreases as P_f increases or decreases from the .50 level.

The relationships enumerated above are clarified by making some simple transformations in Atkinson's model. There is only one degree of freedom among the four environmental determinants of behavior (P_s, I_s, P_f, I_f). The model for achievement-related behavior therefore can be represented as:

$$T_A = (M_S - M_{AF})[P_s \times (1 - P_s)] \qquad [2]$$

Equation 2 clearly indicates that the strength of M_S relative to M_{AF}, or the capacity to experience pride in success relative to the capacity to experience shame in failure, determines whether individuals will approach or avoid achievement tasks. The motive measures, therefore, may be considered weights given to the functions that relate motivation to success probability. If $M_S > M_{AF}$, greater value is given to the approach than avoidance tendency, and vice versa. Further, when $M_S > M_{AF}$, resultant achievement motivation is positive and maximum when $P_s = .50$. On the other hand, when $M_{AF} > M_S$, resultant achievement motivation is negative and most inhibitory when P_f (and P_s) = .50.

Needless to say, this brief review does not do full justice to Atkinson's conception, and as previously indicated, many recent conceptual developments are ignored. Nevertheless, the summary does include many of the essential concepts in his model and manages to convey Atkinson's general theoretical approach. In the tradition established by Hull, Atkinson attempts to isolate the determinants of behavior and to specify their mathematical relationships. The influence of Lewin and Tolman is also evident, for the primary experiential component in the model is an "expectancy" concerning the likelihood of success. Hence, Atkinson's conception is labeled as cognitive, rather than mechanistic.

Evidence Supporting the Theory. The experimental evidence cited in support of this conception may be sorted into four general categories: data reflecting the free choice to become engaged or not in achievement activities, data concerning the particular achievement task chosen when the subject must choose one, intensity or magnitude of task performance, and the persistence of achivement-oriented behavior. This evidence is not reviewed in detail here, nor are appropriate references cited; see Atkinson [1964] and Weiner [1970]. Rather, hypotheses or derivations from the achievement model are presented, and a general summary statement concerning the empirical evidence is offered.

In a *free choice* setting, Atkinson's model specifies that when $M_S > M_{AF}$, T_A is positive; these individuals therefore are expected to approach achievement-related tasks. Conversely, when $M_{AF} > M_S$, T_A is negative; these individuals consequently should avoid achievement activities. When subjects classified according to strength of achievement needs are given an opportunity to perform an achievement-related activity, it does appear that those high in achievement motivation are more likely to undertake that task than subjects low in achievement motivation.

Subjects in a *forced choice* setting are typically required to select and perform a task from a number of achievement-related problems that differ in reported or objective level of difficulty. The hypothesis generally tested is that subjects in whom $M_S > M_{AF}$ will be more likely to choose tasks of intermediate difficulty ($P_S = .50$) than subjects in whom $M_{AF} > M_S$. This prediction has been confirmed by many investigators, providing the best evidence for the validity of the 1957 conception of achievement motivation.

Magnitude or *intensity of performance* has not been used frequently as a dependent variable in studies pertinent to the validation of the 1957 model. However, the general prediction that subjects in whom $M_S > M_{AF}$ will perform with greater intensity or work harder than subjects in whom $M_{AF} > M_S$ also finds support in the experimental literature.

The most sophisticated experimental hypotheses derived from Atkinson's conception employ *persistence of behavior* as the dependent variable. Predictions in these investigations are often rather complex, for interactions are expected between level of achievement needs and the initial P_S at the task. In general, however, it has been predicted and found that individuals in whom $M_S > M_{AF}$ persist longer in situations of failure than those in whom $M_{AF} > M_S$. That is, subjects high in achievement-related needs are more likely to display positive goal striving following nonattainment of a goal than subjects low in achievement needs.

In sum, there is experimental evidence indicating that individuals high in achievement motivation are more likely to undertake achievement activities, select tasks of intermediate difficulty, work harder, and persist longer in the face of failure than individuals low in achievement motivation. These predictions are directly derivable from the model of motivation formulated by Atkinson.

Achievement Behavior and Attribution Theory

Our task now is to reinterpret the foregoing results within an attributional framework. The guiding general proposition is that antecedent conditions (including level of achievement-related needs, prior pattern and level of performance, and information about performance norms) determine whether success or failure experiences are ascribed to the perceived causal elements of ability, effort, task difficulty, or luck. These ascriptions give rise to approach or avoidance behavior, persistence or resignation in the face of failure, selection of easy or hard versus intermediate difficulty level tasks, and intense or weak performance.

Free-Choice Behavior

How might the tendency for individuals in whom $M_S > M_{AF}$ to approach achievement activities, and the tendency for individuals in whom $M_{AF} > M_S$ to avoid achievement activities, be conceptualized in attributional language? It has been suggested [Heckhausen 1967, Weiner & Kukla 1970] that the reward value of an achievement-related goal is a function of the degree of perceived personal responsibility for the outcome of the action. Feather [1967], guided by Atkinson's 1957 model, specifically postulates that I_s be conceived as equal to $C(1-P_s)$, where C represents the degree of perceived internal control. Indeed, it is intuitively reasonable to suppose that pride in accomplishment is contingent upon the extent to which one perceives himself responsible for attaining an achievement-related goal; it is likely that for this reason achievement motivation is believed to be aroused in skill, but not chance, situations. (A more general statement of the relationship between affect and control is that the affect associated with any goal accomplishment will be a direct function of the degree of personal responsibility for the instrumental activity. Thus, affect may be primarily determined by the locus of control, rather than the stability, dimension of causality.)

These considerations led Weiner and Kukla to hypothesize that individuals high in resultant achievement motivation are more likely to attribute success in achievement-oriented contexts to themselves than

are individuals low in resultant achievement motivation. If so, success in achievement activities would be more rewarding to the high than to the low motive group, so that the former would be more likely to approach achievement activities. This hypothesis, therefore, specifies a causal attribution that mediates between the level of resultant achievement motivation and the probability of undertaking an achievement-oriented activity.

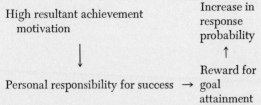

Both correlational and experimental paradigms have been employed to investigate this analysis.

Correlational studies. In the initial study that we conducted in this area, measures of achievement motivation and locus of control were administered to male and female school children in grades 3–6 and to high-school-age males [Weiner & Kukla]. The achievement measure used in the grade school population was untested, although it was modeled after an adult scale validated in prior studies. Achievement motivation in the high school population was assessed with the standard Thematic Apperception Test procedure and with the Mandler-Sarason Test Anxiety Questionnaire. These two measures are conceived, respectively, as assessing the need for achievement (M_S) and anxiety about failure (M_{AF}). The Intellectual Achievement Responsibility (IAR) scale [Crandall, Katkovsky, & Crandall 1965] was employed to ascertain perceived locus of control. The IAR contains thirty-four forced choice items with internal and external alternative responses. The items contain stems with either positive or negative outcomes, and the majority of the internal response alternatives can be classified into either ability or effort attributions. Two exemplary items are:

When you win at a game of cards or checkers, does it happen
  A. because you play very well, or
  B. because the other person doesn't play well?
Suppose you study to become a teacher, scientist, or doctor and you fail. Do you think this would happen
  A. because you didn't work hard enough, or
  B. because you needed some help, and other people didn't give it to you?

A number of theoretical considerations led to the choice of the IAR scale to assess locus of control, rather than the more widely used scale of internal-external control (I-E) developed by Rotter and his students; see Rotter [1966]. First, the items on the IAR scale all pertain to perceived control in achievement-related situations, whereas the I-E test items generally concern social power, leadership, etc. Further, all the items on the IAR scale portray circumstances involving success or failure. This categorization is not attainable with the items on the I-E scale. As indicated earlier, the hypothesis being tested refers to perceived control *given successful outcomes only*. A general tendency toward internality or externality, divorced from information about the outcome of an achievement event, is not anticipated. Hence, the I-E scale is not an appropriate measurement instrument, given the specific conception of control subscribed to in this paper.

Figure 5 illustrates the results of this investigation for the male subjects ($N=258$). In figure 5 the success outcome items (I+) are portrayed separately from the failure outcome items (I−). (The I preceding the + and − indicates an internal response.)

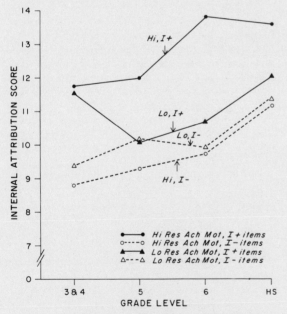

Figure 5. Mean internal attribution scores for positive (I+) and negative (I−) outcome items on the Internal Achievement Responsibility scale, with male subjects (N=258) classified according to resultant achievement motivation and grade level. [From Weiner & Kukla 1970.]

The subjects were classified at the median into high and low resultant achievement motivation. Figure 5 indicates clearly that male subjects high in resultant achievement motivation are more likely to assume personal responsibility for success than are male subjects low in resultant achievement motivation ($p<.02$). Including the data of the female subjects ($N=127$) decreases the level of significance of this finding, although the high motive group still exhibits greater responsibility for success than the low group ($p<.05$). The findings for the females alone generally are nonsignificant.

The I− data, or the assignment of responsibility for failed events, is discussed in detail in the section concerned with the persistence of behavior. It should be noted, however, that males in the high motive group are not internal with respect to failure. That is, they do not display a *general* tendency toward internality.

A second correlational study also provides evidence concerning the hypothesized relationship between achievement motivation and causal ascription for successful events. Weiner and Potepan [1970] investigated some of the differentiating personality characteristics of successful and failing college students. Following a mid-term exam in introductory psychology, 107 students receiving superior or failing grades were administered, in part, measures of resultant achievement motivation and locus of control. The achievement measure was a reasonably well-validated objective instrument developed by Mehrabian [1968], while the measure of control was a variant of the IAR scale. Some of the items were eliminated or altered in the latter instrument so they would be appropriate for a college population.

The first column of figures in table 2 presents the correlations between resultant achievement motivation and causal ascription. In addition to differentiating positive from negative outcomes, the matrix shows the individual ability (A) and effort (E) ascriptions. Again focusing only upon successful outcomes, resultant achievement motivation is significantly related to perceived self-responsibility (I+) ($r=.36$, $p<.01$). This correlation is primarily accounted for by the association between achievement motivation and attribution of success to ability (A+) ($r=.35$, $p<.01$), although there is also a positive correlation between achievement concerns and effort attribution (M+) ($r=.12$).

The correlational data reported in table 2 have been partially replicated in an unpublished study by Harold Segal, which included the assessment of indi-

Table 2. Correlations between Resultant Achievement Motivation and Ascriptions for Success and Failure (N = 107).

Variable No.	Variable	Variable No.					
		1	2	3	4	5	6
1	Resultant achievement motivation						
2	Success ascribed to ability (A+)	.35					
3	Success ascribed to motivation (M+)	.12	−.10				
4	Internality for success (A+(+) M+) = I+	.36	.72	.62			
5	Failure ascribed to ability (A−)	−.33	−.37	−.14	−.37		
6	Failure ascribed to motivation (M−)	.08	.16	.30	.16	−.40	
7	Internality for failure (A−(+) M−) = I−	−.26	−.24	.11	−.24	.67	.42

SOURCE: After Weiner & Potepan [1970].

vidual differences in achievement motivation and locus of control. Among the male subjects (N = 26), he found strikingly high correlations between resultant achievement motivation and A+ (r = .46, p < .05), M+ (r = .43, p < .05), and Total I+ (r = .54, p < .01). None of these correlations, however, approach significance for the 24 females included in Segal's investigation.

In sum, it is stated with some assurance that, among male students, achievement concerns and self-attribution for success are positively related. The result has been found with a variety of measures of achievement motivation and somewhat different indexes of locus of control. Further, the samples tested ranged from third grade through college. On the other hand, the relationship between achievement motivation and locus of control for successful events

is undetermined (nonexistent?) for females. The relative weakness of the findings among the female subjects is not entirely unexpected; prior studies of achievement behavior and locus of control also yield inconsistent results with females; see Crandall, Katkovsky, and Preston [1962].

Experimental Studies. The relationship between achievement motivation and perceived responsibility for success has also been investigated in experimental settings. In one of these studies [Kukla 1970], male subjects (N = 138) classified according to the strength of achievement motivation attempted a task that was ambiguous with respect to the causes of success and failure. The task required the subjects to determine whether a 0 or 1 would be the next digit in a number series. Thus, luck, as well as ability, effort, and task difficulty, could subjectively influence the final performance score. The numbers actually were arranged randomly (see Weiner and Kukla for a more detailed discussion of the procedure). Upon completion of the task and performance feedback, the subjects judged their ability, effort expenditure, and luck, as well as the difficulty of the task.

The subjects were divided at the median according to the level of achievement needs and also according to subjective success or failure at the task. Table 3 gives the mean ratings for the four groups (2 experimental conditions × 2 motive classifications) across the four causal dimensions. The table indicates that ability (p < .001) and luck (p < .01) as well as effort (p < .10) are perceived as greater after success than following failure. The main effect of task difficulty, however, does not approach statistical significance between the success and failure conditions. (These findings are reminiscent of those reported in figure 4.) Further, subjects classified as high in

Table 3. Mean Attribution Ratings in the Success and Failure Conditions for Subjects Classified as High (above the Median) or Low (below the Median) in Resultant Achievement Motivation.

Condition[a]	Ability		Effort		Task Difficulty		Luck	
	High[b]	Low	High	Low	High	Low	High	Low
Success	7.0	6.6	7.1	6.3	5.4	4.8	5.2	5.2
Failure	5.9	4.9	5.8	6.4	5.0	5.8	4.4	4.4

[a]For high success, N = 37; high failure, N = 33; low success, N = 35; low failure, N = 33.
[b]Motive classification

SOURCE: After Kukla [1970].

achievement motivation believe that they have greater ability than subjects low in this motivational classification ($p < .01$). Of more immediate interest are the attributions in the success condition. Table 3 shows that, given success, subjects high in achievement motivation are more likely to attribute the outcome to internal factors (ability and effort) than are subjects in the low achievement grouping (respectively, $p < .20$; $p < .10$), while subjects in the low motive group are more prone to ascribe success to the external factor of task ease ($p < .20$). Further, the subjects high in achievement motivation vary their effort attributions as a function of task outcome ($r = .44$, $p < .01$), while this perceived effort-outcome covariation is not exhibited by subjects in the low motive group ($r = .08$).

Thus, support is again provided for the contention that individuals high in resultant achievement motivation are more likely to attribute success to themselves than are those low in achievement motivation. The differentiated effort and ability comparisons in the success condition only approach statistical significance in this investigation. The pattern of results, however, replicates findings reported earlier by Weiner and Kukla. In the prior experiment conducted by Weiner and Kukla, "skill," rather than ability, was rated following task performance, and direct measures of luck and task difficulty were not obtained. The data indicate that after success the high motive subjects believe themselves to be significantly more skillful at the task than the low motive subjects. Further, in the success condition a significantly greater number of subjects in the low motive group expect to obtain a lower performance score on the next trial, thus intimating that they ascribe their good performance to luck. Finally, the effort ratings of the two motive groups in the Weiner and Kukla study do not differ significantly, although the direction of the results is the same as that reported by Kukla [1970]. In sum, the data obtained in the Kukla investigation appear to be reliable.

Results from a self-reinforcement setting. The predicted relationships between achievement motivation, locus of control, and self-reward have also been tested directly in an investigation conducted by Ruth Cook, Linda Reed, and Patricia Brown. Male pupils in the fourth and fifth grades were placed in a free-operant setting in which they determined their own reinforcements for performance. The subjects ($N = 63$) were given a set of achievement-related puzzles to solve, with half of the puzzles actually being insoluble. On the desk in front of the subjects

was a bowl containing poker chips. The instructions to the subjects indicated that they were to "reward themselves by taking as many chips as they feel they deserve" following each successful trial. In a similar manner, following every failure they were told to "punish themselves" by returning the number of chips which "they feel they should"; see Kanfer and Marston [1963] and Mischel, Coates, and Raskoff [1968], for related self-reinforcement methodologies. Unknown to the subjects, the experimenter was able to monitor how much reward and punishment the subjects self-imposed on each trial. A number of experimental precautions ensured that the subjects never ran out of chips, failed and succeeded an equal number of trials, and perceived the solved and failed puzzles as equally difficult. Two months prior to this testing the IAR and a measure of resultant achievement motivation had been administered.

The results of this study are reported in detail in a 1970 dissertation by Cook and in Weiner, Heckhausen, Meyer, and Cook. Table 4 shows that the

Table 4. *Mean Self-Reward Minus Self-Punishment in a Free-Operant Setting, According to Individual Differences in Resultant Achievement Motivation and Self-Ascription for Success and Failure (Locus of Control).*

Personality Variable	Classification ($N=63$)		
	Low	Medium	High
Resultant achievement motivation	1.59	2.60	3.72
Locus of control[a]	.87	3.54	3.47

[a]A resultant of the tendency to ascribe success to oneself minus the tendency to ascribe failure to oneself.

SOURCE: After Cook [1970].

mean level of reinforcement (which is a composite of reward minus punishment) is a function of resultant achievement motivation ($p < .10$) and resultant internality for success ($p < .05$). (The latter measure is a composite of self-ascription for success minus self-ascription for failure.) That is, individuals high in resultant achievement concerns compensate themselves more for achievement performance than individuals low in achievement concerns, and the greater the tendency to believe that success, but not failure, was caused by oneself, the greater the resultant self-rewarding behavior. Figure 6 shows the separate reward and punishment behavior as a function of resultant internality for success.

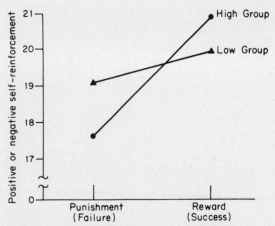

Figure 6. Resultant reward (mean reward minus mean punishment) for individuals classified as high or low in resultant internality for success (internal attribution for success, or I+, minus internal attribution for failure, or I−). [From Cook 1970.]

Summary of Research Relevant to Free-Choice Behavior. Individuals high in resultant achievement motivation approach achievement-related tasks because they experience enhanced reward for success at those tasks. The heightened satisfaction is realized because success tends to be attributed by the high motive group subjects to their own actions, and self-attribution results in augmented reward value for success. Both the achievement-attribution and the attribution-reward links of the model diagrammed at the beginning of this section are relatively well substantiated. The two remaining relationships specified in the diagram between achievement motivation and approach behavior and between reward and response probability are well documented in the experimental literature.

Persistence of Behavior

The second cluster of empirical findings we will attempt to reinterpret pertains to the persistence of behavior. Loosely summarized, individuals high in achievement motivation persist longer at achievement-related tasks than do individuals classified as low in achievement-related needs. An attributional analysis of this behavior requires further consideration of the causal dimension of stability. We have suggested that attributions to the stable elements of ability and task difficulty imply that consistencies between past and future behaviors are expected. More specifically, it is hypothesized that if failure at an achievement task is believed to be caused by a low level of ability or high task difficulty, future failures will be anticipated. (Heider would label this attributional constellation as a perceived shortcoming in the "can" determinant of behavior.)

Conversely, it is submitted that attributions to the unstable elements of effort and luck imply that inconsistencies between past and future behaviors will probably occur. More specifically, it is hypothesized that if failure at an achievement task is believed to be caused by lack of effort or bad luck, future success may be expected. Thus, the individual should engage in repeated instrumental actions. This analysis directly leads to the hypothesis that ascriptions of failure to a lack of effort will result in greater persistence in the face of failure than will ascriptions to a deficiency of ability.

The data summarized in the prior pages provide evidence that differential attributional tendencies for failure do characterize the high and low motive groups. The data pertaining to *failure* reported in table 2 reveal that resultant achievement motivation is inversely related to the self-attribution of low ability $(A-)$, $(r = -.33, p < .01)$ and directly related to the self-ascription of low effort $(M-)$, $(r = .08)$. The study conducted by Segal replicated this attributional pattern for the male subjects. The correlations in that study between achievement motivation and $A-$ and $M-$, respectively, are $r = -.49$ $(p < .01)$ and $r = .17$. Table 3 also reveals that subjects low in achievement concerns, relative to the high motive group, believe that their failure is caused by a lack of ability $(p < .05)$. On the other hand, subjects in the high motive group tend to impute failure to a deficiency of effort $(p < .20)$. Further, in the similar digit-sequence experiment reported in Weiner and Kukla, the subjects high in resultant achievement motivation also rate their effort significantly lower than the low motive subjects, given a failure outcome $(p < .05)$.

In sum, the data generally support the hypothesis that, in situations of failure, individuals high in resultant achievement motivation attribute their poor performance to a lack of effort, while individuals low in resultant achievement motivation perceive failure as being due to insufficient ability. It is submitted that the fixed versus variable nature of the mediating attributional elements of ability and effort produce discrepancies in the persistence of behavior.

Still further evidence supporting these hypotheses is presented later.

Forced Choice (Risk Preference)

Atkinson [1957] has proposed that achievement motive level relates to preferences for or against taking risks in a performance setting. Individuals highly motivated to achieve success prefer tasks of intermediate difficulty more than do individuals low in achievement motivation. Atkinson derived the differential risk-taking hypothesis by assuming that the incentive value of success (I_s) and the probability of success (P_s) are inversely related to each other and multiplicative. In other words, the tendency to approach (strive for) achievement includes the components $I_s \times P_s$ (see formula 1).

Just as M_S (the stable disposition to strive for success) can be construed in the language of attribution theory, the relationship between I_s and P_s can also be accounted for by attributional processes. According to Kelley [1967], the allocation of causality is guided by an examination of "variations in effect" (p. 194). Given an easy task, the majority of people undertaking that task succeed. Correspondingly, most of the individuals attempting an objectively difficult task fail. Hence, these modal success and failure performance outcomes should be attributed primarily to external factors (the task), rather than to internal sources. On the other hand, the occasional performance that contrasts with results produced by others, that is, success at a difficult task or failure at an easy task, should be ascribed to the individual undertaking the task. In sum, given a successful outcome, internal attributions should be inversely related to probability of success. Correspondingly, given a failure experience, internal attributions should be directly related to the ease of the task.

Weiner and Kukla tested these hypotheses using a simple simulation paradigm. Their subjects ($N=76$) rated the perceived internal versus external locus of causality ("degree to which performance was due (not due) to the ability and efforts of person") in eighteen hypothetical conditions. The conditions differed according to the results of the action (success or failure) and the percentage of others designated as succeeding (.99, .95, .90, .70, .50, .30, .10, .05, .01).

The data from this experiment are shown in figure 7. It is evident that internal attribution for success increases as the task becomes more difficult (P_s decreases), while the internal attribution for failure increases as the task becomes easier. Therefore, it is

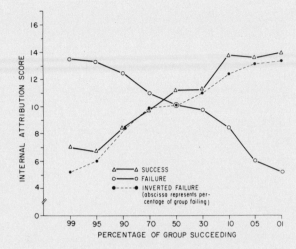

Figure 7. Mean internal attribution scores for success and failure outcome conditions as a function of task difficulty. [From Weiner & Kukla 1970.]

suggested that one experiences more pride (I_s) given success at a difficult task, because there is greater self-attribution for success at low P_s tasks. Similarly, it is contended that more shame ($-I_f$) is experienced given failure at an easy task, because there is greater self-attribution for failure at high P_s tasks. (Feather [1967], has contended that I_s be conceptualized as $C(1-P_s)$, where C symbolizes the degree of internal control. However, P_s is also an index of locus of control when considered in conjunction with task outcome. Hence, Feather's formula for the incentive value of success is a composite of locus of control derived from a stable personality disposition and locus of control as determined by the stimulus situation.)

In addition to further explicating the achievement model in attributional language, these data may have a direct bearing upon the understanding of the disparate risk-taking behavior that characterizes the extreme motive groups. If very easy or very difficult tasks are predominantly selected, respective success or failure (which are the usual outcomes) give rise to information concerning the characteristics of the task rather than to knowledge about the person attempting the task. That is, a person who selects easy or difficult tasks is also opting for external attributions. On the other hand, success or failure at tasks of intermediate difficulty will, over trials, yield definite information about the capabilities of the person undertaking the task. That is, selection of tasks of intermediate difficulty may indicate a preference for internal attribution situations, or self-evaluation.

It is therefore suggested that individuals high in achievement motivation select tasks of intermediate difficulty because performance at such tasks has the greatest self-informational (rather than hedonic or consummatory) value. On the other hand, individuals low in achievement motivation prefer to avoid feedback concerning their relative abilities and select activities that are likely to result in task attributions.

This interpretation finds support from other data in the achievement literature, such as the differential knowledge of results that the motive groups desire. McClelland [1961] states: "From the psychological point of view, it does not automatically follow that all kinds of people like to have concrete knowledge of results of their choices of action. Such knowledge is a source of anxiety because it cuts both ways: it provides not only proof of success, but also inescapable evidence of failure . . . . There is every theoretical reason to suppose that . . . subjects with high n Achievement . . . should be drawn to activities in which they have a chance to show objectively how well they can do" [pp. 231, 233]. This argument is directly applicable to an understanding of the risk-preference literature. The association between task difficulty and causal ascription, when considered in conjunction with task outcome, yields information pertinent to the "proof of success."

Intensity of Performance

There are a number of attributional interpretations of the data indicating that subjects in whom $M_S > M_{AF}$ perform with greater vigor than subjects in whom $M_{AF} > M_S$. Individuals high in achievement motivation perceive outcome and effort to be highly associated, while this relationship is not evident among individuals low in achievement motivation. Thus, effort is perceived only by the high motive group as an important determinant of success. They may, therefore, be expected to work harder at achievement tasks than the low motive group (given the assumption that there is a consistency between belief systems and actual behavior). Further, individuals in whom $M_{AF} > M_S$ ascribe failure to low ability. Perhaps this results in their "giving up," and not engaging in further instrumental actions to reach the goal.

Meyer [1970] used a population of German male school children ($N = 39$) to investigate the relationship between achievement needs, attributions for failure, and intensity of performance. The subjects, who were about fourteen years old, were given five digit-symbol substitution tasks to complete. On each trial they were interrupted before finishing. Following every failure, the subjects attributed the outcome to the four causal elements of ability, effort, task difficulty, and luck. The attribution ratings were in percentage figures and were required to total 100 per cent. Meyer also measured the speed of performance as the subjects attempted the digit substitution task.

As hypothesized by Meyer, subjects above the median in resultant achievement motivation attribute their failures to a lack of effort more than do subjects below the median in the resultant achievement needs (see figure 8). Figure 8 also reveals that

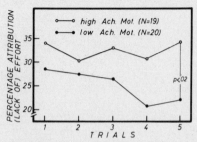

Figure 8. Percentage attribution to lack of effort following failure as a function of motive classification and trials. [From Meyer 1970.]

over trials the differential effort attributions become more pronounced. On the other hand, children low in achievement concerns were more likely to ascribe their failures to a lack of ability (see figure 9). Further, a trials × motive interaction was again displayed.

Meyer then examined the relationships between the attributional ratings and performance speed. He contended that attributions for failure to the unstable elements would result in better performance than attributions to stable elements. The correlations between the attributions and performance speed are: ability ($r = -.05, n.s.$), effort ($r = .25, p < .10$), luck ($r = .23, p < .10$), and task difficulty ($r = -.38, p < .01$). The correlation between intensity of performance and ascription to the combined unstable elements is $r = .43$, $p < .005$. Thus, speed of performance is directly related to the attribution of failure to bad luck and lack of effort.

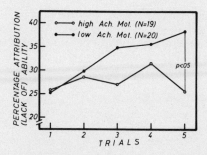

Figure 9. Percentage attribution to lack of ability following failure as a function of motive classification and trials. [From Meyer 1970.]

Relationship between risk preference and performance intensity. Perhaps the disparate risk-taking behavior exhibited by the motive groups gives rise to the differential perceptions of effort as a causal determinant. It has been well documented that subjects in the high motive group prefer tasks of intermediate difficulty, while subjects in the low motive group are attracted to relatively easy or difficult tasks. It is conceivable that performance at intermediate difficulty tasks actually does vary with effort, while outcomes at very easy or difficult activities are generally unaffected by effort expenditure. Thus, past reinforcement histories might account for the contrasting effort ascriptions and vigor of performance.

In addition, there is an intuitively reasonable explanation of why persons work hardest at tasks of intermediate difficulty. It is likely that individuals feel that great effort is not required at easy tasks and is a "waste" of energy at very difficult tasks. To explore this possibility, Weiner, Heckhausen, Meyer, and Cook asked subjects to indicate at which of five tasks effort was the most important determinant of outcome. The task differed only in the percentage of others designated as succeeding (90%, 70%, 50%, 30%, or 10%). Subjects also were asked at which of these tasks it would be most functional to expend effort. The results of this study are shown in figure 10. It is clear from that figure that subjects believe effort is the most important determinant of outcome at tasks of intermediate difficulty and that it is most functional to work hardest at $P_s = .50$ tasks.

General Summary

Individual differences in achievement motivation, as well as cues such as task difficulty, affect mediating cognitions concerning the causes of behavioral outcomes. These causal inferences then influence subsequent achievement behavior. More specifically, our prior discussion indicates that:

A. Individuals high in resultant achievement motivation
  1. Approach achievement-related activities (mediated by the attribution of success to high ability and effort, thus producing heightened reward or pride in accomplishment)
  2. Persist in the face of failure (mediated by the ascription of failure to a lack of effort, which is presumed to be modifiable)
  3. Select tasks of intermediate difficulty (mediated by an interaction between task difficulty, performance outcome, and causal ascription, which results in tasks of intermediate difficulty yielding the most self-evaluative feedback)
  4. Perform with relatively great vigor (mediated by the belief that outcome is determined by effort, and learned in part because performance at intermediate difficulty tasks is greatly influenced by effort)
B. Individuals low in resultant achievement motivation
  1. Do not approach achievement-related activities (mediated by the relative attribution of success to external rather than internal factors and the exclusion of effort as a causal factor, thus resulting in modulated reward for goal attainment)
  2. Quit in the face of failure (mediated by the belief that failure is caused by a lack of ability, which presumably is unchangeable)

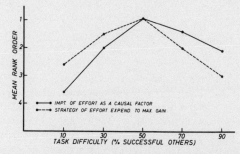

Figure 10. Judged importance of effort as a causal factor, and strategy of effort expenditure to maximize gain, as a function of perceived task difficulty (percentage of successful others). [From Weiner, Heckhausen, Meyer, & Cook in press.]

111

3. Select easy or difficult tasks (because such tasks yield minimal self-evaluative feedback)
4. Perform with relatively little vigor (mediated by the belief that outcome is comparatively independent of effort, and learned in part because performance at very hard or very easy tasks is relatively little influenced by effort)

Contrasting the Attributional and Atkinsonian Models

The aim of the preceding section was to accommodate the data generated by Atkinson's theory of motivation within the framework of attribution theory. No attempt was made to "refute" Atkinson's conception nor to devise definitive experiments that would permit a choice between the two approaches outlined in the paper. There are, nonetheless, a number of points of contrast between the attributional and Atkinsonian models. Consider first the definition of achievement motivation. Atkinson defines the achievement motive as a "capacity for experiencing pride in accomplishment" [1964, p. 214]. Further, the affective anticipations of hope of success and fear of failure, which are emotional reactions elicited by appropriate achievement cues, theoretically determine whether an achievement-related goal is approached or avoided. On the other hand, the attributional model suggests that the achievement motive be defined as a "capacity for perceiving success as caused by internal factors, particularly effort." More pride is then experienced in success by the high motive group because of their particular mediating beliefs about causality. Thus, the achievement motive is a cognitive, rather than affective, disposition. It has been contended in this paper that affect follows cognitive appraisal.

It therefore appears that two fundamentally different conceptions of motivation are represented by the two achievement models. On the one hand, Atkinson's conception of achievement motivation may be portrayed:

$$Stimulus \rightarrow \frac{Emotional}{Anticipation} \rightarrow Instrumental\ Response$$

Conversely, the theoretical structure of the attributional model is:

$$Stimulus \rightarrow \frac{Mediating}{Cognitions} \underset{\searrow Expectancy \nearrow}{\overset{\nearrow Affective \searrow}{Response}} \frac{Instrumental}{Response}$$

Further, it appears that a schematization of the mediating causal cognitions results in differential influences on affect and expectancy:

$$Stimulus \rightarrow \frac{Mediating}{Cognitions} \underset{\searrow Stability \rightarrow Expectancy \nearrow}{\overset{\nearrow Locus\ of\ Control \searrow Affect \searrow}{}} \frac{Instr.}{Res.}$$

[See Lazarus 1968 for a detailed discussion of "emotion-as-response," as opposed to "emotion-as-motivation." Further, see Leventhal 1971 for a similar model concerned with the effects of communications on affect and persuasion.]

The analysis above suggests a number of rather intriguing conjectures. Weiner and Kukla have shown that the amount of pride and shame experienced in success and failure are, in part, a function of the magnitude of the attributions to ability versus effort (see figure 1). Most pride in success, and greatest shame for failure, occur when attributions are made, respectively, to high and low effort. Further, individuals high in achievement motivation ascribe personal failure to a lack of effort. It therefore follows that they should experience more shame given failure than individuals low in achievement needs. Precisely the opposite prediction is derived from Atkinson's conception.

A related point worth noting is that, according to the attributional model, both negative affect and subsequent approach behavior are linked with ascriptions of failure to a lack of effort. Hence, in opposition to current thoughts about the relationship between affect and behavior, a *positive* correlation is expected between the intensity of negative affect (punishment for failure) and the subsequent probability of repeating the achievement activity.

In prior research, achievement motive arousal procedures generally utilize "ego-involving" instructions or induce success or failure, which are believed to heighten affective concerns. Another implication of the position that the achievement motive be viewed as a cognitive disposition is that it should be possible to arouse achievement motivation by inducing appropriate causal ascriptions. In one test of this hypothesis, Breit [1969] had subjects compose essays in which success was attributed either to oneself or to external factors. Subjects in the internal success condition subsequently exhibited behavior associated with high achievement needs more than did subjects in the external success ascription condition.

In a similar manner, Kukla contrasted the performance of subjects given different attributional sets for success and failure. In one condition the subjects were told that the relative success of their performance would be determined, in part, by their effort expenditure. This is the attributional set maintained by subjects high in achievement motivation. In a second condition subjects were informed that performance outcome is determined by ability and that effort has little effect on success or failure. This apparently is the attributional set maintained by subjects low in achievement needs. Subsequent behavior at the task revealed that high-achievement-oriented subjects in the effort condition worked with greater intensity and were more likely to choose tasks of intermediate difficulty than were the subjects low in achievement motivation in that condition. However, this differential behavior was not exhibited in the ability-only condition.

Attribution, Schedules of Reinforcement, and Resistance to Extinction

The attributional framework developed here is generalizable to another psychological problem—experimental extinction. Repeated withholding of a reward, which establishes the procedure for extinction, is analogous to inducing continued failure in an achievement-related context. Hence, the principles employed to explain persistence of behavior in the face of failure are directly generalizable to the analysis of resistance to extinction.

It is postulated that the magnitude of the attributions to the four elements of causality determine resistance to extinction. More specifically, it is hypothesized that any antecedent condition of failure that gives rise to ascriptions of bad luck or a lack of effort (unstable factors) will produce greater resistance to extinction than antecedents that give rise to ascriptions of low ability or high task difficulty (stable factors). This prediction is made because an attribution by the actor to low ability or high task difficulty implies that the negative outcome on the previous trial will result again, while attributions to bad luck or deficient effort indicate that on a subsequent occasion the goal might be attained. It also follows that antecedents that generate attributions during nonreinforcement to low ability and high task difficulty will produce faster extinction than antecedents that result in the relative maintenance of a high ability–easy task pattern of inference.

In one test of these hypotheses, Meyer [Weiner, Heckhausen, Meyer, & Cook] induced five trials of repeated failure at a digit-symbol task. Prior to each trial the subjects indicated their expectancy of success for the next trial, and following each failure they attributed the outcome to the four causal elements. As already indicated, the attributions were in percentage figures and were required to total 100 per cent.

The relationship between subjective expectancy of success and the magnitude of attributions to the four causal elements is shown in figure 11. The figure reveals clearly that when attributions for failure to low ability and task difficulty are high, probability ratings fall rapidly. On the other hand, when attributions to lack of effort and bad luck are high,

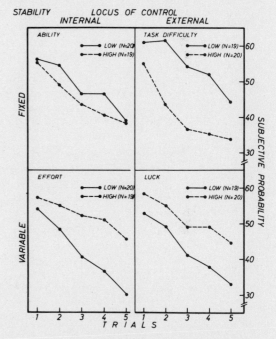

Figure 11. Expectancy of success as a function of above versus below median ascription to the four causal elements. High ascription indicates that a lack of ability, a difficult task, lack of effort, and bad luck are the perceived causes of failure. [From Weiner, Heckhausen, Meyer, & Cook in press.]

decrements in subjective expectancy of success are minimized. In figure 12 subjective expectancy of success is related to the combined attributions of failure to the stable elements (which is inversely related to attributions of failure to the combined unstable

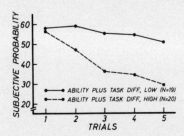

Figure 12. Expectancy of success as a function of above versus below median ascription to the fixed attributional elements (corresponds respectively to below versus above median ascription to effort plus luck). [From Weiner, Heckhausen, Meyer, & Cook in press.]

elements). When failure is attributed to stable rather than to unstable factors, expectancy decrements are displayed. It is evident from figure 11 that combining attributions over the locus of control rather than the stability dimension would eliminate the relationship between causal ascription and expectancy shift.

Schedules of Reinforcement

One widely investigated variable that might influence attributions during extinction is the schedule of reinforcement during acquisition. The studies manipulating reinforcement schedules most pertinent to the attributional viewpoint have been conducted by Rotter and his colleagues [Holden & Rotter 1962, James & Rotter 1958, Rotter, Liverant & Crowne 1961]. These investigators use human subjects and vary skill-versus-luck instructions along with the percentage of reinforcement. Some of these findings are now examined in detail.

Extinction Related to Task Instructions and Reinforcement Schedules

James and Rotter examined resistance to extinction at a "perceptual-acuity" task. The subjects reported whether an X or an O was flashed during a supposed tachistiscopic presentation. False feedback to the subjects enabled the experimenter to control the reinforcement schedule, or percentage of correct responses. Two schedules were employed: 100 per cent success and 50 per cent success. Further, half of the subjects within each reinforcement condition were told that "successful guessing is purely a matter of luck," while the remaining half of the subjects were informed that "there is evidence that some people are considerably skilled at this."

Following ten reinforcement trials, extinction procedures were initiated, with all subjects receiving 0 per cent reinforcement. To assess resistance to extinction, the subjects estimated their expectancy of success prior to each trial. Extinction was assumed when the subjective expectancy of a correct response was .10 or less. (In a subsequent replication experiment Holden and Rotter inferred extinction from the monetary bets subjects were willing to place on the next trial.)

The mean number of trials to extinction, standard deviations, and significance tests are shown in table 5. It can be seen that, given skill instructions, there are greater trials to extinction in the 100 per cent than in the 50 per cent reinforcement condition (C versus D). This is a reversal of the usual partial reinforcement effort. On the other hand, in the chance situation there are greater trials to extinction in the 50 per cent than in the 100 per cent reinforcement condition (A versus B), thus replicating the pattern of results in most extinction investigations employing lower organisms as subjects. Table 5 also reveals that there is greater resistance to extinction in the chance than in the skill condition, given a 50 per

Table 5. Mean Trials to Extinction, Standard Deviations, and Significance Tests between Groups Differing in Percentage of Reinforcement during Acquisition and Task Instructions.

Group	Percentage of Reinforcement	Instructions	Trials to Extinction	S.D.	P
A	100	Chance	15.55	9.86	A vs. B p < .001
B	50	Chance	29.05	9.41	C vs. D p < .10
C	100	Skill	22.90	4.84	A vs. C p < .01
D	50	Skill	19.75	7.27	B vs. D p < .001

SOURCE: After James & Rotter [1958].

cent schedule (B versus D), while the reverse pattern characterizes the continuous reinforcement schedule (A versus C). Holden and Rotter report a replication of the B versus D comparison.

An Attributional Interpretation. The data of the James and Rotter study are interpretable within the attributional framework developed in this paper. Consider first the results when the task is introduced as skill determined. The instructions in that condition connote that performance is a function of ability. Following acquisition, subjects in one condition (100 per cent reinforcement) are likely to infer that they have considerable ability at the task, while the performance of subjects in the 50 per cent condition indicates that they have only a moderate amount of ability. (Performance in the 50 per cent condition does slightly exceed the chance level, given the procedure used by James and Rotter.) Then the percentage of reinforcements changes; subjects in both conditions are given a reinforcement schedule (0 per cent) that connotes that they have little ability. When the attributions generated by the 0 per cent schedule are established, that is, when the subjects believe that they have insufficient ability to perform the task, extinction will occur. The change in self-perception from high to low ability at this novel task should take longer than a change from moderate to low ability. That is, beliefs consistent with ascriptions to low ability are more likely to be produced in the 50 per cent than in the 100 per cent reinforcement condition. This is merely repeating a supposition stated earlier: perceived ability is, in part, a function of prior success at the task.

The results in the chance condition are less readily interpretable. Within the chance condition one subgroup receives random 50 per cent reinforcement. Hence, two sources of information (instructions and outcome) combine to produce ascriptions that performance is completely determined by good or bad luck. But during extinction the 0 per cent schedule now intimates that chance alone cannot determine the outcome. Causal elements in addition to luck must be employed to explain consistently poor performance. (Indeed, were luck the only perceived causal attribute, extinction might not occur in this condition. James and Rotter do report that only in the 50 per cent chance condition were there subjects who never extinguished. These persistent subjects were "poor scientists," for they apparently ignored the new source of outcome evidence.)

The second group within the chance condition receives 100 per cent reinforcement. Hence, the pattern of actual performance contradicts the luck ascription elicited by the instructions, for repeated success indicates that luck is not the sole outcome determinant. If, as Heider [1958] suggests, the "common man" employs the logic of experimental comparison, he should reject the hypothesis that he is engaged in a chance task. Further, during the extinction phase of the 100 per cent chance condition the subjects must become even more confused. They are first instructed to believe that the outcome was determined only by luck; they then find out that they are skilled performers; and the final pattern of reinforcement conveys that they have little skill at the task.

Given the above phenomenological analysis, it would be difficult for the present attributional scheme to predict the relative trials to extinction in the chance conditions. However, the analysis does suggest that greater variability should be displayed in the chance than in the skill condition. This expectation is borne out (see table 5); variability is also much greater in the chance than in the skill instruction condition in the Holden and Rotter study. In the 100 per cent chance condition, which theoretically generates the greatest attributional confusion, the mean number of trials to extinction is 15.5, with a standard deviation of nearly 10. James and Rotter also note these disparities in variance but ascribe the inequalities to individual differences in the tendency to perceive a situation as internally or externally controlled. They state: "There were conceivably some subjects in the chance groups who responded to the task as a skill situation despite instructions" [p. 402]. We agree with this statement but believe it to be a reasonable inference that any subject might draw.

An Investigation of Causal Attributions during Extinction as a Function of Reinforcement Schedules

Some of the shortcomings in the James and Rotter study occur because subjects must alter their attributional schemes during both acquisition and extinction. Further, the relatively high chance probability of a correct response greatly weakens their extinction procedure. (One certainly wonders what the subjects in their experiment are thinking when they repeatedly fail a task at which they have a reasonable probability of being correct merely because of lucky guessing. In a similar manner, the extreme high performance in the 100 per cent chance condition renders the assumed belief in the chance instruction questionable.)

To overcome some of these difficulties, we conducted an experiment in which the task employed

115

was ambiguous with regard to its chance versus skill structure. Further, there was no a priori probability of success at the task. The particular task required subjects to trace over all the lines on a figure without lifting the pencil from the paper or retracing a line [Weiner 1970]. Insoluble figures can be constructed that naive subjects cannot discriminate from soluble figures, thus making it possible for the experimenter to exercise some degree of control over task outcome.

Three experimental conditions were created by varying the percentage of soluble puzzles that the subjects received prior to the initiation of the extinction procedure. For one group of subjects ($N=9$) all puzzles were soluble (S condition); for a second group ($N=15$) half were soluble and half insoluble (R or Random condition); a third group ($N=11$) received all insoluble puzzles (F condition). After eight learning trials extinction procedures were initiated, with all puzzles being insoluble. Seven extinction trials followed.

Prior to every trial the subjects estimated their probability of success (P_s) on a scale ranging from 0 to 10. Then, following success or failure at the task, attributions concerning the outcome were made to each of the four causal elements. Ratings ranged from 0 to 7 in both the success and failure outcomes.

Figure 13 shows the P_s estimates for the subjects in the three reinforcement conditions. It can be seen that the experimental manipulation systematically affected the P_s ratings. Subjective expectancy of success increases in the S condition, remains relatively constant and near .50 in the R condition, and steadily declines in the F condition. Further, during extinction the P_s decreases in all conditions.

Table 6 gives the mean attribution ratings during extinction for the causal elements. A Kruskal-Wallace analysis of variance between the three reinforcement conditions yields significant main effects for task difficulty ($p < .05$) and luck ($p < .02$), while the ability and effort main effects only approach significance (respectively, $p < .30$; $p < .10$).

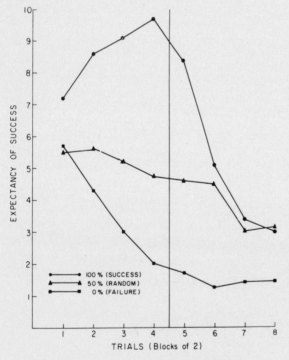

Figure 13. Subjective expectancy of success as a function of the percentage of reinforced trials (experimental conditions). The vertical line indicates the onset of extinction. Trial block 8 represents one rather than two trials.

Table 6. Mean Attributional Ratings during Extinction as a Function of Reinforcement Schedule.

Attribution Dimension	Reinforcement Schedule		
	100%(S)	50%(R)	0%(F)
Ability[a]	2.3	3.0	3.4
Task difficulty	5.6	6.2	6.8
Luck	2.1	2.9	1.3
Effort	1.7	2.8	2.1

[a]High means indicate failure is perceived as due to low ability, hard task, bad luck, or lack of effort.

Inspection of the total pattern of results reveals that in the F condition the subjects infer that stable factors (low ability and high task difficulty) are the causes of failure. Further, they are least likely to believe that the outcome is attributable to a composite of the unstable factors of low effort or poor luck. This overall attributional pattern suggests that subjects in the F condition would be the first to stop responding, for they should not expect the outcome to improve on subsequent occasions. Figure 13 does indicate that during extinction the lowest P_s ratings are displayed in that condition.

The attributional pattern of subjects in the S condition reveals that they are least likely to infer that failure was due to the stable attributional elements. That is, they maintain, relative to others, a high ability–easy task inferential pattern. (In general, subjects in this condition are unable to "explain" the sudden and repeated sequence of failures.) Conversely, the subjects in the R condition most believe that bad luck and lack of effort, the unstable factors, are responsible for their failures during the extinction trials. Differential resistance to extinction for subjects in the S and R conditions is therefore indeterminate, inasmuch as subjects in each condition are associated with two factors that theoretically retard extinction. The P_s estimates support this null hypothesis (no difference in trials to extinction between the S and R conditions); subjective expectancies in the S and R conditions are virtually identical following trial 10.

Although there are no phenotypic differences in the P_s estimates between the S and R conditions during the final extinction trials, the attributional data indicate that there are genotypic disparities between the two conditions. Further, these genotypic differences should be manifest given different instructions. On the one hand, skill directions are expected to result in greater weighting of the ability-task factors and produce slower extinction for the 100 per cent (S) group. Conversely, chance instructions should result in greater salience of the luck dimension and cause slower extinction for the 50 per cent (R) group. These are the findings reported by James and Rotter in their skill-versus-chance instruction conditions.

Some Additional Speculations Concerning Extinction

Can this analysis be employed to explain some of the vast quantity of data produced in animal studies? The suggestion that infrahumans can ascribe nonreinforcement to a lack of effort or low ability might require attributing greater cognitive skills and thought processes to lower animals than is warranted. There is evidence, however, that organisms other than humans are capable of differentiating between some of the causal dimensions outlined in table 1. For example, Maier, Seligman, and Solomon [1968] gave dogs classical aversive conditioning training in which shock unavoidably followed a conditional stimulus. Following training many of these animals

could not learn an instrumental escape response. These data can be interpreted as indicating that a procedure that imposes an "external causation" set retards subsequent learning when the animals are placed in a situation in which they are responsible for event outcome. That is, attributional errors are being made because the dogs have been taught that the aversive outcomes are externally controlled. Maier and his colleagues label this phenomenon "learned helplessness." (A reverse attributional error characterizes "superstitious" behavior—outcomes externally determined are believed to be internally controlled.)

Perhaps animals can differentiate between unstable-stable conditions as well as internal-external situations. The former cognitive discrimination may be inferred from the greater resistance to extinction displayed under 50 per cent than under 100 per cent reinforcement schedules. In addition, it has been found that speed of extinction is inversely related to the effortfulness of an instrumental response; see Lawrence and Festinger [1962]. This suggests that when effort is established as a major determinant of outcome, nonattainment of the goal is ascribed to insufficient effort, and extinction is retarded. Needless to say, inferring the cognitions of animals is a vulnerable practice. Yet a number of current investigations in the animal literature seem to invite cognitive interpretations.

Achievement Predispositions and Reinforcement Schedules: A Review

Both achievement motives and reinforcement schedules affect mediating cognitions concerning the causes of behavioral outcomes. These mediating cognitions then influence subsequent behavior. More specifically, individuals high in need for achievement persist longer in situations of failure than individuals low in need for achievement. In a similar manner, in chance situations, and in most animal experimentation, resistance to extinction is greater given partial rather than continuous reinforcement. It is

Table 7. Genotypic Representations for Phenotypically Dissimilar Behaviors.

Antecedent Conditions	Mediating Causal Cognitions	Causal Schema	Behavioral Consequences
1. Individual diff. in ach. needs	Ability, Task difficulty, Effort, Luck	Locus of control; Stability	Affect; Expec. shift	Persistence of behavior (resistance to ext.)
2. Reinforcement schedules			

117

postulated that these antecedent-consequent relationships are primarily mediated by differential attributions to the unstable causal factors (respectively, lack of effort and bad luck) that give rise to differential persistence of behavior. Thus, similar genotypic representations may be employed for phenotypically dissimilar behaviors, as in table 7.

Educational Implications

Social Class and Racial Differences

It appears that high achievement-oriented behavior is associated with (produced by?) self-attribution for success, and ascription of failure to low effort. Conversely, low achievement-oriented behavior is associated with relative external attribution for success and a belief that failure resulted from low ability. These attributional patterns might be differentially represented in the various social class and racial groupings. For example, Katz [1967] describes low-achieving Negro boys as follows: "What they seem to have internalized was a most effective mechanism of self-discouragement . . . . The child, in a sense, has been socialized to impose failure upon himself" [p. 164]. The general implication of this alleged ascription is that the study of attributional processes might aid in the understanding of some of the disparities in achievement motivation and intellectual performance that are evident between racial and social class groupings.

Teacher Expectancy and Performance

Weiner and Kukla previously noted the relevance of attributions for success and failure to some of the work concerned with teacher expectation and performance. Rosenthal and Jacobson [1968] aroused false teacher expectations concerning the abilities of certain students. Teachers were told that a selected subset of students, who actually had been chosen randomly, would exhibit unusual intellectual growth. Subsequent testing of these students supposedly revealed that they did display greater intellectual development than control students not paired with the fraudulent expectations.

The teachers' behaviors that gave rise to these stated intellectual gains is yet unknown. The framework presented in this paper, however, provides some possible clues to this problem. The false expectancies undoubtedly led the teachers to believe that the selected students had high ability. Hence, it is unlikely that the occasional failures these average students presumably experienced would be attributed by the teacher to a lack of ability. That is, in situations of failure the teachers are likely to infer that the students did not expend sufficient effort.

Attribution of failure to a lack of effort, rather than to low ability, is one characteristic of the attributional schema employed by individuals high in resultant achievement motivation. Hence, the teachers may be communicating ascriptions that, if introjected by the pupils, would facilitate subsequent achievement strivings. More generally, the intent of this interpretation is to convey that false ability expectancies have implications for teacher attributions concerning the causes of success and failure, and these attributions may have motivational consequences.

Attributional Errors and Conflict

In a recent study Beckman [1970] manipulated the temporal pattern of performance feedback to teachers who believed that they were communicating mathematical skills to two students. False feedback concerning the performance of one of the students indicated that his test outcomes were consistently high. Performance of the second student was conveyed as either changing from high to low (H-L), low to high (L-H), or remained constantly low. Subsequent data revealed that the teachers believe that they are more responsible for the behavior of the L-H than the H-L children. On the other hand, a group of "observers" stated that the teachers are more responsible for the H-L than for the L-H performance! The reader is invited to imagine a conference between a teacher and an observer (perhaps a mother) in which opposing attributions are made concerning the good or poor performance of a pupil.

There also are potential conflicts caused by self versus other attributions of effort. It has been suggested that individuals tend to attribute their own behavior to environmental factors, while the behavior of others is ascribed to personal characteristics or traits [Jones & Nisbett 1971]. This suggests that effort may be perceived as a stable attribute when making judgments concerning others, but an unstable attribute in self-ascriptions. As Jones and Nisbett point out, student advisees often feel that they can improve with effort, whereas their advisors are convinced that their problem is attributable to more stable factors, such as low ability or laziness.

Conclusion

A major shortcoming of the psychology of motivation is the failure to unite theories of action with theories of thought. To be sure, psychologists such as Atkinson and Tolman employ cognitive concepts such as "expectancy." But these theorists are content merely to use cognitive terminology, while not systematically concerning themselves with phenomenal experience, or the relationship between thought and action. In contrast to these approaches, we have attempted to formulate a theory of achievement motivation in which the "facts of consciousness" and the "facts of behavior" are synthesized and of equal import.

The cognitive (attributional) approach to motivation advocated here has been illustrated within the context of achievement-related behavior, for a substantial body of empirical facts and a carefully formulated theory already exists in that area. But other motivations, such as affiliative behavior or power seeking, should be amenable to similar analyses. This requires a specification and taxonomic scheme of the causal attributions for attainment or nonattainment of an appropriate goal, designation of the antecedent conditions and decision rules that give rise to particular causal ascriptions, and statements concerning the linkages between the mediating cognitions and behavior. It is hopefully expected that some of the principles that will ultimately be incorporated into a general theory of motivation are contained in the present work.

BIBLIOGRAPHY

John W. Atkinson, "Explorations Using Imaginative Thought to Assess the Strength of Human Motivation." In M. R. Jones, ed., *Nebraska Symposium on Motivation*, University of Nebraska, 1954.

John W. Atkinson, "Motivational Determinants of Risk-Taking Behavior." *Psychological Review*, 1957, 64:359–372.

John W. Atkinson, *An Introduction to Motivation*. Van Nostrand, 1964.

John W. Atkinson, "Change of Activity: A New Focus for the Theory of Motivation." In T. Mischel, ed., *Human Action*. Academic, 1969.

Alfred L. Baldwin, "A Cognitive Theory of Socialization." In D. A. Goslin, ed., *Handbook of Socialization Theory and Research*. Rand McNally, 1969.

Linda J. Beckman, "Effects of Students' Performance on Teachers' and Observers' Attributions of Causality." *Journal of Educational Psychology*, 1970, 61:76–82.

Robert C. Bennion, "Task, Trial by Trial Score Variability of Internal versus External Control of Reinforcement." Unpublished doctoral dissertation, Ohio State University, 1961.

Saul Breit, "Arousal of Achievement Motivation with Causal Attributions." *Psychological Reports*, 1969, 25:539–542.

John Cohen, *Chance, Skill and Luck*. Penguin, 1960.

Ruth Cook, "Relation of Achievement Motivation and Attribution to Self-Reinforcement." Unpublished doctoral thesis, University of California, 1970.

Virginia C. Crandall, Walter Katkovsky, and Vaughn J. Crandall, "Children's Beliefs in Their Own Control of Reinforcements in Intellectual-Academic Achievement Situation." *Child Development*, 1965, 36:91–109.

Vaughn J. Crandall, Walter Katkovsky, and Anne Preston, "Motivational and Ability Determinants of Young Children's Intellectual Behaviors." *Child Development*, 1962, 33:643–661.

Norman T. Feather, "The Relationship of Persistence at a Task to Expectation of Success and Achievement-Related Motives." *Journal of Abnormal and Social Psychology*, 1961, 63:552–561.

Norman T. Feather, "Valence of Outcome and Expectation of Success in Relation to Task Difficulty and Perceived Locus of Control." *Journal of Personality and Social Psychology*, 1967, 7:372–386.

Norman T. Feather, "Attribution of Responsibility and Valence of Success and Failure in Relation to Initial Confidence and Task Performance." *Journal of Personality and Social Psychology*. 1969, 13:129–144.

Jerome D. Frank, "Individual Differences in Certain Aspects of the Level of Aspiration." *American Journal of Psychology*, 1935, 47:119–128.

Irene Frieze and Bernard Weiner, "Cue Utilization and Attributional Judgments for Success and Failure." *Journal of Personality*, in press.

Heinz Heckhausen, *The Anatomy of Achievement Motivation*. Academic, 1967.

Fritz Heider, "Social Perception and Phenomenal Causality." *Psychological Review*, 1944, 51:358–373.

Fritz Heider, *The Psychology of Interpersonal Relations*. Wiley, 1958.

Kenneth B. Holden and Julian B. Rotter, "A Nonverbal Measure of Extinction in Skill and Chance Situations." *Journal of Experimental Psychology*, 1962, 63:519–520.

Fritz Hoppe, "Erfolg und Misserfolg." *Psychologische Forschung*, 1931, 14:1–62.

Clark L. Hull, *Principles of Behavior*. Appleton, 1943.

William H. James and Julian B. Rotter, "Partial and 100% Reinforcement Under Chance and Skill Conditions." *Journal of Experimental Psychology*, 1958, 55:397–403.

Herman M. Jenkins and William C. Ward, "Judgment of Contingency Between Responses and Outcome." *Psychological Monographs*, 1965, 70(1) (whole No. 594).

Edward E. Jones and Richard deCharms, "Changes in Social Perception as a Function of the Personal Relevance of Behavior." *Sociometry*, 1957, 20:75–85.

Edward E. Jones and Richard E. Nisbett, "The Actor and the Observer: Divergent Perceptions of the Causes of Behavior." General Learning Press, 1971. (Also in Edward E. Jones, David Kanouse, Harold H. Kelley, Richard E. Nisbett, Stuart Valins, and Bernard Weiner, *Attribution: Perceiving the Causes of Behavior*, General Learning Press, 1971.)

Edward E. Jones, Leslie Rock, Kelly G. Shaver, George R. Goethals, and Lawrence M. Ward, "Pattern of Performance and Ability Attribution: An Unexpected Primacy Effect." *Journal of Personality and Social Psychology*, 1968, 10:317–340.

Fred H. Kanfer and Albert R. Marston, "Determinants of Self-Reinforcement in Human Learning." *Journal of Experimental Psychology*, 1963, 66:245–254.

Irwin Katz, "The Socialization of Academic Motivation in Minority Group Children." In D. Levine, ed., *Nebraska Symposium on Motivation*. University of Nebraska, 1967.

Harold H. Kelley, "Attribution Theory in Social Psychology." In D. Levine, ed., *Nebraska Symposium on Motivation*. University of Nebraska, 1967.

Andy Kukla, "The Cognitive Determinants of Achieving Behavior." Unpublished doctoral dissertation, University of California, 1970.

John T. Lanzetta and T. E. Hannah, "Reinforcing Behavior of 'Naive' Trainers." *Journal of Personality and Social Psychology*, 1969, 11:245–252.

Douglas H. Lawrence and Leon Festinger, *Deterrents and Reinforcement: The Psychology of Insufficient Reward*. Stanford University, 1962.

Richard S. Lazarus, "Emotions and Adaptation: Conceptual and Empirical Relations." In W. J. Arnold, ed., *Nebraska Symposium on Motivation*. University of Nebraska, 1968.

Herbert M. Lefcourt, "Internal Versus External Control of Reinforcement: A Review." *Psychological Bulletin*, 1966, 65:206–220.

Howard Leventhal, "Findings and Theory in the Study of Fear Communications." In L. Berkowitz, ed., *Advances in Experimental Social Psychology*, vol. 5. Academic, 1971.

Kurt Lewin, *The Conceptual Representation and the Measurement of Psychological Forces*. Duke University, 1938.

Steven F. Maier, Martin E. P. Seligman, and Richard L. Solomon, "Pavlovian Fear Conditioning and Learned Helplessness: Effects of Escape and Avoidance Behavior of (a) The CS-US Contingency and (b) The Independence of US and Instrumental Responding." In B. A. Campbell and R. M. Church, eds., *Punishment*. Appleton-Century-Crofts, 1968.

Mary D. Maselli and John Altrocchi, "Attribution of Intent," *Psychological Bulletin*, 1969, 71:445–454.

David C. McClelland, *The Achieving Society*, Van Nostrand, 1961.

Albert Mehrabian, "Male and Female Scales of the Tendency to Achieve." *Educational and Psychological Measurement*, 1968, 28:493–502.

Robert Merton, *Mass Persuasion*. Harper, 1946.

Wulf U. Meyer, "Selbstverantworklichkeit und Leistungsmotivation." Unpublished doctoral dissertation, Ruhr Universität, Bochum, Germany, 1970.

Walter Mischel, B. Coates, and A. Rashoff, "Effects of Success and Failure on Self-Gratification." *Journal of Personality and Social Psychology*, 1968, 10:381–390.

E. Jerry Phares, "Expectancy Changes in Skill and Chance Situations." *Journal of Abnormal and Social Psychology*, 1957, 54:339–342.

Robert Rosenthal and Lenore F. Jacobson, "Teacher Expectations for the Disadvantaged." *Scientific American*, 1968, 218:19–23.

Julian B. Rotter, "Generalized Expectancies for Internal Versus External Control of Reinforcement." *Psychological Monographs*, 1966, 80(1) (whole No. 609).

Julian B. Rotter, Shephard Liverant, and Douglas P. Crown, "The Growth and Extinction of Expectancies in Chance Controlled and Skill Tests." *Journal of Psychology*, 1961, 52:161–177.

David R. Schmitt, "The Invocation of Moral Obligation." *Sociometry*, 1964, 27:299–310.

Kenneth W. Spence, *Behavior Theory and Conditioning*. Yale University Press, 1956.

Edward C. Tolman, "The Determinants of Behavior at a Choice Point." *Psychological Review*, 1938, 45:1–41.

Bernard Weiner, "New Conceptions in the Study of Achievement Motivation." In B. Maher, ed., *Progress in Experimental Personality Research*, vol. 5. Academic, 1970.

Bernard Weiner, Heinz Heckhausen, Wulf U. Meyer, and Ruth C. Cook, "Causal Ascriptions and Achievement Behavior: The Conceptual Analysis of Effort." *Journal of Personality and Social Psychology* (in press).

✓Bernard Weiner and Andy Kukla, "An Attributional Analysis of Achievement Motivation." *Journal of Personality and Social Psychology*, 1970, 15:1–20.

✓ Bernard Weiner and Penelope A. Potepan, "Personality Characteristics and Affective Reactions toward Exams of Superior and Failing College Students." *Journal of Educational Psychology*, 1970, 61, 144–151.

[This paper grew out of a workshop on attribution theory held at UCLA in August, 1969, supported by Grant GS-2613 from the National Science Foundation. The reported research was supported in part by the Office of Economic Opportunity, Early Childhood Research and Development Center of Los Angeles, CG 9938. Support for Bernard Weiner by Grant MH-12603-05 from the National Institute of Health is also acknowledged.]

7 · Language, Labeling, and Attribution

DAVID E. KANOUSE

University of California, Los Angeles

Tʜɪs discussion reviews some recent work in a rather offbeat area of psycholinguistics. It is motivated by a conviction that much of this work bears on problems and issues raised by attribution theory. The relationship between the two lines of work is not altogether self-evident, so it may be useful to begin with an illustrative problem through which the two can be compared.

Let us suppose that there are two friends, P and O, and that O has just seen the film Z and recommends it most enthusiastically to P. This recommendation poses a small attributional problem for P: why does O like Z? Let us consider P's major attributional alternatives. First, P might simply attribute O's liking to the quality of the film: "O likes it because it's a good movie." On the other hand, P might attribute O's liking to something about O himself. For example, P might know that O is a relatively undiscerning cinemaphile: "He likes anything from early Eisenstein to the Late Late Show." Finally, P might make a more complex attribution, such as "O selectively likes films similar to Z, or Z is liked only by people similar to O."

To frame our example in general terms, O is a person who has a certain relation (liking) to an object (a film). Each of the attributions above attempts to "explain" the relation by pointing to some causal factor in the person on the one hand, or the object on the other. Other things being equal, a person attribution is more likely to be made if the relation is *unique to the person* or *general across objects*, while an object (entity) attribution is more likely to be made if the relation is *unique to the object* or *general across persons*.

Of course, attributors seldom attain anything resembling a state of omniscience; usually they have rather limited information as to how unique or general a particular relation is across persons and objects. Thus they are often forced to make intuitive probability judgments about the generality or uniqueness of a given relation; that is, they must fill in missing cells in the data matrix with reasonable guesses. Returning to our example, the attributional analysis sketched above would clearly suggest that if P knows that many people like Z, he will probably form an object attribution; and if he knows that O wholeheartedly recommends anything on celluloid, he will probably form a person attribution. But what if O is a recent acquaintance whose cinematic standards are completely unfamiliar to P, and Z is a new film about which P knows nothing other than that O likes it? It seems rather unlikely that he would attach no significance whatsoever to the recommendation and would prudently await the appearance of further data. It seems more probable that in the absence of any further knowledge about O in particular or Z in particular, P would evaluate the recommendation on the basis of his knowledge about how many films the *average* person recommends and how much agreement exists concerning the quality of the *average* film. His implicit reasoning might go something like the following:

O recommended Z; therefore he must have liked it a great deal. (After all, most people don't recommend every film they see.) If O liked it a great deal, probably a lot of other people like it too. (Usually, there is moderate to high agreement about the quality of films.) If a lot of people like it, it must be fairly good.

Such a reasoning process simply involves applying a set of normative assumptions in a case where $N = 1$, then making the "normative" attribution that follows from these assumptions. Normative assumptions might be specific to a particular type of situation, like the assumptions about cinematic tastes parenthesized above, or they might be more general, like Abelson's [1968] "implicational principles." The central contention here is that, in the absence of information about the generality of a given relation over persons or objects, individuals make normative assumptions about generality and that these assumptions in turn allow them to form attributions. If this is the case, then in order to gain an understanding of the attribution process, it is necessary to learn something about the rules that people use in making such assumptions. Most of the psycholinguistic work discussed here bears on just this problem: namely, how individuals form inferences concerning the generality of a given event or relation.

Subjective Induction

A series of studies reported by Gilson and Abelson [1965] and Abelson and Kanouse [1966] approached the problem of inferences about generality by ex-amining how individuals utilize the information contained in simple sentences to make subjective generalizations of various types. In these studies, respondents were presented with simple assertions containing a subject, verb, and object. In addition, they were given mixed evidence bearing on the truth of the assertion; that is, some of the evidence supported the assertion, while some contradicted it. The respondent's task was to indicate whether he felt that the assertion was true or false in the light of the given evidence. Two forms of evidence were used, as shown in the examples below.

Altogether there are three kinds of tribes: Southern tribes, Northern tribes, and Central tribes.
  Northern tribes buy bees.
  Southern tribes do not buy bees.
  Central tribes do not buy bees.
Do tribes buy bees?

Altogether there are three kinds of bees: Honey bees, bumble bees, and carpenter bees.
  Tribes buy honey bees.
  Tribes do not buy bumble bees.
  Tribes do not buy carpenter bees.
Do tribes buy bees?

Two things are noteworthy in these examples: (1) the evidence in the first example pertains to the sentence subject, and in the second to the sentence object. For convenience these contrasting evidence forms are denoted *subject-specific* and *object-specific*, respectively. (2) In both examples, the task requires the respondent to accept or reject a generalization on the basis of *inconsistent* evidence; that is, some tribes buy bees while others do not, or some kinds of bees are bought while others are not. Thus, an affirmative response requires that the respondent make an inductive leap; for example, from "Southern tribes" to "tribes" in general.

Respondents in the Abelson and Kanouse studies were given a large number of items such as those in the examples, with sentence elements systematically varied from item to item. Instructions emphasized that the task should not be regarded as a test of logic but that subjects' answers should be based on their intuitive reactions to the evidence.

The results of these studies yielded two findings of major substantive interest. (1) There was a significantly greater tendency to generalize across sentence *objects* than across sentence *subjects*; that is, object-specific evidence produced greater agreement than did subject-specific evidence. Thus, in the examples above, respondents were much more likely to feel that tribes buy bees if tribes buy at least some bees than if at least some tribes buy bees. We shall have more to say about this phenomenon later. (2) Although the particular subject and object appearing in a sentence has little effect on agreement with the generalization, agreement was strongly affected by the sentence verb; the proportion of respondents agreeing to generalizations with particular verbs varied quite dramatically, from 24 per cent to 92 per cent. Moreover, the pattern of differences among verbs appeared to be largely describable by two semantic dimensions. The most important of these dimensions has been labeled "manifest-subjective." This dimension appears to be a close conceptual cousin of Heider's [1946] distinction between unit and sentiment relations. It distinguishes verbs that denote feelings or subjective orientations (for example, love, understand, trust) from those that denote actions or objective orientations (for example, produce, use, have). Subjective verbs produced a rather low rate of agreement to generalizations. In sharp contrast, sentences containing manifest verbs produced high agreement rates.

A secondary dimension, producing a weaker effect, was the affective sign of the verb. In general, verbs expressing positive sentiments or actions elicited higher agreement rates than verbs describing negative sentiments or actions. For example, people were somewhat more willing to agree that "artists like magazines" if artists like some kinds of magazines than to agree that "artists hate magazines" if artists hate some kinds of magazines.

Thus an unanticipated finding emerged from these studies; namely, that the ease with which individuals form inductive generalizations from a given set of information is sharply dependent on the nature of the verb in the generalization. We shall pursue the question of what these verb differences might mean in a later section. First, however, we shall turn our attention to a different form of subjective inference, complementary to that just considered.

Subjective Deduction

Inductive inference proceeds by establishing an abstract generalization on the basis of one or more concrete instances, as shown in the examples given in the foregoing section. Frequently, however, inferences are made in reverse fashion; an abstract generalization is invoked as evidence to be applied in a concrete case. Abelson and Kanouse [1966] investigated the process of deductive inference by presenting subjects with items such as the following:

All bees are flying, stinging, furry insects.
   Tribes buy flying insects.
   Tribes buy stinging insects.
   Tribes do not buy furry insects.
Do tribes buy bees?

Once again, both subject-specific and object-specific evidence forms were used, and sentence elements were systematically varied across items.

The results for deductive evidence forms were for the most part a mirror-image reversal of the results for inductive forms. (1) There was a significant tendency for subject-specific evidence to yield *more* agreement than object-specific evidence. Respondents were more likely to conclude that tribes buy bees if entities with tribelike qualities buy bees than if entities with beelike qualities are bought by tribes. This stands in marked contrast to the results for inductive inference, where subject-specific evidence produced *less* agreement. Thus, inductive inferences seem to be made most readily when the evidence bears on the sentence *object*, while deductive inferences seem to be made most readily when the evidence pertains to the sentence *subject*. (2) As was the case with inductive evidence forms, the particular sentence verb played a critical role in determining evaluations of the evidence, while the other elements in the sentence made little difference. However, in this case the *positive-negative* verb dimension was more critical than the *manifest-subjective* dimension. Respondents were much more willing to make deductive inferences when the verb denoted a negative orientation of the actor toward the object. For example, if artists were said to *hate* topical, periodical publications, respondents readily agreed that artists hate magazines. But if artists were said to *like* topical, periodical publications, respondents were reluctant to conclude that artists like magazines. In addition, there was a slightly greater tendency to agree with the conclusion when the verb was subjective than when it was manifest.

In general, then, these studies show a striking inverse relationship between the pattern of results for inductive and deductive inferences. Verbs and evidence forms that produce strong inductive inferences yield rather feeble deductive inferences, and vice versa. For both types of inferences, however, the verb appears to be of critical importance, and there are significant differences between subject-specific and object-specific evidence.

The Impact of Supportive and Nonsupportive Evidence

In the studies described above, the evidence presented to subjects for evaluation always contained both supportive and nonsupportive instances. Tribes were said to buy some types of bees but not others, etc. The reader may have wondered about the relative weight given by respondents to supportive and nonsupportive evidence in making their judgments. For example, manifest verbs may produce greater inductive agreement than subjective verbs for either of two reasons. First, these verbs may provide stronger positive support for the generalization; or alternatively, nonsupportive instances may be less damaging to the generalization. Data pertinent to this question would be provided by studies that either vary the amount of supportive and non-supportive evidence orthogonally or eliminate one kind of evidence altogether. Two such studies are described below.

Jones and Abelson [1967] presented a group of respondents with a collection of items such as the following:

1. *Inductive*
Ohioans hate snakes.
Bill is an Ohioan.
Does Bill hate reptiles?

2. *Deductive*
Ohioans hate reptiles.
Bill is an Ohioan.
Does Bill hate snakes?

Note that the evidence in both cases is exclusively supportive of the generalization and that it bears on the object of the sentence. That is, the inference proceeds from snakes to reptiles in the first example and from reptiles to snakes in the second. At the same time, however, both examples require an additional inferential leap involving the sentence subject; that is, from "Ohioans" in general to "Bill" in particular. This latter feature is constant across items, and was introduced to lessen the impact of the exclusively supportive evidence, so that substantive verb differences would not be obscured by a ceiling effect.

The pattern of verb differences emerging in the results of the Jones and Abelson study is essentially the same as that found by Abelson and Kanouse [1966] and by Gilson and Abelson [1965]. Thus, the verb differences found in these studies are not dependent on the presence of instances that do not support the generalization but appear even when the evidence is exclusively supportive.

Additional data relevant to this issue are provided by a recent study by Trabasso, Kanouse, and Weichel. In this study, subjects were run individually and a reaction time was obtained for each response. The subject's task was to press a button labeled "yes" or "no" in answer to items of the following form:

1. Henry does not avoid martinis.
It is true that Henry avoids drinks.

2. Paul likes candy.
It is false that Paul does not like peppermints.

This simple format conceals no fewer than six independent variables: (1) a single evidence sentence, either supportive or nonsupportive; (2) the "preface" to the conclusion ("it is true that" or "it is false that"); (3) positive or negative conclusion (e.g., avoids or does not avoid); (4) manifest or subjective verb; (5) positive or negative verb; (6) inductive or deductive inference.

The second and third of these variables made it possible to construct four different forms of the conclusion, as indicated in the following example:

Evidence

John has oranges.

Conclusion
a. It is true that John has fruit.
b. It is false that John does not have fruit.
c. It is false that John has fruit.
d. It is true that John does not have fruit.

The reader will note that conclusions *a* and *b* are logically equivalent, as are *c* and *d*. However, as Johnson-Laird and Tagart have recently noted, "It seems that the negation of falsity is not psychologically equivalent to truth" [1969]. For example, Wason [1959] found that confirmation of a positive statement is performed more quickly and accurately than disconfirmation of its opposite.

Previous studies of subjective inference always posed a conclusion in positive terms (e.g., "Does John have fruit?"). This leaves open the possibility that there is a difference between disconfirming an assertion directly and merely failing to confirm it. Indeed, the meaning of the subjects' responses in previous studies is often ambiguous with respect to this distinction. For example, if a subject were to answer "No" in response to the question "Does John have fruit?", he might mean either (*a*) "The evidence does not establish that John has fruit," or (*b*) "The evidence establishes that John does not have fruit."

The design of the Trabasso, Kanouse and Weichel study permitted direct examination of this distinction by providing subjects with an opportunity to agree or disagree with a positive or negative conclusion on the basis of supportive or nonsupportive evidence.

Although statistical analyses of the results are not yet completed, the data clearly support the following conclusions. (1) Verb differences paralleling earlier findings are apparent, regardless of whether the evidence presented is supportive or nonsupportive. Thus "John buys oranges" is seen by the subjects as clear indication that "John buys fruit," while "John hates oranges" does not establish that "John hates fruit." Conversely, the negative evidence that "John does not buy oranges" appears to be only weakly inconsistent with the statement "John buys fruit"; while similar evidence that "John does not hate oranges" is very damaging indeed to the general statement that "John hates fruit." (2) These verb differences appear regardless of the form of the conclusion (true affirmative, false negative, false affirmative, and true negative).

An additional finding of substantive interest is worth noting here, namely, that subjects exhibited in their *inductive* inferences a much greater tendency to agree to conclusions beginning "It is false that . . ." (54 per cent) than to logically equivalent conclusions beginning "It is true that . . ." (32 per cent). This occurred regardless of the type of verb involved and regardless of whether the evidence supported or did not support the generalization. Moreover, this effect seemingly reflects more than a simple set to disconfirm statements rather than to confirm them, since there was no difference between these forms when the inference was deductive (52 per cent versus 50 per cent). Thus the results support the contention that false affrmatives are not psychologically equivalent to true negatives but suggest a qualification: false affirmatives seem to elicit substantively different responses from true negatives only for inductive reasoning.

The Nature of Verb Differences

As we have seen, the emergence of substantial verb effects in studies of subjective inference is a persistent and reliable phenomenon. Experimental subjects typically respond to a given type or quantity of evidence very differently for different verbs. Thus it becomes important to achieve some theoretical understanding of why these differences occur.

One approach to this theoretical problem begins with a finding first reported by Abelson and Kanouse [1966]. These investigators presented their subjects with a set of assertions composed of systematic combinations of sentence elements and asked them to indicate on an "implicit quantifier scale" (consisting of alternatives such as "a few," "many," "most," or "all") the *minimal* amount of evidence they felt would justify a given assertion. That is, if a subject felt that the unqualified assertion "Artists

buy magazines" would be minimally justified if "Some artists buy a few magazines," he so indicated by checking the appropriate quantifiers on the scale.

Abelson and Kanouse found that the quantifier that subjects selected depended for the most part on the verb in the sentence. For example, respondents indicated that the sentence "George avoids magazines" implies "most" or even "all" magazines, whereas the sentence "George buys magazines" implies only "a few" or "some" magazines. Implicitly, fewer magazines are bought than avoided, despite the fact that the number of magazines is in both cases unspecified. Interestingly enough, the verb differences appearing on this implicit quantifier scale were highly correlated with the verb differences in inductive and deductive generalization described earlier. Specifically, those verbs that show strong inductive generalizing power (for example, "buy," "produce," "have") tended to elicit rather low implicit quantifier ratings, such as "some" or "a few." At the same time, verbs displaying weak inductive generalizing power (for example, "hate," "avoid," "fear") tended to be associated with high implicit quantifiers, such as "most" or "all."

These findings have two implications of substantive interest: that verbs may differ systematically in the implicit quantifiers commonly understood to accompany them and that these implicit quantifiers may play a role in the processing of evidence bearing on a given generalization. The first of these implications is somewhat surprising from a psycholinguistic point of view, since it is, after all, the subject and object in a sentence that are quantified, not the verb. Two studies reported by Kanouse [1968] explicitly examined the notion of implicit quantification by verbs. In the first of these, respondents were asked to indicate the implicit quantifiers in a large number of sentences that included a diverse range of verbs and objects (for example, "James harms baskets," "Bill finds pens," "John hates watches," etc.).

The implicit quantifiers given by the respondents differed substantially depending on whether the verb was manifest or subjective, whereas the positivity of the verb made only a slight difference, and the particular sentence object virtually none at all. In a second study, subjects were presented with a list of sentences to learn via a cued recall procedure. Some of the sentences contained an explicit object quantifier presumably "appropriate" to the verb (for example, "Helen uses one or two wigs," "Margo fears all chairs"), while for some sentences the quantifier was presumably "inappropriate" to the verb ("Helen uses all wigs," "Margo fears one or two chairs"). Sentences in which the quantifier was inappropriate to the verb were significantly harder to learn. Thus the notion of implicit quantification of the object in a sentence by the verb appears to have solid empirical support.

What of the role of implicit quantifiers in the processing of evidence bearing on a given assertion? The phenomenon of implicit quantification suggests an appealingly simple hypothesis; namely, the reason that some assertions are more readily agreed to than others is that some assertions are implicitly more general than others. To all outward appearances, the statement "Maurice buys musical instruments" is as sweeping and unqualified as the statement "Harry hates musical instruments." The former, however, is construed to mean "Maurice buys some musical instruments," while the latter is taken to mean "Harry hates all musical instruments." Thus it seems only natural that in order to establish that Maurice buys musical instruments, all one need do is point out that he has bought, say, a *viola da gamba* and a ukelele or two, while one must point to a very large number of specific instances indeed to establish that Harry hates musical instruments. More generally, whenever the implicit quantifier in an assertion is on the order of "some," proof of the assertion by induction should be relatively easy; but if the implicit quantifier is "all," inductive proof is probably at best tedious and at worst futile.

For deductive inferences, however, the situation is quite different. If Harry hates musical instruments, it follows quite readily that he hates ukeleles; after all, he hates *all* instruments. But if Maurice buys musical instruments, it does not follow that he buys oboes; he buys only some instruments, and one does not necessarily know which ones.

The above analysis suggests that the differential susceptibility of verbs to inductive and deductive evidence may be mediated by the implicit quantifiers associated with the verbs. That is, the inference may be dictated, as it were, by the "logic" of the implicit quantifier. This notion implies that verb differences appear by virtue of the fact that quantifiers are not explicitly stated but are left for the individual encountering the assertion to "read in." The obvious empirical implication of this notion is that verb effects should disappear when quantifiers are held constant by being made explicit. For example, it should require no more evidence to establish that Harry *hates some* musical instruments than that Maurice *buys some* musical instruments.

This hypothesis has recently been tested by Leaf [1969], with the following results: consistent with the analysis presented above, differences between manifest and subjective verbs do indeed disappear when quantifiers are made explicit. Differences between positive and negative verbs, however, though lessened, remain even when quantifiers are explicitly provided. Assertions containing negative verbs are significantly more susceptible to deductive proof than those containing positive verbs. The results of Leaf's study, then, seem to establish that implicit quantifiers mediate the inferential differences between manifest verbs and subjective verbs. The question of why positive and negative verbs display different inferential properties, however, is still very much open. This leaves us with two pressing questions for speculation: What critical features distinguishing manifest from subjective verbs might account for their having different implicit quantifiers? Why do positive and negative verbs differ so strikingly in their inferential properties?

With respect to the first of these questions, there are several possible distinctions between manifest verbs and subjective verbs that are potentially important in explaining implicit quantifier differences, but the following is the one presently favored by the author: verbs will have low implicit quantifiers (for example, "some") if, and only if, the relation described by the verb limits either the *availability of the object* or the *resources of the subject*. Pure subjective orientations or affective states do neither; for example, I can dislike all the kumquats in the entire universe without limiting the availability of kumquats to be disliked by anyone else who cares to, and without decreasing my own ability to dislike all the prickly pears in the universe as well. In contrast, for many verbs this is not the case. For example, if I *have* a kumquat, this kumquat is not available for anyone else to have. And if someone else has a kumquat, that kumquat is not available for me to have. Thus, no one can reasonably expect to have all the kumquats, because of their limited availability for "having."

In addition there are many verbs that, although they do not restrict the availability of the object, do use up the resources of the subject. Among these are verbs of perception, such as "see." Thus, although my seeing a given kumquat does not preclude anyone else from seeing it too, there are only so many that I can see at once. I cannot see all the kumquats in the world at once, because they are too many and scattered. In seeing some, I am of necessity not seeing others. The act of seeing does not use up the objects that I see, but it does use up my own resources.

The point of our examples is that for two rather different reasons one can ordinarily have only some of an object class and see only some of an object class. Thus the implicit quantifiers commonly understood to accompany these verbs are low. The general point here is that the implicit quantifiers associated with a given verb may simply reflect the number of subjects who *can* "verb" an object, and the number of objects that *can* reasonably be "verbed."

Turning now to the question of positive and negative verbs, we may find it helpful to note that the sharpest difference between these two types of verbs occurs when subjects are making deductive inferences, that is, when they are called upon to apply one or more relevant general principles to a specific case. Suppose, for example, that we are asked to predict the reaction of Mr. X to a painting that is brightly colored, angular, and abstract. Suppose further that we know how Mr. X feels toward brightly colored paintings in general, toward angular paintings in general, and toward abstract painting in general. How might we go about combining this information to make a good guess about how Mr. X will feel toward a painting that has all three properties? The empirical phenomenon under consideration indicates that most college sophomores, at least, would do this differently, depending on the sign of the verb describing Mr. X's predominant affect. That is, they would be much more willing to assert that Mr. X dislikes the painting if he dislikes two of its three attributes than to assert that he likes the painting if he likes two of its three attributes.

Why might this be? There is no clear answer at present. One line of speculation having intuitive appeal, however, centers around the notion that people tend to use different *attributional rules* for explaining positive and negative affect. For example, it is generally understood that objects may be disliked because of single "overriding" negative attributes; for example, "I hate this soup because, although otherwise delicious, it has too much salt." It is much less often the case that an object is considered likable because of one single "overriding" positive attribute; thus the absurdity of "I like this soup because, although otherwise rancid, it is salted just right." The view that negative attributes more frequently cancel out positive attributes than vice

versa has some empirical support in the impression formation literature. Anderson [1965] and Feldman [1962] found that negative adjectives exert a greater influence on an overall impression of a stimulus person than equally polarized positive adjectives (see Kanouse and Hanson [1971] for a review of the literature bearing on this "negativity" effect).

These observations suggest that negative affect toward an object is often considered to be justified on the basis of the presence of one single negative attribute. In contrast, one single positive attribute is seldom enough to ensure likability. Rather, there seem to be three criteria that must be satisfied for an object to be considered likable: it must have no negative qualities of any importance; it must have some positive attributes; and these positive attributes must combine into a positive *Gestalt*.

While it is probably true that most of the time positive qualities form a pleasing combination, it is also clear that in many cases they do not. One can like both lasagne and cherries jubilee without liking them together in the same dish. Indeed, a *Gestalt* can fail to be as positive as its component parts for either of two reasons: *stimulus incompatibility*, as in the case of lasagne and cherries jubilee; *response incompatibility*. The latter state obtains whenever the (positive) response to one attribute is incompatible with the (positive) response to the other attribute. For example, one can like two friends very much, yet be uncomfortable with both of them at the same party if the behavioral orientation required to enjoy the one is incompatible with that required to enjoy the other.

There may well be many cases in which two negative attributes form a positive combination, but it is certainly more difficult to think of examples. Two disliked foods seldom make a favorite dish, nor two bores a lively party.

Generalizing over Subjects and Objects

In this section we shall return to a phenomenon noted earlier; namely, that people appear to be more willing to form inductive inferences when the evidence bears on the object of the sentence, and more willing to form deductive inferences when the evidence bears on the subject of the sentence. For example, if we tell an individual that supermarkets sell some kinds of flowers but not others, he is quite likely to agree that "Supermarkets sell flowers." But if we tell him that some supermarkets sell flowers while others do not, he is likely to hesitate before agreeing to the generalization that "Supermarkets sell flowers." In this case, it is easier to generalize from particular types of flowers to flowers in general than from particular types of supermarkets to supermarkets in general.

When the inference is deductive, however, the reverse is true. If the individual is told that "Supermarkets sell flowers," he is likely to be more willing to infer that a particular type of supermarket sells flowers than that supermarkets sell a particular type of flower. In short, inductive inferences proceed more readily for sentence objects than for subjects, while deductive inferences proceed more readily for sentence subjects than for sentence objects.

In discussing this phenomenon, Abelson and Kanouse expressed doubts about its validity, pointing to the possibility that respondents in these studies had simply been more confused by subject-specific evidence and had treated it more noncommittally. After mature consideration (and more data), the present author believes the phenomenon to be a real one, not an artifact. Assuming this to be the case, what interpretation can be made of the phenomenon?

There are three prominent possibilities. The first of these is that the explanation is a syntactic one—that the grammatical subject of a sentence is treated differently from the grammatical object of a sentence, either because it occurs first or for some other reason. While not very compelling, this explanation has the virtue of being easily testable by changing the voice of the sentence from active to passive. Leaf and Abelson did this and found that changing the voice of the sentence leaves the phenomenon unaltered.

This leaves two substantive explanations for the effect. (For a comprehensive description of these, the reader is referred to Gilson and Abelson [1965]). The first rests on the notion of *class homogeneity.* Sentence subjects are often people—or, as in the example above, institutions and collectives. All of these may well possess a greater number of salient individual differences than do the sorts of things that typically occur as sentence objects. Thus it may be easier to generalize from an object to the class of objects to which it belongs than from a person to the class of people to which he belongs simply because the object class is more homogeneous; that is, objects are perceived as more interchangeable than people.

The second possibility is that the effect is due to perceived differences in the *role of the actor* versus the *role of the "acted upon."* In other words, the attributional assumption underlying the subject-object effect may be that people differ more with respect to how they act or feel than they do with respect to how they are acted upon or felt toward. If so, a given assertion is likely to be "understood" as providing more information about the subject than about the object. Thus, presented with an assertion such as "Artists detest businessmen," individuals may be more likely to interpret the statement as meaning "Artists are such that they detest businessmen," rather than "Businessmen are such that they are detested by artists." To put the matter another way, it may be that such assertions implicitly locate the cause primarily with the actor rather than with the object. This line of explanation suggests that there is a bias to form *person attributions* rather than *entity attributions* even when the entities in question are in fact themselves persons, such as the businessmen in the foregoing example. Indeed, data consistent with this notion have recently been collected by Leslie McArthur [1970], who found that person attributions do seem to be more common than entity attributions in explaining a large variety of actions. (See Jones and Nisbett [1971] for a more comprehensive discussion of this general issue.) A test of this explanation, as opposed to the animate-inanimate explanation, would be readily provided by a study in which both subjects and objects are classes of persons.

Note that in addition to providing an explanation of the greater inductive power of object-specific evidence, this analysis also helps to explain the greater deductive power of subject-specific evidence. We have suggested that the sentence "Artists detest businessmen" is taken to mean that there is something special about artists that makes them detesters of businessmen, rather than that there is something special about businessmen that makes them detestable to artists. If so, the assertion seems to permit a greater number of exceptional businessmen who are not detested than artists who do not detest. In other words, the implicit quantifier for artists should be greater than that for businessmen. Empirically, such is indeed the case [Abelson & Kanouse 1966]. It seems quite reasonable, then, that the generalization has greater deductive applicability to particular kinds of artists than to particular kinds of businessmen.

This line of reasoning is, of course, eminently testable, and empirical clarification of the general phenomenon of subject-object differences is much to be desired.

From Specific Acts to General Dispositions

So far we have examined only cases in which an inference is made concerning the subject or object of an invariant relation. One major class of inferences is clearly omitted, namely, those in which an overt action is taken as evidence for an intention, motive, or disposition [Jones & Davis 1965].

The following example illustrates the problem discussed in this section. Suppose that P sees a man yelling at a small boy. P is quite likely to form some hypothesis about the subjective state or enduring characteristics of the man that have causal significance for his behavior. The many attributions P can make include: (1) the man is angry with the boy; (2) the man dislikes the boy; (3) the man dislikes children; (4) the man is a misanthrope. Obviously, these attributions are arranged in order of ascending generality. The question is what determines the level of generality of a dispositional inference. That is, under what conditions are such inferences likely to be most general?

A recent study by Kanouse and Gross [1970] examined this problem within the psycholinguistic framework that is by now familiar to the reader. Translated into this framework, the problem involves the probability of a *simultaneous* inferential leap from a specific object to a more general one, and from a manifest verb (act) to a subjective verb (disposition).

Below is a schematic representation of the problem, using a different example. In the lower left corner is a hypothetical sentence, or "given": "O destroys *Reader's Digest*s." In the upper right is the conclusion, "O hates magazines." The parenthetical statements represent intermediate steps between evidence and conclusion.

Evidence   *Conclusion*

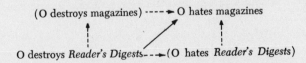

It is apparent from the diagram that there are three different inferential "paths" that P can follow in proceeding from the evidence sentence on the lower left to the conclusion on the upper right. First, he can make a direct inference, symbolized by the diagonal line. Second, he can proceed by way

of the *intermediate* inference that "O destroys magazines." This represents a two-step process: "O destroys *Reader's Digest*s; therefore he destroys magazines; therefore he hates magazines." Finally, he can proceed by way of the intermediate inference on the lower right: "O destroys *Reader's Digest*s; O hates *Reader's Digest*s; therefore he hates magazines." If these two latter paths sound very similar, it is because they are. The only difference is in the intermediate inference: "O destroys magazines" versus "O hates *Reader's Digest*s."

Assuming P follows a two-step inferential path, does it make any difference which path he follows? The results of the Abelson and Kanouse [1966] study suggest that it does. Suppose that the probability of agreeing to the final conclusion is roughly equal to the product of the probabilities of making each separate inference in the chain, that is, the probability of making the inductive leap from *Reader's Digest*s to magazines times the probability of making the leap from destroy to hate. Abelson and Kanouse's findings with respect to verb differences indicate that the probability of making the inductive leap is likely to be quite different for the two paths. As we have seen, manifest verbs facilitate inductive inferences much more readily than do subjective verbs. Thus, one is much more likely to agree that someone *destroys* magazines given that he *destroys Reader's Digest*s than to agree that he *hates* magazines given that he *hates Reader's Digest*s. If we accept the additional assumption that the other inferential leap (from destroy to hate) is equally likely for the two paths, it follows that the intermediate inference "O destroys magazines" should be more conducive to final agreement with the conclusion.

In the Kanouse and Gross experiment subjects were presented with a number of items such as the one above and experimentally induced to follow a given path. This was done by presenting different experimental groups with one or the other intermediate inference as a question. For example:

A. O destroys *Reader's Digest*s.
   Does O destroy magazines?
   Does O hate magazines?
B. O destroys *Reader's Digest*s.
   Does O hate *Reader's Digest*s?
   Does O hate magazines?

Thus both groups received the same evidence and responded to the same conclusion. The only difference between the groups is in the intermediate question. If the intermediate question technique effectively "pushes" subjects into different inferential paths, condition A should lead to greater agreement with the final conclusion than condition B.

The results clearly corroborate this predicted path difference effect. Subjects were significantly more willing to agree with the final conclusion following the intermediate question in condition A, despite the fact that the initial evidence is the same in both conditions. The effect occurred across six different replications in which the specific content (that is, verbs and objects) was varied.

Additional analyses and groups were run in an attempt to pinpoint the reasons for this effect. These are worth discussing in some detail, since the results are instructive. First, an analysis of covariance established that path differences in acceptance of the final conclusion were not mediated by differential agreement with the intermediate question. Thus, although subjects tended to respond more favorably to the intermediate question in the "strong path" condition (A), their greater willingness to endorse the conclusion in this condition represents more than the effect of a favorable response set established by the intermediate question and carried over into the conclusion.

In order to provide information on the effects of simple order differences between the paths (for example, whether the inductive inference occurs first or last), additional experimental conditions, in which the inductive power of the two verbs did not differ and hence no path difference might be expected, were included in the design. Specifically, there was a *manifest-manifest* condition (for example, "O tears up *Reader's Digests*; Does O destroy magazines?") and a *subjective-subjective* condition ("O abhors *Reader's Digests*; Does O hate magazines?"). As anticipated, no path differences emerged when both verbs were subjective. This indicates that path differences occur only for specific types of verbs and are not due simply to the order in which the inductive inference occurs.

In the *manifest-manifest* condition, the results are more complex, though equally informative. When both verbs described manifest actions, path differences emerged *if, and only if, the direction of inference was from a specific verb to a more general one.* Consider the following example:

A. O tears up *Reader's Digests*.
   Does O tear up magazines?
   Does O destroy magazines?
B. O tears up *Reader's Digests*.
   Does O destroy *Reader's Digests*?
   Does O destroy magazines?

Here condition A elicited significantly more agreement than condition B, despite the fact that both verbs are roughly equal in inductive strength. Note, however, that "tearing up" is a more specific verb than "destroying," in the sense that tearing up is a specific means of destruction, not vice versa. Significantly, path differences were apparent for manifest verbs only when the two verbs bore this sort of means-end relationship and were absent when the means-end relationship was reversed.

How might we account for this phenomenon? It seems clear that more is involved in path differences than the differential inductive power of verbs, since the effect sometimes occurs even when the two verbs are approximately equal in inductive power. One line of explanation, however, seems to be consistent with all the data: *path differences occur when the intermediate inferences in the two paths differ with respect to their ability to explain or account for the initial evidence sentence.* The point is obvious when one verb is manifest and the other subjective; thus, hating *Reader's Digests* "explains" destroying them, while destroying magazines does not. Less obviously, specific manifest actions often seem to be "explained" by more general actions in the same class. That is, general actions can explain specific actions by invoking a superordinate goal; for example, "destroying" explains "tearing up," because one tears up in order to destroy (but not vice versa). To put the matter another way, general action verbs like "destroy" often seem to contain more implicit *intentionality* than specific action verbs like "tearing up" and hence possess much more of the explanatory power of subjective verbs.

Further data on the issue of intentionality is provided by an additional set of experimental conditions included in the Kanouse and Gross study. In these conditions an intention was created out of an action by the simple device of prefixing a manifest verb with the phrase "want to," as in the following example:

A. O destroys *Reader's Digests*.
   Does O destroy magazines?
   Does O want to destroy magazines?
B. O destroys *Reader's Digests*.
   Does O want to destroy *Reader's Digests*?
   Does O want to destroy magazines?

Once again there was a path difference in agreement with the final conclusion; that is, subjects were more willing to agree that "O wants to destroy magazines" in condition A than in condition B.

To summarize the findings of the Kanouse and Gross study, the strongest inferential path (the path leading to greatest agreement with the final conclusion) is that in which the original action is generalized to a larger object class before it is "explained" by invoking an intention, feeling, or disposition. Moreover, path differences seem to occur for three types of inferences: from an action to a disposition, feeling, or subjective state; from an action to a more general, goal-directed action with implicit intentionality; from an action to an intention. Path differences do not seem to occur when the inference proceeds from one subjective state to another or from an action that is general and goal-directed to a more specific form of that action. In all three cases in which path differences emerge, the verb appearing at the end of the inferential chain contains more implicit affect or intentionality than the verb at the beginning of the chain and hence possesses explanatory value with respect to the action described in the original evidence sentence.

Interpretation of these results raises a number of issues of special concern to the attribution theorist. In the sections that follow, we shall consider two of these in some detail, relating them to a number of recent social psychological experiments that raise similar issues. The first issue concerns the nature of the naive criteria that individuals apply in considering a given statement to be "explanatory"; the second concerns the relationship between the labeling of a phenomenon and causal attributions for that phenomenon.

Necessity and Sufficiency in Causal Attributions

Any given action can ordinarily be attributed to many different causes. In our earlier example of a man yelling at a small boy, the observer may attribute to the man anything from momentary anger to an enduring mean streak; alternatively, he may attribute to the boy anything from temporarily annoying behavior to a lifelong history of juvenile delinquency. The results of the Kanouse and Gross study suggest that very general attributions or explanations for an action are most likely to be made if the action is first generalized and then explained rather than first explained and then generalized. That is, whenever the intermediate inference in their study seems to explain the initial evidence sentence in some way, the inferential chain appears to stop, and further inferential steps to a more general explanation are less likely to be made. It is as if subjects are willing to make inferences until the datum is satisfactorily explained, and then proceed no further. There is no direct indication in the Kanouse and Gross study that this is in fact what subjects are

doing, but this possibility is entirely consistent with the evidence.

A more general statement of this notion is that individuals may be primarily motivated to seek a single sufficient or satisfactory explanation for any given event, rather than one that is the best of all possible explanations. That is, individuals may exert more cognitive effort in seeking an adequate explanation when none has as yet come to mind than they do in seeking for further (and possibly better) explanations when an adequate one is already available. This bias may reflect a tendency to think of unitary events and actions as having unitary (rather than multiple) causes; individuals may assume, in effect, that no more than one sufficient explanation is likely to exist for a single phenomenon. Thus, when more than one satisfactory explanation is potentially available to an individual, which one he adopts may depend primarily on which of the various possible explanations is most *salient*.

This viewpoint has considerable intuitive appeal when applied to the results of more traditional social psychological experiments. Consider, for example, a recent experiment by Kiesler, Nisbett, and Zanna [1969]. Under the guise of an experiment to determine the optimal number of arguments to use in a persuasive communication, these investigators led subjects to believe that they were going to engage in an action that was entirely consistent with their beliefs, namely, delivering anti-air-pollution arguments to passers-by in the street. At the same time, an experimental confederate was asked to deliver similar arguments on the importance of promoting auto safety. There were two experimental conditions. In the "belief relevant" condition, the confederate stated that he was willing to argue in favor of promoting auto safety because he believed strongly in it; in the "belief irrelevant" condition, the confederate stated that he was willing to do so because the experiment was scientifically valuable.

Kiesler, Nisbett, and Zanna deliberately chose to investigate a behavior that the subject had more than one adequate reason to engage in. Clearly, strong antipollution beliefs are a sufficient reason for delivering anti-air-pollution arguments to strangers; and clearly, so is science. The point of the confederate's manipulation was to emphasize to the subject a set of reasons for his behavior that was either relevant or irrelevant to his attitudinal convictions. The results show that the confederate's statement did indeed have an effect. Subjects in the belief-relevant condition expressed stronger anti-air-pollution attitudes on a postexperimental questionnaire than did subjects in the belief-irrelevant condition. Kiesler, Nisbett, and Zanna offer the following interpretation of their results:

> It is . . . possible to view the subjects in the present experiment as the victims of an attribution error. When led to think that a consonant behavior was relevant to belief, subjects "attributed" their behavior to their belief and erroneously became more extreme in their beliefs and more strongly motivated to perform the behavior [p. 326].

In discussing the results of their experiment, Kiesler, Nisbett, and Zanna suggest that the subject may undergo an (unconscious) inferential process such as the following: "My fellow subject has agreed to do what I'm doing because of his beliefs; I guess that's my reason, too. In fact, my beliefs about air pollution must be pretty strong if I'm willing to proselytize strangers on the street." Whether or not this is the actual process involved, it is interesting that the process is apparently *not* anything like the following: "My fellow subject has agreed to do what I'm going to do because of his beliefs. I guess that's partly my reason too. At the same time, however, this seems like a valuable scientific experiment, the experimenter is a likable sort and I'd like to help him out, it's a beautiful day outside, and I've already accepted $1.50 to do it so I really can't get out of it without impugning my family name." It seems intuitively unlikely that these additional possible causes for their behavior would occur to the subjects unless the first reason is subjectively insufficient or the additional possible reasons are made salient by situational cues.

The point here is rather simple. Assuming that some sort of attributional process is occurring, the very fact that a salience manipulation has some effect indicates that all possible attributions are not otherwise salient. This in turn suggests that the criteria individuals use in accepting causal explanations are not so stringent as to require them to think of every conceivable explanation and then select the best. Rather, the results of the Kiesler, Nisbett, and Zanna experiment suggest that individuals are more likely to accept the first causal explanation that is sufficient by itself to account for the phenomenon.

Indeed, the results of a recent experiment by Lepper, Zanna, and Abelson [1970] suggest that once a given causal explanation is accepted, it may be retained even when the individual is later presented with an opportunity to accept a better alternative. These investigators employed a variant of the classical "forbidden toy" dissonance situation [Aronson & Carlsmith 1963]. Children were forbidden to play with an attractive toy by either a mild or severe threat. Following a temptation period, the children were asked to rank their preferences for a number of toys, including the forbidden toy. In this situation, the typical finding is that the children given a mild threat devalue the toy more than children given a severe threat. To this standard experimental situation, Lepper, Zanna, and Abelson added an orthogonal manipulation: either *before* or *after* the temptation period, the experimenter supplied the child with a social consensus justification for obedience by casually remarking, "You know, sometimes I've played with these toys with other children and sometimes I have had to leave the room and I have left one of these toys up on the table so that they will not play with it. And do you know what? When I asked the other children if they played with the toy I left up on the table, they all told me that they hadn't played with the toy at all."

The effect of this social consensus information is presumably to make the child's otherwise puzzling behavior ("How come I'm not playing with that attractive toy?") somewhat more understandable to him. He is told that *no one* plays with the toy under these conditions, so that his obedience is quite normal. While the consensual information does not exactly explain the child's behavior to him, it does tend to suggest that there is very little to be explained. Thus, when this consensual information is presented prior to the temptation period, one might expect that it would obviate the necessity for dissonance reduction, since the child has no need to devalue the toy in order to explain his obedient behavior. This is precisely what occurs. The strong dissonance effect that is apparent in the mild threat condition when no consensual information is provided is totally absent when the child is provided with this information.

However, what if the same information is provided only *after* the temptation period? Lepper, Zanna, and Abelson reasoned that in this case the consensual information would be "too late" to inhibit dissonance reduction, since the children in the mild threat condition would already have reduced dissonance by derogating the toy. The children would be, in effect, successful problem solvers who have already achieved a satisfactory solution and are reluctant to reconsider their solution. The results provide striking support for this hypothesis. Indeed, consensual information in the "after" condition did not reduce derogation at all. Thus, information that was completely effective in inhibiting dissonance reduction when presented before the temptation period was completely ineffective when presented afterward.

The results of the Lepper, Zanna, and Abelson study clearly show that the cognitive implications of consensual information that are present in the before condition are *not* present in the after condition; unfortunately, there is no indication in the data of what implications might be present in the after condition in their place. There are two prominent possibilities. The first is that there are in fact no cognitive implications in this condition; that is, the children simply ignore or avoid thinking about the information when it arrives too late to help them resolve the attributional dilemma. The second and more intriguing possibility is that the children actually *assimilate* the consensual information so that it conforms with the dissonance-reducing attribution they have already made. How this might occur can easily be seen if we compare the context in which the information is given at each of the two points in time. In the before condition, the child has just been threatened and told not to play with the toy. When the experimenter then remarks that no one else has played with the toy in this situation, it seems likely that the child will regard this information as indicating social consensus about the severity of the experimenter's threat: "All the other kids were scared to play with it too." In the after condition the same statement may mean something quite different to the child. In this condition the child has just managed to emerge from the temptation period with his obedience intact and in the process has succeeded in convincing himself that the toy is really not very attractive. When he learns that other children have not played with the toy, he might naturally infer that "they didn't like the toy either." Thus an identical item of information could easily support either of two quite different attributions, depending on which attribution is most facilitated by situational cues and salient cognitions present at the time.

Although the three studies differ markedly in method and substance, taken together they suggest the existence of a *primacy effect* in the formation of attributions. In the Kanouse and Gross study subjects were less likely to accept a sentence offering a general explanation of an act when the opportunity to accept a more specific explanation was presented first. In the Kiesler, Nisbett, and Zanna experiment subjects appeared to attribute their own consonant behavior to whichever of two plausible reasons was made salient by a confederate. Both of these findings suggest that before a stable attribution has been reached the attributional process tends to be highly sensitive to incidental events such as choice of language and momentarily salient situational cues. However, the results of the Lepper, Zanna, and Abelson study suggest that once a stable attribution has been achieved individuals are relatively unresponsive to new information.

The sort of primacy effect suggested by this data makes a great deal of sense. It seems likely that at least part of the individual's motivation in forming causal attributions is to make sense of the world around him. If so, it is hardly surprising that once he has found a "conceptual good figure" that accounts for a particular phenomenon he is likely to assimilate new information into an existing conceptual structure wherever possible. Only when new data are uninterpretable in terms of existing explanatory systems is the individual likely to seek a new explanatory structure.

Labeling and Attribution

The way in which a given phenomenon is described is almost certain to affect the way in which it is explained. There are at least two ways in which labeling can affect causal attribution. First, the language used to describe events and actions frequently contains implicit attributions in itself. Second, the level of generality used in describing a given phenomenon is likely to influence the level of generality at which the phenomenon is explained. Pertinent details and facets that are omitted in description are unlikely to be reinstated in explanation.

The language studies described earlier provide an illustration of both these points. The first point is really a limited form of the Whorfian hypothesis and is illustrated by the phenomenon of implicit quantification. As we have seen, the generality of a given relation over objects is implicitly specified by the verb. To the extent that a given verb implies extensive or limited generality over objects, it tends to locate the source of the relation either in the subject or the object. This effect seems to be "built in" to the language; that is, implicit quantifiers seem to form part of the *meaning* of verbs, agreement concerning which is shared by language users.

The notion of implicit causal attribution is not limited to connotative differences in quantification. It is likely that other dimensions of connotative meaning involve implicit causal distinctions as well. For example, consider the two verbs "detest" and "abhor." Although both denote intense negative affect, the two seem to differ connotatively with respect to the source and "direction" of the affect. When an actor detests an object, the affect seems to flow from the actor as source to the object as target. But when an actor is said to abhor an object, his role seems more passive. His feeling is essentially *reactive* rather than *active*. Thus the two verbs differ in the extent to which they point to the actor or the object as the source and target of the feeling.

A third example of implicit causal attribution in description is provided by adverbial modifiers. Consider the sentence "Trueblood slammed the door angrily." Although ordinarily considered descriptive, such sentences obviously contain implicit causal information: "Trueblood slammed the door because he was angry." This is readily seen when the sentence is compared with the alternative: "Trueblood slammed the door clumsily."

A second way in which labeling can affect causal attribution is illustrated by the Kanouse and Gross study. Earlier we interpreted the results of this study in terms of the stage at which an explanatory inference was introduced in a chain of inferences. Another way of viewing the results, not incompatible with the first, is that explanations for an action tend to parallel or "match" the level of generality with which that action is described. Thus, when an individual is led to accept a description of an action at a higher level of generality, he apparently becomes more willing to accept an explanation of that action at a corresponding level of generality.

If, as we have suggested, the way in which a phenomenon is labeled affects the way it is explained, it becomes extremely important to understand what determines how individuals describe a given phenomenon. Ordinarily, there are many ways in which the same event can be described. Indeed, a persistent problem in social psychological experiments has been that there is typically a great deal of ambiguity with respect to how the individual cognitively represents a given situation or behavior. In the Kiesler, Nisbett, and Zanna study, for example, it is not clear whether subjects, when left to their own devices, are likely to think of their own (anticipated) behavior as "proselytizing against air pollution," "delivering persuasive communications," "fulfilling experimental obligations," or whatever. Our analysis suggests that these alternative ways of cognizing the same behavior would have quite different attributional implications. Indeed, it is not clear whether the effect of the

confederate's manipulation in this experiment is to make different *reasons* for the subject's behavior salient to him directly or to do so indirectly by influencing the way in which he defines the behavior itself.

This problem of ambiguity as to how the subject cognitively represents a phenomenon is not present in the language studies we have reviewed. The experimenter controls the information he gives the subject to deal with. Thus, working with the process of attributional inferences at the level of the individual sentence has much to recommend it. At the same time, however, language studies lack the motivational and cognitive importance of real-life attributional situations. What seems to be required to enlarge our understanding of the naive reasoning process is imaginative, conjunctive use of both the situational experiment and the pure cognitive study as sources of data.

Summary and Conclusions

Studies of the way in which individuals form naive inferences using everyday language were examined from the standpoint of attribution theory. Of particular interest to the attribution theorist is the implicit *level of generality* of a given item of linguistically encoded information. A number of semantic variables that affect implicit level of generality were discussed. It was suggested that the extent to which a particular linguistic rendering of information readily permits inductive or deductive inferences can affect attribution in either of two ways. First, statements about a phenomenon that, on the face of it, are merely descriptive may often contain implicit causal hypotheses and assumptions. Second, the level of generality with which a phenomenon is described may substantially determine the level of generality at which it is explained.

In addition, a number of studies were examined that suggest the existence of a *primacy effect* in attribution formation. When several adequate attributions are potentially available to an individual, the attribution he adopts appears to be heavily influenced by the particular situational or linguistic cues available to him. Once the individual has formed an attribution that is sufficient to account for a given datum, however, he is unlikely to give other potentially satisfactory alternatives much consideration. It is as if individuals in their attributional endeavors are satisfied with *sufficient* explanations and do not require explanations to be *necessary* as well.

BIBLIOGRAPHY

Robert P. Abelson, "Psychological Implication." In Robert P. Abelson et al., eds., *Theories of Cognitive Consistency: A Sourcebook.* Rand McNally, 1968.

Robert P. Abelson and David E. Kanouse, "Subjective Acceptance of Verbal Generalizations." In Shel Feldman, ed., *Cognitive Consistency: Motivational Antecedents and Behavioral Consequents.* Academic, 1966.

Norman Anderson, "Averaging Versus Adding as a Stimulus-combination Rule in Impression Formation." *Journal of Experimental Psychology*, 1965, 70:394–400.

Elliot Aronson and J. Merrill Carlsmith, "Effect of Severity of Threat on Valuation of Forbidden Behavior." *Journal of Abnormal and Social Psychology*, 1963, 66:584–588.

Shel Feldman, "Evaluative Ratings of Adjective-adjective Combinations, Predicted from Ratings of Their Components." Unpublished Ph.D. dissertation, Yale University, 1962.

Charlotte Gilson and Robert P. Abelson, "The Subjective Use of Inductive Evidence." *Journal of Personality and Social Psychology*, 1965, 2:301–310.

Fritz Heider, "Attitudes and Cognitive Organization." *Journal of Psychology*, 1946, 21:107–112.

P. N. Johnson-Laird and Joanna Tagart, "How Implication Is Understood." *American Journal of Psychology*, 1969, 82:367–373.

Edward E. Jones and Keith E. Davis, "From Acts to Dispositions: The Attribution Process in Person Perception." In Leonard Berkowitz, ed., *Advances in Experimental Social Psychology.* Academic, 1965.

Edward E. Jones and Richard E. Nisbett, "The Actor and the Observer: Divergent Perceptions of the Causes of Behavior." General Learning Press, 1971.

James M. Jones and Robert P. Abelson, "Semantic Generalization of Sentences as a Function of Verbs, Auxiliaries, and Class Relevance." Paper read at Eastern Psychological Association convention, Boston, 1967.

David E. Kanouse, "The Effects of Verb Type on the Cognitive Processing of English Sentences." Unpublished doctoral dissertation, Yale University, 1968.

David E. Kanouse and David Gross, "From Specific Acts to General Dispositions." Unpublished manuscript, University of California at Los Angeles, 1970.

David E. Kanouse and L. Reid Hanson, Jr. "Negativity in Evaluations." General Learning Press, 1971.

Charles A. Kiesler, Richard E. Nisbett, and Mark P. Zanna, "On Inferring One's Beliefs from One's Behavior." *Journal of Personality and Social Psychology*, 1969, 11:321–327.

William A. Leaf, "Subjective Processes in the Acceptance of Verbal Generalizations." Unpublished Ph.D. dissertation, Yale University, 1969.

Mark R. Lepper, Mark P. Zanna, and Robert P. Abelson, "Cognitive Irreversibility in a Dissonance Reduction Situation." *Journal of Personality and Social Psychology*, 1970, 16:191–198.

Leslie Z. McArthur, "The How and What of Why: Some Determinants and Consequences of Casual Attribution." Unpublished Ph.D. dissertation, Yale University, 1970.

Peter C. Wason, "The Processing of Positive and Negative Information." *Quarterly Journal of Experimental Psychology*, 1959, 11:92–107.

[Preparation of this paper grew out of a workshop on attribution theory held at UCLA in August 1969, supported by Grant GS-2613 from the National Science Foundation.]

8 · Attribution Processes in the Development and Treatment of Emotional Disorders

STUART VALINS

State University of New York at Stony Brook

RICHARD E. NISBETT

University of Michigan

An increasing number of experimental studies of attribution processes are relevant to the problems encountered by psychotherapists (see Nisbett and Valins 1971 for a review of these studies). In this paper we attempt to describe systematically how attribution processes may help explain the development of some emotional disorders and how attribution processes may be incorporated into treatment procedures. We hope that this undertaking will help to create a common language with which the problems of clinical practice and the experimental analysis of attribution processes may speak to one another.

Attribution Processes and Emotional Disorders

Attribution is a process whereby the individual "explains" his world. In doing so he often uses social consensus as a criterion for validating his explanations. Indeed, when objective evidence is not available, it is the opinion of relevant others that largely determines the confidence he has in his explanations of the world. Social comparison theory [Festinger 1954] and research on affiliation [Schachter 1959] have provided the major impetus for investigations of the conditions under which we actively seek out the opinions of other people. This research, however, has identified circumstances in which individuals seem to avoid obtaining the opinions of others. To the degree that our preliminary evaluations indicate that our attitudes or behavior are bad or shameful, we may not want to check the validity of our evaluations by discussing them with other people [Sarnoff & Zimbardo 1961]. Likewise, to the degree that other people are dissimilar or do not share our experiences, we may not want to use them as a source of information against which to check our evaluations [Schachter 1959]. It is thus apparent that effective social comparison often *cannot* take place, even though the individual might desire it or benefit from it. Effective social comparison is impossible when there are no individuals available who could provide adequate information and unlikely when the comparison process is personally painful. Social comparison is also unlikely when the person does not realize that there is a social comparison question to be asked, as when he thinks he already has correct explanations for his experiences.

In this section we argue that the failure or inability to use social consensus to check shameful evaluations can lead to self-ascriptions of mental abnormality and personal inadequacy that can be profoundly debilitating. We also argue that under conditions in which no one else shares the individual's experiences he is apt to distrust other people, and left alone he may develop incorrect and seemingly bizarre interpretations of his experiences. In the absence of social consensus, unusual feelings or events may be explained by delusional systems—a symptom characteristic of the paranoid schizophrenic.

Attributions of Abnormality

There exist in the popular culture ready explanations for feelings or behaviors that the individual believes to be inappropriate or wrong. The concepts of modern psychology, in particular those of Freud, have had a profound impact on the naive psychology of the common man. George Miller [1969] has referred to man's changed conception of himself as the major effect of the psychological enterprise on society. One consequence of this new conception is that we have all become amateur psychologists and are quite ready to infer unconscious or hidden motives to account for all sorts of behavior. In most cases attributions of this nature are relatively harmless and have few important implications, even if they are correct. They are evident in cocktail party banter and function more as jokes or to highlight the wit of the observer than to explain the motives of the actor. These attributions take the form of "You spilled that drink because you dislike me and want to stain my carpet," or "She dresses like that because she's afraid of growing old," or "He's a flirt because he's very insecure about his masculinity."

In other contexts these attributions have more serious effects. If one evaluates his own behavior as inadequate or explains it by referring to hidden motives that are shameful or pathological, profound personal upset can occur. Unfortunately, pathological interpretations of behavior now abound in the popular culture. Educated people use the concepts of repression, projection, and defensiveness with as much facility as they use terms such as emphysema and gastritis. The characters in soap operas are likely to be motivated by devious and unconscious forces. The media continually present us with "expert" opinion on the underlying unconscious and often unsavory reasons for our behavior. Magazine articles feature self-administered tests that allow us to evaluate our success or failure in such roles as parent, spouse, or lover. Medical columns in the newspaper saddle us with psychic responsibility even for our physical aches and pains. (The individual who avoids reading popular psychodynamics is likely nevertheless to encounter it in the physician's office. A young married woman of our acquaintance complained of abdominal pain at bedtime and was informed that it had its origin in "sexual fears." A more old-fashioned physician subsequently diagnosed the ailment as a tomato allergy, with symptom onset roughly six hours after consumption of tomatoes. The young woman dropped tomatoes from her diet, and her sexual fears diminished greatly.) Although much of this information may be shrugged off or taken with a grain of salt, most of us are frequently faced with "scientific evidence" of our inadequacy or psychological abnormality. It is thus not surprising that there are individuals who are continually monitoring their behavior and who interpret behaviors that are common and normal as being "abnormal."

Consider as an example of such a person a case study described by John Neale [personal communication 1970]. The client, a twenty-five-year-old black, unmarried male, came for therapy because he thought he was homosexual. Deeply upset by this prospect, he found himself frequently in states of severe anxiety and depression. His attribution of homosexuality was based on several observations. Sexual intercourse was unsatisfactory, he often found himself looking at the crotch area of other men, and he believed that his penis was abnormally small. This latter belief appeared to be the major source of his difficulties. As he put it, "black people are supposed to be hung like horses and I'm not." Therapy was initiated by explaining the laws of optics—to wit, viewed from above objects in the same plane as the line of vision appear shorter. The client was advised to view himself in a mirror and this procedure helped convince him that his penis, though not of superhuman proportions, was of "normal" size. The therapist also explained that the client's glances toward the crotch area of other men were a natural consequence of his belief that his own penis was small. The client was thus persuaded that this behavior was an indication of self-evaluation and not homosexuality. It was "normal" for him to be curious about the size of other men's penises. Finally his unsatisfactory sexual experiences were explained as not being a result of inadequate heterosexual interest but a "normal" consequence of anxiety about possible inadequate performance. Neale reports that these discussions subsequently relieved the symptoms with which the client entered therapy. The client no longer considered himself homosexual and his anxiety and depression substantially diminished.

Neale's therapy, which may be called "attribution therapy" (after Ross, Rodin, & Zimbardo's 1969 suggestion) or (as Davison 1969 has labeled a similar technique) "assessment therapy" evidently consisted of providing "normal" explanations for the behavior the patient presumed to be "abnormal." Such explanations did not support a homosexual attribution and as a result reduced the client's fears. Note, however, that to correct the patient's attributions a psychotherapist may not have been required. A therapist was necessary mainly because the client was too ashamed of his possible homosexuality to check his beliefs with other people. His fears about homosexuality led to incorrect interpretations of behavior. These interpretations might very well have been corrected had he spoken to friends and been influenced by their interpretations. Many beliefs, however, are simply too undesirable to discuss, and in such cases we often do not check their validity through social consensus. Under these circumstances normal behaviors can be used incorrectly to generate a diagnosis of abnormality.

Attributions of Inadequacy

Attributions damaging to mental health are not limited to erroneous interpretations of one's own behavior but also include interpretations of the behavior of others toward oneself. *Time* magazine [1969] reported an important development in military psychiatry practiced in Vietnam. Army psychiatrists observed that the men in long-established combat units were in the habit of greeting new arrivals with strong suspicion and hostility. The new man, ignorant of battle and the unwritten rules of his new unit, seems stupid and unsocialized to his seasoned but uncharitable companions. The pattern, which the psychiatrists labeled the f.n.g. (for "f——g new guy") syndrome, produces a considerable number of psychiatric casualties among the new men. In a program that might be called "preventive attribution therapy," field commanders are now urged to prepare the new man for his cold reception. When the new man joins his unit he is equipped with the attribution "they hate the f.n.g." instead of the far more distressing attribution "they hate me."

The Vietnam psychiatrists recommend a similar preventive technique when rotating unit commanders. Often a departing commander relaxes discipline and lets his hair down with his men, aware that the taut control that psychological distance helps to maintain will soon be unnecessary. The new commander, intent on establishing authority, looks like a martinet by comparison and is sometimes engulfed by the rejection and anger he encounters. Army psychiatrists now urge the departing commander to tighten discipline and control before he leaves. This serves to prevent anger against the new commander and the subsequent damaging self-evaluations.

These techniques have obvious applications to civilian life. There are many life situations that regularly produce severe stress, and there are probably regularities in the damaging attributions that individuals employ to account for their tension and unhappiness in these situations. The new job is probably one of these situations. Damaging self-attributions are likely when the individual observes himself worrying excessively about the prospect of job change, or when he makes the job change and finds himself making errors, or when he incurs criticism from his new colleagues, or when he observes himself upset and tense in his new job.

Clearly to the extent that the problems associated with situations like the job change are universal, self-attributions of inadequacy are not merely damaging but erroneous. These errors are not likely to be discovered, however, because a given individual experiences such situations too seldom to perceive the situational nature of the stress and apparent inadequacy. Reassuring social comparison agents are often not available, even if the individual were motivated to seek them out. And, unfortunately, the explanations offered by the cultural milieu are as likely to reinforce as to counteract self-attributions of inadequacy. The individual who is inclined to label his stress-produced anxiety as "neurotic" readily finds support for that interpretation in the new naive psychology.

Attributions to Account for Unusual Sensory Phenomena: Schizophrenic Delusional Systems

Certainly some interpretations of one's behavior and the behavior of others toward oneself can be quite damaging. The interpretation can generate additional unhappiness and an unflattering self-concept and, as we shall emphasize later, can exacerbate through worry and anxiety the very symptoms the interpretation seeks to explain. The unflattering self-attributions in our examples, however, are not themselves evidence of pathological belief systems. They are not neurotic or "crazy" interpretations and no one would take them as evidence of a thought disorder. They are simply attributions that are wrong or damaging or both. Other explanatory systems, however, usually are taken as evidence of deranged thinking. These are the delusional systems characteristic of the schizophrenic. We shall argue in this section, following Brendan Maher [1970], that it is fruitful to treat such delusional systems as explanatory devices, which like the other attributions we have discussed are not pathological in their own right but merely the results of the patient's attempts to understand certain phenomena.

Let us begin by discussing Davison's [1966] treatment of a schizophrenic by "cognitive restructuring." The client, a forty-four-year-old married male, sought treatment because of twitches over his eye, heart, and solar plexus. He was particularly worried about "pressure points" over his right eye. These pressure points were interpreted as being caused by a "spirit" that was helping him to make decisions. The "messages," however, had begun to impart conflicting information, which troubled the client. When he was admitted to the hospital, "his speech was described as tangential, with loose associations, its content concerned with grandiose schemes and persecutions by others, but centering around information from his pressure points. There was no evidence of hallucinations" [p. 177]. The diagnosis was paranoid schizophrenia.

Therapy consisted of systematically teaching the client that his pressure points were situationally induced and an indication of extreme tension and upset. The client was shown that a tense situation (a game of blackjack with the therapist) produced these pressure points and that muscle relaxation exercises reduced them. Given a "normal" explanation for these pressure points, the client began to refer to them as "sensations" and gradually stopped referring to them as spirit-induced. Furthermore, realizing that his previous spirit explanation was an indication of crazy or abnormal behavior, the client was now considerably relieved to have a "normal" explanation for his pressure points.

Davison's therapy, like Neale's, can best be described as attribution therapy. Just as Neale provided his client with a "normal" explanation for his "homosexual" behavior, Davison provided his client with a "normal" explanation for his "spirit-induced" sensations. Both clients were greatly relieved to realize that they were less deviant than they had supposed. The cases were different, however, in that Neale's client was merely holding a false belief whereas Davison's client had developed a delusional system. Davison's client held a belief with which anyone else would have disagreed and which even the client realized was "crazy." Why did he develop this delusional system? The answer is at the core of the problem we are faced with in understanding and treating the schizophrenic. Brendan Maher has begun to outline an answer that is quite speculative but worthy of close attention.

Maher points out that schizophrenic delusions have usually been regarded as evidence that the patient has an underlying thinking disorder. This view rests on the assumption that the same sensory data are available to the patient as to others. The patient is assumed to be incapable of making reasonable inferences from these data. Maher opposes to this view the possibility that the schizophrenic's inference processes are intact, but that the data available to him really are very different from those available to others. Citing evidence from, among others, Payne [1962] and Venables [1964], Maher argues that an impairment in the patient's sensory input channels may distort the available information. These impairments are probably of biochemical origin, and might conceivably result from a malfunction of the central nervous system arousal mechanisms, perhaps an overactivity of the reticular formation. Such an impairment of arousal mechanisms might reasonably be expected to produce a good many of the other bizarre experiences and behaviors of schizophrenics, including the phenomenon of "word salad" (perhaps from overactive associative links between words and phrases that ordinarily have low associative values), hallucinations, and a variety of somatic sensations.

If it is correct that schizophrenic experiences are "real," then delusional beliefs may appropriately be seen simply as the patient's attempts to explain his unusual experiences. Since other people apparently do not share his experiences, the schizophrenic must reject their opinions when evaluating his experiences. Indeed, by virtue of the fact that others do not share his experiences, the schizophrenic is pushed toward delusions of self-reference. His experiences are considered unique because others are in a conspiratorial fashion producing them, or, because of his special qualities, he has been "chosen." Maher thus argues that there is no reason to assume that the cognitive activity by which patients arrive at their delusions (explanations) is distinguishable in any way from that employed by nonpatients, or for that matter by scientists. The intelligence of the particular patient determines the structural coherence and internal consistency of the explanation. The cultural experiences of the patient determine the content—political, religious, or scientific—of the explanation. In brief, "a delusion is an hypothesis designed to explain unusual perceptual phenomena and developed through the operation of normal cognitive processes" [p. 4].

There is an intriguing similarity between Maher's analysis of schizophrenia and Schachter's analysis of emotion. Schachter [1964] has proposed that the individual in a state of autonomic arousal has a need to explain the arousal. If the explanation is consistent with emotion, the individual will feel emotional. Maher proposes that the schizophrenic has unusual, arousal-producing experiences he needs to explain. If the explanation he hits upon is unusual enough, the individual is called "crazy" and his explanation a "delusion." The implied cure for these delusions is similar to the technique used by Schachter and his colleagues to forestall an emotion, which is to provide a nonemotional explanation for the arousal. Maher proposes that schizophrenic delusions may be similarly circumvented by acknowledging the reality of the patient's experiences and by providing the patient with a "normal," that is, biological, explanation of them. The patient might be told, in effect, that just as some people have weak hearts or inefficient gall bladders, he has an overactive reticular formation. Such an explanation might effectively undermine the delusional system, which the patient himself often knows to be crazy but which he perhaps finds more acceptable than the traditional demand of the therapist that the patient deny the reality of his experiences.

Maher's proposal (which has been anticipated by Davison and Neale) seems to us to be of great importance. It is also thoroughly consistent with recent attribution research indicating that the explanation accepted by an individual for his experiences is of paramount importance for subsequent cognitive, emotional, and motivational processes. Nevertheless, we would like to distinguish between two features of Maher's argument. The reluctant reader can agree that delusions may profitably be viewed as incorrect explanations for the schizophrenic's experiences without however acceding to Maher's belief that these experiences arise from atypical or unusual biological phenomena. It is possible to hold the traditional view that the arousal mechanisms and sensory apparatus of the schizophrenic are intact but still agree that the *context* in which he receives and evaluates stimuli may be radically different. Just as a subject in a sensory deprivation experiment is apt to develop minor delusions, the isolated, distrustful individual who persistently ignores consensus information would be apt to develop bizarre explanations for his "normal" experiences.

Therapeutic Undermining of Dispositional Self-Diagnoses

Diverse as these examples are, it seems to us that they have several elements in common. Neale's "homosexual," the Vietnam soldier, and Davison's schizophrenic resemble one another in the following ways. (1) Each of the individuals had developed a dispositional explanation to account for some behavioral effect. Neale's client attributed various effects to a homosexual disposition, the Vietnam soldier to personal inadequacy, and Davison's client to an ability to communicate with spirits. (2) Each went about making his dispositional interpretation in perfectly logical ways, but because of a lack of social consensus for the observed effect or an inability or unwillingness to seek social comparison agents each arrived at an erroneous belief that there was a relatively unique, personal cause for the observed effects. (3) Each suffered in one or more of the following ways for his erroneous causal attribution: from depression and anxiety caused by an unfavorable view of the self; from a consequent exacerbation of the very symptoms that gave rise to the attribution; from an increasing distance and sense of difference from his fellow men.

The treatment for each of the three types of client may also be described in terms of common elements: (1) In each case the individual's underlying dispositional assumption was challenged (or in the military case prevented). The result was to render the symptom more "normal," which is to say, more nearly a result of situational forces than of personal dispositions. Neale's client did not have a homosexual disposition but a common worry and a natural response to it. The Vietnam soldiers were told to expect a set of reactions that would be common to anyone in their situation. Davison's schizophrenic was assured of a reality base for his "pressure points" but was offered an explanation that served to relate the symptoms to specific situational determinants and to a form of stress reaction that was not unique. (2) In each case the new interpretation resulted in symptom improvement, presumably because the interpretation did not support the anxiety and depression generated by the old attribution and did not have the effects either of furthering a sense of differentness and apartness or of prompting behaviors that would serve to exacerbate the symptoms.

We should say that the tone of this analysis is very much out of step with prevailing clinical practice, which is to make inferences about the patient's personality and dispositions and to share them with the patient in the hope that he will change the disabling dispositions. Whether the dispositional interpretations of the therapist are generally correct or not, we wish to point out that a given patient can sometimes be helped most by attacking the dispositional interpretations he has already made for himself and supplying less damaging situational attributions. The dispositional interpretations generated by the client, it should be noted, will often (and probably increasingly) be misapplications of psychodynamic principles developed since the beginning of the twentieth century.

Attribution Processes, Drugs, and the Treatment Situation

There is reason to be concerned about a patient's attributions even when faulty attributions are not the source of his emotional disorder. All aspects of the treatment situation—including drugs, the conversations between therapist and patient, and the new behaviors the patient is encouraged to attempt— together with the shifting elements of the patient's life situation, are fair game for the patient's attribution processes. Change or lack of change, improvement or worsening, are effects whose causes the patient is likely to try to infer. Knowledge of the attributions patients are likely to make should be helpful to the clinician who wishes to maximize his treatment effects.

Just as a distinction between dispositional and situational causes of behavior was useful earlier, a distinction between stimulus and circumstance causes will be useful here. Nisbett and Valins [1971] have developed a distinction between causal factors seen as *intrinsic to a given stimulus* and those seen as *extrinsic or circumstantial*. In contrast to the dispositional-situational distinction that is concerned with the causal role of the person versus the causal role of the environment, the stimulus-circumstance distinction is concerned with the allocation of cause to various aspects of the environment. A *stimulus attribution* occurs when an individual attributes his reaction (e.g., visceral arousal, subjective fear, avoidance behavior) in the presence of a particular salient stimulus to the stimulus itself (for example, electric shock). A *circumstance attribution* occurs when an individual attributes his reaction to some aspect of the situation other than the particular salient stimulus (e.g., to a drug taken before the electric shock is given). There is a relationship between the two types of distinction. Logically, stimulus and circumstance are subcategories of situational causes, as distinct from dispositional causes. However, dispositional inferences can be coordinated to either type of situational cause. Thus an individual may infer that he has low or high *tolerance for shock* or that he has low or high *susceptibility to a drug* that influences the effects of electric shock.

The remainder of this paper is concerned with the consequences of stimulus attributions and circumstance attributions. In the next section we deal with situations in which it may be beneficial for an individual to attribute his behavior more to extrinsic circumstances than to an intrinsic reaction to the salient stimulus. We believe this to be generally so when (*a*) attribution to the stimulus is likely to result in maladaptive behavior (extreme fear, phobic or inappropriate avoidance) and (*b*) attribution to the stimulus is likely to result in a damaging dispositional inference (e.g., neuroticism, inadequacy). Then we deal with situations in which it may be beneficial for an individual to attribute his behavior more to an intrinsic reaction to the salient stimulus than to extrinsic circumstances. We believe this to be generally so when (*a*) attribution to the stimulus is likely to result in adaptive behavior (e.g., effective coping behavior) and (*b*) attribution to the stimulus is likely to result in a self-enhancing dispositional inference (e.g., belief that he is capable, healthy, etc.).

Almost all the research we discuss has dealt exclusively with drugs as the alternate (circumstance) attribution. Although drugs are often an important part of the treatment regimen and at times constitute the entire treatment, we believe that our discussion is also relevant to treatment situations where drugs are not used.

Therapeutic Effects of Attributing Undesirable Symptoms to an Extrinsic Cause

The distinction between extrinsic and intrinsic causes of behavior is grounded in Schachter's [1964] theory of emotion. We have thoroughly discussed Schachter's theory elsewhere [Nisbett & Valins 1971], but it will be helpful briefly to review the central experiment of the theory. Schachter and Singer [1962] gave subjects epinephrine (adrenalin), a drug that produces marked bodily sensations of autonomic arousal. Subjects were then placed in situations designed to elicit either euphoria or anger. When the arousal symptoms were attributed to the situation (what we would call the salient stimulus), the subjects reacted differently than when the arousal symptoms were attributed to the true source of the sensations—the drug (what we would call the circumstance). When arousal sensations were attributed to the situation, the subjects "caught" the salient emotion present in the situation. They became more angry or euphoric than subjects who attributed the source of their sensations to the drug. Subjects who attributed their arousal to the drug actually tended to be less emotional than subjects who had received no external boost to their arousal at all.

While Schachter and Singer were the first to demonstrate this phenomenon in the laboratory, experiences in the dentist's office suggest that it may occur in many real-life situations. Dentists often inject local anesthetics such as procaine in a solution that includes a vasoconstrictor. The purpose of the vasoconstrictor is to retard the absorption of the anesthetic to maintain its effectiveness. The vasoconstrictor typically used is epinephrine—the same drug Schachter and Singer used to produce the visceral groundwork of emotion! Consider how a bright and well-informed individual, Bertrand Russell, reacts in such a situation.

> On one occasion my dentist injected a considerable amount of adrenalin into my blood, in the course of administering a local anaesthetic. I turned pale and trembled, and my heart beat violently; the bodily symptoms of fear were present, as the books said they should be, but it was quite obvious to me that I was not actually feeling fear. I should have had the same bodily symptoms in the presence of a tyrant about to condemn me to death, but there would have been something extra which was absent when I was in the dentist's chair. What was different was the cognitive part: I did not feel fear because I knew there was nothing to be afraid of. In normal life, the adrenal glands are stimulated by the perception of an object which is frightful or enraging; thus there is already a

cognitive element present. The fear or rage attaches itself to the object which has stimulated the glands, and the full emotion arises. But when adrenalin is artificially administered, this cognitive element is absent, and the emotion in its entirety fails to arise [1927, p. 226].

It seems clear from the Schachter and Singer experiment that if dental patients are not informed about the side effects of the anesthetic (the circumstance), as Bertrand Russell was, they will often find a cause in the situation. We might expect that an uninformed patient would readily find an adequate stimulus explanation for his arousal while the dentist is hovering over him. A clear implication of the laboratory research is that dental patients should be informed of the symptoms that these drugs might produce. Certainly enough fear is experienced in the dental situation without compounding it by allowing patients to misattribute their drug-produced symptoms to fear. Although we are aware of the limitations of informal observation, we should report that we are familiar with at least one dentist who knows of attribution processes and who has found that his patients are "easier to handle" when they are correctly informed of the side effects of anesthetics.

From the standpoint of our concern with psychotherapy, it is intriguing to consider more fully what our dentist may be doing for the emotional processes of his patients. It is likely that the chief source of a given dental patient's arousal symptoms is not the drug but the state of fear he is in. If fear is the true cause of the side effects, or at least one cause, then our dentist may be engaged in a form of attribution therapy with potentially broad applications. It may be that he gives his patients a "drug-attribution" for symptoms actually produced by fear. His patients may be less fearful as a result of this reattribution. The research of Nisbett and Schachter [1966] indicates that such a reattribution is entirely possible. Under conditions in which subjects could be convinced that the arousal symptoms produced by electric shock—palpitations, tremor, and so on—were caused by a capsule they had taken (the circumstance), considerably more intense shocks were tolerated than when subjects attributed their symptoms to the true cause, the shocks themselves (the stimulus).

Ross, Rodin, and Zimbardo [1969] have replicated Nisbett and Schachter's finding in a setting with strong implications for the therapeutic situation. By a clever juxtaposition of stimuli they persuaded their subjects to attribute arousal symptoms accompanying fear of anticipated electric shock to a loud noise piped in over a headset. Subjects were then allowed the opportunity to work on either of two insoluble puzzles while listening to the noise. They were led to believe that the solution of one of the puzzles would allow them to escape the electric shock, while the solution of the other puzzle would bring them a monetary reward. The extent to which subjects spent time working on the shock puzzle, as opposed to the reward puzzle, could thus be used as a behavioral indicator of fear of shock. Subjects who were encouraged to attribute their arousal symptoms to the noise (the circumstance) quickly abandoned work on the shock puzzle and spent more time working on the reward puzzle than did subjects who were left to attribute their symptoms to fear of the shock alone (the salient stimulus).

Ross et al. argued that a version of this reattribution technique might successfully be employed as therapy for phobic patients. For example, an acrophobic might be told that his symptoms are "a common physiological consequence of the optical effects of viewing converging vertical lines" [p. 288]. Such a reattribution of arousal symptoms might counter the emotional response to height. Similarly, the individual with a great fear of flying might be told that autonomic arousal is produced by other factors associated with flying—the anticipation of a trip, entrance into a confined space filled with people, the marked acceleration of takeoff, and so on. When arousal symptoms occur, an airplane phobic with this information would have a ready explanation in circumstantial, nonfearful terms.

A variant of this reattribution device was employed, with therapeutic results, by Storms and Nisbett [1970]. Some of their subjects, all of whom were insomniacs, were given placebos described as drugs capable of producing alertness, heart-rate increase, and high temperature—the arousal symptoms accompanying insomnia. It was reasoned that subjects taking the pills would be able to attribute their arousal to the "drug" (the circumstance) instead of to the emotional thoughts accompanying and intensifying their state of insomnia. Such a nonemotional symptom attribution would be expected to result in lowered emotionality and quicker sleep onset. Such subjects did in fact report getting to sleep about 12 minutes sooner on the nights they took the placebo "pep pills" than they had on nights without the pills.

The exact cognitive process that made it possible for insomniac subjects to get to sleep more quickly was unclear to Storms and Nisbett. The investigators had made the initial assumption that insomnia is produced in part by emotionality at bedtime—the rehearsal of angry, fearful, or exciting memories or anticipations. They reasoned that if they offered their subjects an alternative explanation of the arousal produced by their emotions, the emotions would diminish and sleep would ensue correspondingly quickly. However, comments volunteered by the subjects suggested to Storms and Nisbett that a rather different process might have occurred. Several of the subjects made it clear, in informal conversation, that they were worried about the fact that they were insomniacs—about their inability to control such a basic function as sleep and about the state of insomnia as evidence of more general pathology. There is good reason to believe that the experimental manipulation would have had an effect on a worrisome dispositional inference of this sort. Subjects were told, in effect, that on certain nights their insomnia would be caused by a drug. On those nights, therefore, subjects did not have to view their symptoms as evidence of inadequacy or pathology. They may have worried less about their condition and may have got to sleep more quickly for this reason. The drug attribution, then, may not have resulted in a general reduction in emotionality, but only in a reduction in the degree of worry about being an insomniac. To the extent that such worries interfere with sleep, such a change could have produced the experimental results.

Although it was not possible to be certain as to just what kind of process occurred in their experiment, Storms and Nisbett speculated that:

> It is quite likely that there are pathologies involving a vicious cycle of the following type: (1) occurrence of symptoms, (2) worry about symptoms, (3) consequent exacerbation of symptoms. For example, males with problems of impotence probably respond with alarm to signs of detumescence in the sexual situation. Alarm, of course, would increase the likelihood of continued loss of erection. If it were possible to change the meaning which detumescence has for the individual, alarm and consequent impotence might be prevented. Such an individual might be given a "drug," for example, and told that it might occasionally produce momentary detumescence, or he might be assured that occasional detumescence in the sexual situation was characteristic of most normal males. A cycle of symptoms, worry about symptoms, and intensified symptoms might be expected to occur with a number of other behaviors as well, including perhaps stuttering, extreme shyness, and excessive awkwardness in athletic situations. With each condition, an externalization of the symptoms or a reinterpretation of the symptoms in nonpathological terms might help to break the cycle [p. 326].

We would argue, therefore, that it may often be

beneficial for patients to attribute their reactions to "extrinsic" or circumstantial causes. We suggest that it may be valuable for the individual to attribute his reactions to extrinsic sources when stimulus attribution would lead to maladaptive behavior, when the reactions are regarded as undesirable or as evidence of pathology, or when his worries about his reactions and efforts to change them are likely to result only in further exacerbation.

Yet in the next section, we argue that it is sometimes beneficial to encourage the patient to attribute his behavior or symptoms to the salient stimulus and to discourage attribution to an extrinsic agent. In general, the circumstances where this is true are the reverse of the circumstances where attribution to an external agent is desirable. Attribution to the stimulus is likely to be beneficial when the symptoms are desirable or indicative of psychological health or when there is in fact something that the individual can do through his own efforts to produce the desired behavior or symptoms. In addition, we argue that when the clinician includes external agents such as drugs in his treatment regimen, it may be unwise to encourage the patient to attribute too much causal effectiveness to them. This is especially true when the clinician cannot be sure that the external agent will in fact produce the desired improvement or when it appears likely that the patient's faith in the external agent may leave him uncertain of his ability to maintain the improvement when the agent is withdrawn. As we shall see, these recommendations directly contradict much current clinical theory and practice.

Therapeutic Effects of Attributing Desirable Symptoms to an Intrinsic Cause

Most clinicians are well aware of the "placebo effect." They assume that the effectiveness of a drug is the additive result of its pharmacological effect and the psychological effect of the "suggestion" that the patient will improve. The practitioner is typically not unwilling to capitalize on the possibility of a placebo effect. Thus, when he is treating an individual with drugs or some other procedure, he often describes the treatment's effectiveness in a strong and exaggerated fashion ("This drug is a very effective tranquilizer. Relax, you need not worry any longer"). Although the literature dealing with the placebo effect certainly implies that this procedure is correct, we speculate on its possible negative consequences. In the present terminology, such a procedure is an attempt to get the patient strongly to attribute desirable effects to an extrinsic agent. However, describing

a drug as very strong may lead an individual (a) to rely solely on the drug's curative powers and thereby apply himself less to other aspects of the treatment procedure; (b) to infer extreme illness if the drug does not work in the expected manner; and (c) to become psychologically dependent on the drug and to infer negative consequences when he is taken off the drug.

Exclusive Reliance on Drugs. Let us first consider the possibility that an individual may rely exclusively on the curative power of a drug. Interest has recently been expressed in the use of drugs to facilitate the effectiveness of systematic desensitization therapy. The therapy is based upon the notion that "If a response antagonistic to anxiety can be made to occur in the presence of anxiety-evoking stimuli so that it is accompanied by a complete or partial suppression of the anxiety responses, the bond between these stimuli and the anxiety responses will be weakened" [Wolpe 1958, p. 71]. The client is usually trained to relax his musculature and is then asked to imagine various anxiety scenes while he is relaxed. This therapeutic procedure obviously requires the client to expend much effort. He must maintain his state of relaxation and he must try to imagine vividly the anxiety scenes.

Davison and Valins [1968] have discussed the possibility that such efforts are necessary features of desensitization and have expressed doubts about the efficacy of drugs to relax clients. Without going into their entire argument, we would point out one consequence of using a drug to relax during the desensitization procedure. Individuals so treated may become passive and contribute less to the treatment procedure. They may, for example, try less hard to imagine the required scenes. Since according to the theory a vividly imagined scene must be paired with the relaxation response, the failure to do so should adversely affect treatment. Perhaps as a consequence, there has been some confusion in the literature as to whether a muscle-relaxing drug (methohexital sodium) is effective during desensitization. Among those who have found it to be effective, Brady [1967] reports that he tells clients that the drug will help them to relax but that they must work along with it to achieve the desired results. Brady's observations suggest that it may be unwise to "oversell" the effectiveness of drugs. It may be better to tell the client that the drug is not so powerful as to cure completely by itself. Instead, the patient should believe that he must actively engage himself in the therapeutic process. We suggest that the drug or circumstance attribution·be weakened so that the client can be encouraged to contribute to the therapeutic situation.

The Negative Placebo Effect. Let us now consider a situation in which the placebo effect might literally backfire. What might happen if an individual takes a drug described as strong and effective, but the drug does not change his behavior? The present line of reasoning leads us to expect that he might get worse. If he knows that his functioning has remained at the predrug level, but also "knows" that he is under the influence of a strong medication, he might be expected to reach the logical conclusion that his functioning has in reality deteriorated. He would thus infer a worsening of his state from the failure of a presumably strong medication. Some evidence relevant to this expectation has been accumulated in the context of experiments designed to evaluate the effectiveness of various tranquilizers.

Rickels and his colleagues [Rickels, Baumm, Raab, Taylor, & Moore 1965, Rickels & Downing 1967, Rickels, Lipman, & Raab 1966] have performed a series of evaluations of tranquilizers, always including control conditions where subjects were given placebos but told that they had been given tranquilizers. The present line of reasoning leads to the expectation that subjects in the control conditions would get worse. They might be expected to say to themselves, in effect, "I still feel about the same as I did before taking the tranquilizers, so I must be getting more anxious." The data reported by Rickels and his colleagues, while not presented in a form that makes it possible to determine the extent of worsening, do indicate that at best placebo patients do not improve as a group and that certain categories of patients get decidedly worse. The characteristics of the patients least likely to improve are quite interesting from the standpoint of attribution theory. Patients in the placebo condition did not improve if they had had previous experience with tranquilizers, if their anxiety state was a long-standing one, or if their anxiety state was severe. Each of these circumstances would provide the patient with clearer information about the effects of anxiety and tranquilizers and would increase the probability that he would make the attribution that the pill is not working.

The hypothesis that an unfulfilled expectation of improved psychological state results in a worsened condition has been directly tested by Storms and Nisbett [1970]. In this experiment (of which one condition was described above), self-reported insomniacs were asked to take a drug before bedtime, which, they were told, would serve to reduce alertness, heart rate, and body temperature. These symptoms are, of course, the symptoms of an effective

sleeping pill, but the "drug" was actually a placebo. The investigators reasoned that if insomniacs believed themselves under the influence of an arousal-reducing drug, they would regard anything less than a noticeable reduction in arousal as evidence that their emotional thoughts and insomniac state were unusually intense. This in turn should result in a worsening of the insomnia. Subjects given the "sleeping pills" did in fact report taking about fifteen minutes longer to get to sleep than on nights without the pills. The experiment thus provides confirmation of the proposition suggested by Rickels' work: "placebo effects" may backfire when subjects can infer a deterioration of their state from the absence of a promised improvement.

The phenomenon of "suggestion" therefore cannot necessarily be counted upon when patients are given a placebo. In some circumstances, the clinician can expect "suggestion" to work against him. What can we expect when patients are given not placebos, but genuine psychoactive drugs? A clear answer is not currently available. Three investigations have been made of the effects of "overselling" versus "underselling" psychoactive drugs (Uhlenhuth, Canter, Neustadt, & Payson 1959, Uhlenhuth, Rickels, Fisher, Park, Lipman, & Mock 1966, Kast 1961]. The results of these investigations are rather confused and contradictory, indicating that overselling sometimes, with some populations, lessens the effectiveness of psychoactive drugs and sometimes enhances their effectiveness. However, without exception the studies allowed a confounding of overselling with the relative warmth of the therapist and underselling with relative coldness of the therapist.

The most suggestive evidence on the question to date comes from a study by Valins, Adelson, Goldstein and Weiner [1971]. They found some evidence for the negative placebo effect in an experimental situation in which a psychoactive drug was first administered but then withdrawn. Their S's participated in two experimental sessions. During the first session all S's were given nitrous oxide (N_2O), a gas that many modern dentists use to relax their patients. At customary dosages people typically feel quite relaxed, a bit lightheaded, and in general mildly intoxicated. The study was described as an investigation of the psychological effects of N_2O. After experiencing N_2O for ten minutes, subjects completed various questionnaires and were then scheduled for a second session several days later. During this session, all the S's were administered pure oxygen. However, half the S's were told that the same dosage of N_2O was being administered while the remaining S's were told that a considerably weaker and imperceptible dosage was given. All S's were also led to expect that a test of their tolerance for electric shock would be given after the experience with the gas. It was hypothesized that S's who thought they were getting the strong dose of N_2O, and thus expected to be relaxed, would explain their failure to be relaxed by reference to the shocks they thought they would be getting. As expected, these S's said they were more frightened of the forthcoming shocks than did S's who thought that they were receiving a very weak dose ($p = .05$). This study is further evidence that negative placebo effects can occur if a drug is oversold or if an individual is not told that the drug might not work. In this instance, we again advise that the drug or circumstance attribution be weakened in advance. If a drug is described in somewhat less than enthusiastic terms and if it then does not work, the individual does not then have to search among the disturbing stimuli in his life situation to find an explanation for his failure to improve.

Maintenance of Drug-Produced Improvement. Finally, let us consider the problem of transferring a drug-produced behavior change to the nondrug state. Current use of psychoactive drugs follows this general pattern. The patient takes the drug, knows what he is taking, expects a particular effect, usually experiences the effect, and at some point sees himself being withdrawn from his "crutch" in order to test whether he can function without the drug in a manner similar to his improved behavior while under its influence. This is particularly likely to be the modus operandi in the outpatient treatment of "neurotics," individuals who are unduly upset about certain aspects of daily life. That this procedure leads to only very poor generalization from drugged to undrugged conditions has been cited numerous times as a major problem in the therapeutic use of psychoactive drugs.

Neal Miller's [1966] systematic work with rats constitutes some of the most clear-cut evidence of the failure of drug-induced behavior change to generalize to the nondrug state. In one experiment in Miller's paradigm, rats were shocked for pressing a food lever until the lever-pressing response was completely suppressed. Then the shock was turned off and animals were allowed access to the lever for several trials. During these trials without shock, some animals were given the tranquilizer amobarbital sodium while some were given only placebos. As expected, the tranquilized animals were more likely to press the lever than the animals given placebos. The following day, all animals were given placebos and again allowed access to the lever without shock.

Animals previously given placebos were somewhat more likely to press the lever than they had been the previous day, the extinction process having advanced somewhat further. Animals previously given tranquilizer, however, were less likely to press the lever than on the preceding day and actually somewhat less likely to press the lever than animals previously given placebos. The experiment is especially discouraging from the standpoint of drug therapy carry-over effects, because, as Miller points out, "the drug had allowed the animals to resume pressing the bar, a response which not only gave them an opportunity to discover that the shock was no longer present, but also to secure rewarding pellets of food which might have been expected to countercondition the fear" [p. 7].

Fortunately, when the subjects are people instead of rats, it is possible to encourage them to attribute improved functioning to a new-found reaction to the stimulus. Taking note of the transfer problem, Davison and Valins [1969] have suggested that maintaining drug-produced changes in behavior might be facilitated by allowing individuals to think that part of their behavior change is due to themselves rather than being solely the result of the drug. The Davison and Valins experiment, reviewed in Nisbett and Valins [1971], found that subjects who attributed increased shock tolerance to themselves (because they had previously received only a "placebo") subsequently continued to tolerate more shock than subjects who attributed increased shock tolerance to a "drug." Davison and Valins speculated that when a patient can attribute his behavior change to himself:

> the patient would now have to accept the responsibility for his changed behavior and because of this might make three inferences: (*a*) "The world can't be that frightening after all" (he will reevaluate the stimulus situation); (*b*) "I have succeeded and am competent" (he will feel happy and proud of himself); (*c*) "I will subsequently be able to behave differently when in stressful situations" (his expectations and aspirations for improved behavior will be higher). These kinds of inferences would seem to facilitate the maintenance of the behavior change once we have actually terminated the drug. Such subjects should maintain their improved behavior to a greater degree than those who have a drug-attribution for their behavior change [p. 26].

The implications of the Davison and Valins experiment seem clear. The maintenance of a drug-produced behavior change is likely to be greater if the individual can attribute part of the change to his new reactions to stimuli. Such an attribution will be facilitated if the drug is described as being *not* very strong. If the drug or circumstance attribution is relatively weak, the patient's view of the salient stimulus is more likely to change and his improved behavior more likely to carry over into the nondrug situation.

In summary, we have good reason to suspect that it may not always be wise to trust to the "placebo effect" in the drug-taking or general treatment situation. Describing a drug as very strong can have negative consequences. If the drug is effective an individual may not apply himself to relevant aspects of the treatment procedure, and, furthermore, whatever change is produced may disappear when the drug is withdrawn. If the drug is not effective, the individual may infer extreme illness and this belief can further exacerbate his condition. We would like to emphasize that, while we have spoken almost exclusively of drugs as the extrinsic, circumstance attribution, it is possible to think of all aspects of the treatment situation as potential circumstance attributions. The individual should benefit to the extent that he can attribute change to new-found reactions to the stimuli that constitute his life situation. He should fail to benefit to the extent that he believes that behavior change is due merely to the circumstances of his treatment regimen. When the patient behaves in healthier ways, the therapist should stress the causal role of the patient's new attitudes in prompting the behavior.

A Note on Deception

There may be those who feel that the deception described in some of the present research is unwise or even unethical. It should be made clear, however, that none of the principles underlying our recommendations for clinical practice rest upon any necessity to deceive the patient. While we have used deception in our therapy-relevant research, we have done so not because we believe that deception is usually necessary or desirable but because deception techniques are economical ways of answering research questions. In the therapeutic situation it is usually sufficient merely to withhold information that could be harmful and to emphasize those aspects of the truth, as the clinician sees it, most likely to help. For example, our recommendations for the use of psychoactive drugs do not intrinsically involve deception. Practitioners could simply tell their patients little or nothing about the strength of the drug they are being given, rather than state that the drug is very weak. Similarly, no deception is necessary either in persuading the patient that he must work

along with the drug or, upon withdrawal, that his efforts have been responsible in part for his improvement.

Deception is even less necessary for attribution therapies that do not involve drugs. On the contrary, most of our recommendations involve giving the patient explanations for his symptoms that are closer to the truth as the scientist and therapist see it than those that the patient himself has employed. It is unlikely that Neale was telling his patient a benign lie: it is very implausible that his patient was the homosexual he supposed himself to be. And as evidence mounts that schizophrenia is a biological phenomenon and that psychosis-like phenomena can be produced by drugs, it becomes more and more likely that an acceptance of schizophrenic experiences as "real" is scientifically correct, as Davison [1966] and Maher [1970] suggest. Even the proposal that arousal symptoms be reattributed to extrinsic causes does not necessarily involve deception. For example, it is plausible that insomnia is produced in part by an inconvenient diurnal rhythm or by a high resting level of autonomic activity. If so, insomniac patients might be told this, and the resulting nonemotional attribution might be effective in helping them to sleep. To the extent that nonpathological, nonemotional factors work to produce the patient's symptoms, it is scientifically valid as well as therapeutically helpful to emphasize them.

Summary and Conclusions

We have suggested that an understanding of attribution processes may help to account for the development of some emotional disorders and help to modify various treatment procedures. People usually need other people to help them evaluate their behavior, yet social comparison is often not obtained when the individual considers his behavior to be "bad" or shameful or when he distrusts other people. Under such circumstances people may develop dispositional explanations for their behavior when situational explanations may be more appropriate. Dispositional explanations of homosexuality, inadequacy, and the ability to contact spirits were discussed, and we suggested that therapy should sometimes consist of a systematic attack on the dispositional explanations individuals make and that less damaging situational attributions should be supplied.

We also suggested that it might often be valuable for an individual to attribute his reactions to an extrinsic source (for example a drug) when a stimulus attribution would likely lead to maladaptive behavior, when the individual regards the reactions as undesirable, or when he cannot improve and may possibly exacerbate his untoward reactions by his worries about them and efforts to conquer them. We also suggested that it might be beneficial for an individual to attribute his reactions to intrinsic sources (for example, a new-found attitude toward the stimulus) when such a stimulus attribution would be likely to lead to adaptive behavior, or when the reactions are indicative of psychological health.

Much of our discussion centered on research in which drugs or placebos were given. This research suggests that it may be unwise to try to capitalize on the "placebo effect" in the drug-taking situation. Describing a drug as very strong can have negative consequences. If the drug is effective, the individual may not apply himself to other relevant aspects of the treatment procedure and any change that is produced might disappear when the drug is withdrawn. If the drug is not effective, the individual may infer extreme illness and this belief can further exacerbate his condition.

BIBLIOGRAPHY

John P. Brady, "Comments on Methohexitone-Aided Systematic Desensitization." *Behavior Research and Therapy*, 1967, 5:259–260.

Gerald C. Davison, "Differential Relaxation and Cognitive Restructuring in Therapy with a 'Paranoid Schizophrenic' or 'Paranoid State.' " *Proceedings of the American Psychological Association*, 1966, 177–178.

Gerald C. Davison, "Appraisal of Behavior Modification Techniques with Adults in Institutional Settings." In Cyril M. Franks, ed., *Behavior Therapy: Appraisal and Status*, McGraw-Hill, 1969.

Gerald C. Davison and Stuart Valins, "Drug-Produced and Self-Produced Muscular Relaxation: Letting Go and the Issue of Attribution." *Behavior Research and Therapy*, 1968, 6:401–402.

Gerald C. Davison and Stuart Valins, "Maintenance of Self-Attributed and Drug-Attributed Behavior Change." *Journal of Personality and Social Psychology*, 1969, 11: 25–33.

Leon Festinger, "A Theory of Social Comparison Processes." *Human Relations*, 1954, 7:117–140.

Edward E. Jones and Richard E. Nisbett, "The Actor and the Observer: Divergent Perceptions of the Causes of Behavior." General Learning Press, 1971. Also in E. E. Jones, D. E. Kanouse, H. H. Kelley, R. E. Nisbett, S. Valins, and B. Weiner, *Attribution: Perceiving the Causes of Behavior*. General Learning Press, 1971.

Eric C. Kast, "Alpha-Ethyltryptamine Acetate in the Treatment of Depression: A Study of the Methodology of Drug Evaluation." *Journal of Neuropsychiatry*, 1961, 2, suppl. 1:114–118.

Brendan Maher, "Delusional Thinking and Cognitive Disorder." Paper presented at annual meeting of the American Psychological Association, 1970.

George Miller, "Psychology as a Means of Promoting Human Welfare." *American Psychologist*, 1969, 24: 1063–1075.

Neal Miller, "Some Animal Experiments Pertinent to the Problem of Combining Psychotherapy with Drug Therapy." *Comprehensive Psychiatry*, 1966, 7:1–12.

Richard E. Nisbett and Stanley Schachter, "Cognitive Manipulation of Pain." *Journal of Experimental Social Psychology*, 1966, 2:227–236.

Richard E. Nisbett and Stuart Valins, "Perceiving the Causes of One's Own Behavior." General Learning Press, 1971. Also in E. E. Jones, D. E. Kanouse, H. H. Kelley, R. E. Nisbett, S. Valins, and B. Weiner, *Attribution: Perceiving the Causes of Behavior*, General Learning Press, 1971.

R. W. Payne, "An Object Classification Test as a Measure of Over-Inclusive Thinking in Schizophrenic Patients." *British Journal of Social and Clinical Psychology*, 1962, 1:213–221.

K. Rickels, C. Baumm, E. Raab, W. Taylor, and E. Moore, "A Psychopharmacological Evaluation of Chlordiazepoxide, LA-1 and Placebo, Carried out with Anxious, Neurotic Medical Clinical Patients." *Medical Times*, 1965, 93:238–242.

K. Rickels and R. Downing, "Drug- and Placebo-Treated Neurotic Outpatients." *Archives of General Psychiatry*, 1967, 16:369–372.

K. Rickels, R. Lipman, and E. Raab, "Previous Medication, Duration of Illness and Placebo Response." *Journal of Nervous and Mental Disease*, 1966, 142:548–554.

Lee D. Ross, Judith Rodin, and Philip G. Zimbardo, "Toward an Attribution Therapy: The Reduction of Fear through Induced Cognitive-Emotional Misattribution." *Journal of Personality and Social Psychology*, 1969, 12:279–288.

Bertrand Russell, *An Outline of Philosophy*. George Allen and Unwin, London, 1927.

Irving Sarnoff and Philip Zimbardo, "Anxiety, Fear, and Social Affiliation." *Journal of Abnormal and Social Psychology*, 1961, 62:356–363.

Stanley Schachter, *The Psychology of Affiliation*. Stanford University Press, 1959.

Stanley Schachter, "The Interaction of Cognitive and Physiological Determinants of Emotional State." In L. Berkowitz, ed., *Advances in Experimental Social Psychology*, Academic Press, 1964.

Stanley Schachter and Jerome E. Singer, "Cognitive, Social and Physiological Determinants of Emotional State." *Psychological Review*, 1962, 69:379–399.

Michael D. Storms and Richard E. Nisbett, "Insomnia and the Attribution Process." *Journal of Personality and Social Psychology*, 1970, 16:319–328.

Time Magazine, October 10, 1969, p. 60.

E. H. Uhlenhuth, A. Canter, J. O. Neustadt, and H. E. Payson, "The Symptomatic Relief of Anxiety with Meprobamate, Phenobarbital and Placebo." *American Journal of Psychiatry*, 1959, 115:905–910.

E. H. Uhlenhuth, Karl Rickels, Seymour Fisher, Lee C. Park, Ronald S. Lipman, and John Mock, "Drugs, Doctor's Attitude and Clinical Setting in the Symptomatic Response to Pharmacotherapy." *Psychopharmalogia*, 1966, 9:392–418.

Stuart Valins, Richard Adelson, Joel Goldstein, Michael Weiner, "The Negative Placebo Effect–Consequences of Overselling a Treatment." Paper presented at the International Association for Dental Research, 1971.

P. H. Venables, "Input Dysfunction in Schizophrenia." In B. A. Maher, ed., *Progress in Experimental Personality Research*, Academic Press, 1964.

Joseph Wolpe, *Psychotherapy by Reciprocal Inhibition*. Stanford University Press, 1958.

[*This paper grew out of a workshop on attribution theory held at UCLA in August 1969, supported by Grant GS-2613 from the National Science Foundation. The paper was written while Richard Nisbett was supported by a Morse Faculty Fellowship from Yale University and a National Science Foundation postdoctoral fellowship. The writing of the paper and some of the research reviewed was facilitated by NSF Grant 2587 to Nisbett and by NIMH Grant 14557 to Valins.*]

9 · Causal Schemata and the Attribution Process

HAROLD H. KELLEY

University of California, Los Angeles

This essay develops the idea that attributions and causal inferences, particularly those made on the basis of partial information, are derived from causal schemata. A causal schema is a general conception the person has about how certain kinds of causes interact to produce a specific kind of effect. Each schema can be described in terms of a hypothetical matrix of data that summarizes the attributor's beliefs and assumptions about the distribution of the effect over various combinations of the causal factors. After specifying the general properties of causal schemata, this paper reviews the relevant social psychological literature for what it has to say about the types of schemata likely to be found in the typical attributor's repertoire. The research bearing on causal schemata reveals how they manifest themselves, the types of causal inferences they permit from different sets of incomplete evidence, and, derivatively, how they can be identified. Existing evidence also suggests some generalizations about the conditions under which various schemata are brought into play. The attempt here is to delineate these potentialities of a causal schematic analysis of the attribution process as well as to indicate some of its major limitations.

In an earlier paper, I argued that people often make causal attributions as if they were analyzing data patterns by means of the analysis of variance [Kelley 1967]. That is, effects are attributed to those causal factors with which they uniquely covary rather than to those of which they are relatively independent. To take a simple example, a given individual's reaction of dislike to a particular animal is attributed to him if it is more or less unique to him and consistently associated with him, but is attributed to the animal if other persons, each consistently and all consensually, have the same reaction. Similarly, a successful action on a given task is attributed to the actor if he uniquely and consistently completes it but the action is attributed to the task if uniquely and consistently associated with it.

This description is clearly an accurate account of the basic method of causal analysis that underlies scientific investigation. From Inhelder and Piaget's observations [1958] it seems also an appropriate description of the mode of causal thinking of which an adolescent of thirteen or fourteen is capable. On reaching the developmental stage of "formal operations," the youngster is able to think in terms of possible combinations of causal factors as they relate to a given effect, to plan ways to gain the information necessary to separate their effects (as by varying one at a time), and to draw conclusions about competing causal hypotheses such as those indicated above. In a sense, he knows how to design experiments properly and to interpret their results logically.

While the attribution process implied by the analysis of variance (ANOVA) model is appropriate for certain cases in which the person conducts a full-dress causal analysis, it is clearly an idealized model and not descriptive of most everyday, informal attributions. In these more common instances, the causal problem is not important enough to warrant gathering, retrieving, and processing the data necessary for the ideal analysis. Or even if the problem warrants a detailed analysis, time may not permit it, a decision or action being required before the complete analysis can be made. In any case, the person rarely needs to conduct a complete new analysis in order to make a causal attribution. He has made many (partial or complete) analyses before and can draw attributional conclusions from them. Furthermore, the mature individual undoubtedly has acquired a repertoire of abstract ideas about the operation and interaction of causal factors. These conceptions afford him a solution to the need for economical and fast attributional analysis, by providing a framework within which bits and pieces of relevant information can be fitted in order to draw reasonably good causal inferences. These conceptions, referred to as *causal schemata* (singular: schema), are considered in this paper.

The Concept of Causal Schema

In general, a causal schema is a conception of the manner in which two or more causal factors interact in relation to a particular kind of effect. A schema is derived from experience in observing cause and effect relationships, from experiments in which deliberate control has been exercised over causal factors, and from implicit and explicit teachings about the causal structure of the world. It enables a person to perform certain operations with limited information and thereby to reach certain conclusions or inferences as to causation.

Specifically, a causal schema is *an assumed pattern of data in a complete analysis of variance framework.* What the person learns at a conceptual level about causes and effects is how certain types of effects tend to be distributed in a matrix of relevant causes. Given information about a certain effect and two or more possible causes, the individual tends to assimilate it to a specific assumed analysis of variance pattern, and from that to make a causal attribution. This view of causal schemata has the heuristic advantage of maintaining a link between the present analysis of the processing of incomplete data and the earlier description of the more idealized process suited for complete data. Additionally, it seems reasonable to assume that the conceptual organization resulting from the individual's learning about causation corresponds rather closely to the explicit external organization that he imposes upon complex and complete sets of data in order to interpret them.

An example will clarify the above points. Perhaps the most common experience the individual has with causation is that different causes produce the same effect. From this experience, he learns that there are several sufficient causes for a given effect and that the effect will occur if any one of them is present. This condition of multiple sufficient causes may be represented by the type of schema shown in figure 1. For the two causes, A and B, the effect E is shown to occur when either A or B is present or when both are present. The figure summarizes a pattern of data an individual might obtain from an experimental analysis of the relationship between the two independent variables, A and B, and the dependent variable, E. For our present purposes, the figure portrays a causal schema, that is, the person's conception of the

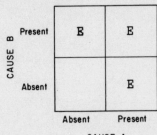

Figure 1. Causal schema for multiple sufficient causes.

action of the two causes in relation to the given effect. Thus, it might reflect his notion of the manner in which an actress' statement endorsing an automobile (the effect) results from either a belief in its merits (B present), a proper payment from an advertising agency (A present), or both. Similarly, this particular schema might reflect our understanding of the way in which a student's correct answer to a particular test item reflects either his specific knowledge of the assigned material, the obvious nature of the answer, or both.

The answers to some simple direct questions will probably determine whether this (or any other) particular schema characterizes a particular person's thinking about a particular causal problem: Why do actresses make such statements? Is an actress likely to do so even if she knows nothing about the particular automobile? If so, why? Furthermore, the existence of such a schema can be inferred from the causal attributions the person draws from partial information regarding the facts summarized therein. Most importantly, knowing that a certain schema characterizes a particular attributor's thinking about a given causal problem, we can make predictions about the interpretations he will make of partial data. For example, to take a case familiar to the student of attribution literature, if you know that with very little external inducement a person agrees to make an unusual speech, what attitude do you judge him to have with regard to the topic of the speech? In contrast, if you know he has agreed when subjected to strong external pressure, what estimate would you make of his attitude? The schema in figure 1 implies an inference of a favorable attitude in the first case: with cause A (the external inducement) being absent, in order to account for E, cause B (the favorable attitude) must be assumed to be present. Similarly, the schema implies uncertainty about the attitude in the second case: if cause A, the external inducement, is present, the effect is explained and we know nothing about whether cause B is also present or not.

The Properties of Causal Schemata

Causal schemata form an important subset of the cognitive schemata characterized and investigated by Piaget [1952, 1954]. Causal schemata reflect the individual's basic notions of reality and his assumptions about the existence of a stable external world—a world comprised of permanent, though moving and apparently variant, objects; a world separate from and independent of himself; and a world seen by other persons in the same way as by himself.

Derived from the individual's sensory and manipulatory experience with the external world, the causal schemata enable him to integrate and make use of information gained from temporally and spatially distinct occasions. Once it is learned, a schema may be activated by any of a number of appropriate sets of data or cues, and it thereby has "mobility" in that it is applicable to a broad range of objects and situations.

Causal schemata are of various forms, each appropriate to particular cause and effect circumstances. When activated, a schema provides a framework, or system, within which certain operations and their inverses can be performed. These operations constitute the *implications* of the schema, as when, in the example above, the person draws an inference regarding cause A from information about the effect and cause B. The schema is characterized by "reversibility" in that it permits going in various opposite implicational directions, as from B and E to A but also from A and E to B, or from A and B to E but also from E to A and B. The set of possible implications has the properties of organization that Piaget specifies as characteristic of an "operational system." That is, any actual implication is drawn against a background of knowledge about other potential implications and their inverses, so the individual has some implicit sense of where he is within the system at all times and how he might reach other points within it. This means that he can provide explanations for any implication he draws (explain how he got to where he is) and can indicate the evidence necessary to permit a different or more precise implication (explain how to reach another point).

While the concept of schema is adopted here from Piaget, it has been used in social psychology in ways that are largely consistent with the present one. Some of these uses and related concepts are noted here because they highlight various facets of the meaning presently intended. As will become clear in subsequent sections, the users of the concept provide us with a broad range of suggestions about the identification and consequences of schemata.

The concept of schema was used in early studies of thinking to refer to a blank form or frame to be filled in. Solution of a thought problem was viewed as depending upon the adequacy of the schema brought into play and the amount of information supplied for filling it in [Woodworth 1938]. Although not entirely satisfied with the connotations of the term, Bartlett adopted it in the interpretation of his classical observations on the social psychology of remembering. He defined schema as "an active organization of past reactions, or of past experiences" and repeatedly remarked upon the ability of man to "turn round upon his own schemata" and "rove more or less at will in any order over the events" upon which they are based [1932, pp. 201, 301, 203].

More recently, DeSoto refers to a schema as a theory about social structure "marked by certain essential properties but doubtlessly skeletal and sketchy in other respects . . ." [1960, p. 420]. His colleague Kuethe describes a "social schema" as being employed when a person is asked about relations existing between two or more people [1962]. The meaning of "relation," particularly as illustrated by the earlier research of DeSoto and Kuethe [1959], is such that it is perhaps not stretching the concept too far to consider it as an "effect" of which people are in some manner the possible "causes." Clearly central to the present analysis is Kuethe's emphasis on the function that schemata serve in structuring ambiguous or minimal information. From this emphasis he derives a general implication as to methodology: "The study of preferred modes of organization of unstructured situations reveals the schemas that typically operate" [p. 38]. In a similar vein, Singer describes schemata as "pre-existing assumptions about the way the world is organized" that can aid in the processing of information [1968, p. 338].

Another concept in social psychology that is similar in meaning and purpose to schema is Abelson's notion of implicational molecule. He argues that "the basic principles by which human beings manipulate the symbols they cognize are few in number and structurally rather simple, although the nature of things cognized can be of enormous variety" [1968, p. 132]. Corresponding to each such principle is an implicational molecule, which consists of "a self-contained set of statements which, taken together, are psychologically self-consistent" according to the particular principle. An example would be the *intention* principle, with the set of sentences in the "molecule" being of the form "P took action X which produced effect E. P knew that X would produce E. P desires the occurrence of E." Similarly, the molecule for the *compulsion* principle would be "P does X. P does not want to do X. P was forced to do X."

Closely related to Abelson's implicational principle and very similar to the present notion of schema are what Kanouse describes as "normative assumptions." Kanouse assumes that, when forced to make attributions from limited information, attributors "fill in missing cells in the data matrix with reasonable guesses." He continues, "in the absence of information about the generality of a given relation over persons or ob-

jects, individuals make normative assumptions about generality, and . . . these assumptions in turn allow them to form attributions" [1971, p. 2].

Types of Causal Schemata

Various kinds of social psychological research can be interpreted in terms of causal schemata. A review of the relevant research indicates the major types of causal schemata and the kinds of causal inferences they variously make possible. This review also suggests something of the conditions under which each type of schema is evoked and some of its manifestations in learning, judgment, and expectation.

Multiple Sufficient Causes

A wide variety of experiments have been conducted according to the following paradigm: subjects are given information regarding an effect and the state of one possible cause for it and are asked to judge the magnitude (or presence versus absence) of another possible cause. Typically, the subjects in a "low" condition are told or shown that the one possible cause was at low strength (or was absent) and that the effect occurred, while subjects in a "high" condition are told the one cause was at high strength (or was present) and that the same effect occurred. The results from a comparison of these two conditions typically suggest that the subjects use the causal schema illustrated in figure 1, the schema for multiple sufficient causes. Subjects in the low condition tend to report or otherwise indicate the other possible cause as being present (or of high magnitude), whereas those in the high condition more often report it as absent (or of medium magnitude). It is as if (1) the description of the situation is such as to elicit for all or most subjects the schema shown in figure 1, (2) the two patterns of information are fitted into the schema (A absent and E present versus A present and E present), and (3) the appropriate implications are drawn (B present versus B may or may not be present). An intrinsic property of this particular causal schema is that these two sets of information lead to inferences of different degrees of ambiguity. It is certain that B is present in the first case but uncertain whether or not it is present in the second.

The case of multiple sufficient causes is illustrated by the numerous experiments on judgments of *others' behavior* that demonstrate the discounting principle [Kelley 1971b]. For example, in the studies by Thibaut and Riecken [1955] and by Jones, Davis, and Gergen

154

[1961] a stimulus person is seen to exhibit a certain behavior either in the presence of a plausible external cause or in its absence. The attributor-subject is asked to judge the causes for the behavior that are internal to the stimulus person: his intrinsic interest in the action or his personal predisposition to act in that manner. The discounting principle, supported by these and many similar and derivative experiments, is simply a statement of the implication of the multiple sufficient cause schema: with the plausible external cause absent, an appropriate internal cause is inferred to be present; with the external cause present, the presence of the internal cause is cast in doubt. In the latter case, the behavior is discounted, so to speak, as an indicator of personal disposition. From a different theoretical perspective, similar instances are provided by Bem's interpersonal simulations of certain forced-compliance experiments [1967]. Given the statement of a rather unexpected opinion by a stimulus person, a corresponding attitude (the appropriate internal cause) is attributed to him to a greater degree when there is no sufficient external explanation for his statement than when such external explanation is present.

In the cases just mentioned, the effect of the presence of one cause (for example, the external one) is to render ambiguous the inference regarding the other cause. However, there are certain cases in the literature on interpersonal perception where the effect of the external cause is just the opposite. In these cases, the cause is inhibitory and tends to operate against the occurrence of the specified effect. The clearest example is the phenomenon of external social pressure against taking a certain action. In this case, the same multiple sufficient cause schema would be applicable but in a slightly different form, as shown in figure 2. As can be seen there, the weak state of the facilitative cause is sufficient to produce the effect unless the inhibitory cause is present and the strong state of the facilitative cause serves to override the in-

hibitory one. In this situation, if the attributor knows that the effect occurred with inhibitory cause B present, he can conclude unequivocally that facilitative cause A was present in its strong form.

Many of the experimental results relating to attributions of *own behavior* [Nisbett & Valins 1971] are also interpretable in terms of the schema for multiple sufficient causes. For example, Storms and Nisbett [1970] provided insomniacs with an external explanation for their problem in the form of a pill described as creating the symptoms associated with sleeplessness. Under these conditions, the subjects reported getting to sleep more quickly than usual. This result suggests that when the external cause was present, the subjects inferred that their own internal cause was relatively weak or absent.

Storms and Nisbett also provide an instance of an inhibitory cause. When they were given a pill that they believed would reduce their feelings of sleeplessness but that was in fact a placebo, the insomniacs, who presumably felt as sleepless as ever, acted as if their internal causal state was strongly present by taking longer to get to sleep. Valins and Nisbett [1971] note the relevance of this result to the interpretation of the "negative placebo effect." In many cases, persons who are given placebos and told they will feel better report later that they feel worse. Interpreted in terms of figure 2, this phenomenon suggests that the person believes the external inhibitory cause to be present and, believing his own facilitative causal state to be a weak one, expects no effect. When he experiences an effect, he concludes, not that the inhibitory cause was absent (he accepts what the doctor has told him), but that his own internal state must be stronger than he had thought. The end result of this inference is his report that he feels worse than he had previously.

With respect to causal attributions for success or failure, the alternative causes involved in a given schema may be internal and external, as in the case of ability and task difficulty, but they may also be entirely internal to the stimulus person, for example, ability and motivation. From the research on achievement attributions by Weiner and his colleagues [1971], it seems that these causal inferences often follow the implications of the multiple sufficient cause schema. For example, part of their data has to do with interpreting a person's success on a given task. If the task is sufficiently difficult, its properties do not provide an external cause for success, and an attribution is made to some internal cause, such as ability, and/or to a different external one, such as good fortune.

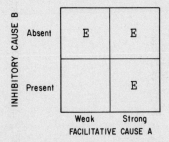

Figure 2. Causal schema for multiple sufficient causes with inhibitory cause.

Multiple Necessary Causes

The conjunction "and/or" must be used above because the reported averages do not reveal whether some subjects attribute the success to ability and other subjects attribute it to luck or whether all subjects attribute the success to both. This question is important because the answer would tell us something about the complexity, in terms of number of dimensions or causes, our attributors can and do employ in their schemata. At a more basic level, the question leaves us uncertain about the kind of causal schema being used. Consider the problem of accounting for a person's success on a very difficult problem. It seems intuitively plausible that such an effect requires the joint action of several causes (for example, ability *and* motivation or, perhaps, perseverance *and* luck). This being so, the appropriate causal schema is shown, not in figure 1, but in figure 3, which represents multiple *necessary* causes.

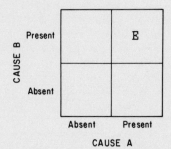

Figure 3. Causal schema for multiple necessary causes.

This latter causal schema permits inferences rather different from those we have been considering. If only information that the effect is present is given, the schema for multiple necessary causes permits the inference that *both* causes were present. For example, both ability and motivation may be inferred from success on a difficult task. It may be noted, however, that the same is true in figure 1 for information that the effect is *absent:* the absence of both causes is unequivocally indicated. Figures 1 and 3 are, of course, merely rearrangements of each other produced by redefining "effect" and re-ordering the causal conditions. Thus, logically, they permit analogous inferences from analogous information. Psychologically, however they are different. The inference of "no causes" from "no effect" is ordinarily less informative than the inference of "both causes" from "effect." It may also be noted here that the causal schema in figure 3 involves the same asymmetry of ambiguity as

does the earlier schema, except that in figure 3 ambiguity is greatest when there is known to be *no* effect. If cause A is absent and there is no effect, one is uncertain about the state of B; if A is known to be present, however, and there is no effect, one is certain B is absent.

As our examples suggest, the causal schema for multiple sufficient causes (figure 1) is probably evoked to explain success on easy tasks, and the schema for multiple necessary causes (figure 3), to interpret success on very difficult tasks. In the first case, success would imply the presence of either one or both causes, and in the second, the presence of both causes. Different interpretations would be expected when the effect is failure. Failure would imply the absence of both causes in the first case (for easy tasks) but the absence of one or both in the second case (for difficult tasks). The hypothesis can be proposed that *the more extreme the effect to be attributed, the more likely the attributor is to assume that it entails multiple necessary causes.* For example, a boy's behavior of extreme social delinquency would be likely to be attributed to both his coming under a bad influence and his weak character.

The hypothesis can also be suggested that *the multiple sufficient cause schema is assumed when the two causes are strong, and the multiple necessary schema, when they are weak.* In the latter case, if both causes are marginal in strength, the presence of both would be assumed necessary to produce the effect. This hypothesis may further afford a basis for explaining perceived differences between reward and punishment as they are used to produce behavioral compliance. If, other things being equal, punishment tends to be seen as a stronger cause than reward, the schema in figure 1 would usually be evoked when punishment is used to influence behavior, and the schema in figure 3, when reward is used. As a consequence of the different inferential asymmetries present in these schemata we would expect different causal inferences to be drawn from the identical compliant behavior. For compliance in the presence of punishment, there would be ambiguity about the presence of the other cause (that is, about the complier's own motivation to perform the behavior). In contrast, for compliance in the presence of reward the schema in figure 3 would yield the unambiguous inference that the other cause (internal to the person) was also present. This implication is consistent with Kite's evidence that influence agents who bring about a change in another person's behavior by use of punishment attribute more causality to the external power than do agents who produce the same effect by use of reward [1964]. The analysis is also consistent with Bramel's hypothesis that persons acting under the threat of punishment are seen to have less freedom than are those acting to gain positive incentives [1969].

Compensatory Causes

Our attributor is undoubtedly able to distinguish, not only between the mere presence or absence of causes and effects, but degrees of both. If we consider first the case in which degrees of cause are discriminated, generalizations of the notions of multiple sufficient and multiple necessary causes yield the causal schema shown in figure 4. Here the effect is assumed to occur if either cause is strong (a simple generalization of the schema in figure 1) but also when *both* causes are at medium levels (a generalization of the schema in figure 3). It can be seen that the two causes are assumed to act in a mutually compensatory manner. The effect occurs with strong A and weak B, but a reduction in A, rather than eliminating the effect, can be compensated for by an increase in B, the effect occurring with medium A and medium B.

The pattern of compensatory causes affords a basis for calibrating one cause against the other. In scientific practice the schema appears in the form of Guttman's procedure for scalogram analysis [1950], which affords a scaling of persons in terms of the degree of test item they pass (in ability assessment) or endorse (in opinion assessment). This practice undoubtedly has its parallels in everyday attribution. For example, the degree of one cause (ability) may be judged on the basis of the minimum degree of a compensatory cause (effort, or task ease) necessary in combination with it to produce the effect (task success). Thus, the less the apparent effort required for a given success, the greater the attributed ability.

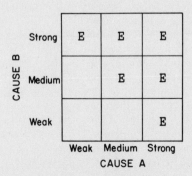

Figure 4. Causal schema for compensatory causes.

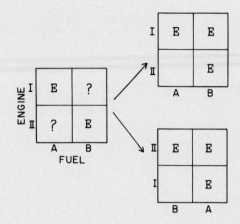

Figure 5. Triangular patterns enabling ordering of causes.

A key idea in scalogram analysis is that the presence of a compensatory causal schema can be determined by seeing how well the triangular pattern, illustrated in figure 4, can be formed by placing the columns and rows in proper order. For this purpose the investigator need not know anything at the outset about the relative magnitudes of the causal factors constituting the rows and columns. (For this reason the scalogram logic is also quite appropriate to the analysis of the interplay between *sets* of causal factors, as illustrated in the example below. Schemata entailing this interplay are discussed later.) If, in figure 5, the attributor finds engine I powered by fuel A to produce some criterial degree of horsepower and engine II powered by fuel B to produce the same effect, whether he will be able to order I and II (and A and B) with regard to a common underlying causal dimension will depend on where else the effect appears.

If, as shown in the upper right-hand portion of figure 5, the effect also occurs for the combination of I and B, then those two causes represent the greater degrees of their respective causal factors. On the other hand, the occurrence of the effect for the combination of II and A has the same implication for them, as shown in the lower right-hand portion of figure 5. Either occurrence, together with the original observations indicates that the motors and fuels act to create a compensatory causal schema with the two causal continua, relating to the same effect, arrayed respectively along the columns and rows. Of course, the attributor may observe the effect to occur in all four cells (a trivial case) or in neither of the two cells in question. The latter, a type of "complex" pattern to be considered below, suggests that different causal processes are involved in the two effects, corresponding to something unique about each specific pairing of engine and fuel. The presence of the effect in the third position, as in figure 5, assures us that the corresponding pair of causal states is not somehow incompatible and this suggests that we are dealing with degrees of the same cause, not with qualitatively different causes.

In investigations of the attribution of task difficulty and ability the triangular pattern, which is the distinguishing characteristic of a compensatory cause schema, is manifested in the common tendency to evaluate the difficulty of tasks by how many subjects succeed on each one and to rank the subjects by ability according to how many tasks each successfully completes. Evidence for these attributional tendencies is provided by Weiner et al. [1971].

When a compensatory causal pattern may be assumed, that is, when the triangularity requirement is fulfilled, then once the lower left boundary of effects is located, the rest of the effects in the schema are implied. For each pair of causes located above the boundary, at least one cause must be more favorable to the effect than some minimally effective pair on the boundary. For example, in figure 4, knowing that medium B plus medium A produce the effect, the attributor can infer that the effect also occurs for strong B plus medium A, medium B plus strong A, and strong B plus strong A. The general implication of this property of the compensatory schema seems to be that it is very important for the attributor to know the boundary between effect and no effect. It provides a convenient summary for him of *all* the conditions, among those represented in the schema, under which the effect will occur. Of course, the boundary may not follow the diagonal of the schema but may have irregularities, as in figure 6.

The compensatory cause schema can easily be confused with schemata to be described later (see figures 8 and 9), which warrant simple person- or entity-attributions. Instead of the triangular pattern characteristic of the full-blown compensatory schema, under special conditions there may be rectangular patterns, with the effect located only across rows or along columns. Distribution of the effect across rows would occur in figure 4, for example, if only very weak and very strong degrees of cause B were paired off against a series of finely graded intermediate degrees of cause A. Similarly, distribution of the effect along columns would occur if only medium degrees of cause B were paired with extremely high and low degrees of cause A. The point is that the triangular pattern requires

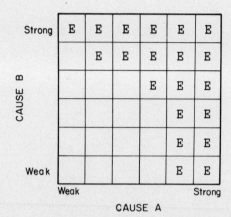

Figure 6. Compensatory schema with irregular boundary between effect and no effect.

appropriately matched ranges of magnitude variation in the two causes. This technical requirement (which in scalogram analysis is the requirement that the test items be graded along a range of difficulty appropriate for the test population) may not be well understood by lay attributors and may therefore create confusion for them as between the compensatory schema and certain others. This confusion is exhibited in the tendency to attribute the success of the consistently successful person to him (his ability) and the completion of a given task by many persons to the task (its easiness), without recognizing the joint and compensatory causal roles of ability and task difficulty in the total schema of which these consistent cases are only the extremes.

Graded Effects

If the attributor distinguishes degrees of a given *effect*, he is likely to assume that it increases with the cumulative strength of relevant causes. A simple causal schema entailing such an assumption—specifically, one with additive effects—is shown in figure 7. The degree of effect is designated by the number of E's entered in each cell. Once again, this schema is a generalization of the multiple sufficient and multiple necessary causal patterns: with either cause present to any degree, the effect occurs, but high degrees of the effect require both causes to be present in high degrees.

The schema with additive effects makes more explicit the hypothesis presented earlier for the multiple cause schemata, that the greater the effect, the clearer the inference that *both* causes are present to a strong degree. The additive schema also permits more unambiguous inferences than those considered heretofore.

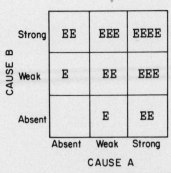

Figure 7. Causal schema with additive effects.

If the attributor gauges the degree of effect together with the degree of one cause, an unequivocal inference can be drawn as to the degree of the other cause. We are no longer faced with the asymmetrical ambiguity of inference characteristic of the simpler schemata (that, for example, B absent and the effect implies A present, but B present and the effect carries no clear implication regarding A).

The additive effect schema also makes clear the necessity of the assumption of *constancy of effect* that was stated elsewhere [Kelley 1971b] in connection with the "discounting principle" (that a given cause is discounted as producing a given effect if other plausible causes are also present). Referring to figure 7, this means that the strength of cause B is judged to be less in relation to the effect if cause A is known to be, say, strong, than if A is known to be absent. Obviously, this implication assumes that the same degree of effect (for example, EE) is present in the two instances being compared. If with strong A the effect is EEEE, but with A absent the effect is less (say, EE), the variation in A may warrant no change in the exaluation of B. For example, the extremely favorable view a person expresses under strong social pressure may warrant no different inference about his true attitude than does the weakly favorable statement he makes in private. The general point is that constancy of effect must be assumed if the presence of one cause is to afford a basis for discounting the effect of a second cause, relative to the case where only the latter is known to be present.

The additive effect schema has implications for inferring the level of a given causal factor when its action is observed on repeated occasions but with probable variations in another relevant cause. Under these circumstances the average, the maximum, or even the minimum degree of effect provides clues to the level of the stable causal factor, because across each row, for example, the magnitude of effect reflects

the magnitude of the cause defined by the columns. Assume that in figure 7 cause A is a person's ability, presumably a stable property, and cause B is his effort, likely to vary over successive test situations. If his performance is observed on successive occasions, the maximum magnitude of success he attains (for example, whether E, EE, EEE, or EEEE) suggests the level of his ability.

Of the possible indicators usable in this manner for ability inferences, the maximum performance level may have special appeal: it is easy to remember and provides a characterization of the person in terms of the best performance of which he is capable. Weiner et al. report a study by Rosenbaum showing that attributors infer a person's ability from the maximum performance level he has attained [1971]. They show that the person who hits the higher peak performance is attributed more ability even though his average is no higher than that of the person with whom he is being compared. One wonders whether attributors are aware of the hidden assumption entailed in such inferences when ability comparisons are made between different persons—an assumption that plagues psychologists in their efforts to assess abilities—namely, that the variable cause (effort) must range as high, over successive observations, for one person as for others.

Interplay between Sets of Causes: Simple Patterns

In the preceding sections, we have considered schemata in which the causes are distinguished by their presence or absence or by their degree of strength. That is, each schema we have considered is a conception of how a given effect occurs as a function of variations in presence-absence or in degree of a limited number of causes. We now turn to cases in which *sets* of causal factors are played off against each other. Each row (or column) in the schema represents the presence of a causal state or factor qualitatively different from the other rows (or columns). In a common example, the rows correspond to different persons and the columns to different impersonal entities, with the effects referring to a given type of reaction by each person to each entity. There is no a priori basis for ordering the persons or entities.

For the person-entity schema we will first consider instances where the effects are thought to vary in a simple manner, as a function of one set of causal factors but not of the other. In a subsequent section we will consider instances in which the effects are thought to occur in complex patterns, as a joint function of members of the two sets of causes.

In an earlier paper [1967] I proposed that when persons interact with things by observing them, tasting them, evaluating them, acting upon them, and so on, an effect, such as a reaction, evaluation, change in the shape or location of the thing, and so on, is attributed to the particular thing if it is (1) distinctively associated with it, (2) the same for various persons, and (3) consistent for each person over time and different modes of interaction with the entity. This pattern was asserted to be basic to the person's knowledge of external reality. The properties of entities in the external world are known by way of effects from person-entity interactions that fall into the pattern satisfying these conditions. The appropriate data pattern can be represented, omitting the factor of consistency, by the schema in figure 8. The effect E occurs only for entity X—not for W, Y, or Z— and occurs for all persons. On the other hand an attribution of the effect to the person is indicated by its occurring (1) only for him, (2) in his interactions with various different things, and (3) consistently so. The appropriate data pattern is represented, again

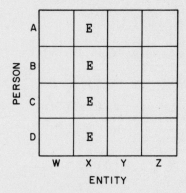

Figure 8. Person-entity schema with evidence for an entity-attribution.

partially, by figure 9, in which the effect occurs only for B and in his reactions to all the entities. In both these schemata, the effect is a simple one, occurring only for a given cause and independently of the cross-cutting set of causes.

These ideas have to do with the data pattern forming the basis for different attributions. They relate to our present discussion of causal schemata insofar as they suggest patterns of effects an attributor will assume to exist when he has reason to believe a person- or entity-attribution is warranted. Research by Leslie McArthur [1970] bears on both these points. She tested directly the different attributions made when individuals are given different data patterns.

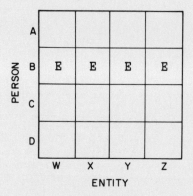

Figure 9. Person-entity schema with evidence for a person-attribution.

In her analysis of different verbs, which designate different effects, she also obtained evidence as to what schematic patterns are assumed for various effects.

To test the hypotheses about data patterns underlying various attributions, McArthur presented subjects with person-entity statements ("Tom is enthralled by the painting") and three accompanying statements providing information about high or low degrees of consensus (low: "Hardly anyone who sees the painting is enthralled by it"), distinctiveness (low: "Tom also is enthralled by almost every other painting"), and consistency (high: "In the past, Tom has almost always been enthralled by the same painting"). For each such set of information, the subject was asked to decide what probably caused the event to occur, expressing his decision in terms of whether it was something about the person, something about the entity, something about the particular circumstance, or some combination of two or more of the first three factors. McArthur's basic results are clear. Attributions of the effect to the person or to the entity follow the pattern suggested above. Person-attribution occurs with highest frequency for low distinctiveness, low consensus, and high consistency. This is illustrated by the example sentences given above. Given the accompanying information, Tom's reaction to the painting is explained by something about Tom. In contrast, the effect is attributed most frequently to the entity when the attributor is given evidence of high distinctiveness, high consensus, and high consistency. We learn something about the properties of the painting from knowing that Tom reacts similarly to hardly any other painting and that his reaction to this one is consistent and shared by other observers.

Not surprisingly, McArthur's data make it clear

that the attribution of the effect to "the particular circumstances" is overwhelmingly determined by evidence that the effect is a unique one. This uniqueness is indicated primarily by its low consistency over time and secondarily by its high distinctiveness (Tom does not make the same response to other paintings). This is perhaps an appropriate place to raise a question about the causal significance of time. We may guess that its main significance lies in its permitting unspecified unstable causal factors to vary. Depending on the particular attributional problem, these factors might include those within the person, such as satiation, fatigue, and, as Weiner et al. suggest, effort, but also shifting and transient external ones such as McArthur's "circumstances" and Weiner et al.'s "luck." As noted in our earlier discussion of the problem of estimating ability from successive performances, the attributor may also assume variations in the specific tasks or entities encountered by the person.

In addition to investigating the attributional consequences of specified patterns of data, McArthur analyzed how the direction of attribution depends on the type of verb. According to the present view, the verbs in her sentences describe the effects resulting from the person-entity interactions. Thus, her results here bear on the question of what schemata are assumed for different effects. The four types of verbs compared are: *accomplishment* (George translates the sentence incorrectly); *action* (Steven puts a bumper sticker advocating improved automobile safety on his car); *opinion* (Bill thinks his teacher is unfair); *emotion* (Tom is enthralled by the painting). The results indicate that *accomplishments* and *actions* are attributed predominantly to the person, and *opinions* and *emotions* to the stimulus. McArthur notes that the distinction between actions and accomplishments on the one hand and opinions and emotions on the other corresponds to a general distinction between manifest and subjective verbs. The former have been shown in other studies to yield more person-attribution than the latter. This distinction will be of interest to us below. In the present instance, the main result seems to be the obvious one: actions are attributed to the person, and reactions to the entity. The first category of effects apparently tends to evoke the schema illustrated in figure 9, and the second category, the schema in figure 8.

Interplay between Sets of Causes: Complex Patterns

In the preceding section, we have been considering simple person- or entity-attributions and their under-

lying data patterns. We now consider more complex attributions and the associated data patterns. One such pattern is suggested by McArthur's data. She permitted her subjects to account for the observed effect in terms of combinations of simple factors and found that a common explanation was in terms of a combination of something about the person and something about the stimulus. This attribution was made only with evidence of high consistency and then only for two cases: high consensus and low distinctiveness (case I) and low consensus and high distinctiveness (case II). As shown in figure 10, case I seems to be our old friend, multiple sufficient causes. It suggests there are two possible explanations for the effect, something about person A or something about entity X. In terms of our earlier example, there is evidence both that there's some-

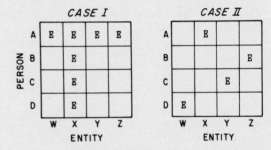

Figure 10. Person-entity schemata yielding joint person- and entity-attributions (after McArthur).

thing about Tom that results in his being enthralled by paintings and that there's something about this particular painting that results in persons generally being enthralled by it. While the pattern logically warrants an explanation in terms of "one *or* the other *or* both," it apparently is described by the subjects in terms of "a combination of one *and* the other."

Case II is more significant for our present discussion. As shown in figure 10, person A distinctively (and consistently, not represented in the figure) responds to entity X in a way no other person does, implying that the effect is, as McArthur puts it, "a more specific habit or attitude characterizing the interaction of the person with this particular stimulus" [p. 60]. The reader will recognize in this statement a specific instance of the schema of multiple necessary causes: both A and X must be present for the effect to occur. But, of course, as shown in case II of figure 10, the effect may occur for other specific combinations of persons and entities in a pattern of "each to his own." It is not likely our attributor knows how to construct or conceive of a one-to-one pattern, as in figure 10 (which, like the distribution of one element in a Latin square, is generated by the knight's move from chess). However, he undoubtedly has a conception of the simple version illustrated by figure 11, which is a mere rearrangement of case II in figure 10.

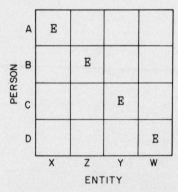

Figure 11. Person-entity schema for effects occurring from unique person-entity pairings (from rearranging case II of figure 10).

The one-to-one schema presumably applies to instances in which an effect produced by some particular combination of P and E precludes both causal factors from creating the same effect in combination with different ones. Examples are provided by such diverse phenomena as legal marriage, exclusive possession, and fastening as an effect of different sizes of nuts and bolts.

Presumably the schematic pattern in figure 11 affords a highly precise basis for inferring one cause from knowledge of the other cause and the presence of the effect (though, a less clear basis for inferring anything from knowledge of one cause and the absence of the effect). For example, if I know what type of movie each of several critics reacts to most favorably, a reading of a favorable review of a particular movie should enable me to infer the author of the review. However, as the pattern in case II makes clear, unless I have the entire schema in mind, I am not able to use it. Knowing only certain "locations" of an effect does not help me infer its other locations. Knowing that Edward G. Robinson possesses a particular Van Gogh does not help me infer who possesses a different one. If I can assume the one-to-one (one to a customer) relationship of figure 11, I can only conclude that he owns no other

Van Gogh and that no one else owns that particular Van Gogh.

The implications of the patterns in figures 10 and 11 have been little explored. In her comparison of verb types in their contributions to attribution, McArthur obtained some evidence that emotions and accomplishments are most frequently attributed to combinations of person and stimulus properties. These are probably instances of case I, there being nothing about her instances of either emotions or accomplishments (see examples above) that would preclude other person and entity combinations from producing or experiencing the same effects.

The one-to-one pattern in figure 11 has been shown to play a role in "verbal generalization." It seems to afford a basis for the attributor to make a generalization of the sort "people have entities" or "people like entities" (where the effect refers to "having" or "liking"). This result comes from Gilson and Abelson's inquiry into the information a subject requires to endorse such a generalization [1965]. The rate of endorsement was found to be high if each of the several kinds of persons was found to have (or like) a different one of the several kinds of entities, as depicted in figure 11.

More generally, the research on "verbal generalization" [Gilson & Abelson 1965, Abelson & Kanouse 1966, Kanouse 1971] seems to concern under what circumstances an effect is seen to characterize the interaction between a *class* of persons and a *class* of entities. Certainly, the general statement "people verb entities" for specified classes of people and entities would be warranted by evidence that the effect ("verbing") occurs in every cell of the schema—in the interaction between each and every member of the person class and each and every member of the entity class. These investigators' results suggest, however, that with considerably less evidence (and some encouragement to their intuitive impressions) a large majority of subjects will accept the generalization as justified. For example, around 75 per cent of a sample of Yale undergraduates accepted the generalization "people have entities" when told something like: "There are three kinds of people, *As*, *Bs*, and *Cs*. *As* have the entities, *Bs* do not have them, and *Cs* do not." The rate of acceptance was somewhat (and consistently) higher if the information was as follows: "There are three kinds of entities, *Xs*, *Ys*, and *Zs*. People have *Xs*, they do not have *Ys*, and they do not have *Zs*." The advantage of the latter, "object-specific" form of the evidence over the former, "subject-specific" form implies that the generalization depends somewhat more on uniformity of the effect over persons than on its uniformity over entities. There is a similar implication in results from investigations of "implicit quantifiers." The generalization "people verb entities" appears typically to mean something like "*many* of the people verb *a few* of the entities." In sum, then, the generalization "this class of people interacting with this class of entities generally produces this effect" implies a schema something like that in figure 11 or the one shown in figure 12. The one-to-one instance in figure 11, shown to be effective in Gilson and Abelson's pilot study, has not been investigated further. Figure 12 is drawn simply to show the relatively greater importance for the generalization that the effect be distributed over

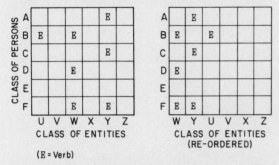

Figure 12. *Person-entity schema for the generalization "persons verb entities."*

the persons than that it be distributed over the entities. This latter configuration seems to be related to the grouping schema to be described later. The basic property of this schema is that people are grouped (as would be suggested by their being members of the same class) on the basis of making similar distinctions in their reactions to other persons or entities. This property of the schema in figure 12 is highlighted in the right-hand version of the schema, in which the entities have been re-ordered so as to emphasize the consensually distinctive reactions the members of the person-class make to them, generating the effect with the left-hand members of the entity class but not with the right-hand members.

While the foregoing statements are true for many of the verbs studied, certain verbs reveal a different pattern of results. We encounter here once more the distinction between manifest and subjective verbs. The manifest verbs (epitomized by *have, buy, produce,* and *use*) show the results described above: there is considerable agreement with the generalization given the information in either the subject-specific or the object-specific form, there is more agreement for the object-specific form, and the im-

plicit quantifiers for the generalization are "*many* people verb *a few* entities." In contrast, for subjective verbs (epitomized by *understand, hate, trust,* and *avoid*), agreement with the generalization is low for both types of information (on the order of 45 or 50 per cent), the two forms of evidence do not differ in endorsement rates, and the implicit quantifiers for the generalization are something like "*many* people verb *many* entities." The latter two facts are, of course, intimately related. If a generalization implies that the effect occurs for many entities, the object-specific evidence, which designates two entities for which the effect does not occur, provides little support for it.

In short, for the type of effect described by the subjective verbs, the generalization seems to imply a schema with a greater density of the effect and its equal distribution over persons and entities. The interpretation of these verb effects is discussed more fully elsewhere [Kanouse 1971], so it will suffice to mention briefly two possible aspects of the difference that are most relevant here.

First, the manifest verbs seem intuitively to refer to relations people tend to have with only one of a kind of entity. As Kanouse suggests, limited resources of the persons and/or limited supply of the entities usually mean that people produce, buy, have, or use a limited number of the entities in a given class. The extreme instance of this is the one-to-one relation. By legal marriage, the husband uses up his capability to produce the effect and, at the same time, removes the wife from the supply of marriage partners available to others.

Second, a schematic way to view the subjective verbs is that they describe effects commonly appearing in grouping schemata. This type of schema will be described below, but an intuitive understanding of the meaning of "groups" is adequate for the present purpose. Some of the subjective verbs seem highly appropriate to the characterization of relations between and within groups of people: *we* hate and avoid *them; we* understand, like, and trust *one another.* Through their involvement in these ingroup-outgroup relationships, the effects these verbs denote may evoke a grouping schema in which all members of the one causal class tend to have the specified relation with all members of the other causal class. (Grouping patterns are probably especially common in person-person schemata, as described below, but they undoubtedly also exist in person-entity schemata.) Given a subjective verb, then, the "persons verb entities" generalization refers to a segment of a grouping schema, as shown in figure 13. For the evoked schema to be satisfied, the evidence regarding the interaction between the two classes, P and M, must indicate that most of the persons in the one class generate the effect in combination with most of the entities in the other class.

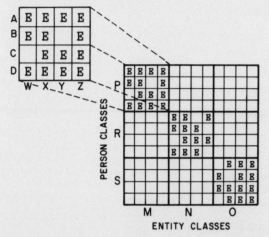

Figure 13. The person-entity schema for particular classes as a portion of a grouping schema.

The reader will recall McArthur's evidence regarding manifest versus subjective verbs, that the former are attributed to persons, and the latter to entities. One wonders how McArthur's observation relates to the present discussion, since there seems to be some contradiction between her results and my interpretation of the verb types. As figure 12 suggests, manifest verbs seem to evoke configurations suggestive of entity properties, and my interpretation of the subjective verbs suggests, if anything, a person-by-entity determination. For me, the relation between these two sets of data is uncertain. While the categories of verbs are common to the two lines of work, little else is. Greatest uncertainty exists as to the schematic implications of the "verbal generalization" procedure. If, as suggested here, it introduces the problem of the interaction between *classes* of causes, then much remains to be worked out as to the psychological relations to the simpler schemata involving *individual* causes. For example, it may be entirely consistent to attribute effects designated by action verbs to the person and yet to assume that these actions are taken consensually and distinctively with respect to the members of a given class of entities. Similarly, there is no necessary inconsistency between the attributor's assuming, on the one hand, that subjective reactions are generally attributable to entities and, on the other hand, that in intergroup interactions there

are both high consensus and low distinctiveness in group members' reactions. My hating another person reflects his disagreeable properties, but I am not surprised to learn not only that most other members of my group also hate him, but that we all tend also to hate other members of his group.

Interplay between Sets of Causes: Symmetric Patterns

We finally consider schemata in which there is symmetry between pairs of causes acting in different functions or "roles." This property has been investigated in person-person schemata, so we first turn to a general consideration of these schemata to introduce the topic of symmetry. Of special interest to social psychologists are the attributor's beliefs about how persons act jointly to produce effects. Some of the relevant schemata are ones we have already considered. For example, in figure 14, we have two familiar instances. The first one, the compensatory cause pattern, might represent the outcome of observing three actors in their verbal exchanges with three target persons, the effect being that the actor succeeds in dominating the conversation. As before, the schema provides a coordination between actors and

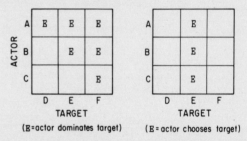

Figure 14. Some examples of person-person schemata.

targets, the former arranged from most to least dominant, and the latter from least to most submissive. The second, similar to a simple person-entity schema, might represent the outcome of an informal sociometric procedure in which three boys, A, B, and C, are asked to name their preferred dancing partner from among three girls, D, E, and F. The pattern suggests that the effect indicated by choice is to be attributed to the properties of the fortunate girl, E.

Beyond these familiar examples, person-person schemata entail some unique and interesting attributional problems. It is typical of personal causation (and of animate causal agents in general) that the individual may be both person and entity, actor and target. This means that the same set of causes can be considered in both roles—the same persons can be lined up along both axes of the schema. This property of person-person schemata generates several new logical possibilities for the configuration of the schema, and these possibilities seem to have their psychological counterparts. The possibilities are that A, both as person and as entity, may create the effect (the logical property of reflexivity); that given A as person and B as entity create the effect, it follows that B as person and A as entity also create it (the property to be emphasized here—symmetry); and that given A as person and B as entity create the effect, and given further, that B as person and C as entity create the effect, it follows that A as person and C as entity create the effect (transitivity).

The last property, transitivity, is basic to the compensatory cause schema when it involves the same set of factors arrayed along both causal dimensions. If A dominates B and B dominates C, then given the compensatory schema, the attributor can infer the further effect that A will dominate C. The presence of the compensatory schema in this case means that the attributor assumes there is a complete or strong ordering of the set of persons with respect to the given effect, dominance. Knowing the lower left boundary of effects is to know the dominance hierarchy of the set and from it can be inferred all the other possible dominance effects.

We owe much to DeSoto, Kuethe, and their colleagues for our knowledge of person-person schemata (or *social* schemata, as they refer to them). Their methodology also represents some sharp departures from what we have seen so far. In contrast to McArthur's procedure, in which she more or less directly gave information about the distribution of an effect over the schema, the methods used by these men are more indirect. One procedure [DeSoto 1960, DeSoto, Henley & London 1968] requires the research subject to learn the distribution of effects. For example, he is presented, one at a time, with the relations existing between each possible ordered pair of four persons (Bill influences Jim, Jim influences Jack, Jim does not influence Bill, and so forth, twelve in all) and learns them to the point that he can proceed twice through the list without prompting and without errors. His rate of learning is compared for different patterns, for example, one in which all effects are asymmetrical and transitive versus one in which they are asymmetrical but not necessarily transitive. The assumption is that the pattern in the subject's schema (the kind of social structure he

assumes) is revealed by the pattern of evidence he most easily learns.

The second procedure [DeSoto & Kuethe 1958, 1959] provides the subject with information about a specific effect in the schema and then quizzes him as to other probable locations of the same effect. The five most important types of such information-question problems are illustrated in figure 15. Given, for example, that B trusts C, (1) does A trust C (generalization over actors), (2) does B trust A (generalization over targets), (3) does C trust B (symmetry), (4) does B trust himself (reflexivity), and given additionally that C trusts D, (5) does B trust D (transitivity)?

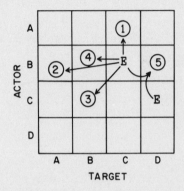

Figure 15. Major types of inferences from given effects (see text).

The first and second of these questions are ways of detecting schemata in which the effects are attributed to the target or to the actor, according to the simple patterns we have considered earlier. Of the ten interpersonal verbs (effects) DeSoto and Kuethe studied, none appears uniquely to evoke a simple person- or entity-attribution [1959]. The one verb assumed to generalize most strongly across targets is "lies to." In other words, this is an effect that tends to be attributed to the actor. If B lies to C, he is seen as likely also to lie to A (and to D). This is consistent with the hypothesis of social desirability proposed by Jones and Davis [1965]: the less socially desirable the consequences of a behavior, the more informative it is as to the attributes of the person enacting it. Perhaps a latent assumption the attributor makes here is that the effect would be rare in other rows of the schema. This fact is reflected in the relatively low rates of affirmative replies to the control, information-free question "Does X lie to Y?" and to the question "If B lies to C, does A lie to C?" As we will see below, however, "lies to" also has high assumed transitivity and symmetry, so the schema it evokes is not primarily the simple person-attribution schema of the type shown in figure 9.

DeSoto and his colleagues' results bearing on transitivity suggest that the schema for the complete ordering of persons is the one commonly assumed by attributors. In a learning study involving four persons as actors and targets, and *influence* as the effect, DeSoto [1960] found the asymmetrical, transitive, and complete set (all relationships specified) to be most easily learned. Transitivity seems to be the key factor in this efficient learning because an asymmetric and completely specified set of relations not characterized by transitivity was by far the most difficult to learn.

Additional effects for which the ordering schema is apparently the assumed one are revealed by the information-question method. These effects are defined by verbs for which transitivity, but not symmetry, is assumed (reflexivity was not measured), namely, *feels superior to, is happier than, dominates,* and *is afraid of.* These are the effects, then, that are assumed to satisfy the triangular pattern of the compensatory cause schema. Referring to figure 15, if we know B dominates C, the probability is low (.12 in the data) that C dominates B. If we know both that B dominates C and that C dominates D, it is rather probable that B also dominates D (.70 is the obtained value). *Is happier than* affords even stronger evidence of the asymmetric and transitive triangular pattern, the perceived likelihood of symmetry being estimated as .09, and of transitivity, as .89. This is perhaps a trivial case inasmuch as there is an implication in the verb of an external agent making the comparison. Interestingly, the more truly subjective comparison item, *feels superior to,* is not characterized by low symmetry (the obtained value is .37). Some attributors apparently make the not unreasonable assumption that it is possible both for B to feel superior to C and for C to feel superior to B.

A new (and final) set of schematic configurations is provided by effects for which the property of symmetry is present. The two different patterns, referred to as pairing and grouping, depend on whether or not transitivity is also present. Without transitivity, the schema describes a set of pairings as shown in the left-hand portion of figure 16. Each effect is matched by another effect symmetrically around the axis extending from the upper left-hand corner to the lower right-hand corner. Given one effect, the attributor can infer the other, but nothing more. Thus, if actor A and target C produce the effect, it also occurs for

actor C and target A. With transitivity, the schema tends to portray groupings, as in the right-hand schema of figure 16. There, the number of effects is

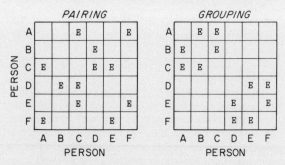

Figure 16. Person-person schemata characterized by symmetry.

the same as in the left-hand schema, but they are located so that it is true for all pairs of instances in which X acting on Y produces the effect and Y acting on Z produces the effect, that X acting on Z also produces the effect. To use the familiar sociometric example in which the effect is "choice," if C chooses A and A chooses B, it follows that C chooses B.

Holding constant between the two schemata the limited number of effects, as in figure 16, we are forced to arrange the symmetric and transitive pattern into *two* subgroups. This has the consequence of extending the kind of implications the attributor can draw from the distribution of effects. This schema not only affords him the transitivity inferences described above, but provides the basis for a special kind of inference based on between-group relations. Thus, if A chooses C and C does not choose D, the attributor can infer A also does not choose D. This means simply that if A and C are known to be in the same group, the information that D is in a different group from C implies he is also in a different one from A. This operation is also "reversible": knowing that A and D are in different groups and that D and C are in different ones, the attributor can infer that A and C are in the same group. The reader will, of course, recognize the "balance" ideas contained in these transitivity implications [Heider 1958].

With more persons than shown in figure 16 and a proportional increase in the frequency of the effect, the grouping schema would reveal three or more subgroups. One wonders whether this logical consequence has its parallel in the unsophisticated attributor's expectations for the grouping schema. Would it be true that with an increase in the number of persons he considers to be related via an effect of a certain probability, his schematic expectations will reflect an increase in the number of groupings? (It should be noted that with more than two subgroups, certain of the transitivity operations are *not* reversible in the way they are for two subgroups.)

DeSoto and Kuethe [1959] reveal something about the effects, as characterized by verbs, that conform to one or the other of the two schemata in figure 16. Their information-question method suggests that the pairing pattern is assumed for *dislikes* and *hates*. Intuitively, these seem like appropriate characterizations of the intense relationships that most commonly develop between two persons, as in relationships of spiraling hostility, and do not necessarily extend beyond them to their common acquaintances. The latter extensions are, by DeSoto and Kuethe's results, more characteristic of less intense positive feelings. Specifically, *likes* and *trusts* were found to evoke the grouping schema, both symmetry and transitivity being assumed for them. Two other verb phrases, *confides in* and *lies to*, are not clearly identified by the data as to their underlying schematic patterns. *Confides in* conforms more to the pairing pattern, and *lies to*, more to the grouping pattern, an outcome that gives us pause about concluding that the primary difference is one of negative versus positive effects.

DeSoto, Henley, and London have raised the further problem, in the context of "balance" versus grouping principles, of whether there is a tendency to assume interpersonal relationships to be organized into only *two* groupings [1968]. Their results, obtained with the learning technique, suggest that two groupings are expected where the effect is friendship (and the non-effect is enmity), three groupings being more difficult to learn in this case. In contrast, three groupings appear to be not unexpected when the effect is simple acquaintance. Once again, more evidence is needed because the point is an important one. An interesting and clear outcome of this particular study is that two slightly incomplete groupings (ones in which two effects are not specified) constitute a difficult learning task. This result suggests that attributors assume the groupings to be complete ones.

The psychological consequences of the two schemata entailing symmetry have not been studied in detail. When compared with the person-entity schema supporting an entity attribution (figure 8), the pairing schema suggests an interesting sense of "interpersonal agreement." In the former schema, persons A and B agree in their reaction to a third thing or person, but in the pairing schema they agree both in their reactions to each other and in their stimulus value for each other. That is, the one person responds to the other as an entity in the same way the other responds to him as an entity, and at the same time, the one person serves as a stimulus to the other in the same way the other serves as a stimulus to him. In terms of emotional reactions, this implies for the individual that he is liked or hated for the same reasons, by the same criteria, that he likes or hates the other. For jointly produced actions or products, the symmetry implies an interchangeability of roles as between the more and the less active one (two children pulling each other on a sled and similar reciprocity arrangements).

Our examples of these causal schemata have been given with persons as both actors and entities, but there are undoubtedly parallels in schemata for other causal agents, such as tools, that are interchangeable as to their functions (heavy objects either of which may serve as hammer to the other's anvil).

The grouping schema also affords an interesting contrast with the entity-attribution pattern (figure 8). Within each subgroup there is both consensus and distinctiveness of reaction: all group members have the same pattern of reaction to the various persons-entities. For example, the effect occurs in their ingroup reactions and not in their outgroup reactions. The consensus does not exist, however, *between* the groupings. As applied literally to intergroup relations, the pattern suggests the operation of group norms, unique to each group but uniform within it. In the two-group case, there may also be an implication of norm definition by contrast with the other group: we choose whom they do *not* choose.

The nonpersonal versions of the multiple grouping schema would represent two or more sets of causal factors such that within each set any possible pair of causes serves to produce the effect. Furthermore, for each pair there is interchangeability of causal role. Good examples of nonpersonal causes satisfying these requirements are difficult to think of, which suggests that the grouping schemata may be learned primarily from instances of person-causation.

Potentialities and Limitations of the Schematic Analysis

The evidence reviewed above suggests that each person has a repertoire of causal schemata, each one of which is evoked under certain conditions. Once evoked, a schema affords the attributor a basis for drawing causal inferences from limited information. The schemata can be discovered by providing appropriate cues and information and observing the way the information is used. Our final purpose is briefly to draw together and summarize some of the diverse observations made above and to make some general comments about this particular theoretical approach to causal attribution.

Varieties of Schemata and Inferences

It is not proposed here to provide a taxonomy of causal schemata but merely to indicate that it might be profitable to construct one. The schemata reviewed above seem to have a hierarchical organization in which certain of the more complex ones incorporate as elements the simpler ones. As noted, the compensatory pattern can be viewed as combining the properties of the schemata for multiple sufficient causes and multiple necessary causes. Similarly, the row and column patterns related to person- and entity-attribution have a resemblance to the simple multiple sufficient cause schema, and in contrast, the patterns implying pairings and groupings bear a resemblance to the multiple necessary cause schema. Of course, these observations are based merely on configurational properties of the various schemata. The important question is what schemata are psychologically similar for the attributor. Such psychological similarity might be indicated, for example, by his confusions between them as he draws causal inferences or learns the lists of information they contain.

The varieties of schemata may also be explored developmentally. An obvious hypothesis is that the more complex ones, combining properties of the simple configurations, are acquired and used only by the older attributor, who has had more experience with causal phenomena. For example, on the basis of a comparison of fourth graders and college students DeSoto and Kuethe indicate that pairing may be a more fundamental way of seeing interpersonal relations than grouping. The latter schema, they suggest, may be the outcome of long experience in observing people as they interact in cliques and friendship groups [1959]. Their evidence on this point is not very convincing but the question raised is certainly important. A different but important aspect of complexity, mentioned earlier, is the number of causes the attributor can readily deal with in schematic terms. Developmental studies should attempt,

among other things, to determine the dimensionality of the schemata employed at different levels of mental maturity.

If we disregard some of the finer distinctions among the various schematic configurations, they seem to be of three broad types:

1. The horizontally or vertically linear pattern associated with the single predominant cause. This pattern reflects the consistent effect a particular cause generates regardless of the presence of other factors. It is epitomized by the schemata underlying simple entity- and person-attributions. Each condition under which, or each time at which, the cause is present, the effect is also present. This pattern affords the indications of the stable, simple causal events present in the attributor's world.

2. The triangular pattern characteristic of the compensatory cause schema. It affords a basis for comparing the sets of causes that jointly form the schema and for evaluating the members of each set according to an ordering of causal magnitude.

3. The pattern of special combinations, exemplified by the simple pattern of multiple necessary causes and by the more complex pairing and grouping schemata. The psychological connotations seem to include notions such as reciprocity, role interchangeability, and we-they differentiation.

One wonders about the ramifications of this tripartite classification of the causal schemata. If these schemata constitute the foundations of the person's understanding of causality, the three patterns imply three basically different conceptions—ones that might be labeled something like *reality, mastery,* and *reciprocity.* These concepts happen to correspond to three bases of moral evaluation described in a recent paper [Kelley 1971a]. The argument there, perhaps illustrative of the general implications of a taxonomy of causal schemata, is that moral evaluation has its basis in more primitive evaluational systems and, consequently, varies in its properties and criteria depending on which basic system is given most emphasis. It is suggested that the more basic systems underlying moral evaluation have to do with reality evaluation, achievement evaluation, and reciprocity evaluation. The corresponding schemata may suggest something about the criterion of judgment involved in each kind of moral system. In the first case, a person will be favorably evaluated for contributing to the moral consensus through his agreement with others' moral stands. In the second case, he will be favorably evaluated for demonstrating a high degree of moral mastery, as by producing a moral effect in the presence of external causal conditions when few other persons are able to do so. In the third case, favorable evaluation will follow from his contributing to the pattern of symmetric and transitive considerateness required by the defined boundaries of his moral ingroup. Similarly, the three causal patterns suggest the different sources of moral behavior, whether it is seen to stem from an external "reality," from personal strength vis-à-vis counterforces of evil, or from the relationship with special others. The reader can extend the tripartite analysis to include the nature of the personal disposition making for immoral behavior, whether it be wrongheadedness, weakness, or ingratitude; the inferences to be made from knowledge that a person is morally good or bad; and so on.

The analysis of types of schemata will ultimately include systematic generalizations about the kinds of causal inferences they variously permit. Different types of inferences may be defined in terms of the initial information at the attributor's disposal and the question he answers with it. A common problem is the one in which the attributor knows one cause and the presence or absence of the effect and is asked to infer the other cause. An important difference among the various schemata is in the degree of unequivocality of inference they permit for different sets of information. This difference was noted in comparing the multiple sufficient cause schema to the one for multiple necessary causes. The former permits a less equivocal inference from the absence of one cause than from its presence (given that the effect is present in both cases). There are, of course, similar asymmetries for other schemata. For example, when the compensatory pattern characterizes the interaction between a set of persons of varying ability and a set of tasks of varying difficulty, the inferential asymmetry is reflected in the fact that an able person's success on a given task tells us less about the difficulty of that task than does the less capable person's similar success.

Another type of inference, often used to determine the configuration of the schema, provides the attributor with information about a particular location of an effect and asks him whether or not the effect also occurs in certain other locations. The equivocality of this type of inference also varies with the type of schemata. As noted earlier, if the attributor can assume the schema to be a compensatory cause one, he need only know the set of "boundary" locations of the effect in order to infer all the other locations. The boundary in this case constitutes a kind of threshold between no effect and some effect, so it very efficiently summarizes the entire schema. An interesting problem for investigation concerns what similar simplified encodings or mnemonic devices are available to the attributor for learning and using the various kinds of schemata, the reduction of groupings to two being a possible example.

The Evocation of Causal Schemata

DeSoto appropriately comments upon "our crippling ignorance of the dynamics of schema arousal and application" [1961, p. 22]. Systematic use of the theoretical notions outlined here will require a thorough understanding of the conditions under which each type of schema is brought into play. The present literature suggests the variety of factors to be considered in this connection. The most evidence exists with regard to verbs, which have been interpreted here as effects. While far from complete, the research makes it clear that verbs play a central role in the kind of schematic configuration the attributor assumes. Certain verbs—the action verbs, particularly those describing actions that, because of their low social desirability, are uncommon—tend to define effects attributed to the person (in person-entity schemata). Verbs describing accomplishments were also found by McArthur to elicit person-attributions, though we might expect them to be involved in compensatory causal patterns. This point is perhaps one at which the simple person or entity patterns merge with and become confused with the triangular patterns. More subjective verbs, defining feelings and opinions, seem to evoke entity-attribution patterns. Verbs involving clear interpersonal comparisons and, more interestingly, those referring to dominance-submission aspects of interpersonal relations evoke the triangular compensatory cause pattern. Finally, pairing schema seem to be aroused by verbs denoting close interpersonal relations and intense feelings, whereas those denoting less intense relations tend more to evoke the grouping schema.

Our review reveals little about types of *causes* as they relate to the schematic patterns. We have had occasion to base our illustrations of various patterns upon different types of causes, such as easy versus difficult tasks, persons versus nonpersonal entities, quantitatively graded causal states versus assorted sets of qualitatively different causal states, and unrelated, individual causal agents versus classified or grouped causal agents. Certain schematic properties seem more common to one type than another. For example, the functional differentiation and inter-changeability at the basis of symmetry (in pairing and grouping patterns) seem less readily exemplified by nonpersonal entities than by persons (for example, transient role differentiations common to exchange relationships, such as speaker-listener roles). It seems highly probable that the evocation of the compensatory cause schema depends upon perception of the causal states as graded. Our interpretation of the "verbal generalization" studies suggests that the assumed distribution of a given type of effect may depend upon whether it is treated in relation to independent causal states (for example, a set of unrelated persons) or in relation to a class of such states (a group of persons sharing some property or class name).

Other social psychological literature can be examined as it bears upon this point. For example, social conformity pressures are stronger with respect to certain entities and judgments than to others. Attributors are likely to be aware of distinctions of this sort and then to make different assumptions about the degree of consensus present in the given person-entity schema depending upon the kind of entities or effects involved. Thus, "A supports X" will carry a stronger implication that "B also supports X" if X refers to a goal of high importance within the social collectivity than if it designates a matter of taste or aesthetic preference. The schema for the first would tend to be that in figure 8, and for the second, case II in figure 10. Similarly, greater consensus will be assumed for attribute judgments than for expressions of preference. In a different vein, a grouping schema is likely to be assumed for reactions to political issues or candidates inasmuch as these tend to follow party or other group lines.

A fascinating recent line of research bears in a more general way upon the problem of schema evocation. This is the work on "cognitive activation" [Abelson 1968] and perceived relevance of behavior to belief [Kiesler, Nisbett & Zanna 1969]. The experimental demonstrations are that internal (belief) attributions for a given behavior, enacted under mild external pressure, are greater if the actor is gently reminded that his behavior has potential belief relevance, which seems to imply that his belief is a possible cause for his behavior. The broad implication is that not all plausible causes for a given effect may be salient to the attributor at any given time. Not surprisingly, he may simply overlook some of the possibly relevant causes and thereby delimit or shift the class of causal inferences he might draw from the occurrence of the effect. Those inferences can apparently be externally manipulated by cues and reminders as to the possible relation to the effect of certain plausible causes. According to the present view, these cues have their effect by virtue of the particular schema they lead the attributor to consider as he interprets the observed cause-effect evidence.

The Identification of Causal Schemata

Here are drawn together the suggestions provided by existing research and writings about how to identify the schema evoked in a given situation. The range of procedures is a broad one because every demonstrated manifestation of a schema is a potential indicator of its existence. Thus, Singer's view of schemata as serving to structure the individual's perceptions and learnings implies that perceptual distortions and differentially rapid learning are useful as reflections of the underlying schema [1968]. And we have seen rate of learning used by DeSoto and Kuethe for exactly that purpose.

The simple direct question is perhaps a useful device for determining what causes are considered relevant to a given effect (the very first matter to be determined in identifying the schema). Abelson provides an illustration in his naive question game: "Here is X. How come?" [1968]. A different and more focused line of questioning requires the subject to work from specified causes to effects. The most direct way to determine the configuration of the matrix was suggested to me by Jae-Ho Cha: given this degree of cause A and that degree of cause B, how likely is the occurrence of the effect? Queried about all possible combinations of states of A and B, the attributor's set of answers directly portrays his assumptions about how the effect is distributed over them. We have also seen several instances in which the subject is provided with partial sets of cause and effect information and asked his expectations about other facts. One illustration is provided by DeSoto and Kuethe's information-question procedure summarized in figure 15: given that the effect occurs for one or more specified combinations of causes, what is the likelihood of its occurring for certain other combinations? In a similar vein there is the causal inference question: given the effect and one cause, what was the state of the other cause? We have been considering this type of inference primarily as a consequence of the schema, but it may also, in some research contexts, serve as an indicator of the type of schema at work.

The research on verbal generalization suggests that schemata can be evoked by general statements of the sort "Boys grow vegetables." The subject can then be given various sets of data and questioned about their compatibility with the general statement. Do they justify it? Are they consistent with it? Alternatively, he can be asked to indicate specific statements he would think likely to follow from the general statement. This alternative might require him to generate some instances he would regard as compatible with it as well as some contrasting incompatible ones.

A somewhat more abstract version of the same procedure might consist of describing a schematic configuration as follows: "I'm thinking of a verb that is appropriate for filling in the blank in the sentence 'Boys _____ vegetables.' I can tell you that all boys _____ tomatoes and corn, but few boys _____ rutabagas and onions." The attributor would be asked what the effect might be, perhaps working from a checklist of verbs. Alternatively, the verb could be specified and either the persons or entities not specified. Such procedures would seem useful in broadening our knowledge of what types of effects and causes elicit which types of schemata.

An even more abstract procedure (perhaps approaching the limits of the capacities of our subjects for abstract thinking) would set the subject to thinking about a certain list of persons as they act toward or react to a certain list of entities in some particular way. The subject would then fill in the distribution of "effects" for a list of person-entity combinations or characterize several such lists as to their appropriateness.

The last method comes very close to the list-learning methods that DeSoto [1960] and Zajonc and Burnstein [1965a, 1965b] have used to investigate assumptions regarding social structure. The independent variables of rate of learning, trials to criterion, and types of errors made during learning are interpreted as indicating those sets of data most consistent with the subjects' preconceptions about patterns of social relationships. The procedure has been applied only to person-person and person-entity schemata but is in principle applicable to other cases as well.

With experience, this list of identification procedures will undoubtedly be extended, possibly to include methods to assess selective attention to and long-term retention of information consistent with the schema, and the attributor's formulation of informal experimental tests and designs to identify causal factors and their interplay.

Limitations of the Schematic Analysis

As in the earlier use of the analysis of variance as a model of the layman's attribution processes [Kelley 1967], the present paper runs the danger of confusing his attributional concepts and procedures with the sophisticated and complex procedures that scientists have laboriously evolved for similar purposes. One is uneasy about using the scalogram analysis of ability and attitude scales or the matrix analysis of sociometric data for the identification of cliques and groupings as an analogue for the manner in which the lay attributor organizes and interprets cause and effect data. However, the underlying assumption here is that there are only a limited number of ways of making sense out of the available data about the world and that the scientific procedures are merely refined and explicit versions of methods upon which the common man also comes to rely. If there is a continuity between the scientific and the everyday procedures for organizing information, it is proper to draw upon the more explicit processes for insights into the more implicit ones.

By "implicit" we mean to indicate that there is no necessary assumption here that the lay attributor explicitly thinks about causal problems in terms of data matrices of the kind drawn here. There *is* the assumption (and the evidence) that he acts on information (learns, remembers, fills in, assumes, infers) *as if* he were using these matrixlike schemata. But strictly speaking, the data matrices are *our* means for summarizing his activities, for thinking about them, and for making predictions about his use of information under various conditions. From a longer view, it must be admitted that this question cannot forever be dodged. We do indeed wish and need to know the terms in which the lay attributor thinks about causal problems. It seems unlikely that an "as if" model that has little correspondence to the attributor's actual modes of information processing will succeed in anticipating and summarizing all the important details of his activities.

While we are not, then, assuming much about the attributor in his explicit use of matrices and complex configurational analyses, there are several respects in which we are probably assuming too little about him. The first underestimate we make of his causal sophistication lies in the hidden assumption that he treats causes as if they occurred independently. For example, he was portrayed as being likely to be uncertain in his inference about the difficulty of the task from knowing merely that a capable person had succeeded on it. Or, at least, we expected him to be more uncertain than if, in contrast, he knew only that an incapable person had succeeded on it. The attributor may, however, draw his inference in this situation on the basis of the stereotype that people select tasks in accordance with their ability, and therefore he would be as certain that the task completed by the capable person was difficult as that the one completed by the incapable person was easy. The general point is that there are many instances in which it is entirely reasonable for the attributor to assume that the causes do not occur independently but that they covary. Such covariance can be assumed on many grounds: that one cause affects the other (for example, in the realm of behavioral compliance, external pressure kills the person's internal interest, or external inducements arouse the person's positive motivation with respect to the behavior) or that some third factor or process induces the two causes to covary (for example, maintenance of self-esteem induces selection of tasks consistent with one's ability).

Again, the point is clarified by reference to scientific procedures. In scientific work we know that causes do not naturally occur independently and in all combinations (as the schema represents). This knowledge is a major reason for conducting scientific experiments—to induce the causes to occur independently and in all combinations so we can assess their independent and joint effects. Undoubtedly, the lay attributor is also aware of the lack of independence in the natural occurrence of causes, and his use of causal schemata probably takes this into account. It is as though he were dealing with the problem in terms of a truncated schema in which only certain combinations of the sets of causal factors are assumed to exist.

A second way in which the present analysis underestimates the attributor is in his ability to distinguish different kinds or qualities of effects. For example, we ask the attributor to infer the strength of a student's attitude from his compliance with his teacher's assignment to write an essay in favor of stiffer penalties for marijuana use. But we do not permit the attributor to take account of the nature of the effect (the immediacy and thoroughness of the compliance versus its slowness and grudgingness), or at least our analysis takes no account of what information he might draw from the nature of the compliance.

Rather, our analysis simply defines the effect in all cells of the schema as "compliance" and permits discriminations only as to degree. It is the essential point of Michotte's experiments on perception of causality that observers can and do distinguish qualitatively different kinds of effects [1963]. Indeed, the distinction between the impressions of *l'effet déclenchement* (in which one object is seen to trigger the movement of a second, which then appears to move of its own accord) and *l'effet entraînement* (the first object is seen to encounter, push, and carry along the second) suggests the kind of qualitative discriminations between effects likely to be common to a variety of causal schemata. Thus, in a schema for multiple sufficient causes (figure 1), in which presence and absence of an internal cause are played off against the presence and absence of an external one, something like *l'effet déclenchement* would be assumed to be a more characteristic indication of the presence of the internal cause, and *l'effet entraînement*, an indicator of the presence of the external cause.

A more positive point to make in this context is that the schematic analysis here proposed represents what the attributor is able to do with minimal qualitative distinctions among effects. It suggests the possibilities available to him by virtue of schematic configurations that reflect only gross distinctions as to the presence or absence, or degree, of the given effect. In view of the undoubted ability of the attributor to make distinctions among different kinds of effects that are distributed unevenly over the schema, his inferential powers are underestimated by the present view.

Another facet of the problem raised in the preceding paragraphs has to do with the interchangeability or equivalence of effects. While the attributor may make fine distinctions among different types of effects, certain effects that appear to be different are, for all practical purposes, equivalent. This is particularly true in human behavior, where different sequences of action have a functional equivalence for the actor and are to be taken as reflecting similar causal states. The equivalence problem also appears in the necessity for coordinating information gained through different modalities of interaction with an entity. For there to be a sense of "object constancy" (that is, entity-attribution by way of intermodality consistency), the feel of the entity must be coordinated with the sight of it, the visual image of it from one perspective with that from another perspective, and so forth. Similarly, the contribution of consensus to the definition of the external reality requires the coordination of the diverse views different people have of the same thing—a problem the solution to which is undoubtedly facilitated by labeling. An important task for attributional analysis is to provide an understanding of the basis of these perceived equivalences and coordinations of different kinds of effects.

This paper has undoubtedly raised more questions than it has answered. For example, one wonders how much sense it makes to treat personal and impersonal causation in the same terms, as has been attempted here. One senses the potentiality in schematic analysis of a unique approach to the understanding of language, with the possibility of providing causally relevant distinctions among parts of speech, within the verb category, and so on. A salient question concerns when it is that the attributor relies upon existing schemata for his causal inferences and when it is he suspends them in order to gather more data and to make a full-blown ANOVA analysis. This matter has been discussed in general outline elsewhere [Kelley & Thibaut 1969], but the schematic analysis suggests some new ways of thinking about the problem. An effect may be observed to occur at an unexpected juncture in the schema, or in other ways the set of information at the attributor's disposal may be internally inconsistent. Similarly, conflicting or ambiguous cues may evoke schemata that lead to contradictory inferences or may leave the attributor without a clear schema to use. And as we have noted, certain schema-data combinations do not permit unambiguous inferences. Any of these circumstances, if occurring for an important problem, may provide the impetus for setting aside the assumptions and stereotypes embodied in the causal schema and carrying out a more informed analysis. The individual's repertoire of conceptions about the operation and interaction of causal factors—his repertoire of causal schemata—provides a marvelously versatile and comprehensive means for making sense of incomplete data about particular causal phenomena. However, one must identify the many important instances in which the appropriate schema is brought into play only tentatively and inferences from it are withheld until additional information can be gathered as to the distribution of effect in relation to causes.

BIBLIOGRAPHY

Robert P. Abelson, "Psychological Implication." In Robert P. Abelson, Elliot Aronson, William J. McGuire, Theodore M. Newcomb, Milton J. Rosenberg, and Percy H. Tannenbaum, eds., *Theories of Cognitive Consistency: A Sourcebook*, Rand McNally, 1968.

Robert P. Abelson and David E. Kanouse, "Subjective Acceptance of Verbal Generalizations." In Shel Feldman, ed., *Cognitive Consistency: Motivational Antecedents and Behavioral Consequents*, Academic, 1966.

Frederic C. Bartlett, *Remembering*. Cambridge University Press, 1932.

Daryl J. Bem, "Self Perception: An Alternative Interpretation of Cognitive Dissonance Phenomena." *Psychologcial Review*, 1967, 74:183–200.

Dana Bramel, "Determinants of Beliefs about Other People." In Judson Mills, ed., *Experimental Social Psychology*, Macmillan, 1969.

Clinton B. DeSoto, "Learning a Social Structure." *Journal of Abnormal and Social Psychology*, 1960, 60:417–421.

Clinton B. DeSoto, "The Predilection for Single Orderings." *Journal of Abnormal and Social Psychology*, 1961, 62:16–23.

Clinton B. DeSoto, Nancy M. Henley, and Marvin London, "Balance and the Grouping Schema." *Journal of Personality and Social Psychology*, 1968, 8:1–7.

Clinton B. DeSoto and James L. Kuethe, "Perception of Mathematical Properties of Interpersonal Relations." *Perceptual and Motor Skills*, 1958, 8:279–286.

Clinton B. DeSoto and James L. Kuethe, "Subjective Probabilities of Interpersonal Relationships." *Journal of Abnormal and Social Psychology*, 1959, 59:290–294.

Charlotte Gilson and Robert P. Abelson, "The Subjective Use of Inductive Evidence." *Journal of Personality and Social Psychology*, 1965, 2:301–310.

Louis Guttman, "The Basis for Scalogram Analysis." In Samuel A. Stouffer, Louis Guttman, Edward A. Suchman, Paul F. Lazarsfeld, Shirley A. Star, and John A. Clausen, eds., *Measurement and Prediction*, Princeton University Press, 1950.

Fritz Heider, *The Psychology of Interpersonal Relations*. Wiley, 1958.

Bärbel Inhelder and Jean Piaget, *The Growth of Logical Thinking from Childhood to Adolescence*. Basic, 1958.

Edward E. Jones and Keith E. Davis, "From Acts to Dispositions: The Attribution Process in Person Perception." In Leonard Berkowitz, ed., *Advances in Experimental Social Psychology*, Vol. 2, Academic, 1965.

Edward E. Jones, Keith E. Davis, and Kenneth J. Gergen, "Role Playing Variations and Their Informational Value for Person Perception." *Journal of Abnormal and Social Psychology*, 1961, 63:302–310.

David E. Kanouse, *Language, Labeling, and Attribution*. General Learning Press, 1971.

Harold H. Kelley, "Attribution Theory in Social Psychology." In David Levine, ed., *Nebraska Symposium on Motivation, 1967*, University of Nebraska Press, 1967.

Harold H. Kelley, "Moral Evaluation." *American Psychologist*, 1971a, 26:293–300.

Harold H. Kelley, *Attribution in Social Interaction*. General Learning Press, 1971b.

Harold H. Kelley and John W. Thibaut, "Group Problem Solving." In Gardner Lindzey and Elliot Aronson, eds.,

The Handbook of Social Psychology, Vol. 4, Addison-Wesley, 1969.

Charles A. Kiesler, Richard E. Nisbett, and Mark P. Zanna, "On Inferring One's Belief from One's Behavior." *Journal of Personality and Social Psychology*, 1969, 11:321–327.

W. Richard Kite, "Attribution of Causality as a Function of the Use of Reward and Punishment." Ph.D. thesis, Stanford University, 1964.

James L. Kuethe, "Social Schemas." *Journal of Abnormal and Social Psychology*, 1962, 64:31–38.

Leslie A. McArthur, "The How and What of Why: Some Determinants and Consequences of Causal Attribution." Ph.D. thesis, Yale University, 1970.

Albert E. Michotte, *The Perception of Causality*. Basic, 1963.

Richard E. Nisbett and Stuart Valins, *Perceiving the Causes of One's Own Behavior*. General Learning Press, 1971.

Jean Piaget, *The Origins of Intelligence in Children*. International Universities Press, 1952.

Jean Piaget, *The Construction of Reality in the Child*. Basic, 1954.

Jerome E. Singer, "Consistency as a Stimulus Processing Mechanism." In Robert P. Abelson, Elliot Aronson, William J. McGuire, Theodore M. Newcomb, Milton J. Rosenberg, and Percy H. Tannenbaum, eds., *Theories of Cognitive Consistency: A Sourcebook*, Rand McNally, 1968.

Michael D. Storms and Richard E. Nisbett, "Insomnia and the Attribution Process." *Journal of Personality and Social Psychology*, 1970, 16:319–328.

John W. Thibaut and Henry W. Riecken, "Some Determinants and Consequences of the Perception of Social Causality." *Journal of Personality*, 1955, 24:113–133.

Stuart Valins and Richard E. Nisbett, *Attribution Processes in the Development and Treatment of Emotional Disorders*. General Learning Press, 1971.

Bernard Weiner, Irene Frieze, Andy Kukla, Linda Reed, Stanley Rest, and Robert M. Rosenbaum, *Perceiving the Causes of Success and Failure*. General Learning Press, 1971.

Robert S. Woodworth, *Experimental Psychology*. Holt, 1938.

Robert B. Zajonc and Eugene Burnstein, "The Learning of Balanced and Unbalanced Social Structures." *Journal of Personality*, 1965a, 33:153–163.

Robert B. Zajonc and Eugene Burnstein, "Structural Balance, Reciprocity, and Positivity as Sources of Cognitive Bias." *Journal of Personality*, 1965b, 33:570–583.

[*Preparation of this paper grew out of a workshop on attribution theory held at UCLA in August 1969, supported by Grant GS-2613 from the National Science Foundation, and was made possible by NSF Grant GS-1121X.*]

INDEX

INDEX

A

Abelson, Robert P., xi, xii, 50, 58, 60, 61, 76, 77, 122–125, 128, 129, 132, 133, 135, 154, 162, 163, 170, 173, 174

ability, attribution of, 37–40, 80, 81, 98–100
    and maximum performance level, 159

abnormality, attributions of, 138–139

Abrahams, Darcy, 17, 26

achievement behavior,
    and attribution theory, 104–112
    forced choice, 109–110
    free choice, 104–108
    intensity, 110–111
    perceived determinants, 96
    persistence, 108–109
    risk preference, 109–110

achievement motivation(s), 102–119
    Atkinson's theory, 102–104, 112–113
    attributional model, 112–113

achievement predispositions, 117–118

acrophobia, reattribution therapy, 144

actor, in attribution processes, ix, 79–94
    naive psychology, x, 88–92

actor vs. observer, divergent attributions, 79–94

adaptive behavior, 142

Adelson, Richard, 146, 150

Aderman, David, 87, 94

adjectives, 32, 48, 49, 60
    combinations, 30–32
    modifying capacities, 49

negative, 48, 49, 127
    polarized, 48
    positive, 48, 49, 127

adolescents, causal thinking, 152

Adrenalin (*see* epinephrine)

adverbs, 134

affect, negative (*see* negative affect)

affiliation, x

aggression, ix

airplane phobia, reattribution therapy, 144

Alexander, C. Norman, 6, 24

Allison, Joel, 14, 24

Allport, Gordon W., 91, 94

Altrocchi, John, 97, 120

amobarbital sodium, 147

analysis of variance (ANOVA) models, of attribution process, 86, 88, 151, 152, 173

Anderson, Norman H., 28, 30–35, 38, 42, 43, 45, 48, 49, 60, 61, 127, 135

anesthetics, local, 143

animals
    attribution in, 117·
    cognition in, 117
    dislike for, 151

ANOVA models (*see* analysis of variance (ANOVA) models)

antonyms, 31

anxiety,
    desensitization therapy, 145

apathy, attribution in murder witnesses, 79

Arnold, W. J., 45, 120